The Arts and Cognition

The Ar

Edited

nd *Cognition*

David Perkins
d Barbara Leondar

The Johns Hopkins University Press
Baltimore and London

The poem "Adam's Curse" is reprinted with permission
of Macmillan Publishing Co., Inc., from *The Collected
Poems of W. B. Yeats*. "My Dear, You Are Like This Public
Park," copyright © 1965 by Barry Spacks, from the book
The Company of Children, by Barry Spacks, is reprinted
by permission of Doubleday & Co., Inc.

Manufactured in the United States of America

The Johns Hopkins University Press, Baltimore, Maryland 21218
The Johns Hopkins Press Ltd., London

Library of Congress Catalog Card Number 76-17237
ISBN 0-8018-1843-5

Library of Congress Cataloging in Publication data
will be found on the last printed page of this book.

 Contents

Acknowledgments

This book represents the collective effort of Harvard Project Zero, an informal and largely voluntary collaboration of individuals concerned with the arts, with human cognition and symbol processing generally, and with their implications for education. Many of the authors make their own special acknowledgments, but here the editors welcome the opportunity to thank those who have lent their general support and encouragement to Project Zero and to this volume. Our effort was founded in the fall of 1966 by Professor Nelson Goodman, who directed activities for some years thereafter and remains active in the project. Our thanks to him can only fall short; Professor Goodman has been model and mentor, guardian and gadfly to all of us. David Perkins succeeded Professor Goodman, and recently he and Howard Gardner have jointly directed the project; we look forward to further fruitful enterprise under their guidance.

Under Deans Theodore Sizer and Paul Ylvisaker, the Harvard Graduate School of Education has offered our project colleagueship and a home for which we are most grateful. Associate Dean for Academic Affairs Arthur Powell and, after him, Assistant Dean John Butler have served as heartening sources of enthusiasm, encouragement, and advice. Professor Israel Scheffler, a Project Zero member, though not represented in this volume, has both welcomed our viewpoint and activity at the Harvard Graduate School of Education and contributed his own considerable insights to our effort.

Over Project Zero's history, many agencies have provided invaluable financial support for the progress of the project as an entity. In accordance with common government and foundation policy, we offer here the general disclaimer that the opinions expressed in this volume do not necessarily reflect the positions or policies of any of our supporting agencies, and no official endorsement should be inferred. Currently the National Institute of Education (Grant no. NE-G-00-3-0169) and the Spencer Foundation are funding major research programs here. Martin Engel of the National

Institute of Education has offered us valuable guidance. From September 1971 through February 1974, a grant from the National Science Foundation (Grant no. GB-31064) supported project activities. Funding from the United States Office of Education distributed through the Committee for Basic Research in Education (Grant no. OEG-0-9-310283-3721[010]) provided support for the period September 1969 to September 1971; we especially thank Patrick Suppes for encouraging our effort. In the years 1968-71 the Old Dominion Foundation made possible a series of lecture-performances produced by Project Zero and offered without charge to the Harvard and Greater Boston communities. An earlier grant from the National Science Foundation assisted Nelson Goodman's germinal work on symbol systems and the writing of *Languages of Art*.

Finally, we express our appreciation to the many individuals over the past years who, as project members or not, have lent their time and intelligence with little or no recompense to forward our enterprise. Their influence echoes throughout the pages of this volume, and we can only regret that more of them are not represented directly.

The Arts and Cognition

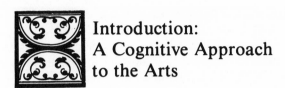

Introduction:
A Cognitive Approach
to the Arts

In three phrases, William Butler Yeats defined a central paradox of artistic creation:

—A line will take us hours maybe;
Yet if it does not seem a moment's thought,
Our stitching and unstitching has been naught.

His words become doubly apt as a sample of what they describe. Easily accessible, gracefully put, they indeed "seem a moment's thought." Yet one would like to know what labor they cost Yeats.

Yeats refers to the conscious expense of effort in the service of grace; the poet's exertion begets the reader's ease. Sometimes art reverses this sequence so that invention seems effortless while comprehension must strain and labor. But the philosopher or psychologist exploring the nature of perceiving and creating finds no paradox either way. Whether consciously or not, the work of discriminating, searching, selecting, and fabricating must in every case be done. Thus our own unstudied resonance to Yeats's lines deceives us; the easy appropriateness of "stitching and unstitching" conceals our active mental patterning. As we remake Yeats's metaphor in our response we realize, covertly at least, that stitching is a fussy, painstaking business, and that organic thread and cloth, not rivets and girders, are its materials. We recognize, too, that "stitching and unstitching" means trying over and over, not building up and tearing down once. We follow many further threads of association—thread as line, as a line of poetry, the thread of a line as the thread of an idea with which the poet stitches. Mostly this happens beyond ready scrutiny. Yet happen it must; otherwise "doing and undoing" would serve as nicely as Yeats's figure.

Of course this small analysis offers no substitute for a reader's natural response. Its aim is different—to explain the experience, not re-create it. The explanation, so much longer than the lines themselves, underscores the wealth of knowledge, of discrimination, of expectation that serves our least encounter with these few words. *Cognition*, the act of knowing, gives a name to this wealth—and to this book as well.

Whatever else the appreciation and creation of art may be, the premise of this work is that acts of cognition constitute our perceiving and making and that cognitive skills divide more from less competent efforts. Recommending this view is the fertile research in cognitive psychology which has recently illuminated such complex human performances as language, problem solving, memory storage and retrieval, perceptual discrimination, and learning. Cognition, or "knowing," is too easily construed as solely a matter of words and their silent manipulation. But recent work in cognitive psychology emphasizes that such nondiscursive matters as perception, motor control, personality, and emotion may be embraced within this approach. To see why this is so is to see why a study of cognition and the arts can succeed without trivializing its subject.

One premise of a cognitive approach holds that all human activity occurs relative to a *knowledge base*. Perception, for instance, amounts not just to seeing what is there but to apprehending in accordance with—and sometimes through painful revision of—previously accumulated experience and established dimensions and categories. In the arts, not only everyday knowledge of the world but also specialized knowledge of history, genre, and style inform the apprehension of particular works. Again, in art as well as life, emotional reactions depend on how a situation is *understood*. Whether the rogue is hated, loved, or pitied depends crucially on what kind of a rogue he is taken to be.

A second theme holds that our reactions, while indeed dependent on knowledge, also constitute *ways of knowing*. Most obviously, through perception we find out how the world is. But the same is so of emotions as well. To note that a real or fictional plight moves one or leaves one cold is to say something about the plight as well as about oneself; emotional reactions offer not simply personal highs and lows but ways of registering and comprehending the situation "out there." To complicate this picture, discovery, insight, and similar cognitive achievements themselves carry strong emotions which enrich our experiences of making and perceiving. Thus affect becomes both a manner and a product of knowing.

Third, cognition includes *knowing how* as well as *knowing that*. We act on the world as well as apprehend it, guided by both conscious and nonconscious knowledge of how to accomplish aims. In this light, personality becomes a characteristic way of dealing with the world, a notion which sometimes goes under the name "cognitive style." Errors in diverse enterprises often reflect not mere lapses but systematic if misguided plans to deal with problems in another way. Even insanity can be seen not as a deviation but as an effort to cope. Likewise such subtle matters as invention in the arts may be probed for the underlying know-how—the methods, the concepts, the strategies, the accidents and their fertile use which conspire to promote the effective artistic product.

But *knowing how* reaches further yet, for on a cognitive account perception itself is action. The stimulus does not so much assert as hint, and perceptions do not so much accept as interpret. Generally we proceed unaware of the busy-work involved in perceiving because much of it proceeds rapidly and nonconsciously. But when the unexpected happens —when we unknowingly leave the elevator on the wrong floor or taste milk thinking it to be water—we discover through our confusion how much perceiving depends on a continually updated preconception. By their nature, the arts constantly challenge our expectations and throw into prominence perception as action.

These points emphasize that cognitive psychology represents a style of approaching many phenomena rather than a topic restricted to a few. As such, a cognitive perspective questions many sanctified contrasts in the arts and construes them in new ways. One popular dichotomy makes much of the emotional versus the cognitive, proposing the arts to be the special dominion of the former. But as just sketched, emotions are a way of reading the world; further, emotions, like the most coolly reasoned of conclusions, can be appropriate or inappropriate to their objects. On this account emotions do not oppose but become a mode of cognition.

Another dichotomy classifies artistic production and perception as the special province of the subjective as contrasted with the objective. Certainly immersion in the arts often involves listening to inner reactions, hunches, and intuitions and crediting these as significant indices of a work's quality or direction. But "subjective" has a more precarious sense when it is used to argue that one can make whatever he wants of, or for, a work of art. In contrast, a cognitive approach holds that perception and production, invention and innovation involve crucial know-how and that an artist or audience member, though he may fool himself more easily, can no more disregard realities than can an engineer or politician.

A third dichotomy proposes that the arts require special exercise of the spontaneous versus the deliberate. Certainly laborious mastery of a work is less efficient and thus less delightful than intuitive, effortless engagement. A cognitive perspective, however, views spontaneous performance as no less intricate and inferential than deliberated performance. The one contrasts with the other in routinization—relegation of the activity to nonconscious mechanisms—rather than in the authenticity of results. Accordingly a slowly and painfully evolved response or product may prove as valid as a spontaneous effort. Further, any valuing of the spontaneous over the deliberate in an unqualified way emphasizes the superficially spontaneous over the more deeply deliberated, and by this topsy-turvy philosophy denigrates the awkward rehearsal that generally must precede discerning spontaneity itself.

Finally, talk about art is traditionally deprecated in favor of action and experience. Here again no one would deny that a written description of a painting or a piece of music makes a poor substitute for direct viewing or listening. Indeed a special venture of this book is to underscore some fundamental differences among linguistic, pictorial, and other means of symbolizing. But knowledge can be acquired through many different routes and can be couched in many different codes. A cognitive view allows for a rich and supportive interplay among man's many sorts of symbols. If there is obtuse talk about the arts, there is also talk which leads the eye or ear to discern in a new and deeper way. Further, the conductor may guide music with gesture, the choreographer may diagram a dance, the viewer may mimic the posture of a painted figure to better perceive its grace and balance. Interactions among language, gesture, picture, dance, music, and so on appear both persistent and fruitful. An isolationist doctrine whereby each art disdains illumination through any other mode of symbolizing flies in the face both of actual practice and of the capacity for dialogue suggested by a cognitive model.

These paragraphs thus argue that a cognitive approach to the arts entails reconsidering and reconstruing many traditional attitudes. The essays which follow flesh out that injunction; they illustrate what happens when the mandate to reconstrue is taken seriously. But they illustrate only. Rather than map the whole of cognitive aesthetics—an endeavor doomed to superficiality—these essays study single issues intensively. Thus the volume need not be read straight on but may be sampled according to taste. The reader is cautioned, however, against too narrow an interpretation of his own interests. By and large the essays transcend their announced topics and enlighten not only adjacent subjects but some which, at first glance, seem wholly remote. Such extended implications inform the commentary preceding each division. Some readers will prefer to postpone these remarks until the essays themselves have been studied; others will find them a useful companion along the way. Both prior reading and subsequent review would best frame the articles within the larger themes of a division.

The perspective proposed furnishes rich fare for many tastes. The rewards can best be surveyed by reading further here and in other sources as well. As to the form of those rewards, this volume does not aim to channel artists, tell off critics, rectify teachers, or straighten out audience members. The aim, rather, is some comprehension of how works of art are made and made sense of and how people come to be able to do both. Yeats's process of stitching and unstitching itself becomes the cloth for cautious fashioning of insight.

ONE  # Symbol Systems:
The Stuff of Art

One thing certain about the arts is the uncertainty of what the arts are about. Communication of emotions, self-expression, sophisticated play, seeing the world fresh, sublimation, intrinsic value—all these fall among the many ways the arts have been construed. That formulas abound need not in itself invite dismay: no rule requires that something must be *one* thing. Even a chair is a piece of wood, something to sit on, a part of the living room's layout, and so on. Not the multiplicity of descriptions but their inaptness makes for a problem. Explanations of the arts contract to do at least two jobs. First, they should *subsume* all instances of art, though in pointing up links with other kinds of human activity they may include more than art. Second, they should, as the underlying concepts are elaborated, *differentiate* kinds of art from one another and art from other kinds of things.

Simple-sounding enough, these standards confound most easy-going answers. Whatever role communication of emotion sometimes plays, some paintings by Mondrian or string quartets by Webern are no less art for being emotionally cool. However self-expressive Van Gogh may be, Bach more culminates a tradition than conveys individual whimsy. If Bach's Little Fugue is playful, his B Minor Mass is not. Though most artists we know by name have offered us some fresh vision, the work of artists within rigid traditions is nonetheless regarded and revered as art. And so on.

Such confusion pleads for clarity. To find it, this volume returns to that ancient philosophical tradition which defines man as a rational animal. For Kant, to characterize man as rational was to recognize that all his experience is cognitive—mediated by mind. Rather than encountering the world directly, man interprets and explains it to himself. All human intellection is thus concerned not so much with knowledge of things "out there" as with man's interpretations and representations of these things. In this sense, man inhabits a universe of his own invention. Wordsworth's description of "the mighty world/ Of eye and ear—both what they half create,/ And what perceive" echoes Kantian doctrine in acknowledging the creative role of perception in the construction of the human world.

To this conception of mind as an intermediary between man and his environment, Cassirer (and in his wake Langer and the European semioticists) added a further distinction. The conceptual instruments which man uses to label, classify, and explain his world—to represent it to himself—are systems of symbols. It is illuminating to think of symbol systems as languages provided the limitations of that analogy are acknowledged, as they will be below. Such a system would consist of a set of elementary units, a vocabulary, together with a corresponding set of rules or conventions governing their permissible relations. On this view, the table of elements together with the laws of chemical combination constitute a symbol system, as does the web of belief and ritual called Catholicism or the set of theorems and proofs of Euclidean geometry. Cassirer argued that the great symbol systems of myth and religion, language, art, history, and science constitute the foundation of human culture. But he fully recognized the presence of the symbolic in the quotidian and the mundane as well. Even the practical world of hard facts is an artifact of mind.

Art, then, becomes above all an act of intelligence, whether overt, covert or unconscious, reflective or reflexive. And the several arts, as symbol systems, constitute instruments for interpreting the world, tools for transforming sensation into experience. This theme finds its most recent expression in Nelson Goodman's book *Languages of Art*. The present sketch draws from that work directly but without promising its rigor or complexity.

For a start, then, symbols must subsume the arts and thus all art works, including performances, must be symbols. The enterprise fails at the outset unless *symbol* takes its most generic sense, ranging over speech and writing of any sort, musical scores, gestures, maps, diagrams, cattle brands, traffic lights, paintings, sculptures, dance performances, and so on. Two further points sharpen the concept. First, parts of symbols may also be symbols. A whole painting is a symbol, and the man in the center is also a symbol read in the context of the whole. Second, symbols become so through functioning as members of a symbol system. A chess piece used as a paperweight is not used symbolically at all. Employed in playing chess, it becomes a symbol signifying board position within a conventional system. To regard the chess piece as a sculpture is to read it as yet another sort of symbol.

If workable, this theory of symbols promises some order in a careless household. Challenging the vague notion that the arts lie isolated from other realms of human endeavor, the concept of symbol systems acknowledges unity in human communication, whether artistic or not. Sharpening the hunch that the arts are "somehow different," the concept of symbol systems can hope to deal precisely with how an art form differs from—or indeed cleaves closely to—other art forms or symbolic types employed in the sciences and elsewhere. Emphasizing that works of art occur within a system, the notion underscores a real and all too often ignored objective component in the making and reading of art.

But the quest to subsume and differentiate the arts as symbols is not so easily accomplished. Letting *symbol* be generic for things that refer does not obviously suffice even for subsumption. How is a work of music or an abstract painting symbolic? What does it refer to? Music and abstract painting depend crucially on formal properties such as balance, theme and variation, and fugue as well as on expressive properties such as friskiness, dolor, and calm. When paintings or poems treat of some subject, formal and expressive properties still remain important. Unless an account of the arts as symbol systems accommodates expressiveness and formal properties, it misses the point quite as much as "self-expression" or "play" theories.

Goodman's theory of symbols meets this problem. His article following this introduction resolves the puzzle by reminding us that symbols symbolize in different ways. Where words or representational pictures may denote things in the world, other symbols may *exemplify*—show forth as salient—features, properties, or labels. Once recognized, exemplification proves commonplace, including store samples of all sorts, movie previews, a critic's quotations from books, and demonstrations of anything from archery to zeppelin flying.

Exemplification is the means of subsuming formal aspects of art, and thereby music and abstract painting, under the umbrella of symbolism. Though a poem does not denote its sonnet form, a painting its balance, or a symphony its structure, all of these can be thought of as exemplifying their formal properties.

In *Languages of Art*, Goodman also explains how the concept of exemplification extends to include expression. The tailor may offer a tweed swatch to his customer to exemplify the label "tweed." Expressiveness in works of art also emerges in the labels we apply to them. To note that a jig is frisky, for example, is to take the work as exemplifying the label "friskiness." Such a label cannot of course apply *literally* to a work of art; here, as in metaphor, labels operate outside their usual range. But they do so with discretion—a morose piece of music cannot be called frisky nor a frisky one morose. With this in mind, expression can be understood as one sort of *metaphorical* exemplification.

Crucial here is the break between expressed and induced emotions. A jig played mistakenly at a funeral will prompt indignation, not friskiness, yet it will not thus become indignant rather than frisky. The same jig played at an Irish wake might indeed heighten the spirit of the occasion. The jig performed in theme-and-variations virtuoso arrangement for a conservatory exam might feed only the cool analysis of a panel of critics. Yet still the jig is properly called frisky regardless of feelings induced.

Here psychological issues rear up. How is it that we apply metaphorical labels consistently to music or anything else? For that matter, how is it that we apply nonmetaphorical labels with consistency? The humdrum use of labels in fact holds quite as many mysteries as the metaphoric use. But to expect an answer here to this essentially psychological question is to mistake the method. The philosophical tactic in these paragraphs is to shear off the logical from the psychological side of symbol use.

That tactic lays a base for a more precise psychological treatment of symbol use. Far from ignoring psychology, the theory of symbols finds its premises reverberating throughout contemporary inquiry into human thought and behavior. A central interest of cognitive or constructivist psychology, for example, has concerned the interaction between information supplied by the environment and that imposed by the observer. Here again one meets Wordsworth's conception of a world half-created, half-perceived by the thinking subject. Another center of interest has been the relationship of languages to thought, languages being symbol systems which encourage certain formulations of experience and inhibit others. Still another has been the study of relationships themselves ("next to," "taller than," "as bright as") since these are patently mental constructs made available to intellection only by virtue of man's symbolizing propensity. Later sections of this volume take up these possibilities and extend them to the realm of the arts.

Yet if symbols subsume the arts, this speaks to only half the problem. Indeed, the many characterizations that fail to subsume the arts also fail to differentiate them. If the arts sometimes communicate emotions, it is far from clear that some art forms do so any better than others—that music is more moving than drama or poetry than painting. Nor does the communication of emotions tag a symbol as artistic, for words (from epithets to endearments) may both express emotion and move the hearer without counting as art. Similarly, self-expression or intrinsic value seems no more characteristic of one art than another. And one may "self-express" through playing football or running traffic lights and pursue the intrinsically valuable through mastering chess or astronomy without these being arts.

Goodman's concept of *notationality* maps one way of sorting symbol systems. Notationality consists in five formal requirements. Satisfying all of these requirements is conventional music notation. Satisfying some but not others are written and spoken languages. Picturing satisfies none. Further mention of the somewhat technical conditions for notationality will be left to the articles in this section. Here one additional point suffices: notationality is not an ideal toward which all symbol systems should strive but simply a neutral characterization of types of symbol systems, a manner of sorting them. Symbol systems are neither better nor worse but are simply different as the degree of notationality varies and as they differ in the styles of information processing they require of the maker or reader.

Fundamental to philosophy, the aims of subsuming and differentiating—of "getting it all in" and "sorting it all out"—continue through the contributions of this section. More precise description of particular symbol systems is the aim. Such new venturings as conceptual art and found objects pose a modern problem for traditional boundaries. Can works of these sorts post legitimate claims as art, or has that title become an unwilling accomplice to a shifty game of words? Goodman's essay explains how such works earn their claim by taking on symbolic functions characteristic of art.

In film, "sorting it all out" makes special trouble. The "grammar" of motion pictures has been variously construed as a system of images, as a sequence of scenes which are concatenations of images, as a chain of narrative events, and in diverse other ways. Søren Kjørup, drawing on both the framework of European semiotics and the theory of symbols, takes many prior accounts to task for oversimplifying the situation. Film, he argues, is peculiar among the arts in combining a variety of symbol systems, each of which makes more isolated appearances elsewhere. Not just the multiplicity of systems but their interaction becomes a keynote of Kjørup's presentation in "Film as a Meetingplace of Multiple Codes."

Graham Roupas's essay, "Information and Pictorial Representation," returns to a classic theme in semiotics, the demarcation of the linguistic from the pictorial. Casual discourse often renders this as the verbal versus the visual. Yet this distinction is poorly drawn, reading being manifestly both verbal and visual. Other thinkers have advanced the notion of "icon," where reference depends not on convention but on resemblance. Roupas begins from two bases—the theories of J. J. Gibson, who approaches resemblance from a psychological rather than a philosophical standpoint, and those of Nelson Goodman, who rejects resemblance as too vague a notion to provide a sharp account. A drawing of an apple, for instance, resembles its subject much less than does another apple, yet drawings of apples denote apples while actual apples do not. Buttressing Gibson's undeveloped notion of information to provide further machinery for Goodman's approach, Roupas offers a new conception of the pictorial.

Because they fail to subsume and differentiate the arts, most casual aesthetics collapse at the outset. After all, many bizarre systems might include and sort the arts to no good purpose. One value of Goodman's theory of symbols lies not just in subsuming and differentiating but in doing so in trenchant ways. At the same time it rescues aesthetic activity from an untenable isolation and locates its source in a universal, indeed *the* universal, human characteristic. One need scarcely say that the distinctions adduced by Goodman may apply with equal power to symbol systems other than the arts and that his little volume may thereby prove to be a guidebook for the study of human intellection. Here Kjørup and Roupas show how Goodman's philosophical machinery can do further work in someone else's hands. But more than that, his thought has set a style and standard informing the psychological research which the other sections of this book present. Some of these build directly on Goodman's terminology. All reflect his larger enterprise—to map the symbolic functioning of man.

1

When Is Art?[1]
Nelson Goodman

If attempts to answer the question "What is art?" characteristically end in frustration and confusion, perhaps—as so
often in philosophy—the question is the wrong one. A
reconception of the problem, together with application of some results from
a study of the theory of symbols, may help to clarify such moot matters as
the role of symbolism in art and the status as art of the "found object" and
so-called "conceptual art."

One remarkable view of the relation of symbols to works of art is
illustrated in an incident bitingly reported by Mary McCarthy:

> Seven years ago, when I taught in a progressive college, I had a pretty girl
> student in one of my classes who wanted to be a short story writer. She was not
> studying with me, but she knew that I sometimes wrote short stories, and one
> day, breathless and glowing, she came up to me in the hall, to tell me that she
> had just written a story that her writing teacher, a Mr. Converse, was terribly
> excited about. "He thinks it's wonderful," she said, "and he's going to help me
> fix it up for publication."
>
> I asked what the story was about; the girl was a rather simple being who
> loved clothes and dates. Her answer had a deprecating tone. It was about a girl
> (herself) and some sailors she had met on the train. But then her face, which had
> looked perturbed for a moment, gladdened.
>
> "Mr. Converse is going over it with me and we're going to put in the
> symbols."[2]

Today the bright-eyed art student will more likely be told, with equal
subtlety, to keep out the symbols, but the underlying assumption is the same:
that symbols, whether enhancements or distractions, are extrinsic to the
work itself. A kindred notion seems to be reflected in what we take to be
symbolic art. We think first of such works as Bosch's *Garden of Delight* or
Goya's *Caprichos* or the Unicorn tapestries or Dali's drooping watches, and
then perhaps of religious paintings, the more mystical the better. What is

remarkable here is less the association of the symbolic with the esoteric or unearthly than the classification of works as symbolic upon the basis of their having symbols as their subject matter—that is, upon the basis of their depicting rather than of being symbols. This leaves as nonsymbolic art not only works that depict nothing but also portraits, still lifes, and landscapes where the subjects are rendered in a straightforward way without arcane allusions and do not themselves stand as symbols.

On the other hand, when we choose works for classification as nonsymbolic, as art without symbols, we confine ourselves to works without subjects; for example, to purely abstract or decorative or formal paintings or buildings or musical compositions. Works that represent anything, no matter what and no matter how prosaically, are excluded; for to represent is surely to refer, to stand for, to symbolize. Every representational work is a symbol, and art without symbols is restricted to art without subject.

That representational works are symbolic according to one usage and nonsymbolic according to another matters little so long as we do not confuse the two usages. What matters very much, though, according to many contemporary artists and critics, is to isolate the work of art as such from whatever it symbolizes or refers to in any way. Let me set forth in quotation marks, since I am offering it for consideration without now expressing any opinion of it, a composite statement of a currently much advocated program or policy or point of view:

"What a picture symbolizes is external to it, and extraneous to the picture as a work of art. Its subject if it has one, and its references, subtle or obvious, by means of symbols from some more or less well-recognized vocabulary, have nothing to do with its aesthetic or artistic significance or character. Whatever a picture refers to or stands for in any way, overt or occult, lies outside it. What really counts is not any such relationship to something else, not what the picture symbolizes, but what it is in itself —what its own intrinsic qualities are. Moreover, the more a picture focuses attention on what it symbolizes, the more we are distracted from its own properties. Accordingly, any symbolization by a picture is not only irrelevant but disturbing. Really pure art shuns all symbolization, refers to nothing, and is to be taken for just what it is, for its inherent character, not for anything it is associated with by some such remote relation as symbolization."

Such a manifesto packs punch. The counsel to concentrate on the intrinsic rather than the extrinsic, the insistence that a work of art is what it is rather than what it symbolizes, and the conclusion that pure art dispenses with external reference of all kinds have the solid sound of straight thinking, and promise to extricate art from smothering thickets of interpretation and commentary.

But a dilemma confronts us here. If we accept this doctrine of the formalist or purist, we seem to be saying that the content of such works as

The Garden of Delight and the *Caprichos* doesn't really matter and might better be left out. If we reject the doctrine, we seem to be holding that what counts is not just what a work is but lots of things it isn't. In the one case we seem to be advocating lobotomy on many great works; in the other we seem to be condoning impurity in art, emphasizing the extraneous.

The best course, I think, is to recognize the purist position as all right and all wrong. But how can that be? Let's begin by agreeing that what is extraneous is extraneous. But is what a symbol symbolizes always external to it? Certainly not for symbols of all kinds. Consider the symbols:

(*a*) "this string of words", which stands for itself;

(*b*) "word", which applies to itself among other words;

(*c*) "short", which applies to itself and some other words and many other things; and

(*d*) "having seven syllables", which has seven syllables.

Obviously what some symbols symbolize does not lie entirely outside the symbols. The cases cited are, of course, quite special ones, and the analogues among pictures—that is, pictures that are pictures of themselves or include themselves in what they depict—can perhaps be set aside as too rare and idiosyncratic to carry any weight. Let's agree for the present that what a work represents, except in a few cases like these, is external to it and extraneous.

Does this mean that any work that represents nothing meets the purist's demands? Not at all. In the first place, some surely symbolic works such as Bosch's paintings of weird monsters, or the tapestry of a unicorn, represent nothing; for there are no such monsters or demons or unicorns anywhere but in such pictures or in verbal descriptions. To say that the tapestry "represents a unicorn" amounts only to saying that it is a unicorn-picture, not that there is any animal or anything at all that it portrays.[3] These works, even though there is nothing they represent, hardly satisfy the purist. Perhaps, though, this is just another philosopher's quibble; and I won't press the point. Let's agree that such pictures, though they represent nothing, are representational in character, hence symbolic and so not 'pure'. All the same, we must note in passing that their being representational involves no representation of anything outside them, so that the purist's objection to them cannot be on that ground. His case will have to be modified in one way or another, with some sacrifice of simplicity and force.

In the second place, not only representational works are symbolic. An abstract painting that represents nothing and is not representational at all may express, and so symbolize, a feeling or other quality, or an emotion or idea.[4] Just because expression is a mode of symbolization of something outside the painting—which does not itself sense, feel, or think—the purist rejects abstract expressionist as well as representational works.

For a work to be an instance of "pure" art, of art without symbols, it must neither represent nor express nor even be representational or expressive. But is that enough? Granted, such a work does not stand for anything outside it; all it has are its own properties. But of course if we put it that way, all the properties any picture or anything else has—even such a property as that of representing a given person—are properties of the picture, not properties outside it.

The predictable response is that the important distinction among the several properties a work may have lies between its internal or intrinsic and its external or extrinsic properties; that while all are indeed its own properties, some of them obviously relate the picture to other things; and that a nonrepresentational, nonexpressive work has only internal properties.

This plainly doesn't work, for under any even faintly plausible classification of properties into internal and external, any picture or anything else has properties of both kinds. That a picture is in the Metropolitan Museum, that it was painted in Duluth, that it is younger than Methuselah, would hardly be called internal properties. Getting rid of representation and expression does not give us something free of such external or extraneous properties.

Furthermore, the very distinction between internal and external properties is a notoriously muddled one. Presumably the colors and shapes in a picture must be considered internal; but if an external property is one that relates the picture or object to something else, then colors and shapes obviously must be counted as external, for the color or shape of an object not only may be shared by other objects but also relates the object to others having the same or different colors or shapes.

Sometimes the terms "internal" and "intrinsic" are dropped in favor of "formal". But the formal in this context cannot be a matter of shape alone. It must include color, and if color, what else? Texture? Size? Material? Of course, we may at will enumerate properties that are to be called formal; but the "at will" gives the case away. The rationale, the justification evaporates. The properties left out as nonformal can no longer be characterized as all and only those that relate the picture to something outside it. So we are still faced with the question what if any *principle* is involved—the question how the properties that matter in a nonrepresentational, nonexpressive painting are distinguished from the rest.

I think there is an answer to the question, but to approach it, we'll have to drop all this high-sounding talk of art and philosophy and come down to earth with a thud.

Consider an ordinary swatch of textile in a tailor's or upholsterer's sample book. It is unlikely to be a work of art or to picture or express anything. It's simply a sample—a simple sample. But what is it a sample of? Texture, color, weave, thickness, fiber content . . . ; the whole point of this sample, we are tempted to say, is that it was cut from a bolt and has all the same properties as the rest of the material. But that would be too hasty.

Let me tell you two stories, or one story with two parts. Mrs. Mary Tricias studied a sample book like this, made her selection, and ordered from her favorite textile shop enough material for her overstuffed chair and sofa, insisting that it be exactly like the sample. When the bundle came she opened it eagerly and was dismayed when several hundred two-by-three-inch pieces with zig-zag edges exactly like the sample fluttered to the floor. When she called the shop, protesting loudly, the proprietor replied, injured and weary: "But Mrs. Tricias, you said the material must be exactly like the sample. When it arrived from the factory yesterday, I kept my assistants here half the night cutting it up to match the sample."

This incident was nearly forgotten some months later, when Mrs. Tricias, having sewed the pieces together and covered her furniture, decided to have a party. She went to the local bakery, selected a chocolate cupcake from those on display, and ordered enough for fifty people, to be delivered two weeks later. Just as the guests were beginning to arrive, a truck drove up with a single huge cake. The lady running the bake shop was utterly discouraged by the complaint: "But Mrs. Tricias, you have no idea how much trouble we went to. My husband runs the textile shop, and he warned me that your order would have to be in one piece."

The moral of this story is not simply that you can't win but that a sample is a sample of some of its properties but not others. The swatch is a sample of texture, color, etc., but not of size or shape. The cupcake is a sample of color, texture, size, and shape, but still not of all its properties; Mrs. Tricias would have complained even more loudly if what was delivered to her was like the sample in having been baked on that same day two weeks earlier.

Now in general, which of its properties is a sample a sample of? Not all its properties, for then the sample would be a sample of nothing but itself. And not its "formal" or "internal" or, indeed, any one specifiable set of properties. The kind of property sampled differs from case to case; the cupcake but not the swatch is a sample of size and shape, a specimen of ore may be a sample of what was mined at a given time and place. Moreover, the sampled properties vary widely with context and circumstance. Although the swatch is normally a sample of its texture, etc., but not of its shape or size, if I show it to you in answer to the question "What is an upholsterer's sample?" it then functions not as a sample of the material but as a sample of an upholsterer's sample, so that its size and shape are now among the properties it is a sample of.

In sum, the point is that a sample is a sample of—or *exemplifies*—only some of its properties, and that the properties to which it bears this relationship of exemplification[5] vary with circumstances and can only be distinguished as those properties that it serves, under the given circumstances, as a sample of. Being a sample of or exemplifying is a relationship something like that of being a friend; my friends are not distinguished by any single identifiable property or cluster of properties, but only by standing, for a period of time, in the relationship to me of being my friends.

The implications for our problem concerning works of art may now be apparent. The properties that count in a purist painting are those that the picture makes manifest, selects, focuses upon, exhibits, emphasizes, heightens in our consciousness—those that it shows forth—in short, those properties that it does not merely possess but exemplifies, stands as a sample of.

If I am right about this, then even the purist's purest painting symbolizes. It exemplifies certain of its properties. But to exemplify is surely to symbolize. Exemplification, no less than representation or expression, is a form of reference. A work of art, however free of representation and expression, is still a symbol even though what it symbolizes be not things or people or feelings but certain patterns of shape, color, texture that it shows forth.

What, then, of the purist's initial pronouncement that I said facetiously is all right and all wrong? It is all right in saying that what is extraneous is extraneous, in pointing out that what a picture represents often matters very little, in arguing that neither representation nor expression is required of a work, and in stressing the importance of so-called intrinsic or internal or formal properties. But the statement is all wrong in assuming that representation and expression are the only symbolic functions that paintings may perform, in supposing that what a symbol symbolizes is always outside it, and in insisting that what counts in a painting is the mere possession rather than the exemplification of certain properties.

If we look for art without symbols, then, we shall find none, if we take into account all the ways that works may symbolize. Art without representation or expression or exemplification, *yes*; art without all three, *no*.

To point out that purist art consists simply in the avoidance of certain kinds of symbolization is not to condemn it but only to uncover the fallacy in the usual manifestoes advocating purist art to the exclusion of all other kinds. I am not debating the relative virtues of different schools or types or ways of painting. What seems to me more important is that recognition of the symbolic function of even purist painting gives us a clue to the perennial problem of when we do and when we don't have a work of art.

The literature of aesthetics is strewn with desperate attempts to answer the question "What is art?" The question, often hopelessly confused with the query "What is good art?", is acute in the case of found art—the stone picked out of the driveway and exhibited in a museum—and is further aggravated by the promotion of so-called environmental and conceptual art. Is a smashed automobile fender in an art gallery a work of art? What of something that is not even an object and is not exhibited in any gallery or museum—for example, the digging and filling-in of a hole in Central Park, as prescribed by Oldenburg? If these are works of art, then are all stones in the driveway and all objects and occurrences works of art? If not, what distinguishes what is from what is not a work of art? The fact that an artist calls it a work of art? The fact that it is exhibited in a museum or gallery? No such answer carries any conviction.

As I remarked at the outset, part of the trouble lies in asking the wrong question, in failing to recognize that a thing may function as a work of art at some times and not at others. In crucial cases, the real question is not "What objects are (permanently) works of art?" but "When is an object a work of art?"—or more briefly, as in my title, "When is art?"

And my answer is that just as an object may be a symbol—for instance, a sample—at certain times and under certain circumstances and not at others, so an object may be a work of art at some times and not at others. Indeed, just by virtue of functioning as a symbol in a certain way does an object become, while so functioning, a work of art. The stone is normally no work of art while in the driveway but may be so when on display in an art museum. In the driveway it usually performs no symbolic function; in the art museum it exemplifies certain of its properties—e.g., shape, color, texture. The digging and filling of a hole functions as a work insofar as our attention is directed to it as an exemplifying symbol. On the other hand, a Rembrandt painting may cease to function as a work of art when used to replace a broken window or as a blanket.

Now, of course, to function as a symbol in some way or other is not in itself to function as a work of art. Our swatch, when serving as a sample, does not then and thereby become a work of art. Things function as works of art only when their symbolic functioning has certain characteristics. The same stone in a museum of geology also takes on symbolic functions as a sample of the stones of a given period, origin, or composition, but it is not then functioning as a work of art.

The question just what characteristics distinguish or are indicative of the symbolizing that constitutes functioning as a work of art calls for careful study in the light of a general theory of symbols. That is more than I can undertake here, but elsewhere[6] I have ventured the thought that there are four symptoms of the aesthetic: (1) syntactic density, where the finest differences in certain respects constitute a difference between symbols—for example, an ungraduated mercury thermometer as contrasted with an electronic digital-read-out instrument; (2) semantic density, where symbols are provided for things distinguished by the finest differences in certain respects—for example, not only the ungraduated thermometer again but also ordinary English, which is not syntactically dense; (3) relative repleteness, where comparatively many aspects of a symbol are significant—for example, a single-line drawing of a mountain by Hokusai, where every feature of shape, line, thickness, etc. counts, in contrast with perhaps the same line as a chart of daily stockmarket averages, where all that counts is the height of the line above the base; and finally (4) exemplification, where a symbol, whether or not it denotes, symbolizes by serving as a sample of properties it literally or metaphorically possesses.[7]

These suggest themselves not as defining properties but only as symptoms. Presence or absence of one or more of them does not qualify or disqualify anything as aesthetic; nor does the extent to which these features are present measure the extent to which, or the probability that, an object or experience is aesthetic.[8] Symptoms, after all, are but clues; the patient may have the symptoms without the disease, or the disease without the symptoms. And although I hesitantly conjectured that these four symptoms may be disjunctively necessary and conjunctively (as a syndrome) sufficient, I readily recognize that this would probably result in some redrawing of the vague and vagrant borderlines of the aesthetic. Still, notice that these properties tend to focus attention on the symbol rather than, or at least along with, what it refers to. Where we can never determine precisely just which symbol of a system we have or whether we have the same one on a second occasion; where the referent is so elusive that properly fitting a symbol to it requires endless care; where more rather than fewer features of the symbol count, and where the symbol is an instance of properties it symbolizes, we cannot merely look through the symbol to what it refers to, as we do in obeying traffic lights or reading scientific texts, but must attend constantly to the symbol itself, as in seeing paintings or reading poetry. This emphasis upon the nontransparency of a work of art, upon the primacy of the work over what it refers to, far from involving denial or disregard of symbolic functions, derives from certain characteristics of a work as a symbol.[9]

Quite apart from specifying the particular characteristics differentiating aesthetic from other symbolization, the answer to the question "When is art?" thus seems to me clearly to be in terms of symbolic function. Perhaps to say that an object is art when and only when it so functions is to overstate the case or to speak elliptically. The Rembrandt painting remains a work of art, as it remains a painting, while functioning only as a blanket; and the stone from the driveway may not strictly become art by functioning as art.[10] Similarly, a chair remains a chair even if never sat on, and a packing case remains a packing case even if never used except for sitting on. To say what art does is not to say what art is; but I submit that the former is the matter of primary and peculiar concern. The further question of defining stable property in terms of ephemeral function—the what in terms of the when—is not confined to the arts but is quite general. It is the same for defining chairs as for defining objects of art. The parade of instant and inadequate answers is also much the same: that whether an object is art, or a chair, depends upon intent or upon whether it sometimes or usually or always or exclusively functions as such. Because all this tends to obscure more special and significant questions concerning art, I have turned my attention from what art is to what art does.

A salient feature of symbolization, I have urged, is that it may come and go. An object may symbolize different things at different times, and nothing at other times. An inert or purely utilitarian object may come to function as art, and a work of art may come to function as an inert or purely utilitarian object. Perhaps, rather than art being long and life short, both are transient.

Notes

1. An earlier version of this paper was first read at the Fogg Museum, Harvard University, in 1971, and later at other institutions.

2. Mary McCarthy, "Settling the Colonel's Hash," *Harper's Magazine*, 1954; reprinted in *On the Contrary* (New York: Farrar, Straus and Cudahy, 1961), p. 225.

3. See further "On Likeness of Meaning" (1949) and "On Some Differences about Meaning" (1953), both reprinted in Nelson Goodman, *Problems and Projects* (Indianapolis and New York: Bobbs-Merrill, 1972), pp. 221–238; and Goodman, *Languages of Art: An Approach to a Theory of Symbols* (Indianapolis and New York: Bobbs-Merrill, 1968), pp. 21–26.

4. Motion, for example, as well as emotion may be expressed in a black and white picture; see figs. 1 and 2 in Nelson Goodman, "The Status of Style," *Critical Inquiry* 1 (1972): 799–811. Also see the discussion of expression in Goodman, *Languages of Art*, pp. 85–95.

5. For further discussion of exemplification, see Goodman, *Languages of Art*, pp. 52–67.

6. Goodman, *Languages of Art*, pp. 252–255, and the earlier passages there alluded to.

7. Notice that not only may a symbol function both denotatively and as a sample at the same time, e.g. in a painting that both represents and expresses, but also that representation-as and fictive representation are matters of exemplification rather than denotation. See Goodman, *Languages of Art*, pp. 21–31.

8. That poetry, for example, which is not syntactically dense, is less art or less likely to be art than painting that exhibits all four symptoms thus does not at all follow. Some aesthetic symbols may have fewer of the symptoms than some nonaesthetic symbols. This is sometimes misunderstood.

9. This is another version of the dictum that the purist is all right and all wrong.

10. Just as what is not red may look or be said to be red *at certain times*, so what is not art may function as or be said to be art at certain times. That an object functions as art at a given time, that it has the status of art at that time, and that it is art at that time may all be taken as saying the same thing—so long as we take none of these as ascribing to the object any stable status.

2 Film as a Meetingplace of Multiple Codes
Søren Kjørup

In Jean-Luc Godard's film *Les Carabiniers* (1963) one of the protagonists, a poor and simple peasant, goes to the cinema for the first time in his life. Curiously enough, he even happens to see one of the first films ever produced, Louis Lumière's *The Arrival of the Train at the Gare de Lyon* (1895). This one-minute, unedited film shows the train coming from afar, approaching and approaching, and finally arriving in a medium shot (felt as a close-up). Just like the original audience, the hero gets scared. He feels that he will be run over by the train; he does not distinguish film from reality.

Shortly, however, he learns to do so. The next film in the program happens to be an innocently pornographic movie about a girl bathing. Wanting to join the nude in the bathtub, the hero jumps to the stage. But unable to get into the tub, he pulls down the screen, and the rest of the film is projected on the bleak wall—and on him. He has been forced to realize that film is not reality, even though it may offer a semblance of reality. He has been forced to realize that film is a symbolic medium, a visual language.

1. Film and language

That film is a language is an old notion in film theory, and a still live one. Yet it is not always as clear as it might be what theorists who say this are really asserting. Obviously the statement that film is a language must be taken in some extended, metaphorical, or nonliteral way; nobody has ever wanted to claim that film literally belongs among English, Danish, French, and Chinese.

To make sense, the claim that film is a language must be taken as a pointer to some supposedly significant similarity or set of similarities between film and verbal language. But as everyone has been forced to realize from time to time, and as Nelson Goodman has pointed out so clearly, similarity is a "false friend," "a pretender, an imposter, a quack."[1] Everything resembles everything else in some way or other (just as everything is different from everything else in some way or other). Only if the theorist states explicitly in what respect film is similar to verbal language will he make a real contribution to the understanding of film.

2. Code and medium

An initial problem, however, is that the very terms "film" and "language" are themselves not as precise as one might wish. "Language," to take that first, may mean both what the French call *langage* and what they call *langue*. Tentatively one may say that *langage* is a rather vague word denoting the total linguistic phenomenon, language as a means of communication and as an object for study from many points of view (physiological, psychological, phonetic, social, etc.), among which the linguistic point of view is only one. And just as tentatively one may say that *langue* denotes the specific language system of syntax and semantics inherent in any verbal language and an object for linguistic study only.[2]

This is a valuable distinction that will run through the whole of this essay (getting clearer as it goes along). It is thus regrettable that English has no terms that correspond directly to the French *langage* and *langue* and that possible renderings of the two terms (like "language in the broad sense" and "language in the narrow sense") are unduly clumsy. Instead, a pair of alternative terms will better serve to sustain the distinction between *langage* and *langue*, namely the term "medium" for *langage* and the term "code" for *langue*. These two will also permit discussion without quotes about other "languages," that is, media or codes other than verbal language if such other means of communication can be found. Maybe film is one?

But "film," on the other hand, is not a very clear notion either. There are, for example, many different kinds of films. This essay, however, will be concerned only with sound films like the narrative and fictive features made in Hollywood between 1935 and 1960, although at special places some asides may appear about silents, documentary films, and TV films. But even if this is clear, saying that film is a language cannot be saying that each single feature film is a language. It must rather be saying that each single film is (or may be compared to) an *utterance* within a language of a special kind, the film language.

And this raises the first interesting question of this essay, namely, does "language" here mean "code" or merely "medium"? "Code," probably, as shown by such characteristic titles of books on film theory as *A Grammar of the Film*.[3] The same conclusion is borne out by characteristic formulations such as this (probably the first expression of the idea of the strict parallel between film and verbal language, but expressed repeatedly by many film theorists): "just as in living speech, so, one may say, in editing: there is the word—the piece of exposed film, the image; a phrase—the combination of these pieces."[4] The same interpretation is further supported by common sense; to express the idea that film is a language in a general way, without specifying how this language is built up, is pointless if "language" is to be taken as "medium" and not as "code."

3. The structure of verbal language—and of film

The traditional claim that film is a language seems, then, to be the claim that film is a code, and even a code with a close structural or grammatical similarity to the code of verbal language. Evaluating this claim requires a closer look at the code of a typical verbal language—English, for instance.

One basic aspect of the code of English is that it is a two-level structure. It comprises a primary level (called the *primary articulation*) of meaningful units, the words, and a secondary level (the *secondary articulation*) of units not meaningful in themselves, the phonemes (rendered, approximately, in script by letters), which, however, combine in different ways to form the units of the primary articulation and thereby also their meanings. Substituting an *h* for the *m* in "mouse," for example, yields quite another word with quite another meaning.

The units of the primary articulation, the words, may obviously be combined into sentences, which are the vehicles of actual communication. But this does not mean that sentences constitute some superprimary articulation; units like sentences are rather what is called *syntagms*. Units of a primary articulation differ from syntagms in that the former are composed of units not in themselves meaningful whereas the latter, the syntagms, are composed of already meaningful units which keep their separate meanings even when combined.[5]

Two more things should be pointed out in this connection. First, most verbal languages have (like English) syntactic or grammatical rules that distinguish between correctly and incorrectly built syntagms. Second, the meaning of a word is not some object in the world to which the word refers or that the word stands for but is rather an inherent property of the word as such, a property by virtue of the fact that the phonemic pattern of the word complies with certain semantic rules of the language in question. One might say that a meaningful unit like a word is a two-sided entity consisting of a syntactic and a semantic element, or in other words the signifying element (in French *le significant*, the sound pattern of a word), and the meaning (in

French *le signifie*). The point is that the meaning is part of the sign, not of the world.

The word "unicorn," for instance, has its visible syntactic shape, and it means *unicorn*. But since there are no unicorns in the world, it should be clear that a word can have meaning without reference, that is, that meaning and reference differ. The same holds for words like "typewriter." "Typewriter" has this syntactic shape and means *typewriter*; taken simply as a word of that shape and meaning this, it does not refer to the typewriter from which this essay is now emerging or to any other typewriter in the world. One may use it to refer to (and characterize) any particular typewriter exactly because the word has the meaning it has.

Does film resemble verbal language on these points? Some theoreticians have indeed argued that each shot of a film can be seen as a meaningful unit of a primary articulation resting on a secondary articulation of units that do not have any meanings in themselves. They have argued, moreover, that film does have a grammar for the construction of correctly formed syntagms (that is, sequences or scenes) out of already meaningful units (that is, shots and pictures) by chaining them to suggest single, uninterrupted episodes. Yet one can agree that pictures represent whatever they represent in exactly the same sense as that in which words mean whatever they mean, and one can argue further that there is a striking semantic similarity between film and verbal language, without at the same time accepting the two claims of syntactic similarity.

Casually speaking, it may indeed be both possible and sensible to say that a shot or a picture as a whole is built up through units like lines and dots, and colored or black and white shapes.[6] But such units are not clearly distinguishable and limited in number like phonemes. These characteristics of phonemes are central to the theory of phonemes and articulations; they provide the basis of the economic principle, inherent in the theory, that from a limited number of clearly distinguishable units indefinitely many meaningful combinations can result.[7]

And still, casually speaking, it may also be both possible and sensible to say that a shot or a picture of a man is built up of units like two eye pictures, a nose picture, a mouth picture, and so on.[8] But if that were the case, even if the units proved to be clearly distinguishable and of a limited number (and this is certainly doubtful), they would not be without meaning like the phonemes. Nose pictures, for example, are meaningful units, that is, units belonging rather to the primary than to the secondary articulation. Viewed in this light the picture as a whole would be a syntagm rather than a unit of the primary articulation.

Speaking about an editing code of the film is certainly feasible, too. But this code does not correspond to the grammatical rules of a language like English. If a grammatical rule is one that permits a distinction between correctly and incorrectly formed syntagms (like sentences or sequences), then film has no grammatical rules. Any combination of shots in a film is correct. But this is not to deny the possibility of nonsense sequences, that is, sequences that tell about unlikely or even inconceivable situations or events.

A chain of words like "the man eat his supper" does not belong to any known language (very strictly speaking), not even to English, since it violates a formal grammatical rule of English. But a chain of shots that goes from a close shot of a man looking to the right, over a close shot of a woman looking to the right, to a medium shot of the two persons conversing face to face, is still film. This is true even though the sequence tells about a most unlikely (and probably unintended!) change of position of one of the conversants between shots two and three, and even though this might conveniently be described as violating the well-known editing rule which requires that, to suggest two people looking at one another by juxtaposing a close shot of each, they must look in opposite directions.

A sequence like the one imagined here corresponds more closely to a nonsense sentence like "the man eats his empiricism" than to "the man eat his supper," that is, to semantic rather than to syntactic aberration. Semantic aberration need not violate formal grammatic rules; rather, semantic aberration presupposes adherence to these rules, since the question of sense and nonsense seems only to arise in connection with correctly built sentences.

4. Film as a medium

The fact that film does not correspond structurally to the verbal code need not imply that film is not a code at all. The implicit definition of a code as used so far may be too strict. One might at least argue that even though verbal languages do characteristically have two articulations, and even though verbal languages do characteristically have grammatical rules, calling them codes only adds up to the fact that they are systems of semantic rules which make certain units mean something. Working with this minimum definition of a code does indeed seem quite sensible, since it would permit us to say that not only verbal languages and closely related systems are codes but also, say, the system of traffic signs. Could film be called a code according to this definition?

Again the answer must be no, but this time not a strict no. Taking "film" in the traditional sense of a fictional narrative feature film, then film is not *just* a code; that is, it is not merely a system that lets certain designs projected on a screen, certain moving dots and lines and shapes, mean something, namely persons, things, rooms, cityscapes, and landscapes.

Indubitably such a code is part of what is meant by "film language." But only part; for if this code and film language were identical, film would only be a means through which persons, things, rooms, cityscapes, and landscapes are *depicted* or *represented*. The fictional narrative feature film is not like that. It is a means of communication in which *stories are told* about fictitious persons, things, rooms, cityscapes, and landscapes.

And this counterargument could be used against any other system of semantic rules of the film which might be cited as evidence that the film is a code, namely the code that is this very system. As already indicated above, it is possible to talk about an editing (or montage) code of the film. But one cannot thereby maintain that film is a code because its system of rules makes certain combinations of shots mean things like "the man is looking at an apple" or "the girl enters the house by the front door." Indubitably film does have a code like that; but again, film is not identical with just this code, for the fictional feature film is not a means for the depiction of such minor events but a means of communication in which stories are told. If it is maintained that the film is a code because its system of rules makes certain compositions of elements within the picture frame mean things like "this man is dominating that man," the same counterargument holds once more. Film is not a means for the depiction of such minor situations but a means of communication in which stories are told. Even though film language contains a code like this, it is not identical with just this code.

Therefore, even though film language can be demonstrated to contain or to use several codes (by the minimum definition of "code," namely, as semantic code only), it cannot reasonably be claimed to be identical with any one of them. If film is a language, it is not a code; it is a means of communication in a more general sense, a medium.

But now the concept of a medium can be clarified. The notion that film language contains or uses several codes can now be replaced by the proposal that film language is a medium in the sense of a conglomerate of multiple codes. Here, then, is at least one reason why the comparison between verbal language and film, as ordinarily articulated, seems so awkward. That comparison seeks to relate means of communication of different categories, so to speak, namely a code and a medium.

But the conclusion that film is a medium, and the arguments leading up to that contention, give rise to a variety of questions. Is moving picture representation—or pictorial representation in general—really based on a code? Are the other codes mentioned—the editing code, the picture composition code—really codes at all? What other codes does the film medium use? Are these various codes specific to the film medium? What is the relationship between the codes within the film medium in general and those within each actual film? The rest of this essay is concerned with these questions.

5. Representation and resemblance

An earlier section claimed that representation is a property of pictures corresponding closely to meaning as a property of words. Thus the fact that a picture *P* represents *x* is an institutional fact, one which is a fact only because a semantic rule (a constitutive or institutional rule of a definite kind[9]) makes the design of *P* count as a representation of *x* or rather as an *x*-representation, a representing picture of a certain kind. This is, however, not the usual way of regarding representation in film theory (or in general aesthetics, for that matter). Most theoreticians would probably argue that there is a sharp distinction between "meaning" in pictures and in words (a claim that has its counterpart, by the way, in the reluctance of many film theoreticians to compare film and verbal language on any level other than the grammatical).

If concerned with this problem at all, most film theoreticians argue that verbal meaning and pictorial representation are quite distinct phenomena. Granted, verbal meaning is constituted by way of arbitrary rules (arbitrary not in the sense that they have been made by individual human decision but in the sense that no compelling logic requires a certain sound pattern to mean this rather than that). But, they continue, pictorial representation has nothing to do with rules. Pictorial representation is not an arbitrary or conventional phenomenon, the argument goes, but a natural one. A picture represents whatever it represents for reasons independent of human decision not only in practice but even in theory, for a picture represents whatever it resembles. It is therefore not up to human beings to decide what a certain design should represent but only to find out what it does represent by finding out what it resembles.[10]

As a little reflection will show, however, this argument does not hold. It is quite simply not the case that a picture represents whatever it resembles, as an example will show. Leondardo's Mona Lisa resembles many of the reproductions of it, yet it certainly does not represent any of them. And if it should then be argued that only things can be represented by pictures, not pictures by pictures, it must be pointed out, first, that pictures of pictures are indeed very common (any photograph of a room with paintings on its walls would do as an example), and second, that the argument can be restated. If, for instance, the Mona Lisa should resemble one of my cousins, this does not imply that it represents one of my cousins.

6. Resemblance as a necessary condition for representation

But even if resemblance has thus been shown not to be a sufficient condition for representation, and even if pictures do represent whatever they represent because their designs comply with certain semantic rules belonging to a certain representational code, it might still be maintained that there is nonetheless a fundamental difference between words and pictures, namely that only if a picture does resemble what (according to some arbitrary rule) it represents can it reasonably be called a picture or a representation of its subject. Or, to put it differently, it might still be maintained that if resemblance is not a *sufficient* reason for representation, then at least it is a *necessary* one. Even if a picture need not represent whatever it resembles, it must necessarily resemble whatever it represents in order to be a picture or a representation of it. It might, for instance, be conceded that what looks exactly like a lion nevertheless, according to some idiosyncratic rule, "stands for" a man. But in that case it should not be called a picture or a representation of a man but rather a symbol of a man (as the cross is not a picture of Christianity but a symbol of Christianity).

There are, however, several reasons why even this weaker argument cannot be sustained. One is that the very concept of resemblance or similarity is so vague that anything can be said to resemble anything else in some way or other. To demand resemblance between a picture and what it represents as a necessary condition for its being a picture at all is therefore quite trivial since the condition will always be satisfied. Unless some special kind of resemblance is demanded, pictures and nonpictures cannot be distinguished by means of this condition. And there is even the special problem that the specific condition put forth should not be an arbitrary one, as it is exactly the need to avoid arbitrariness that initiated this line of reasoning.

But another reason is that whatever specific kind of resemblance the theoretician demands (commonly the kind of resemblance that allows the design of a picture to be seen "as" whatever is represented[11]), the resemblance theory must always presuppose the material existence of whatever is represented. For, obviously, a picture *P* cannot resemble *x* if *x* is not an object with a visible appearance; but having a visible appearance presupposes having material existence. So if the condition holds, it should be impossible to represent entities like unicorns and Mr. Pickwick.

Yet it certainly is possible to represent unicorns and Mr. Pickwick and all other fictitious entities, so the theory must be rejected. There is no way out by saying that even though fictitious entities do not exist materially, nevertheless they do have visible appearances in the sense that we know what they would look like if they did exist. An argument like that is simply nonsense, parallel to but worse than arguing that if dogs were cats they would mew and chase mice. Mr. Pickwick would not be Mr. Pickwick if there were any conceivable chance that he might turn up in the material world as a living person, since the fundamental thing to know about Mr. Pickwick is that he is a fictitious person, a person in a novel by Charles

Dickens. To make this clear, however, is not in any way to deny that people do know how fictitious entities look in pictures (how they should be represented, that is); on the contrary, that is exactly the point.

7. Representation and reference

There is, however, even a third reason to reject the theory that representation corresponds to or presupposes resemblance, and this reason is a more complex one. The reason is that the resemblance theory overlooks a fundamental ambiguity in the concept of representation and therefore confuses one kind with another.

The sentence "This picture represents a man" is ambiguous. It may mean that the picture represents a man rather than a woman or a lion; thus the picture "represents a man" in the sense of being a picture of a certain kind. But the sentence may also mean that the picture represents some specific entity that happens to be a man; the picture now "represents a man" in the sense that it is used to refer to and characterize something, and this something is a man, Winston Churchill, say.

If Winston Churchill is being characterized, how is he being characterized? The answer is: as a man, if the picture represents a man in the first sense (and then probably as a man of a certain appearance, character, and so on). But once the distinction has been made between "representation" as a description of the picture (so that it is a picture of a certain kind) and as a term for the relation between the picture and what it refers to and characterizes, it should be clear that, in our example, Churchill need not be characterized as a man. The picture may be a picture of a lion used as a picture of Churchill, that is, a picture of Churchill as a lion.

Obviously this distinction between the two senses of "representation" corresponds closely to the distinction between the meaning and the reference of a word. Just as obviously the distinction must be made in a simple way to avoid the ambiguity of "representation" not least because the arguments used to show that a picture represents an x are quite different in the two cases. Following Nelson Goodman, then, the phrase "the picture represents x" shall be used only to denote cases where the picture refers to and characterizes some x (where there is a relation between the picture and its referent, that is), whereas the phrase "an x-representation" or "an x-picture" shall be used as a description or classification of the picture itself (where no relation is involved).[12]

When theoreticians discuss representation, they discuss it in the "kind" sense and not in the reference sense. For if it were representation in the reference sense they were discussing, they would put forth arguments to show that the pictures are used to refer to and characterize specific things, and this they do not do. Characteristically they offer arguments to the effect that the design of a picture makes it count as an x-picture. Theoreticians do not tend to argue things like "this must be a representation of a man, for I know that the painter wanted it to represent Winston Churchill," but rather to argue things like "this must be a picture of a man (a man-picture, that is), for I can see its design as a man." (Admittedly the ambiguity of the parlance of traditional representational theory does blur this distinction.)

But since talking about pictures in this way is talking about them independently of the things they may or may not represent (in the reference sense)—and this means talking about them independently of anything but the pictures themselves and their rules—their eventual resemblance to these things (or to any other things) simply cannot be relevant to the discussion. When the resemblance theoretician argues that a picture must resemble an x if it is to count as a real picture or representation of x, he overlooks the fact that before anyone lets the picture refer to an x, that is, before any x is pointed out to which the picture may be compared for resemblance or lack of resemblance, the picture may already be an x-representation.

Thus there is not and there cannot be any logical relationship between representation and resemblance. A picture P represents x if and only if there is a representational semantic rule to the effect that the design of P counts as an x-representation. This is the whole answer to the logical question about representation. But to say this is not to deny that all kinds of sensible questions may be raised about why our actual representational rules are as they are, nor again to deny that these etymological questions may have correct answers drawing on resemblance, "seeing as," and other kinds of psychological, historic, or social observations.

8. *Photographic representation*

One might argue against these objections to the resemblance theory of representation, however, that this may all be good and true, but it completely misses the point. And it does so because it simply has nothing to do with *moving* pictures, shots in a film, since these are characteristically photographic pictures. Where photographic representation is concerned, it might be argued, neither resemblance, nor rules, nor distinctions between representation as reference and representation as meaning have any role to play. A photographic picture is something quite different from a word or an ordinary picture, the objection goes, because it represents only and whatever it is a photographic trace of and thus always refers to existing things, representing them as whatever they actually are.

This objection does not hold, however. First, pictures in feature films do not represent existing things and do not represent whatever they are photographic traces of. Feature films do not tell stories about real actors and actresses among props and sets but about fictitious persons at fictitious places. Second, the very fact that a picture P is a photographic trace of x is in no way a guarantee that P is a photographic representation of x. Why should it be, one may ask rhetorically?

The answer to this question might be that anything that is an effect of some cause is a sign of that cause (as footsteps in the snow are signs of the man who walked there, and the position of the weather vane is a sign of the direction of the wind that blew it into position). But any item is the effect of infinitely many causes, yet it is not a sign for all of them (and maybe not even for any of them).

A photograph, for instance, is just as much an effect of the photographer releasing the shutter or of the use of a certain lens as of the subject whose light rays made their imprint on the emulsion in the camera. Why, then, is it not considered a sign for the photographer or the lens, but only for the subject? And to concentrate merely on the relation photograph/subject, why are only fairly well-focused, properly exposed, and perhaps even properly composed photographs recognized as photographic pictures of their motives but not the blurred, overexposed, curiously composed ones that happen every now and then and that are photographic traces of their motives just as much as the acceptable ones? The answer to the last question is, obviously, that only when photographs are focused and so forth can they be read as ordinary pictures, which goes to show that photographs, as far as representation is concerned, are just ordinary pictures made in a special way.

To claim that photographs are just ordinary pictures made in a special way is, however, not to deny three basic facts about photographs. It is not to deny that a natural way of using photographs as pictures is to use them to depict their models or motives (as in family albums and newspapers); nor is it to deny that the fact that photographs characteristically are traces of real persons and things may give them a special importance as evidence of these persons and things;[13] and again, it is not to deny that our knowledge about how photographs are made may have a certain influence on the representational code according to which they are used and interpreted.

One might perhaps speak of a special photographic representational code—some sort of dialect within the general representational code—that lets designs count only as visual-appearance-representations (even when the photographs are not pictures of their models but rather of certain fictitious persons and things), whereas the general representational code may let designs count as visual-appearance-representations *or* as other things, emotion-representations, say. In a photograph a greenish color in a "face-design" would probably indicate a green complexion (the whole design would count, that is, as a face-with-greenish-complexion-representation), whereas in an ordinary picture the whole design might prima facie just as well count as a jealous-man-representation. Yet there are exceptions even to this; in modern Chinese films a greenish-face-design in a photographic man-picture counts as a member-of-Kuomintang-representation (or traitor-representation, or the like).

9. The codes of the film medium

So far these pages have tried to show that if film is a language it is not a code but a medium, a medium in which stories can be told and one that, unlike the medium of verbal language (as distinct from the language of fictive literature, the language of law, the language of trade, and so on) incorporates and uses not only one code but several, among which the photographic representational code is a very prominent one. Now some of the other codes deserve a closer look.

As already discussed, film is not just a language in which persons, things, and places and their visual appearances are depicted photographically. To maintain this position (although no theorist has explicitly done so) would be to disregard the fact that the appearances which characterize persons, things, and places are revealing and meaningful in their own right. Consider how the film maker tells the age, sex, or social status of the fictitious persons on the screen by means of their visual appearances. A person who is characterized as having gray hair and mustache is by these very features further characterized as a man and as rather old. This must mean that a further rule that belongs to a whole code of visual appearances makes a certain visual appearance mean something.

One may doubt, of course, that such things are "coded" at all. Seeing that a man is a man by his mustache and that he is rather old by his gray hair is interpreting the film just as one would interpret visual reality. Who would claim that visual reality is coded? But this is exactly what my claim is. Visual reality *is* coded, although not necessarily in the sense that human beings organize things according to rules to make them convey certain messages or express certain feelings. Rather it is coded in the sense that we interpret certain features of the visual world as signs.[14]

Sometimes this code is used quite deliberately to convey messages and express feelings. Why does one dress in certain ways and have his hair cut in certain ways (or not cut at all!) if not to make a certain impression on people, to tell them something? Visual reality is coded not in the sense that a linguistic system has been constructed, using as syntactic elements things like age, sex, and social status, but rather in the sense that people do in actuality interpret these things in these ways and that such interpretations seem to be based on systems of the kinds indicated.

So the film maker who wants to tell us more about his persons and things than simply their visual appearances may choose to use (or choose to refrain from using) those ready-made codes. Most film makers actually do rely heavily on these codes, not least because the audience is very liable to expect them to do so and is therefore more than liable to misinterpret a whole film fundamentally if these codes are not used. As most moviegoers will know, it may be difficult to experience a fictitious person as, say, rather old or to keep his age in mind if the person is played by a young-looking actor even though it may be unmistakably clear from other features (such as the dialogue) what the age of the fictitious person is. Just think of the curious age relationship between old-looking Hamlet and his young-looking mother in Sir Laurence Olivier's *Hamlet* (1948).

Yet the film maker need not use these codes or use only these codes. He may use other codes to tell the same things, or he may supplement the codes from daily life with less realistic codes, those of "cinema iconography," or others which he invents himself. The film maker may have his hero wear white and his villain wear black (or he may surprise us by doing things the other way around), he may show relationships between persons and places by using certain color schemes (the way a warm red stands for the kidnaped boy in Alfred Hitchcock's *The Man Who Knew Too Much*, 1955), or he may use pictures of things in a symbolic or metaphorical way. Think of all the pictorial metaphors for the sexual act invented in Hollywood between 1930 and 1965: trains, trees, steaming kettles, and so on and on.

10. The codes of composition

The single picture or shot in a film, however, does not comply only with semantic rules on the two levels discussed so far: the first where the designs projected on the screen comply with rules that make them count as representations, and especially as representations of the visual appearances of people, things, and places; and the second where these representations, or parts of them, in their turn comply with rules, either of daily life or of a less realistic kind. The elements on the first level, that is, the x-representations, are also used as signifying elements within systems of pictorial composition, some common to films and photographs only, others to all pictorial media.

By composing his pictures in certain ways, that is, by arranging the elements in certain ways on both the actual two-dimensional plane and in the represented three-dimensional space, the film maker may tell things, for instance, about his persons and the relations between them. To call our attention to one person rather than another, or to emphasize the importance, or the strength, or the social status of one person in contrast to another, the film maker may set him off by framing him against the features behind him (like a door with its panels) or by pointing to him with lines constituted by the contours of background elements, or by other people's gazes. Or he may use the simpler means of having the more important person occupy a larger area than the other or have him appear higher than the other on the two-dimensional plane. Or he may place the more important person in front of the less important, or in an actually higher position, or where the more important person usually stands, or in many other ways. The fact that these spatial relations are readily perceived as meaningful confirms that the codes of composition are widely shared.

11. The codes of movement

So far the discussion has concerned single pictures or single shots only, as if a feature film consisted of only one still photograph or at the most of an unorganized conglomerate of still pictures. But obviously this is not the case. One example of a feature film consisting exclusively of stills is Chris Marker's *La Jetée* (1963), and here the stills are certainly not organized in any haphazard way. But most shots of an ordinary feature film obviously do contain movement (and if a shot does not, especially if it is a frozen shot, this is meaningful in itself in contrast to moving shots, whereas the stillness of ordinary photographs is not a signifying feature). And of course the shots are joined together in organized ways.

Within the single shot there are codes of movements directly related to the codes of still photographs considered so far. In the still, codes from daily life are used to tell about such things as age, sex, or social status. In the same way, codes from daily life are also used in moving pictures, codes that enable the film maker to tell more about the fictitious individuals, both about who and what they are and about their actions.

Their ways of moving and gesticulating (as represented) tell about their age, energy, mood, and so on, and their gestures and actions also contribute to the development of the story. But it should not be forgotten that on this level too the film maker can either refrain completely from using the codes of daily life or, more often, can supplement these with special codes. In early silent movies, for instance, gesture codes common to mime were used to some extent, and even in realistic sound movies certain gestures (like Humphrey Bogart's pulling the lobe of his ear in Howard Hawks's *The Big Sleep*, 1946) may be used in a meaningful, yet symbolic or metaphorical way.

A more interesting field of study is, however, movement on the compositional level, which may be movement made either by letting actors move around among the props or by moving the camera (or merely changing the focal length of the lens, as with a zoom lens) whereby the picture frame may be said to move in relation to the elements of the picture. Through these movements the film maker may tell about changes in relationships between persons in much the same way as he might tell about relationships on the still level. The code used on this level seems to be specific to film, or rather to moving picture fiction, including television plays. It does not seem to be used in TV nonfiction (perhaps because of the speed with which most TV nonfiction is produced) and only to a certain extent in documentary films.

12. *The codes of montage*

The codes sketched thus far are those used by the film medium considered as a means of communication through still pictures or single moving shots. But as everyone knows, a traditional feature film consists characteristically of a chain of shots, despite such famous exceptions as Alfred Hitchcock's 1948 film *Rope* (which should be seen as one unbroken shot, even though it was technically impossible to make it that way). And as I have already pointed out, the principles on which this chain of shots are constructed—the principles of montage—have commonly been regarded by film theorists as the real and only code of the film.

An earlier discussion had to refute this contention because traditional film theoreticians assume too strict a parallel to verbal language. But if the organization of the shots in a feature film does not strictly parallel the grammar of verbal language, this does not mean that the chain is not constructed according to a code at all. Actually, the very argument used to show that this strict parallel does not hold tends to indicate that some code is in fact used on this level. The argument was that whereas it is possible to make chains of English words that do not result in English sentences (because they violate English grammatical rules), any chain of shots in a film will mean something, even though this something may be nonsense. The very fact that these chains do mean something seems to show that there must be some code.

The so-called "grammar of the film" seems to comprise two levels. On one level just two or three shots are put together to form a syntagm with a minimum content such as "the man sits down in a chair" or "the old lady looks at the books" (or one might also say that a minimum content like these is split into two or three shots instead of being shown in just one). On the other level more than two or three shots are joined (or chains of shots of the first level are combined into somewhat larger chains) to form what might be called larger syntagms with a more complex content such as "the man enters the room, takes a seat, lights a pipe, and starts reading a book, but is disturbed in his reading by a knock on the door," or "the girl is chased by the gangsters through the dark street, while the hero tries to find her by asking for her in the coffee shops."

This structural distinction follows a historical one. Originally, silent feature films had no montage at all but consisted of chains of scenes, each presented in one unbroken shot from a fixed camera position. These scenes corresponded to the larger syntagms. But gradually the larger syntagms were broken up more and more, first by the insertion of close shots which served to magnify and to break the continuity of the action, later in shots of "scenettes," in shots of the continuous action from different points of view, and so on until the Soviet montage experiments of the early twenties showed that even a unit like the opening of a hand could be shown in several shots from different angles.

The films with which this paper is concerned, the standard feature films of 1935 to 1960, tended to use a middling style between the two extremes. A scene would invariably be broken up, and most "scenettes" ("a man sits down," "a girl takes a book, opens it, and starts reading") would be broken up into clearly distinguishable (because strikingly composed) shots. Since 1960, however, the tendency has shifted toward scenes shown in unbroken shots but with a moving camera (often called "cutting in the camera"). Instead of cutting to a close shot, for instance, the film maker now often moves his camera from medium into close shot. There has also been a shift toward hiding the montage, for instance by cutting during the movements of the actors instead of between movements.

The rules of montage of the first level are chiefly rules for "cutting continuity" and for what has conveniently been called "film geography."[15] One such rule is that a close shot of a man looking, followed by a close shot of something else, means that the man is looking at whatever is represented in the second shot. (Obviously this can work the other way around, too, even though the signal shot, the one of the person looking, normally precedes the subject shot, the one of what the person is looking at.) Another rule is that a close shot of a man thinking, dissolved into a shot of something else, means that the man is thinking of whatever the second shot shows. There are also less realistic chains of two or three shots, metaphorical or associative shots of flowers or animals, say, followed by shots of whatever is "like a rose" or "like a cat."

13.   Christian Metz's system of larger syntagms

More interesting than these smaller syntagms are the larger ones. Recently the French film theoretician and semiotician Christian Metz has proposed that the traditional feature film has only eight different types of larger units of this kind, "autonomous segments" as he calls them. Any such unit found in a traditional feature film will belong to one of these eight groups, whose distinguishing features are a number of time and place relationships. Since Metz's study of these segments is one of the most exact contributions to the study of film as a language, it deserves to be set forth in some detail.

Metz has tried to present his eight autonomous segments in a way that makes it clear that they constitute a system, namely, by way of six dichotomies.[16] The first dichotomy that he mentions is that between segments consisting of a single shot and segments consisting of several intercut shots, the syntagms. As William Wyler, Orson Welles, and Alfred Hitchcock have shown, it is indeed possible to tell separate parts of a film story without cutting at all within these parts. *Segments of single shots*, therefore, may be mentioned as the first kind of autonomous segment.

Of interest here, however, are the syntagms, the edited segments, and among these one can distinguish, first, between segments that tell about time relationships and those that do not. The latter kind divide into *parallel syntagms* and *parenthetical syntagms*. In parallel syntagms, shots of two or more motives are intercut for contrast or comparison (shots of the rich and the poor, of calm and exaltation, of country and town, and so on). In parenthetical syntagms shots of different aspects of the same motive are intercut, and the whole syntagm will count as a general statement about this usually abstract motive (of "timeless universals" like love, war, city life, childhood, and so on).

The syntagms involving time divide first into *descriptive syntagms* and *narrative syntagms*. In descriptive syntagms shots of different motives are intercut, and the whole syntagm will count as a statement about the simultaneity of everything presented (trees, a river, a group of houses, and so on, are presented in a description of a landscape).

The narrative syntagms, in their turn, divide into *alternated* (*narrative*) *syntagms* and *linear* (*narrative*) *syntagms*. The alternated syntagms are identical with "cross-cut sequences," a kind of cross between segments telling about simultaneity and segments telling about sequential events. Two or more series of events are intercut, and the whole syntagm will count as a statement about the simultaneity of the two series taken as wholes, but about a progress in time within each series (the most familiar examples being pursuits, shown through shots of the pursuers and the pursued mixed in A-B-A-B-form, or last-minute rescues, where shots of the stage coach being attacked by the Indians are intercut with shots of the approaching cavalry).

The linear (narrative) syntagms divide further into what Metz calls *scenes* and *sequences*. Scenes consist of shots intercut to tell about events in a way that lets the time of the telling equal that of the event told. Even though the point of view may alternate between partners in a conversation, for example, nothing is cut out completely, and nothing shown twice. (Actually such scenes are rather rare. Scenes of this apparent kind turn out, on analysis, to be slightly condensed; people are rarely shown walking the whole distance from one chair to another, for instance, even though the fact that the change of position takes time may be made quite clear to, and even "felt" by, the audience.)

Sequences, however, are normally compressed as compared with the time spans of the events they describe. Sequences are divided into *ordinary sequences*, which are compressed after no special scheme (and these are the most ordinary autonomous segments of traditional films), and *episodic sequences*, which present a series of short "scenettes" often separated by dissolves or other optical effects. Episodic sequences usually tell about long time spans in a very economical way, often by showing the same motive again and again as it changes through time (breakfasts at a longer and longer breakfast table to show the development of Kane's first marriage in Orson Welles's *Citizen Kane*, 1941).

14.   Three questions about codes

Obviously the codes mentioned in the preceding paragraphs have been discussed only as examples of the various codes (or perhaps submedia) that make up the film medium as a whole. This list of codes is by no means exhaustive, and all except perhaps the representational code have received only the scantiest treatment. There are, obviously, further codes on the level of single still pictures, on the level of single moving shots, and on the level of chains of shots and of the whole narrative structure of the film. And, just as obviously, the use of verbal language as a submedium of the sound film as well as codes for musical accompaniment and for sound effects have been wholly ignored.

Nonetheless, enough codes have been exemplified to raise three questions. Are the codes specific to the film medium? Do all codes have the same syntactic-semantic structure? And how do the codes relate to one another within the film medium as such, and when used in an actual film?

15.   Specificity of codes and specificity of media

The problem whether the codes incorporated in and used by the film medium are specific to this medium[17] has been touched upon several times in the paragraphs above. Taking the phrase "specific to a medium" to mean used only by this medium, most (and maybe all) of the codes used by the film medium are quite evidently not specific to it. The photographic representational code, for instance, is common to the film and to such media as amateur photography, news photography, and the photo novel. The code that permits us to interpret visual-appearance representations as expressions of the age, sex, or social status of fictitious persons is common to film, the everyday visual world, and various kinds of photography, or, in the case of the special unrealistic codes of film iconography, to the film, painting, and the photo novel, as are codes for the composition of shots. One might even argue that the codes for constructing chains of shots are common to the film, the photo novel, and the comic strip.

So it seems that no code used by the film medium is specific to this medium. But this does not mean that the film medium is not an individual or particular medium. On the contrary, its particularity lies in the combination of the nonspecific codes it uses. The film medium may have codes for building up chains of shots in common with the comic strip, but it differs from that medium because it is based on a photographic representational code and because it has a code for movements within shots or pictures. Again, the film medium shares this latter code with the medium of TV news but is distinguished from it by stricter codes for the composition of shots, not merely for aesthetic reasons but because the spatial relations in a feature film shot may tell about personal relationships (relations of strength or power, for example), whereas this is not true of the TV news film.

To repeat, then, film is a medium in the sense that it is a meetingplace of multiple codes (or submedia) and is defined as a particular medium not by virtue of specific codes but through the characteristic set of nonspecific codes that it uses. Obviously this way of regarding the film medium is inspired by the old thought of the *Gesamtkunstwerk*. The view presented in this essay, however, is much broader than the traditional one. A typical feature film is, indeed, a *Gesamtkunstwerk*, one which unites the arts of literature, drama, music, and painting. But the description of a medium developed in this essay includes not only the arts of *Gesamtkunstwerk* (film, opera, ballet) but also the traditional basic arts. Artistic painting, for instance, is a medium (as that word has been used here) characterized by representational, compositional, iconographic, and other codes.[18] One might, however, argue that film is unique among the arts (although perhaps similar to opera) in incorporating more codes than any other.

16. Three types of codes

So far "code" has not been defined very clearly. An earlier paragraph proposed a minimum definition of "code" to the effect that it is a system of rules which make certain entities (sounds, designs, etc.) count as, that is mean, something. But it seems rather evident that there must be differences between such codes as the basic photographic representational one and the iconographic one exemplified by the rule that the man in white is the hero, the man in black the villain. How can such differences be spelled out in a systematic way?

Nelson Goodman has distinguished three ideal types of codes, which he calls *notations*, *languages*, and *representational systems*.[19] This distinction is based primarily on different syntactic structures. On the one hand, notations and languages are codes whose syntactic elements are so organized that they may be determined unambiguously (in principle at least). On the other hand, representational codes or systems are those whose syntactic elements are not organized in this way.

Verbal languages, in both spoken or written form, are examples of codes in which it is possible to determine the syntactic elements—the words—unambiguously because of the finite number of unambiguously distinguishable phonemes or letters. A certain sound is either this phoneme or that one or none at all; a certain mark on paper (or vellum or stone) is either this letter or that one or none at all. There is no third phoneme in the sound continuum between an *e* and an *a*, for example, and no third letter in the continuum between handwritten *a* and *d*.

Representational codes, however, provide for indefinitely many syntactic elements; between any two designs there is a third, hence indefinitely many. Imagine, for instance, two primitive man representations in which the only prima facie difference is the length of the line that counts as the nose representation. Obviously the very representational code that provides for these two representations also provides for a third one containing a nose representation of intermediate length, and thus for indefinitely many in all.

But this means that each specific man representation cannot be clearly distinguished from every other; the code does not provide any means for deciding whether two man representations which appear completely alike are two instances of the same syntactic element of the code (in the sense in which two marks on paper are instances of the same letter) and not, instead, two marginally different syntactic elements. And this means further that each individual *x*-representation, each single picture, has to be considered as unique. Since there is no criterion for deciding whether two *x*-representations are completely alike or not, and since there is no criterion for distinguishing relevant from irrelevant differences in two *x*-representations, any difference has to be taken as relevant, and any single *x*-representation has to be taken as unique. The claim, for instance, that two *x*-representations are two instances of one and the same syntactic element of the representational code, when no difference can be perceived between them, cannot be maintained, for what cannot be perceived now may be perceived at another time.

Codes like this are called dense, and density in this sense is the defining characteristic of representational systems or codes as against both notations and languages. These latter types are both characterized by clearly distinguishable syntactic elements, but they differ in the structure of their semantics.

One might say that most codes are concerned with specific universes of discourse, according to the meanings of the elements and also according to the items of the world which may be characterized by utterances belonging to the code. The code of traffic signs, for instance, is concerned with such things as curves, bumpy and slippery roads, and railway crossings, and these make up its universe of discourse; the code of musical notation has tones as its universe of discourse; a certain semaphoric code has various situations aboard ships.

Some of these universes of discourse contain only clearly distinguishable items that can be correctly referred to and sensibly characterized by specific elements of the relevant codes. Other universes of discourse, however, have no clear boundaries as a whole, do not contain only clearly distinguishable items, or contain items that can be correctly referred to and sensibly characterized by various elements of the code. The code of musical notation, for instance, has a universe of discourse containing only items that are just as clearly distinguishable as the note signs, namely the tones, wherefore a one-to-one relationship exists between notes and tones in the sense that, just as a certain note sign may be used unambiguously to refer to only one tone, so a certain tone can be correctly referred to only by one specific note sign. Verbal languages, however, do not have specific universes of discourse; their comprehensive universes do not contain only clearly distinguishable items (there is no sharp borderline between youth and adulthood, for instance); and each item may be correctly referred to and sensibly characterized in several ways (a certain "man" is also a "bachelor," a "university professor," a "tennis player," and so on).

Codes like that of musical notation are instances of what Goodman calls *notations*, and codes like those of verbal languages are instances of what he calls *languages*. As for *representational systems*, the fact that their syntactic elements are not clearly distinguishable renders superfluous any question about an unambiguous relationship between elements of the codes and items of their universes of discourse.

17. Notational, linguistic, and representational codes in the film medium

All three types of codes may be exemplified in any traditional feature film, using the very codes cited here as standard examples. In *The Man Who Knew Too Much* (1956), for instance, Hitchcock shows pictures of a score to indicate the approach of the moment when a sniper in one box of the concert hall will shoot a man in another box. In the sound film, verbal language is used to a large extent, and pictures of printed matter or handwritten messages are not unusual. And, obviously, the photographic code is a "representational" code.

But all three types can also be found among the other codes. The iconographic code is a good approximation of a notational system. The syntactic elements are, for the most part, readily distinguishable; it is, indeed, unambiguously clear whether a person is in white or black (and whether there seems to be any point in this at all). And the iconographic code does seem to provide for a good approximation to an unambiguous one-to-one relationship between elements of the code and items of its universe of discourse. The specific iconographic code used as an example is only concerned with heroes and villains, and it unambiguously states that the hero should be characterized by white, the villain by black. The fact that a director may choose not to use this system or to have his hero wear black, his villain white, does not falsify this point; it only shows that there may be iconographical codes other than the one from which a rule has been cited or that this kind of code may not be used in a certain film at all.

The more realistic uses of visual appearances to tell about such things as age, sex, or social position tend to be of the "language" type, once again in Goodman's sense. An audience will not have any trouble seeing that this person is of the mustache-plus-gray-hair type, hence is a rather old man, whereas this other person is of the gray-hair-plus-long-dress-plus-jewelry type, hence is a rich, rather old lady.

But there is no one-to-one relationship between being an old man in a film and being characterized by gray hair and mustache. The old man that the director needs in a certain position in the plot may be characterized in many other ways according to the very same code from daily life, and none of these will be exactly synonymous with the gray-hair-plus-mustache type. The director may characterize the old man as such by his dress and gait rather than by his hair and mustache. Or if the man's position in the plot is not so much a function of his age as of his physical weakness or of his being very wise, the director may choose to characterize him as very thin or partly lame, or as bald or bespectacled, rather than as gray-hair-and-mustache.

So it takes a good deal of creativity to use a code like this to characterize persons in films in a manner consistent with the plot and with the film as a whole. But this is exactly what characterizes the use of any "language." Using a language means, among other things, choosing between alternative characterizations, whereas using a notation means, for example, finding in a rather mechanical way the only correct note for a certain tone. There is opportunity for creativity in composing music but not in transcribing the composition, whereas using a language gives an opportunity for creativity both in finding or inventing what should be described and in the actual description, the actual formulation in words or pictures. This opportunity may be minimally used, of course; stock phrases and stock pictures easily come to mind and threaten to reduce a language to the state of a notation. But the opportunity for choosing subtle and clever and mutually enhancing formulations is always there.

The gray hair may, however, also be used in a "representational" way to mean old if gray is taken as a continuum of shades, each of which has a specific meaning; that is, if, say, more or less whitish gray means more or less old. And several of the other codes used by the film medium are of this representational kind. Telling about the relative strength or importance of the fictitious persons by placing them higher or lower on the picture plane or at more or less accentuated places in the picture space is an example of using a representational code in Goodman's sense. When one is placed higher than the other, not only the question "Who dominates whom?" may be answered (in which case this would exemplify a rule of "language"), but also the question "Who dominates whom by how much?"

18. The system of larger syntagms as a notation

How does Metz's system of "larger syntagms" fit these distinctions? Presupposing that his system does fit the facts in a satisfying way, it could be argued to be an approximation to a notation.

Where the universe of discourse is concerned, this seems clear enough. The system has a limited universe of discourse (logically limited, that is), consisting of seven different time and space relationships within the autonomous segments of feature films that count as syntagms of shots. (The *segments of single shots* stand a little apart, since they are syntactically defined. But their universe of discourse is quite unambiguous; it is everything, and differences between the various parts of "everything" shown in each segment are considered irrelevant.) And, actually, it should be easy to decide in each case whether the part of the plot that the director wants to translate into film is concerned with time relations, or whether the time relations between incidents of each segment (syntagm) are cases of simultaneity, and so forth. What the director wants to tell about must be simultaneous events at different places, or a complete event of short duration, or a relation between "timeless universals," or an extended development of something, and so on.

One might reasonably doubt, however, whether it is possible to distinguish unambiguously between various syntagms on the syntactic side. As a matter of fact, Metz has not given a clear formal description of these various syntagms. Some syntagms have no formal description at all beyond the fact that they are syntagms, chains of shots, and not segments of single shots. Only by understanding their content are we able to distinguish and recognize them. And those that are given a formal description, the parallel syntagm and the alternated syntagm, share the same one, the A-B-A-B-form. Again, only by realizing that one case consists of alternation between shots of such items as the pursuers and the pursued are we able to distinguish between these syntagms.

Yet this does not disqualify Metz's code as an approximation to a notation (or as a code, for that matter, as one might also think). The point in notations (and, on the syntactic side, in languages as well) is not that any syntactic element can be recognized and interpreted unambiguously *out of context*. The point is that it should be possible in principle to recognize and interpret any syntactic element, and to use contextual means (among others) to do so is just as respectable as to use only formal characteristics of the elements.

If contextual means were disallowed, scores would not exemplify notations, and verbal languages would not exemplify languages, since it is indeed possible to imagine marks on paper which, considered apart from any relevant context, might be an inscription in standard musical notation or in some written language, or just a meaningless doodle. Yet the context will ordinarily make this clear. And in the same way, even though the larger syntagms of a feature film are not distinguishable by purely formal means, they are distinguishable in practice. Their construction and context usually leave no doubt as to the classification of particular syntagms.

The few attempts at using Metz's scheme in a systematic way for analysis of a feature film (or part of one)[20] seem to agree that the only problems of classification are some rare cases of difficulty in deciding among parallel, parenthetical, and descriptive syntagms. Parallel shots of the rich and the poor, say, may tend to express a general statement of a "timeless universal" or may tend to describe various activities in two parts of a town.

This is not very serious, however. What is perhaps more serious is that these studies also show more pervasive difficulties in identifying the range of individual syntagms in the discourse of a film, that is, in locating the beginning and end of each. Where a change of syntagm is accompanied by a change of type of syntagm, this difficulty is rare. But where the whole discourse is built up as a chain of syntagms of the same type—and this will normally be a chain of ordinary sequences—the exact number of syntagms and the exact range of each may depend upon arbitrary decisions by the analyst.

So the scheme of larger syntagms is not a perfect notation. Yet it still seems to be a good approximation to one. And above all, the scheme appears to have been conceived as a notation, so that the whole point of the scheme must be the demonstration of a notational system of types of larger syntagms in the traditional feature film.

19. The meeting of the codes

The supportive role of context partly answers the last question about the various codes of the film medium: how do these codes relate to one another in an actual feature film? The answer is that the various codes elucidate the ways in which the other codes are used. And there seem to be at least two different, though not sharply distinct, ways in which this is done.

Some codes elucidate others because they are more basic in the sense that they are presupposed by the others. Most other codes, for example, must rely on the basic photographic code since they take representations, not simply designs or meaningless formal systems, as syntactic elements. It would, quite obviously, be impossible to interpret the gray hair of a man as a sign of his age if the projected blacks and whites and grays on the screen had not already been understood as a man-with-gray-hair-and-mustache representation. Neither would it be possible to understand the small syntagm of a shot of a man looking, plus a shot of an apple, as saying "the man looks at the apple" unless the two single shots had already been understood by way of the photographic representational code.

But the representational code is not the only one that is presupposed by others. Some of the Metz syntagms—most scenes and sequences especially—presuppose that certain smaller syntagms have been understood. The audience would not be able to understand a scene telling about a man entering a room if it were not already able to understand each smaller syntagm within this larger one.

Likewise, an iconographic code may be basic to a compositional code; for instance, the fact that the audience recognizes the man in white as the hero may emphasize his presence in a shot even if he is not placed in any remarkable way, and his gaze may further emphasize other things in the shot. One could say, then, that the shot presupposes not only the photographic representational code but the iconographic code as well.

In addition, codes elucidate one another by making it clear which codes are actually used and how. The audience finds out whether an iconographic code is used not only by seeing whether items that might be taken as syntactic elements of an iconographic code are present but also by seeing whether an interpretation of these elements according to the code makes sense within the larger context of the film, in light of the interpretation of other elements according to other codes. The man in white cannot be interpreted as the hero if he consistently performs villainous acts; thus either the stock iconographic code has not been used or some of the other elements have been misunderstood.

This kind of elucidation works not only between codes presupposing the same more basic codes or from basic codes upwards, so to speak, but also the other way around. The fact that a larger syntagm of the A-B-A-B type makes sense only if taken as an alternated syntagm, say, may indicate how a shot should be interpreted according to the representational code, especially when this is not evident if the shot is seen out of context. For instance, a design that might be either a pursuer representation or a pursued representation may, by its position as an A and not as a B, be revealed as the design of a pursuer representation.

It is tempting to try to formalize the ways in which the various codes of the film medium work together. Yet it would be difficult to extend this analysis beyond the scattered remarks above. In any case, providing more examples would seem to be a better way of amplifying the account. In cases such as this, "the canons of the classification are less clear than the practice," as Nelson Goodman says about the similar temptation to codify representational rules.[21]

The task of the film director is to use the possibilities in the many codes and the ways they work together as creatively as possible, and the task of audiences and critics is to experience and interpret the film presupposing that the medium has been used as creatively as possible, that everything, therefore, hangs together in the most intricate ways, and that each detail may elucidate many others.

20. Toward a semiotics of cinema

Film is not a language, then, if a language is taken to be what the French call a *langue*, a code, a set of syntactic and semantic rules. Above all, film is not a code with a structure strictly parallel to the structure of verbal language. But film is a language if that term is taken to mean what the French call a *langage*, a medium, a means of communication in a more general sense. It is characteristic of the film medium that it is a meetingplace of multiple codes, the photographic representational code being one, and various more or less realistic iconographic, compositional, and narrative codes being examples of others.

Of the various codes which together make up the film medium, none is specific to the medium. They approximate three different ideal types of codes, *notations, languages,* and *representational systems.* In any film the codes work together in such a way as to elucidate one another, some because they are basic to others, and all because they help to clarify which other codes are actually used, and how.

This is an outline of a semiotics of the cinema, an attempt at formulating, through discussion and examples, a rough sketch of the problems and how they may be handled. Obviously this essay has given no final solutions to the more intricate problems of the semiotics of the cinema. But emphasizing the fact that film is a meetingplace of multiple codes and exemplifying some of these codes should at least demonstrate that a semiotics of the cinema must cope with an abundance of codes and their subtle interactions, a point often overlooked by film theoreticians.

So film is not reality, as the young peasant thought at first in Godard's *Les Carabiniers.* Rather it is a language with a strong claim to uniqueness, a uniqueness that lies not in a specifically cinematic code but in the special combination of the many codes it shares in different ways with other languages, other means of communication.

Notes

1. Nelson Goodman, "Seven Strictures on Similarity," a lecture reprinted in Goodman, *Problems and Projects* (Indianapolis and New York: Bobbs-Merrill, 1972), p. 437. See also Goodman, *Languages of Art: An Approach to a Theory of Symbols* (Indianapolis and New York: Bobbs-Merrill, 1968), pp. 3–6. Throughout this essay I am indebted to Goodman's work, especially to the latter book, both in a general way and in more details than I shall be able to pinpoint in these notes.

2. This distinction was originally made by Ferdinand de Saussure, *Cours de linguistique générale*, ed. Charles Bally, Albert Sechehaya, and Albert Riedlinger (1915, reprinted Paris: Payot, 1969), pp. 23–32 (chap. 3, sections 1–2). For a good introduction in English to the basic concepts of modern French linguistics see André Martinet, *Elements of General Linguistics* (London: Faber, 1964). The distinction between film as a *langue* and film as a *langage* has been forcefully made by Christian Metz—apparently the first film theoretician to take the alleged parallel between film and verbal language seriously enough to see that film is not a *langue*—in his essay "Le cinéma: langue ou langage?" *Communications* 4 (1964): 53–90, reprinted in Metz, *Essais sur la signification au cinéma* (Paris: Klincksieck, 1968), pp. 39–93; in English, *Film-Language: A Semiotics of the Cinema* (New York: Oxford University Press, 1974).

3. Raymond Spottiswoode, *A Grammar of the Film* (1935, reprinted Berkeley and Los Angeles: University of California Press, 1950).

4. V. I. Pudovkin, *Film Technique and Film Acting* (1929/1933, reprinted New York: Bonanza Books, 1949), p. 72.

5. Martinet, *Elements*, pp. 22–24, 124.

6. Umberto Eco, *La struttura assente: Introduzione alla ricerca semiologica* (Milan: Bompiani, 1968), pp. 146–147, 156.

7. The "economics" of sign systems has been stressed in particular by Luis Prieto, *Messages et signeaux* (Paris: Presses Universitaires de France, 1966).

8. See Pier Paolo Pasolini, "La lingua scritta dell'azione," *Nuovi argomenti* 2 (April-June, 1966): 67–163.

9. About constitutive rules, see John R. Searle, *Speech Acts: An Essay in the Philosophy of Language* (Cambridge: At the University Press, 1969), pp. 50–53.

10. For a recent example from film theory of this very common thought, see Metz, *Essais*, pp. 67–69 and elsewhere.

11. See, for instance, Göran Hermerén, *Representation and Meaning in the Visual Arts: A Study in the Methodology of Iconography and Iconology* (Stockholm, Göteborg, and Lund: Läromedelsförlagen/Scandinavian University Books, 1969), chap. 2 in particular, and Richard Wollheim, *Art and Its Objects* (New York: Harper & Row, 1968), sections 11–14 in particular.

12. See Goodman, *Languages of Art*, pp. 27–31.

13. It should be noted, however, that using photographs as evidence is not using them as representations. If you want to argue on the basis of a photograph that a certain person was present when the photograph was taken, you would not claim that part of the design of the photograph *represents* the person but that part of the design could hardly have looked the way it does if the person in question had not been present in front of the camera—and this is quite another thing.

14. On visual reality as "coded," and especially on the "languages" of gestures and clothes, see the special issue on *Pratiques et langages gestuels* (ed. A. J. Greimas) of *Langages*, no. 10 (June 1968) with annotated bibliography, and the work of R. L. Birdwhistell and E. T. Hall.

15. The term seems to have been coined by the Danish film editor Christian Hartkop.

16. The final version of Metz's study of the autonomous segments of the feature film is presented in his essay "Problèmes de dénotation dans le film de fiction," in *Essais*, pp. 111–46.

17. This problem has also been treated by Christian Metz in his "Spécificité des codes et spécificité des langages," *Semiotica* 1, no. 4 (1969): 370–96, and again in his *Langage et cinéma* (Paris: Larousse, 1971), pp. 157–90; in English, *Language and Cinema* (The Hague: Mouton, 1974).

18. The point that the arts—and especially the film—are all "media" in the sense of being conglomerates of "heterogeneous" codes has been forcefully made by Emilio Garroni,

Semiotica ed estetica: L'esterogeneità del linguaggio e il linguaggio cinematografico (Bari: Laterza, 1968).

19. Goodman, *Languages of Art*, pp. 127–57, 225–32, and elsewhere.

20. E.g., Metz and Michele Lacoste, "Tableau des 'segments autonomes' du film *Adieu Philippine*, de Jacques Rozier," *Image et Son*, no. 201 (1967): 81–94, reprinted in Metz, *Essais*, pp. 151–75; Jens Toft, "Christian Metz og Eisenstein," *Exil: Tidsskrift for tekstteori* 25 (1973): 15–30; Jorgen Poulsen, *Antonio-das-Mortes* (Copenhagen: Institut for film-videnskab, 1972).

21. Goodman, *Languages of Art*, p. 23.

3 Information and Pictorial Representation
T. G. Roupas

Human beings use symbols—words, pictures, gestures, musical scores, traffic signs, and others—for a great variety of purposes. Not the least of these purposes, and perhaps the most central, is simply to communicate information. In an article published in 1954 the psychologist J. J. Gibson pointed out that although much was known about the manner in which language conveys information, little was known about the way in which pictures do so.[1] Since that time many psychologists, philosophers, art critics, and even linguists have concerned themselves with pictures as vehicles of information, and this essay shares that interest.

When Gibson raised the problem of how pictures convey information he was speaking only of *representational* pictures—those that show within their borders some concrete object, person, scene, or event. He did not intend his remarks to have any bearing upon what is commonly called "abstract" art, as exemplified by, say, the paintings of Kandinsky or Mondrian. Indeed, Gibson was not specifically concerned with art at all. Pictures after all do not just hang in galleries; they also appear in newspapers, in magazines, as illustrations in books, and on television screens. Traditionally the making of pictures may have been associated with artistic production, since it was always done by a craftsman working with brush or pen. But surely since the advent of photography it has become evident, if it was not so before, that there is no essential connection between pictorial representation and artistic purpose. Gibson's treatment of pictorial representation thus cuts across the boundary that separates art from other picturing, and in this respect the treatment here will be no different.

If some pictures are not works of art, it is no less true that some symbols which convey information *are* works of art. Franklin's *Autobiography* is both extremely informative and a work of literature. A self-portrait of Rembrandt gives us as much information about the way Rembrandt looked as a newspaper photograph gives us about the way Gerald Ford looks. If the informative belongs to the province of science, then the province of science intersects the province of art. In being concerned with information, then, the present essay no more excludes art from consideration than in being concerned with pictures it deals exclusively with art.

In order to prevent misunderstanding something ought to be said about the sense given to the word "information" in these pages. Sometimes art critics or others say things like "In this painting the artist is telling us that the world is without purpose and that man can expect no help from a beneficent deity in the struggles of life." Suppose the painting shows a man standing alone on a rocky and barren expanse in a fierce thunderstorm. Now whatever one may think of this remark as a comment on the painting, it does not accord with what I mean by the information conveyed by that painting. "Information" here will have a quite restricted meaning—the information conveyed to an observer by a picture that represents a concrete object, scene, or event is simply whatever the observer can tell from the picture about the object, scene, or event that it represents. Thus to someone looking at it, this painting conveys the information that the terrain represented is bleak, that on this terrain is a man standing alone, and that this man is being battered by a storm; but it does not convey the information that the world in general is without purpose. In the same way, the information conveyed to a person by a verbal description of some object or event is simply whatever that description tells him about the thing it describes. I am not here disparaging the critic's attempt to fathom the "message" of a picture, description, or other symbol in a wider or deeper sense, to draw general philosophical conclusions from it, or to find allegorical meanings in it. The point is only that the topic of this essay is not allegory but rather information in the narrowest and most literal sense of that term. This is the sense that Gibson had in mind when he wondered how pictures convey information; hence the present discussion will follow Gibson in his use of "information" as in his use of "picture."

Calling pictures *symbols*, incidentally, here implies only that pictures are bearers of information in the literal sense just explained. Obviously not all pictures are symbols on a more grandiose conception of a symbol as something with "deep" or allegorical significance. On the view here being adopted, however, all (representational) pictures are symbols in the modest sense intended; they are all bearers of information. It should be noted that not everyone would agree with even this limited claim. Some hold the view that in order for an object to function as a picture what is essential is that it serve as a "prop" in a game of make-believe, and that concurrently with performing this role it may or may not also serve in a symbolic capacity to convey information. But this view would seem to exactly reverse the essential and the incidental. The reader may decide for himself whether when he looks at a photograph of Gerald Ford in the morning newspaper he is aware of engaging in a game of make-believe in which he pretends that the picture is Ford himself. And on the other hand, even when an object serves as a surrogate for some other object in a game of make-believe that someone is playing, it is surely not functioning as a picture if it fails to tell that person anything, to convey any information to him, about that which it stands for.

The argument in these pages will be a response to four interrelated questions raised by Gibson's article of 1954: What is a picture? What is information? How do pictures convey information? What special relationship is there between pictorial representation and visual perception? Since these questions are all closely related, they will not be answered in any fixed order. Instead, in section 1 the views of Gibson's 1954 article will be compared with his more recent views on the same topic as contained in an article published in 1971.[2] Although Gibson rightly links the idea of picturing with the idea of information, not only are both his earlier and later definitions of pictorial representation inadequate but he neglects to offer any general definition of information. In section 2 of this essay such a definition will be provided, for the concept of information is needed both to answer the question how pictures convey information and to define the very concept of pictorial representation itself.

The final section of this essay will examine Nelson Goodman's account of representation in his recent book *Languages of Art*.[3] For Goodman, *pictorial* representation is only one special case of representation in general. Goodman considers the important theoretical distinction to be not between picturing and other kinds of representation but between representation and verbal description. The view to be presented here will follow Goodman in regarding this as the important distinction, and it will draw the crucial insight into the nature of this distinction from *Languages of Art*. At the same time, however, it will recognize that Goodman's specific formulation of that distinction is fraught with difficulties that grow out of his Spartan theoretical framework—a framework within which not only can representation not be precisely defined and distinguished from description but also information cannot be defined. Indeed, the concept that needs to be supplied in order to fashion a philosophically tight definition of representation out of the insight in *Languages of Art* is precisely the concept of information. Within the theoretical framework that will be set up in section 2 of this essay for the sake of defining information, it will be possible in section 3 both to define representation and to say what is distinctive about the way in which pictures, as one kind of representational symbol, convey information.

1. J. J. Gibson on picturing

1.1 The question "What is a picture?" To ask "What is a picture?" is to ask at the outset a possibly misleading question, and we had better be clear as to just what is being asked before proceeding further. As Nelson Goodman reminds us, "Nothing is intrinsically a representation. . . . A picture in one system may be a description in another."[4] The physical object or event itself—be it a canvas covered with pigment, some splotches of ink, a sequence of sounds, or something else—is simply an object; in order to function as a symbol capable of communicating information it must be interpreted in some way. The real issue is this: When is interpreting an object in accordance with a system, standard, or rule that imparts significance to it interpreting it *pictorially*? The classification "pictorial" applies not to a physical object taken by itself but to such an object taken together with a standard of interpretation. Instead of asking "What is a picture?" we should ask "What is it to interpret an object *as* a picture?"

1.2 Gibson's earlier and more recent views: exposition and comparison. In 1954 Gibson proposed, "A faithful picture is a delimited surface so processed that it reflects (or transmits) a sheaf of light rays to a given point which is the same as would be the sheaf of rays from the original to that point."[5] How, in view of the preceding paragraph, is this proposal to be understood? Suppose an interpretative standard is regarded as a declaration of the condition under which one object—the symbol—is to count as being faithful, or applying correctly, to another object. (The word "object" will be used from now on for anything that is concrete—a chunk of matter, a living thing, a scene, and the like.) Different standards will declare different conditions to be the criterion of faithful symbolization or correct application; hence there will be as many different senses of "faithful" and "applies" as there are different interpretative standards. Now there can hardly be any objection to Gibson's proposal if the word "faithful" in it is understood in an appropriate sense. Surely the requirement of matching sheaves of light rays defines one standard for interpreting symbols pictorially, one which might be called the color-photographic standard (although few photographs, even in color, would meet it).

However, since Gibson put forward his proposal as a general definition of pictorial representation, it is doubtful that his intention was merely to claim the color-photographic standard to be one way among others of interpreting a symbol pictorially. More likely he intended to say that this is the *only* pictorial standard there is, that to assess the fidelity or correct application of a symbol to an object on any basis other than the matching of light rays is to interpret the symbol other than as a picture. This reading of Gibson's position in 1954 is borne out by his own recent account of how he reconciled that position to the existence of caricature: "One might try to salvage part of the theory by supposing that distortion in caricatures is exceptional; it is not actually a kind of representation but a kind of graphic symbolism like the using of words. I was tempted by this compromise in 1954." Gibson now repudiates the view that the color-photographic standard is the only pictorial standard there is, for he now regards caricature as a counterexample to that view. He also remarks that "there is no point to point correspondence of brightness or color between the optic array from a line drawing and the optic array from the object represented." This latter observation, it may be noted, is quite conclusive by itself, whatever opinion one holds about caricature. If a monochromatic line drawing is faithful to its multicolored subject according to some pictorial standard S, then S cannot be the color-photographic standard; hence the latter is not the only standard there is for interpreting symbols as pictures.[6]

In his 1971 article Gibson offers a new definition of pictorial representation, one employing the concept of information: "A picture is a surface so treated that a delimited optic array to a point of observation is made available which contains the same kind of information that is found in the ambient optic arrays of an ordinary environment." An immediate question concerns the function of the word "kind" inasmuch as for any group of items, no matter how disparate, there will always be some single kind to which they all belong. But apparently this word can be omitted, for Gibson continues, "The definition is broad enough also to admit the case of caricature, where . . . even the forms are different, but where the high-order information to specify a particular person is common to both arrays. In short the optic array from a picture and the optic array from a world can provide the same information without providing the same stimulation."[7]

Since, as has been emphasized, an object becomes a picture only as interpreted by some interpretative standard, one may wonder what Gibson is saying about the qualifications for a standard to be a pictorial one. Toward this end it may be helpful to note the criticism made by Nelson Goodman of Gibson's use of the term "information" in the passages just quoted: "The information yielded by [pictures] . . . depends not only upon them but also upon the system according to which they are interpreted."[8] For Goodman, it is a shortcoming of Gibson's formulation that the definition fails to state how information is relative to a system or standard of interpretation. Now it is possible at one and the same time to exhibit the relativity of information to an interpretative standard and to construe the term "pictorial" as characterizing such standards, by taking Gibson to be proposing something like this: an interpretative standard S is a pictorial interpretation of an object x if and only if the information a person would get from looking at x and interpreting it by means of S is the same as the information he would get from looking at those things, if any, to which x is faithful in accordance with S.

Before this proposal is criticized, the reader ought to be aware of the larger framework into which it fits. Gibson's new definition is not so much the result of any counterexamples to the earlier definition as it is the consequence of Gibson's unchanged view on the connection between picturing and perception combined with his new account of perception: "The above definition is based on a new theory of perception as well as a new formulation of optics. It assumes that two perceptions can be the same without their accompanying sensations being the same. . . . Perception is based on the pickup of information, not on the arousal of sensation, and the two processes are distinct." For Gibson in 1971 as in 1954, what is characteristic of picturing is that perceiving a picture is very much like perceiving the original. But whereas in 1954 Gibson seemed to assume that sameness of visual perception implied sameness of visual sensation and that this in turn implied sameness of ocular stimulation (qualitative, not numerical, sameness in each case), he now denies any invariable correlation of sensation with perception even to the point of saying that "visual sensations are not necessary for visual perception, strange as this may seem."[9]

Of course, no one expects to obtain the same or even similar visual perceptions from the picture and the original under any and all circumstances. On Gibson's 1954 theory the special circumstances necessary for sameness of perception included that the viewer be looking at both objects through a peephole with one eye. On Gibson's later theory, the special conditions necessary for similarity of perception pertain not to the external setup but to the state of the viewer's mind instead. When someone looks at a picture, according to Gibson, "he can notice only the information for the perception of what is represented or he can pay attention to the picture as such, the medium, the technique, the style, the composition, the surface, and the way the surface has been treated." He can, that is to say, pay attention either to what is "in" the picture or to the picture itself. The visual perception occasioned by the picture is like the visual perception occasioned by the original only to the extent that in viewing the picture the observer takes the first of these attitudes, which might be called "the representational attitude." Gibson's remark "But it is not true that perceiving what is represented can ever be exactly like perceiving it in the world" is to be understood, one suspects, as a denial that a person can ever fully attain to the representational attitude and wholly exclude from attention such features of the picture itself as its surface texture or its arrangement of line and color.[10]

1.3 Ambiguity of the term "information." The distinction Gibson draws between "the information for the perception of what is represented" and the properties belonging to the "picture as such" is extremely important here. When we observe a symbol and interpret it according to some interpretative standard, it *conveys* or *communicates* to us certain properties of whatever object, if any, it is faithful to in accordance with that standard.

The properties conveyed or communicated to us by a symbol under interpretation are not usually the same as the properties we observe to belong to the symbol itself. For example, a portrait showing a bearded man conveys to a normal observer on the customary interpretation the property of being bearded, but the painting certainly does not itself possess the property of being bearded. Conversely, it possesses the property of being covered with paint, but it does not convey this property in its symbolic function—does not tell the viewer that the man depicted is covered with paint. In the same way, the *word* "bearded" conveys but does not possess the property of being bearded, and possesses but does not convey the property of beginning with a "b." The middle section of this essay will offer a formal definition of the notion of conveyance or communication, but perhaps what has been said will make that concept sufficiently clear for immediate purposes.

Recall Gibson's suggestion that the information contained in the optic array from the picture is the same as the information contained in the optic array from the original. Here the two occurrences of the term "information" do not have the same meaning. The first occurrence refers to properties *conveyed* by the picture under interpretation, while the second refers to properties *possessed* by the original. Gibson's proposal would after all be too absurd if "information" referred in both occurrences to properties possessed by the object being observed, since a photograph of Fidel Castro, for instance, unlike Castro himself, does not have a beard.

This is not to say that Gibson's definition of pictorial representation in terms of information becomes immune from criticism once the ambiguity of "information" has been clarified but only that its meaning becomes clearer. When the appropriate equivalents for the two occurrences of "information" are substituted in the earlier restatement of Gibson's definition, the resulting proposal is the following: An interpretative standard S is a pictorial interpretation of an object x if, and only if, for every object y such that x is faithful to y in accordance with S, the properties that x, as interpreted by S, would convey to a person who was looking at x are the same as the properties that would be seen by that person to be possessed by y if he were looking at y.

A virtue of this restatement is that it does away not only with the ambiguous term "information" but also with the metaphorical expression "contained in the optic array." It achieves the effect of locating the information from both picture and original in the optic array by the reference to looking and seeing, while it avoids the error of supposing that the information conveyed by a picture under interpretation is somehow "in" the optic array out of relation to any person who may be observing that picture. What a picture conveys it always conveys *to* someone, as a consequence of what that person notices when he views the picture combined with his general background knowledge. If, for instance, he notices nothing because he has his eyes shut, the picture will convey no information to him at all.

1.4 Criticism of Gibson's recent definition. With a clear proposal on the nature of pictorial representation now at hand, it is time to turn to criticism. In the first place, line drawings make trouble for the present proposal just as surely as they did for Gibson's 1954 definition. A line drawing of someone will fail to tell us the color of his eyes or hair, which we would have discovered if we had looked at him in person. Such a drawing, like a verbal description, is selective in what it conveys about the thing to which it is faithful. Nor let anyone object here that such selectivity is incompatible with fidelity. A faithful symbol conveys *only* properties possessed by the original, but need not convey *all* such properties.

The difficulty posed by line drawings is easily eliminated by replacing the words "the same as" with the word "among" in the proposal. The proposal thus amended, however, is still not acceptable. To see why not, suppose S is the interpretative standard that customarily governs the interpretation of words and phrases of English and let x be a series of ink marks that spells "large and round." Then clearly S is not a pictorial way of interpreting these marks. Yet if one were looking at any object to which they were faithful—i.e., at any large and round object—one would immediately see it to possess that property which the marks convey, namely the property of being large and round. This shows that the modified proposal does not give a sufficient condition for pictorial representation but at best a necessary condition. The phrase "if, and only if" in that proposal should therefore be changed to simply "only if."

To make this change is to abandon the enterprise of giving a complete definition of picturing. What remains is instead a proposed necessary condition only. Nor is even this much beyond all doubt. A picture may reveal to an observer a property of the depicted object that he would have missed if he had been looking at that object directly. Indeed, it may even be false that he *could* have seen the object to possess that property. To be sure, the artist may have originally noticed the property when he observed and painted the object, but those who are less observant might never have noticed what the artist noticed; through emphasis and selection his picture makes available to other people knowledge resulting from a keener observation of nature than their own.

In addition, Gibson seems to be unduly narrowing the concept of pictorial representation by considering only information contained in the optic array, i.e., only information that can be picked up by seeing. X-ray pictures, for example, convey properties, such as the property of having a broken rib, that nobody (Superman doesn't count) could see simply by looking. If ordinary pictures are normally most useful when the pictured object itself is unavailable, an x-ray picture is not rendered superfluous even when the pictured individual is at hand. The same is true of a photograph taken by an electron microscope: the properties that the photograph conveys could not be directly seen. Indeed, whereas the x-ray picture provides only the most convenient access to information that could conceivably be gained in other ways (e.g., by opening the subject up), the electron microscope photograph is perhaps the only way of learning about certain properties of very small objects. Then too, there are pictures of objects too large to be looked at. A picture of the solar system, for instance, is constructed on the basis of many different observations in different directions and from different positions on the earth, and with the help of many mathematical calculations; it makes no sense to talk about the optic array from the solar system to some fixed viewing point, nor is the point where the artist stood when he drew the picture relevant here at all.

If it is admitted that these examples are examples of pictures, then they provide additional reason not only for rejecting Gibson's specific definition of picturing in terms of information contained in optic arrays, but also for rejecting his larger assumption about the likeness of pictorial perception to direct perception. Our perception of an x-ray picture does not in the least resemble our perception of the individual represented, and in the cases of the electron microscope photograph and the picture of the solar system it does not make sense at all to talk about our perception of the objects represented.

It is true, of course, that the manner of picking up information from a picture taken by an electron microscope or a picture of the solar system is by looking at it; the optic array from the picture is still important. But then the optic array from a page of print is no less important in picking up information from that page. The other side of this coin is that one can imagine pictures that are to be perceived by a sense other than sight. For example, the outline of a line drawing can be raised into a ridge so that a blind person is able to perceive the drawing by touch.[11]

1.5 Generalizing the concept of picturing. In all of these examples, it might be pointed out, there is still a geometrical relationship between the spatial layout of the picture and the spatial layout of the object depicted, even though one or both of these layouts may not be accessible to vision. Then perhaps in order to be a pictorial mode of interpreting a symbol, an interpretative standard must at least specify some geometrical relationship between the spatial layout of the symbol and the spatial layout of the object that is symbolized. But while it does seem that picturing, as ordinarily understood, is especially concerned with spatial arrangements, there are several reasons why the preceding sentence will not do as a definition. First, the term "geometrical relationship" is terribly vague and could plausibly include such nonpictorial relations as that which holds between inscriptions of the word "square" and square objects. Second, if one tries to be more specific as to which geometrical relationships a pictorial standard must specify, he finds himself confronted with the task of drawing up a long list that he can never be sure of having completed. Among the geometrical relationships that would seem to merit the title "pictorial" are, to name a few, perspective projection, reverse perspective projection, orthogonal projection, and central projection (of the globe onto a flat surface). Nor is it enough to say that the geometrical relationships that are pictorial are the projective ones, even assuming that the general concept of a projection is clear. A particular pictorial standard may specify that the results of a certain kind of projection are then to be subjected to certain alterations of scale or other distortions in one or more directions. Since surely not every distortion counts as pictorial, the task would remain of drawing up a list of specific geometrical relationships that qualify as pictorial standards of interpretation.

Even if this task could be accomplished, there would still be a reason for not resting content at this point with a definition of picturing in purely spatial terms. This is that the concept of picturing admits of natural extensions to cases where the spatial layout of either the symbol or the object symbolized is not in question. Consider, for example, a relief map in which the projections above the plane of the map indicate not elevations in the land but rather, say, population densities. Here is a kind of three-dimensional picture one of whose spatial dimensions has nothing to do with any corresponding spatial dimension of the territory represented. Or suppose that a spatial succession of bands of color is represented by a temporal succession of sounds, where the pitch, intensity, and duration of the sounds indicate the hue, brightness, and width of the represented bands of color. Again, the sound that arises from playing a phonograph record may be regarded as a sort of sound picture of an original performance, analogous to the image that results from projecting a photographic film onto a screen.

If these latter examples are not examples of pictures in a narrow sense, the term "representation" may be appropriated to express that common feature which accounts for their being regarded as similar in some important respect to more ordinary cases of picturing. Nelson Goodman, taking precisely this approach in *Languages of Art*, says of it, "It allows for full relativity of representation and for representation by things other than pictures. Objects and events, visual and nonvisual, can be represented by either visual or nonvisual symbols."[12]

On the other hand, representation is not so broad that it fails to contrast sharply with description by means of language. The final section of this essay will propose a definition of representation inspired by Goodman's view and will explain how, in the light of that definition, symbols interpreted as representations convey information. But first, it is necessary to become clearer about the concept of conveying information and about the theoretical framework that must be presupposed for the clarification of that concept.

2. The concept of information

2.1 Properties, interpretative standards, and information. What a symbol communicates to an observer who interprets it are *properties* of anything to which it is faithful. But what are properties? To answer this question, it may be helpful to recall what was said about interpretative standards at the beginning of section 1.2: an interpretative standard is a declaration of the circumstances under which one object—the symbol—is to count as being faithful, or correctly applying, to another object. There is no cause to be puzzled over what sort of thing a declaration is. Inasmuch as any declaration can presumably be expressed in English, a declaration may as well be identified with the English expression that would ordinarily be said to express it. An interpretative standard is therefore an expression of English, and more specifically a two-place English predicate "... x ... y. ..."[13] Furthermore, any such predicate may be an interpretative standard, since it may stipulate a criterion of fidelity of symbols to objects, or in other words a sense of the expression "x is faithful to y."

Although there is no reason to suppose that all properties can be expressed in words, the distinction to be drawn in section 3 between representation and description need only refer to verbally expressible properties. These may be construed, on analogy with the preceding way of construing interpretative standards, as also predicates of English, albeit *one*-place rather than two-place predicates. For example, the property of being round gets identified with the one-place English predicate "x is round."

Against this treatment of both interpretative standards and properties (from now on the qualifying phrase "verbally expressible" will be omitted in front of "property") it may be objected that a declaration cannot be identical with the words that express it in English since the same declaration could be expressed in German or any other natural language; and likewise a property must be distinct from its verbal expression in English for the same reason. This objection misconceives the enterprise, however. The intention in this section is not to put forward a metaphysical view of what properties and interpretative standards *really* are, but rather to construe these entities in a way that will enable us to define information and representation and explain how symbols interpreted as representations convey information. For these purposes it will prove quite suitable to regard properties and interpretative standards as expressions of English.

Of course, if the present essay were to be written in German, say, instead of English, then properties and interpretative standards would be regarded as expressions of German rather than English. It is immaterial which natural language properties and interpretative standards are considered as belonging to. What is important, though, is that they be taken to be expressions of a language and not to be *sets* or *classes* of objects. To be sure, to every property P there corresponds a class—called the *extension* of P—containing just those objects that do in fact possess P; and to every interpretative standard S there corresponds a class—called the *extension* of S—containing just those ordered pairs of objects $<x,y>$ such that x is in fact faithful to y in accordance with S. But an interpretative standard cannot be identified with its extension; for, as section 3 will demonstrate, the distinction between a representational interpretation S_1 and a non-representational interpretation S_2 of a given symbol x need not involve any distinction between the extensions of S_1 and S_2.

Neither can a property be identified with its extension, if properties are to be what a symbol conveys to a person as information. To see this, let x be a drawing of a triangle, S be the interpretative standard "x has the same shape as y," and r be a person who is aware at time t that x is triangular. Then x as interpreted by S conveys to r at t the property of being triangular, because r knows at t that anything which has the same shape as x is triangular. Suppose further, however, that r does not know that a triangle has an angle sum of 180 degrees. In that case x as interpreted by S does not convey to r at t the property of being a polygonal figure with an angle sum of 180 degrees, despite the fact that the *class* of polygonal figures having an angle sum of 180 degrees is identical with the *class* of triangular figures. This shows that a property cannot be identified with the class of things that possess it, at least for the purpose of discussing information.

In order to define the concept of conveying information precisely and with full generality, it will be convenient to introduce two technical conventions involving the use of quotation marks. The first convention is to write (1) r knows at t ". . ." in place of (2) r knows at t that . . ., for any English sentence ". . .". Statement (1) is simply an alternative way of phrasing statement (2) and must not be taken to imply that r says the very sentence ". . ." to himself or even understands the language (English) to which that sentence belongs. For example, since Ahmed, a speaker of Arabic who understands no English, knows that the earth is round, Ahmed knows "The earth is round" by the convention here being adopted. The same convention holds for other verbs taking a that-clause, such as "believes," "pretends," "notices," "sees," "fears," "doubts," and "wishes."

The second technical convention to be adopted is the use of quasi-quotation marks, or "corners," an extremely useful device invented by W. V. Quine.[14] Suppose that P is the predicate "x is round" and Q is the predicate "x is flat." Then ⌜Either P (the earth) or Q (the earth)⌝ is the same as the sentence "Either the earth is round or the earth is flat." Notice that what was just asserted becomes incorrect if the quasi-quotation marks are replaced by ordinary quotation marks. For "Either P(the earth) or Q(the earth)" contains the letters "P" and "Q" and fails to contain the words "is round" and "is flat." By contrast, ⌜Either P(the earth) or Q(the earth)⌝ does not contain the letters "P" and "Q" but rather contains P, i.e., the words "is round," and Q, i.e., the words "is flat." The general rule is this: when metalinguistic variables such as "P," "Q," and "S"—variables that refer to expressions of English—appear in contexts of quasi-quotation, what is designated by the whole, including the quasi-quotation marks, is not the very expression within those marks but the expression obtained when the metalinguistic variables are replaced by the expressions they refer to.

With the two preceding conventions at hand, it is now possible to say what properties a symbol x as interpreted by an interpretative standard S conveys to a person r at a time t, for any x, S, r, and t. They are those properties P such that r knows at t ⌜For any object y, if $S(x,y)$ then P(y)⌝.[15] This definition implies that the information conveyed by a symbol will depend upon what properties the observer has noticed the symbol to possess as well as upon his general background knowledge. To return to the triangle discussed above, if an observer notices that this symbol is not merely triangular but triangular with one angle between 20 and 40 degrees, it will convey to him the property of being triangular with one angle between 20 and 40 degrees. If on closer inspection he then ascertains that the angle of this symbol is between 25 and 35 degrees, it will come to convey the additional property of being triangular with one angle between 25 and 35 degrees. If he does not perceive the symbol at all, on the other hand, it will convey no properties to him except trivial ones possessed by all objects.

Not every time an additional property is ascertained to belong to a symbol does that symbol convey additional information. If an observer looking at the triangular figure mentioned above notes that the length of one side is between 3/4 and 1 1/4 inches, that symbol does not come to convey any new properties to him. This is of course assuming that the observer interprets the symbol according to the standard "x has the same shape as y." The situation changes if he interprets it instead according to the standard "x has the same size and shape as y." The effect upon information of ascertaining new properties of a symbol thus depends upon the standard by which the symbol is interpreted, a point that will be considered further in discussing the distinctive manner in which symbols interpreted as representations convey information.

2.2 Varieties of information. Information as just defined is a matter of what a person knows. Another, parallel concept of information is defined by reference to what a person believes rather than what he knows. In this second sense of "conveys," a triangular figure could convey the property of being equilateral to someone who wrongly believes that that figure is equilateral.

A challenge to both definitions—the one in terms of knowledge and the other in terms of belief—is presented by symbols that have application in fiction but do not apply to any actual objects. Let x be a painting that shows a unicorn, and let S be the customary way of interpreting representational paintings in our culture. To a person who knows (and therefore also believes) that there are no unicorns, x as interpreted by S conveys all properties without discrimination according to either definition.[16] What this shows is not, however, that the two previous definitions of information are incorrect, but that there is still a third variety of information. A person who is reading a story that he believes in all seriousness to be false will often, for the sake of not having the story spoiled by contradiction, suspend those of his serious beliefs that conflict with it. At the same time, he may pretend to believe things he does not seriously believe. He processes the story, that is, not through his body of serious beliefs but rather through a pretended body of beliefs. In the same way, if he is looking at the picture x mentioned a moment ago, his pretended body of beliefs will exclude "There are no unicorns" and ⌜For every object y, it is not the case that $S(x,y)$⌝, which he believes seriously, and may contain the opposite statements, which he does not believe seriously. Of course, that body will undoubtedly also contain here many statements that are among his serious beliefs; his pretended body of beliefs overlaps in large part his body of serious beliefs. Hence one must be careful not to confuse the status of being a pretended belief, in a sense in which what is pretended is not held seriously, with the status of belonging to a person's pretended *body* of beliefs.

A third sense of "conveys" can now be defined as follows: x as interpreted by S conveys P relative to r's pretended body of beliefs at t if ⌜For any object y, if $S(x,y)$ then $P(y)$⌝ belongs to r's pretended body of beliefs at t. There are thus at least three concepts of information relative to a person and a time: that which refers to the person's knowledge, that which refers to the person's (serious) beliefs, and that which refers to the person's pretended body of beliefs. In order to reduce this multiplicity to a single concept, one need only make information relative to a class of statements[17] rather than to a person and time: for any such class Γ, x as interpreted by S conveys P relative to Γ if ⌜For any object y, if $S(x,y)$ then $P(y)$⌝ belongs to Γ.[18] The three concepts of information relative to a person r and a time t can then be derived from the single concept of information relative to an arbitrary class Γ of statements by letting Γ be, respectively, r's body of knowledge at t, r's body of (serious) beliefs at t, and r's pretended body of beliefs at t. (For one example, a portrait showing a man with a beard, interpreted according to the customary standard of representation, conveys the property of having a beard relative to some viewer's momentary body of knowledge, provided that the statement "For any object y, if the portrait correctly represents y, then y has a beard" belongs to that body of knowledge.)

A slight variation on the preceding concept of information relative to a class Γ results from substituting "is logically entailed by Γ" for "belongs to Γ" in the definition above. If Γ is deductively closed—that is, if all logical consequences of Γ belong to Γ—then this variation comes to the same thing as the original. Where Γ is the body of knowledge of a normal human being, however, Γ will not be deductively closed; we do not draw all the logical consequences of what we know. Hence the variation defined in terms of entailment by Γ will be a broader concept of information than the original defined in terms of membership in Γ. (Whatever belongs to Γ is also entailed by Γ, but the converse is true only if Γ is deductively closed.) This broader concept captures the idea of the information that a person *would* get from a symbol if he had perfect powers of deductive reasoning, whether he actually gets that information or not. Now as a matter of fact it will prove convenient in the sequel to operate with this broader concept. Where Γ is not deductively closed, not much can be claimed for certain about what statements Γ contains given that Γ contains something else; but on the basis of logic much can be claimed about what Γ *entails* given that Γ entails something else. From now on, therefore, the word "conveys" is to be understood as follows: x as interpreted by S conveys P relative to Γ if Γ logically entails ⌜For any object y, if $S(x,y)$ then $P(y)$⌝.[19] (As an example of the difference between this broader sense of "conveys" and the narrower sense defined in the preceding paragraph, consider a person who is looking at a triangular figure, who interprets that figure according to the standard "x has the same shape as y," and who does not know that a triangle has an angle sum of 180 degrees. Assume that this person nevertheless knows the axioms and postulates of geometry, which logically entail the theorem that a triangle has an angle sum of 180 degrees. Then relative to this person's body of knowledge the figure he is viewing conveys in the broader sense, but not in the narrower sense, the property of having an angle sum of 180 degrees, since that body of knowledge logically entails, but does not contain, the statement "For any object y, if the figure in question has the same shape as y, then y has an angle sum of 180 degrees.")

2.3 Conditional information and strength of information. The concept of conditional information will serve later in defining representation. Conditional information is the information that a symbol would convey to a person if he not only possessed perfect powers of deductive reasoning but also had determined a certain property to belong to the symbol that he has not in fact determined to belong to it. Where x is a symbol, S is an interpretative standard, M and P are properties, and Γ is a class of statements, x as interpreted by S conveys P conditionally upon M relative to

Γ, provided that Γ logically entails ⌜For any object y, if $S(x,y)$ and $M(x)$ then $P(y)$⌝. Clearly if a symbol conveys a property conditionally upon some condition, it conveys that property unconditionally once the condition has been ascertained to hold—that is to say, if x as interpreted by S conveys P conditionally upon M relative to Γ, then x as interpreted by S conveys P relative to Γ′, where Γ′ contains in addition to the statements in Γ the statement ⌜$M(x)$⌝. Suppose, for example, that someone who understands English is looking at an inscription of the word "cat" but for some reason cannot make out the first letter of that inscription. This symbol, as interpreted in English, conveys to him the property of being a bat conditionally upon beginning with a "b," the property of being a cat conditionally upon beginning with a "c," and the property of being fat conditionally upon beginning with an "f." Once he establishes by closer observation that the inscription in fact begins with a "c," it then conveys to him unconditionally the property of being a cat.

For the purpose of defining representation later the following concepts are also needed. (1) $P_1=P_2$ relative to Γ, provided that Γ logically entails ⌜For any object y, $P_1(y)$ if and only if $P_2(y)$⌝; (2) $P_1 \neq P_2$ relative to Γ, provided that it is not the case that $P_1=P_2$ relative to Γ; (3) $P_1 \subseteq P_2$ relative to Γ, provided that Γ logically entails ⌜For any object y, if $P_1(y)$ then $P_2(y)$⌝; (4) $P_1 \subset P_2$ relative to Γ, provided that $P_1 \subseteq P_2$ relative to Γ and $P_1 \neq P_2$ relative to Γ.

It is easily seen that if, relative to Γ, $P_1 \subseteq P_2$ and x as interpreted in a given way conveys P_1 conditionally upon M, then x as interpreted in the same way also conveys P_2 conditionally upon M. For instance, suppose that relative to the knowledge of the observer in the example given a moment ago the property of being a bat $\subseteq$ the property of having wings. In that case, the inscription he is viewing conveys to him the second as well as the first of these properties conditionally upon beginning with a "b." Among the properties conditionally (or for that matter unconditionally) conveyed by a given symbol, then, some will be stronger or narrower than others.

Let Ψ be an arbitrary collection of properties and P belong to Ψ. Then within Ψ, P is a *strongest* property conveyed by x conditionally upon M, provided that x conveys P conditionally upon M and there is no property $P′$ in Ψ such that $P′ \subset P$ and x conveys $P′$ conditionally upon M. (Here the parameters S and Γ are implicit. As an illustration of the present concept take the preceding example and let Ψ contain just the properties of being a bat and having wings. Within this collection the property of being a bat is a strongest property conveyed by the inscription in question conditionally upon beginning with a "b.") It will be useful for future purposes to show that given a certain modest restriction on Ψ there cannot be two nonequivalent strongest properties in Ψ conditionally (or unconditionally) conveyed by a symbol. The restriction on Ψ is that Ψ contain the conjunction of any two or more properties that Ψ contains individually.

Given this restriction, the desired result is obtained as a corollary of a more general theorem: Assume that $(a)\Psi$ satisfies the constraint mentioned, (b) P and P' both belong to Ψ, (c) within Ψ P is a strongest property conveyed by x conditionally upon M, and (d) P' is conveyed by x conditionally upon M. Then $P \subseteq P'$.

To prove this theorem note that $\ulcorner P$ and $P'\urcorner \subseteq P$, $\ulcorner P$ and $P'\urcorner$ belongs to Ψ, and $\ulcorner P$ and $P'\urcorner$ is conveyed by x conditionally upon M. Since it cannot be that $\ulcorner P$ and $P'\urcorner \subset P$, it must be true that $\ulcorner P$ and $P'\urcorner = P$, that is to say, $P \subseteq P'$. The corollary now easily follows: if to the hypotheses of the preceding theorem is added the assumption that within Ψ P' is also a strongest property conveyed by x conditionally upon M, then it cannot be true that $P \subset P'$; and so, by the preceding theorem, $P = P'$.

Thus if Ψ is such that the conjunction of any two properties in Ψ is also in Ψ, then there is at most one strongest property in Ψ conveyed by x conditionally upon M. Of course, the parameters S and Γ are implicit in this result. Where P is such a property, therefore, P is uniquely determined by Ψ, x, M, S, and Γ. Now for reasons that will become apparent in section 3.3, this relation will be written as follows: $P=S(M)$ relative to Ψ, x, Γ; and it will be said, by analogy with the value of a mathematical function at an argument, that P is the *informational value* of S at M relative to Ψ, x, and Γ. (Thus consider again a triangular figure as interpreted by the standard "x has the same shape as y." If Ψ contains not only all properties of the form "y has an angle between so many degrees and that many plus 20 degrees" but also all conjunctions of any properties that it contains, then there will be a *unique* strongest property within Ψ conveyed by that figure conditionally upon itself having an angle between 25 and 35 degrees. This unique strongest property in Ψ—the informational value in Ψ of the interpretative standard "x has the same shape as y" at the property "x has an angle between 25 and 35 degrees"—is of course just the property "y has an angle between 25 and 35 degrees," which is the conjunction of the two properties "y has an angle between 15 and 35 degrees" and "y has an angle between 25 and 45 degrees.") In the remaining section of this essay it will become clear how the notion of the informational value of an interpretative standard at a property is of use in characterizing representation.

3. Information and representation

3.1 Representation is not a matter of extension. Recall that the extension of an interpretative standard S is the class of ordered pairs $\langle x,y \rangle$ such that x is *in fact* faithful to y in accordance with S. What extension an interpretative standard has is thus a matter of the objective state of affairs in the world; if a symbol correctly applies to an object in accordance with some standard, it does so irrespective of whether anyone has knowledge of that fact. Once this is recognized, it is easily seen that the difference between a representational standard and a nonrepresentational one does not always lie in a difference between the extensions of those standards. For consider the traditional Western system of pictorial representation. There are, in the first place, only finitely many actual pictures embraced by this system. The pictures are, after all, concrete objects like pieces of canvas covered with pigment, and clearly there is not room on earth for infinitely many such objects. In addition, each pictorial symbol is faithful to at most finitely many objects, since the depicted objects are also concrete and take up space. It is immaterial to the present point how large these finite numbers are, and so for the sake of simplicity let us pretend that in fact the only picture that ever has or ever will be produced is Gilbert Stuart's portrait of George Washington and that this picture is indeed a faithful representation of the man it portrays. On this supposition the two interpretative standards (1) x is faithful to y in accordance with the customary Western standard of pictorial representation, and (2) x is Stuart's portrait of Washington and y is Washington, have the same extension. But whereas (1) is a representational way of interpreting Stuart's portrait, (2) is not.

To see why not, compare standard (2) with an example given by Nelson Goodman: "If pictures in a commandeered museum are used by a briefing officer to stand for enemy emplacements, the pictures do not thereby represent these emplacements. To represent, a picture must function as a pictorial symbol."[20] Standard (2) is obviously of the same sort as that employed by the briefing officer: a symbol is identified, and its application is independently specified. The only difference is the immaterial one that on standard (2) the object to which the symbol applies is a man instead of a military emplacement.

Although both (1) and (2) have the same extension under these imagined circumstances, they do not yield the same information from the symbol at hand. Information, remember, is relative to the knowledge of a symbol processor. When a person looks at Stuart's portrait and interprets it according to (2), it conveys to him the property of being George Washington. It 'says' in effect "Washington." Beyond that, however, it tells him nothing about Washington that he does not already know. If he does not already know whether Washington had a mustache, Stuart's portrait as interpreted by (2) will not give him information on this matter, any more than will any other object—a pencil, say—interpreted as standing for Washington. Moreover, there is no point to his looking more closely at the portrait in order to obtain more information from it. Once he has identified it as Stuart's portrait of Washington, it conveys to him, as interpreted by (2), all that it will ever convey to him.

How different is the situation when he interprets that same painting according to standard (1)! Suddenly it conveys to him a great number and variety of properties, such as not having a mustache, wearing a wig, and being of ruddy complexion. Moreover, when he looks more closely at the portrait it conveys to him still further properties. For example, if he cares to measure the appropriate areas of the canvas, he can obtain such detailed information as the approximate ratio of the length of Washington's nose to the distance between his eyes. Thus the difference between (1) and (2) in their capacity to provide information from the same symbol is indeed vast. Interpreted according to (2), that symbol is in effect merely a proper name of Washington, whereas interpreted according to (1) it becomes, as the adage says, "worth a thousand words."

3.2 Nelson Goodman's account of representation. The difference between representational and nonrepresentational ways of interpreting symbols need not, therefore, involve any difference in the symbols themselves or in the objects to which those symbols in fact apply. Rather the division seems bound up with a difference in the information they convey to a processer. The relation between representation and information will become clear when a precise definition of representation is given in section 3.3. First, however, it will be instructive to examine the account of representation offered by Goodman in *Languages of Art,* for Goodman's account both illustrates the need to go beyond consideration of which symbols in fact apply to which objects and at the same time contains the crucial insight that will lead here to a correct definition of representation. Unfortunately, explaining Goodman's account requires some of his technical terminology.

Goodman talks about *symbol systems* rather than interpretative standards and means by this something slightly different from what the latter has meant here. A symbol system consists of two components, one syntactic and the other semantic. The purely syntactic component, or *symbol scheme*, is a collection of *characters*, where "characters are certain classes of utterances or inscriptions or marks."[21] Thus the utterances, inscriptions, and marks—the concrete symbols—are sorted into classes, and these classes of symbols constitute the symbol scheme.

The semantic component is a correlation of the symbols with objects to which they apply. If a symbol x is correlated with an object y, then x is said to *denote* y, and y to *comply with* x, under the correlation in question. Goodman thus uses "denotes" in the same way that "applies to" and "is faithful to" have been used here. The class of all objects y denoted by a given symbol x is called the *compliance-class* for x. Now one might suppose that the semantic component of a symbol system is the same thing as that which has here been called an interpretative standard. It is not clear in *Languages of Art*, however, whether Goodman means by the semantic component of a symbol system an interpretative standard, which is a two-place predicate of

English, or the extension of an interpretative standard, which is a class of ordered pairs of objects. What *is* clear is that the compliance-classes for the symbols are classes.

So a symbol system comprises two collections of classes: the characters, which are classes of symbols, and the compliance-classes, which are classes of objects denoted by the symbols. If the compliance-classes for all the symbols belonging to a single character are identical, then that character is said to be *unambiguous*, and the single compliance-class for any of these symbols is said to be the compliance-class for the character. A symbol system is unambiguous as a whole if all the characters belonging to its symbol scheme are unambiguous. In what follows only unambiguous symbol systems will be considered.

The essential requirement for a symbol system to be representational, according to Goodman, is that its symbol scheme be *syntactically dense*, or "provide for infinitely many characters so ordered that between each two there is a third."[22] An example of a syntactically dense symbol scheme is one that takes as its symbols straight ink marks of any length and sorts these marks into characters according to length. This scheme is syntactically dense because between any two lengths, however close, there is a third length. By contrast, the scheme that takes as its symbols inscriptions of letter sequences and sorts these inscriptions into characters according to spelling is not syntactically dense, since there is not a third letter sequence between any two in the usual lexicographic ordering of these sequences.

A representational system is normally also *semantically dense*, or in other words "provides for an infinite number of characters with compliance-classes so ordered that between each two there is a third."[23] Suppose, for instance, that the following semantic component is added to the syntactically dense symbol scheme mentioned in the preceding paragraph: each straight ink mark is to denote any object whose weight in ounces is equal to the length in inches of that mark. The resulting symbol system is semantically dense because it provides for a different compliance-class corresponding to every different character and because these classes are so ordered that between any two there is a third.

If the concepts of syntactic and semantic density, central to Goodman's account of representation, seem clear enough from the definitions quoted and the illustrations given, they become much less so upon closer examination. What does it mean to say that a symbol system "provides for" infinitely many characters? Clearly a representational system need not *have* infinitely many characters in fact. There are only finitely many actual pictures in the domain of the traditional Western system of pictorial representation, and there are only finitely many actual ink marks in the domain of the representational system described above. And if there are only finitely many symbols, there are also only finitely many different characters, since characters are just classes of symbols. Furthermore, if there are only finitely many characters then there are only finitely many compliance-classes for these characters; and so for neither characters nor compliance-classes can it be the case that "between each two there is a third."

Goodman is fully aware that a representational system may embrace only finitely many actual symbols. Of a scheme that sorts pictorial images into characters according to height, he admits that "we still have syntactic density here even if there are only two actual images and they differ conspicuously in height."[24] The requirement for syntactic density, he emphasizes, is only that the scheme *provide for* infinitely many characters, not that there *be* infinitely many characters in fact. Thus Goodman seems to be agreeing with the point made in section 3.1 that in order to define representation one must have regard for more than extension, i.e., for more than simply what symbols exist and what objects they apply to. The problem now is to say *how* representation goes beyond extension.

If characters are classes of symbols and a representational system provides for infinitely many characters, then however "provides for" is construed, such a system must also provide for infinitely many symbols; infinitely many classes of objects requires infinitely many objects. Yet the claim that a representational system provides for infinitely many symbols is false not only if taken in a sense implying that there *are* infinitely many symbols but even if taken in a weaker sense implying that there *could* be infinitely many symbols. Could there be infinitely many pictures made out of canvas or paper covered with pigment? If "could there be" means here "are there, for all anyone knows to the contrary," the answer is that we all know perfectly well only finitely many actual pictures ever have been or ever will be produced. If "could there be" is instead taken counterfactually as meaning "might there have been, even though in fact there are not," the answer may well again be no. Infinitely many pictures made out of canvas or paper would take up an infinite volume of space, since even the thinnest piece of paper has thickness; but according to some modern cosmological theories space itself is finite.

Failing a coherent reading of the words "provides for," one might try reconstruing the notion of a character. Instead of taking characters to be classes of *actual* symbols, as Goodman does, one might try taking them as classes of *possible* symbols. Then "provides for" could be read simply as "has": a syntactically dense symbol scheme has infinitely many characters and so embraces infinitely many possible symbols in its domain. Thus even though only finitely many straight ink marks are ever actually produced, there are infinitely many possible straight ink marks, one for every different length, and this is why the symbol scheme mentioned a few paragraphs back is syntactically dense.

The trouble with this suggestion is that the notion of a possible but not actual object is among the most obscure notions of metaphysics. Quine once asked "How many possible fat men are there in the doorway?" to bring home this obscurity.[25] Not only does no one know the answer to this question, but it is hard to see how the question could have a correct answer at all; and if it does not make sense to suppose that there is some definite number of possible objects of a given kind, then it does not make sense to suppose that there are *any* possible objects of the given kind. Furthermore, even if a coherent metaphysics of possible objects were available, it would seem a mistake to explain the common and everyday phenomenon of picturing in terms of some high-flown metaphysical theory.

Thus Goodman's definitions of syntactic and semantic density are by no means completely clear. Yet Goodman's account greatly illuminates the essential nature of representation. The basic idea is that in a representational system smooth variation along some dimension or aspect of the symbol gives rise to a corresponding variation along some dimension or aspect of the object to which the symbol applies. The same is not true in a linguistic system such as English. Smooth variation in the height of the letters of the word "cat," for instance, does not at all affect what the word applies to; however large or small its letters may be, it always applies to all and only cats. Now the way to clarify this insight of Goodman's into the nature of representation is in terms of the concept of information, and in particular the concept of informational value developed in section 2.3. J. J. Gibson thus deserves belated credit for linking the idea of picturing to the idea of information, even if his particular definition proved incorrect.

3.3 Representation defined. Although the account of representation to be presented here seeks to give precise formulation to Goodman's basic insight, it is not simply an elaboration of his account. One important difference concerns the kind of entity that is called representational. For Goodman, it is a symbol system, which consists of a collection of characters and a rule correlating symbols with objects (or the extension of such a rule). On the account to be offered here, it is the rule alone, or interpretative standard, that is called representational. For the terms "representational" and "pictorial" apply to modes of interpreting a physical symbol presented to a person, as was stated in section 1.1, and there is nothing more to such a mode of interpretation than a rule that declares when a symbol is to count as faithful to an object. Thus suppose S is the rule "x is a straight ink mark and y is an object whose weight in ounces is equal to the length in inches of x." However the different ink marks may be sorted into syntactic characters, the interpretation of a particular ink mark with which a person is presented is the same. He observes the mark and extracts information from it, the information consisting of all properties P such that he knows (or believes) ⌜For any object y, if $S(x,y)$ then $P(y)$⌝. And in obtaining information from the mark x by means of the interpretative standard S, he is interpreting that mark in a representational manner. By the same token the rule "x is an inscription of 'cat' and y is a cat" is a nonrepresentational interpretation of any inscription of "cat," regardless of how the various inscriptions of this word are sorted into characters.[26]

Another difference between Goodman's concept and the concept to be defined here is that for Goodman a symbol system is or is not representational absolutely, whereas on the definition to be offered here an interpretative standard is or is not representational relative to a symbol on the one hand and a class of statements taken as expressing the knowledge or beliefs of a processer at a time on the other. Indeed, it seems conceivable that one and the same rule may be a representational interpretation of one symbol but a nonrepresentational interpretation of some other symbol relative to a given observer, and that a representational interpretation of a symbol relative to one class of statements may not be a representational interpretation of that same symbol relative to some other class of statements. Illustrations of both kinds of relativity will be given later on.

The definition of representation offered here is as follows: An interpretative standard S is a representational interpretation of a symbol x relative to a class of statements Γ, if there are collections of properties Φ and Ψ such that (a) Φ is a *continuous aspect* of x relative to Γ, and (b) Φ *indicates* Ψ relative to S, x, and Γ. (For instance, the color-photographic standard mentioned in section 1.2 is a representational way of interpreting a given picture relative to the knowledge of a normal person who is viewing that picture because there are various continuous aspects of the picture, such as the distance between designated points on its surface, the area of designated portions of that surface, the color of those portions, etc., that are indications to the viewer, when he interprets the picture according to that standard, of corresponding aspects of anything to which the picture may happen to be faithful.) This definition employs two concepts that must now be explained, that of a continuous aspect and that of indication.

The first of these concepts corresponds roughly to Goodman's idea of a syntactically dense symbol scheme. There are, however, perhaps as many differences as similarities. For one thing, a continuous aspect is a collection of *properties* rather than of characters regarded as classes of symbols. This makes it possible to require that a continuous aspect *have*, and not merely provide for in some weaker sense, infinitely many elements. There can be infinitely many properties of symbols even though there are only finitely many symbols, indeed even though there is only a single symbol, because a number of distinct properties may share the same extension.[27]

The properties contained in a continuous aspect are possible properties of the symbol being observed. In contrast to talk about possible symbols, which was seen in section 3.2 to be obscure, talk about possible properties of an actual symbol is perfectly intelligible. For the kind of possibility involved in this way of talking is *epistemic* rather than metaphysical: to say that M is a possible property of an object x relative to a person's body of knowledge Γ is merely to say that for all the person knows to the contrary x has M, or in other words that Γ does not entail ⌜It is not the case that $M(x)$⌝. So different, indeed, is the concept of a possible property of an actual symbol x from the concept of a possible symbol (supposing the latter concept to be clear for a moment) that even if the interpretative standard in question allows for no possible symbols at all besides x, there can still be infinitely many possible properties of x. For instance, if a person is looking at a given straight ink mark and does not know the exact length of that mark, there are infinitely many properties of the form "x is exactly so many inches long" that are possible properties of that mark relative to his knowledge, whether or not there are any possible symbols besides the mark he is looking at.

A second difference between a continuous aspect and a symbol scheme is that while the characters provided for by the latter correspond to individual points on a line, the properties belonging to the former correspond not only to individual points but also to *intervals* of points on a line. For example, the continuous aspect length contains not just properties of the form "x is exactly so many inches long" but also properties of the form "x is between such and such a number and such and such a different number of inches long."[28] The reason for thus expanding the conception of a continuous aspect is that a person who is estimating, say, the length of an object always ascertains the object's length only to within some margin of error. Hence in order to describe the information gained in examining the length of a symbol it is necessary to consider possible properties specifying its length not exactly but only approximately.

When a person observes the symbol before him more closely and refines his estimate of its length, he narrows the limits within which the length of that symbol falls. Since he can never measure its length exactly, the process of narrowing the limits is potentially endless. In this respect a continuous aspect such as length differs from a discontinuous aspect such as spelling. Although the spelling of an inscription may at first be indistinct due to such causes as remoteness of the observer or occlusion of some of the letters, improvement in the observational conditions will eventually disclose the exact spelling of the inscription. As will emerge shortly, this difference between a continuous and a discontinuous aspect is an essential element in explaining how symbols interpreted representationally convey information.

Of course, all symbols equally—indeed, all objects—possess both continuous and discontinuous aspects. The difference between interpreting an object as a representation and interpreting it as a word or some other kind of symbol has to do with the bearing of its continuous aspects upon the information it conveys. When a symbol is interpreted in a representational manner, at least one of its continuous aspects *indicates* some other collection of properties. Indication is defined in terms of the concept of informational value developed in section 2.3: Φ indicates Ψ relative to S,x,Γ if for every two properties M_1 and M_2 in Φ such that $M_1 \neq M_2$ relative to Γ, there are properties P_1 and P_2 in Ψ such that $P_1 \neq P_2$ relative to Γ, and $P_1 = S(M_1)$ and $P_2 = S(M_2)$ relative to Ψ,x,Γ. In less technical terms, Φ indicates Ψ if for every two different properties in Φ the informational values in Ψ at those properties are also different. To put it still another way, Φ indicates Ψ if S is one-to-one from Φ into Ψ. (For example, the distance between designated points on the surface of a given picture indicates to a viewer who interprets that picture according to the color-photographic standard the foreshortened distance between the corresponding points of anything to which the picture may happen to be faithful, because for any two different possible properties specifying the distance between the designated points on the surface of the picture the informational values of the color-photographic standard at those properties will also be different.)

The concept of indication captures at least part of Goodman's notion of semantic density, for the wording of Goodman's definition seems to imply that a semantically dense symbol system provides for a different compliance-class corresponding to every different character it provides for. Again, however, there are important dissimilarities with Goodman's notion. Instead of referring to classes, the concept of indication refers to properties. And instead of talking about the compliance-class that a symbol system provides for corresponding to a character that it provides for, the concept of indication talks about the informational value of an interpretative standard at a property. Moreover, indication is relative to a given symbol that is being observed, and no other symbols actual, possible, or provided for are involved in the definition in any way. If an interpretative standard is such that it provides for no other symbols in its domain besides the one being observed, this fact would presumably prevent that standard from being the semantic component of a semantically dense symbol system on Goodman's conception, but on the present definition of indication there may still be a continuous aspect of that symbol that indicates some other collection of properties.

To better appreciate the concept of indication, consider a straight ink mark and consider the two interpretative standards (1) x is the mark and y is a metal rod having the same length as x, and (2) x is the mark and y is a metal rod one inch in length. The difference between (1) and (2) is parallel in an important way to the difference between (1) and (2) in section 3.1. As interpreted by (1), the mark is a rudimentary picture; as interpreted by (2), it is in effect a word—not a proper name this time but a common noun applicable to any metal rod one inch in length.

Suppose that relative to some normal observer's body of knowledge Γ the mark could have any length between 3/4 and 1 1/4 inches. Let Φ_0

contain all properties *M* such that *M*⊆ "x is between 3/4 and 1 1/4 inches long" relative to Γ and *M* is either of the form "x is exactly so many inches long" or of the form "x is between such and such a number and such and such a different number of inches long"; and let Ψ₀ contain all properties of either of these forms without restriction, as well as the conjunction of any properties it contains. Then Φ₀ is a continuous aspect of the mark relative to Γ, and Φ₀ indicates Ψ₀ when that mark is interpreted by (1) relative to Γ. On the other hand, Φ₀ does not indicate Ψ₀ when the same mark is interpreted by (2) relative to Γ. And this remains true even if it is supposed that in fact the mark is exactly one inch long, so that (1) and (2) have the same extension.

The difference between the representational (1) and the nonrepresentational (2) can be illustrated graphically as in figure 3:1. In both pairs of graphs the properties in Φ₀ correspond to the points and intervals of points

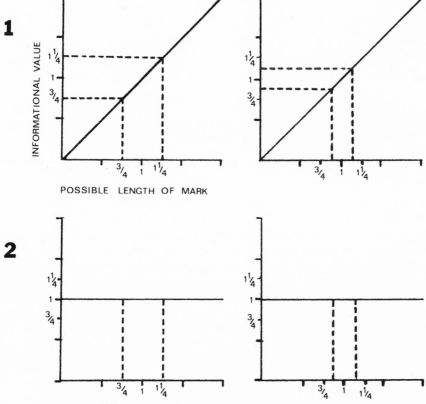

Figure 3:1. Difference between the representational (1) and the nonrepresentational (2).

on the horizontal axis between $3/4$ and $1\ 1/4$, and the properties in Ψ_0 correspond to the points and intervals of points on the vertical axis. The informational value of the interpretative standard (1) or (2) at a point or interval on the horizontal axis is the reflection of that point or interval onto the vertical axis by means of the graph. It is at once seen that standard (1) takes different points and intervals on the horizontal axis into different points and intervals on the vertical axis, whereas standard (2) takes all points and intervals on the horizontal axis into the same single point on the vertical axis.

Notice from the left-hand and right-hand graphs in (1) the effect upon information of going from a weaker to a stronger property in Φ_0. As a general principle, indication of Ψ by Φ relative to S,x,Γ implies that strengthening the condition in Φ always at the same time strengthens the information in Ψ that is conditionally conveyed. This principle is most easily demonstrated by first proving the following theorem: (3) Assume that (a) the conjunction of any two properties in Ψ is also in Ψ, (b) $M_2 \subseteq M_1$ relative to Γ, (c) $P_1 = S(M_1)$ relative to Ψ,x,Γ, and (d) $P_2 = S(M_2)$ relative to Ψ,x,Γ. Then $P_2 \subseteq P_1$ relative to Γ.

Proof: Since x conveys P_1 conditionally upon M_1 by hypothesis (c) and $M_2 \subseteq M_1$ by hypothesis (b), x conveys P_1 conditionally upon M_2. By hypotheses (a) and (d) and the theorem concluding section 2.3, therefore, $P_2 \subseteq P_1$ relative to Γ. From this theorem the desired result now follows as a corollary: (4) Assume that Φ indicates Ψ relative to S,x,Γ. Then for every M_1 and M_2 in Φ and every P_1 and P_2 in Ψ such that $P_1 = S(M_1)$ and $P_2 = S(M_2)$ relative to Ψ,x,Γ, if $M_2 \subset M_1$ relative to Γ then $P_2 \subset P_1$ relative to Γ. (To prove this corollary note that if $M_2 \subset M_1$ then $M_2 \subseteq M_1$ and $M_1 \neq M_2$, and if $P_2 \subseteq P_1$ and $P_1 \neq P_2$ then $P_2 \subset P_1$.)

Now, as was noted in section 2.3, if a symbol conveys a property P to an observer conditionally upon M, then once the observer has established M to actually hold of that symbol it comes to convey P to him unconditionally. Hence the strengthening in what a symbol conditionally conveys to a person when he moves from the hypothesis of a weaker to that of a stronger condition in Φ becomes a strengthening in what the symbol conveys to him unconditionally when, having established that the weaker condition actually holds of the symbol, he then comes to establish that the stronger condition holds of it as well.

It is now possible to answer the question "How do pictures convey information?", taken as meaning "What distinguishes the manner in which pictures convey information from the manner in which symbols interpreted nonrepresentationally convey information?" When an observer interprets a symbol according to a pictorial standard, or more generally a representational standard, as he progressively refines his estimate of the symbol's location along some continuous aspect, the information conveyed to him by the symbol becomes progressively stronger. Moreover, however precisely he measures the symbol with respect to the continuous aspect in question, further refinement in his measurement will yield even stronger information from the symbol. By contrast, when he interprets the same or a different symbol according to a nonrepresentational standard, he does not have to bother estimating the location of the symbol along any of its continuous aspects, since such estimation is irrelevant to the information it conveys.

An interpretative standard is representational not absolutely but relative to a symbol on the one hand and a class of statements on the other. Earlier, examples of both kinds of relativity were promised. To see how an interpretative standard S can be a representational interpretation of one symbol x_1 and at the same time a nonrepresentational interpretation of another symbol x_2 relative to a class of statements Γ, imagine two marks each about one inch long and suppose the interpretative standard to be (3) x is the left-hand mark and y is a metal rod having the same length as x, or x is the right-hand mark and y is a metal rod one inch in length. Obviously (3) is a representational interpretation of the left-hand mark and a nonrepresentational interpretation of the right-hand mark relative to the knowledge of a normal person who is looking at both marks.

Of greater interest is the second kind of relativity. To see how an interpretative standard S can be a representational interpretation of a symbol x relative to one class of statements Γ_1 but not relative to another class of statements Γ_2, let S be (1) mentioned above, x be the mark that was also mentioned there, Γ_1 be the body of knowledge of a normal observer looking at that mark, and Γ_2 be the body of knowledge of an omniscient observer, or in other words the class of all true statements. Now an omniscient being would know the true length of the mark, which is, suppose, one inch. Therefore for every property M such that "x is one inch long" $\subseteq M$, the informational value of (1) at M relative to that mark would be the same for him, namely "y is one inch long." Moreover, all other properties specifying length would fail to be possible properties of that mark relative to his knowledge. Hence there would be no continuous aspect of the mark that indicated to him any other collection of properties. For this reason, standard (1) would not be a representational interpretation of the mark in question as far as this being was concerned any more than standard (2) would be; that is to say, the distinction between a picture and a word evaporates for an omnicient being.

This point is really the same as the point made in section 3.1, that whether or not an interpretative standard is a representational interpretation of a given symbol is not settled by the extension of that standard.

3.4 Picturing and perception. A special case of representation occurs when the collection of properties indicated by a continuous aspect of the symbol is itself a continuous aspect of some object to which the symbol is faithful. In this case progressively refined estimation of the symbol's location along the continuous aspect Φ in question will result in the symbol conveying progressively stronger properties from the indicated collection Ψ. But, since Ψ is now assumed to be a continuous aspect of the object that the symbol faithfully represents, direct inspection of that object would similarly have resulted in establishing it to have progressively stronger properties in Ψ. To trade on the same ambiguity of "information" between properties conveyed and properties possessed that was noted in connection with Gibson's formulations in section 1, it might be said that in these cases of representation an observer can get the same information in Ψ from perceiving the symbol as he can get from directly perceiving the object to which the symbol is faithful (given the assumption that this object is accessible to direct perception at all). Of course, only information *of a certain kind*—namely, properties in Ψ—is being said here to be ascertainable equally by perceiving the symbol and by perceiving the object represented. Certainly not *all* information that can be gained from the symbol need be capable of being gained directly from the object represented.

Moreover, to say that an observer can obtain the same information of a certain kind from perceiving the symbol as he can obtain from perceiving the object represented is not to say that the appropriate modes of perception of the symbol and the object represented are the same. In order to pick up information (properties possessed) of the kind Ψ from the object represented, he must ascertain properties in Ψ to hold of that object; whereas in order to pick up information (properties conveyed) of the same kind Ψ from the symbol, he must ascertain properties not in Ψ but in Φ to hold of that symbol. The mode of perception appropriate to ascertaining properties in Φ may be very different from the mode of perception appropriate to ascertaining properties in Ψ. If tones of sound stand for color samples according to some representational standard, hearing the tone will convey information pertaining to the color of the sample represented by the tone.

As this last example shows, it would be a mistake to equate picturing in the common and everyday sense with representation in which one continuous aspect indicates another. Rather, as was suggested back in section 1.5, picturing as commonly and narrowly understood is especially concerned with the spatial properties of both the picture and what it depicts. It is now possible to delimit the special kind of representation that Gibson may have had in mind when he defined picturing in terms of sameness of information contained in the optic arrays from the picture and the object depicted. This is the kind in which a continuous *spatial* aspect of the picture indicates a continuous *spatial* aspect of the object depicted. In those cases where the indicated spatial aspect can be perceived by vision, it is correct to say that an observer can get the same information of a certain kind (rather than the same kind of information) from looking at the picture as he can get from looking at the object it depicts. This is not, however, quite the same thing that Gibson said, since the claim here is not that *all* information an observer can get from looking at the picture can be gotten equally from looking at the object depicted. Nor is it claimed that the observer's visual perception in looking at the picture is qualitatively the same as his visual perception in looking at the object depicted; indeed, a stick figure whose length indicates the height of the individual represented is an example of the type of representation now being discussed, but nobody would want to maintain that perceiving the stick figure is qualitatively indistinguishable from perceiving the individual it depicts.

In closing, a word may be said about caricature, which Gibson in 1971 regarded as a counterexample to his theory of 1954. As David Perkins has pointed out in a recent paper on the subject, those continuous spatial aspects of the caricature that exaggerate certain continuous spatial aspects of the individual caricatured do not indicate, in the sense here defined, the latter aspects.[29] Gibson therefore seems to have been more correct in 1954 when he regarded distortion in caricature as a "kind of graphic symbolism like the using of words" than he was in 1971 when he regarded it as a species of pictorial representation. What *is* a species of pictorial representation, though, is the distortion that occurs when one looks into a curved mirror such as those found in carnival funhouses. The difference between caricature and reflection in a funhouse mirror, which superficially appear to be similar phenomena, is that in the latter but not necessarily in the former kind of symbolization there are continuous spatial aspects of the image that indicate continuous spatial aspects of the original.

Notes

1. J. J. Gibson, "A Theory of Pictorial Perception," *Audio-Visual Communications Review* 1 (1954): 3–23.
2. J. J. Gibson, "The Information Available in Pictures," *Leonardo* 4 (1971): 27–35.
3. Nelson Goodman, *Languages of Art: An Approach to a Theory of Symbols* (Indianapolis and New York: Bobbs-Merrill, 1968).
4. Goodman, *Languages of Art*, p. 226.
5. Gibson, "Pictorial Perception," p. 14.
6. Gibson, "Information in Pictures," pp. 28, 29. In fairness to Gibson it should be said that in his 1954 paper he considered fidelity as an "extreme case." He meant, presumably, that pictures are not simply faithful or unfaithful, but more faithful according as the light rays they deliver come nearer to matching those of their subjects. But this qualification does not affect the criticisms above. A line drawing may be *perfectly* faithful to an object in accordance with the appropriate pictorial standard, even though that drawing yields nowhere near the same sheaf of light rays as does that object.
7. Ibid., p. 31.
8. Nelson Goodman, "Professor Gibson's New Perspective," *Leonardo* 4 (1971): 360.
9. Gibson, "Information in Pictures," p. 31.

10. Ibid., pp. 32, 33. If the present essay were discussing pictorial representation as an *art*, it would refer at this point to the view of Roger Fry and Clive Bell that the proper aesthetic appreciation of a painting positively demands that the viewer *not* take the representational attitude.

11. See the article by John Kennedy and Nathan Fox in the present volume.

12. Goodman, *Languages of Art*, p. 231.

13. A predicate is an expression obtained from a grammatical sentence by substituting place holders in the form of letters such as "x," "y," and "z" for one or more naming expressions. Examples of one-, two-, and three-place predicates respectively are "x is between Boston and New York," "x is between y and New York," and "x is between y and z."

14. See Quine, *Mathematical Logic* (Cambridge, Mass.: Harvard University Press, 1951), pp. 33–37.

15. The reader who is acquainted with the writings of W. V. Quine will recognize that this definition as it stands commits the fallacy of quantifying into referentially opaque contexts by using the variable "x" to refer to the same thing both inside and outside the quasi-quotation marks. The way to avoid this fallacy is to use the locution "r at t knows Q of x", in which "Q" refers to a property rather than a statement and "x" no longer appears within quotation marks. On this and similar locutions see Quine, *The Ways of Paradox* (New York: Random House, 1966), pp. 183–94. The concept of information is then defined as follows: x as interpreted by S conveys P to r at t if r at t knows ⌜For any object y, if S(x,y) then P(y)⌝ of x. The definition given in the text may now be understood as convenient shorthand for the fully correct definition given in this note.

16. This can be seen as follows. A person who knows that there are no unicorns knows ⌜For any object y, it is not the case that S(x,y)⌝. (Or rather, in view of the preceding footnote, he knows ⌜For any object y, it is not the case that S(x,y)⌝ of x). *A fortiori*, then, he knows ⌜For any object y, it is not the case that both S(x,y) and not P(y)⌝, no matter what property P may be. But "It is not the case that both . . . and not _____" is logically equivalent to "If . . . then _____." He therefore knows (and hence also believes) ⌜For any object y, if S(x,y) then P(y)⌝, no matter what property P may be.

17. The reader must not confuse a class of *statements* with the extension of a property, which is a class of *objects*, or the extension of an interpretative standard, which is a class of ordered pairs of objects.

18. Strictly speaking, in view of n. 15, the definition of information relative to Γ should read as follows: x as interpreted by S conveys P relative to Γ if the property-object pair < ⌜For any object y, if S(x,y) then P(y)⌝, x> belongs to Γ. Γ thus contains property-object pairs in addition to genuine statements.

19. The concept of logical entailment may be easily extended to cover property-object pairs as well as genuine statements by treating any such pair $<Q,x>$ exactly as if it were a genuine statement ⌜Q(c)⌝ in which an individual constant "c" designates the object x. In all such pairs the same object is regarded as designated by the same constant and different objects are regarded as designated by different constants.

20. Goodman, *Languages of Art*, p. 41.

21. Ibid., p. 131.

22. Ibid., p. 136. In the revised edition (1972) a slightly stronger definition of syntactic density is given, one which entails but is not entailed by the definition in the first edition. The difference between the original definition, which has been quoted here because it is simpler, and the revised one need not be of concern here.

23. Ibid., p. 153. As with syntactic density, semantic density receives a slightly stronger definition in the revised edition than in the first edition. Again, the original definition has been quoted because it is simpler, the difference between it and the revised definition being unimportant to present concerns.

24. Ibid., p. 227.

25. W. V. Quine, *From a Logical Point of View* (Cambridge, Mass.: Harvard University Press, 1961), p. 4.

26. If each different height of letters counts as a different character, then the resulting symbol scheme is syntactically dense. But the symbol system consisting of this scheme and the rule that "cat" applies to cats is not semantically dense. A system such as this, which is

syntactically but not semantically dense, is still a representational system according to Goodman, although he says that a *normal* representational system is semantically as well as syntactically dense. (See *Languages of Art*, p. 159, and p. 227 n. 1.) It seems to this writer, however, that systems which Goodman considers abnormal representational systems are not representational at all, since syntactic density without semantic density achieves nothing. The relation between Goodman's conception of a *normal* representational system and the definition of representation offered here is discussed below.

27. To object here that properties are expressions of English and only finitely many such expressions have ever been written down or uttered is to confuse English considered as the background language whose expressions play the role of properties and interpretative standards with English considered as one interpretative standard among others. The elements in the domain of English considered as an interpretative standard—the utterances and inscriptions that a processer observes and interprets—are of course finite in number. They are concrete objects on a par with trees, houses, and other denizens of the physical world, and only finitely many of them ever have been or will be produced. But properties and interpretative standards are not symbols—they are not the sorts of entities that a person could kick—but are rather ingredients in what a person knows or believes. They may therefore be regarded as abstract sequences of letters rather than concrete utterances or inscriptions, so there can be infinitely many of them.

28. Note the ambiguity of the expression "the length of x," which sometimes refers to a continuous aspect of x—i.e., a certain collection of properties—and sometimes refers to a single property of x, namely the unique property that is possessed by x and has the form "x is exactly so many inches long."

29. David Perkins, "A Definition of Caricature" and "Caricature and Recognition," *Studies in the Anthropology of Visual Communication* 2, no. 1 (1975): 1–24.

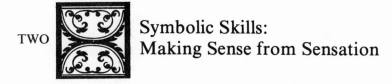

TWO Symbolic Skills:
Making Sense from Sensation

The painter paints, the poet writes, the dancer dances, each hoping the audience will respond with depth and discrimination. Artists work the materials of sensation, fusing them into significant statement; audience members transform the clutter of sensation into the resonant experience of art. Both are intricate feats. Of what are they wrought?

One sort of answer might mention a keen sense of balance, an ear for the vernacular, a gift of mimicry, or an eye for line. Another sort might address visual discrimination, conceptual fluency, motor coordination, or information processing. Whether in everyday or technical parlance, such answers offer explanation in terms of skill—indeed, since symbols are being made and read, explanation in terms of symbolic skill.

But what about the furthest reaches of genius, the pinnacles of insight and synthesis? Surely here is "something more" than skill. The question thus becomes, how much can skill aspire to explain, and where must skill inevitably fall short? The issue is precarious because the explanatory reach of skill depends crucially on what the concept means.

Accounts of skill explain in a certain way. One might instead (or in addition) address the commitment and drive of the artist or audience member, the traditions he may channel or challenge, his childhood, his neuroses, his teachers, his friends and enemies, his theories, enthusiasms, and anathemas. But none of these are skills, and in explaining by skill one necessarily sets aside, at least for a while, these other perspectives. Consider simply questions of motivation. Artistic or other achievement rarely finds a foundation in sloth. Certainly commitment looms as a crucial variable. Yet the adage that "where there's a will there's a way" seems amply contradicted by the many who strive and the few who succeed. Taking the "will" for granted, this book focuses on the "way."

Skills describe the "way." Skills relate to performance as part to whole. A pianist will make accurate left-hand skips in playing a whole piece; his facility with such skips will figure in many pieces; further, he may practice or demonstrate the skill in isolation. Themselves performances, skills do not merely influence but operate within the larger performance they describe. But skills are not just part of one performance; rather they are portable pieces of behavior that can contribute in a variety of contexts and can also operate in isolation from their larger purpose. These properties place the concept of skill in a tradition ranging from atoms and molecules to parts of speech. Particular wholes—whether polymers or artistic processes—are construed as different arrangements of standardized components. This plan seems to be one of man's most powerful analytical inventions. The very family membership of the concept of skill recommends its salience.

Yet skill sacrifices all hope of potent explanation unless the concept stands as sufficiently flexible from the start. In common usage, "skill" connotes routine, technical sorts of activities like left-hand skips. But so narrow a range omits too much. Even complex strategic maneuvers must count as skills, providing they function as units portable from occasion to occasion. Further, the skills described in textbooks or the procedural lore of some art forms may offer considerable help to the learner but certainly do not provide a rich enough base for the immensely complex activities involved in the arts or other domains: most skills must be considered "there" though undiscovered. Nor is a whole performance merely a concatenation of skills; coordinating and integrating individually acquired skills may be more of a problem than learning the skills themselves. Moreover, a flexible conception of skill requires that skills may or may not be conscious, may or may not be learnable or learned, may or may not be acknowledged as such by their possessor. Skills are not atomic and indivisible but hierarchical: a skill may itself be analyzed in terms of subordinate skills. Nor need there be one right hierarchy of skills for explaining human behavior. A putative skill is an explanatory construction of a purposeful observer—the person himself, a teacher, a psychologist—and different analyses of the same performance can certainly vie for attention and relevance. It is this conception of skills rather than the more common and more mechanistic one that informs the work to follow.

The relation of skills to accomplishment—the output or product of effort—introduces further complications. Excellence in a given field does not relate to any single body of skills because excellence takes different forms. One genre demands quite different activities of a painter or poet than another. Further, even relatively specific objectives may not require a specific assemblage of skills. The folk wisdom that "there's more than one way to skin a cat" remains powerfully true throughout human endeavor. However, all tasks unequivocally require particular basic skills. Most crudely put, the painter cannot paint without seeing nor the writer write without knowing a language. In sum, the skills potentially contributing to a given objective comprise a complicated family, some necessary, some inter-substitutable.

Despite these complexities and qualifications, the concept of skill remains a powerful tool in accounting for, predicting, and even educating performance. The same features that fit skills for explanation also fit them for prediction. A person's repertoire of skills delimits his potential performances at a given time in much the same way that his vocabulary delimits his possible utterances. Those skills, like that vocabulary, may combine in infinite ways, but in ways bounded by their own variety. The further and crucial point is that skills, like vocabulary, need not remain static. Skills are slow-changing units of behavior—otherwise they would be too volatile to explain multiple performances by the same person. But old skills do evolve and new ones emerge. Defining what skills a particular objective requires immediately defines a plan for educational intervention. Further, training in skills dodges many ethical issues which arise in aiming to alter other dimensions relevant to a person's accomplishments—his personality, his commitments, and so forth. In all, skills not only define a person's capability but offer a way of mapping performance goals into specific and nonsensitive pedagogical objectives.

In theory this is tidy. In practice, such a system only works as well as the analysis of skills at hand. Unfortunately, analyses of broad performance areas into skills have a notorious reputation for missing the heart of the matter, as numerous episodes warn in the history of both factor analysis and the more recent behavioral objectives movement. Apart from the completeness of an account, there remains also the problem of how well the putative component skills are distinguished. Isolated by factor analytic techniques, subtests supposedly measuring the same skill show a correlation hardly higher than correlations between different skills. Although these "skills" can be separated mathematically, certainly in human functioning they do not stand as sharply distinct.

These falterings and false starts speak less to the concept itself than to the youth of its employment. The Greeks, after all, conceived the atom, but only in the last hundred years has the notion of a universal chemical building block matured into sound scientific theory. If the question is how did Beethoven do it, the answer is not skills. Rather, skills is a proposal for an answer, a style of addressing the question and a form that the answer might take. Uttering "skill" no more resolves the puzzle of human genius than uttering "atom" explains the structure of matter. It is in the details—the particular units, the rules of combination—that the substance of a theory lies. And it is in settling just such questions that the investigator suddenly faces innumerable options, many of them not recognized as such, with only dim signs to steer by.

Being a young science, analysis in terms of skills must be a bold one. This thought recalls the theme that genius involves "something more" than skill. If "something more" means that simply saying "skills" explains nothing, then that is granted. If "something more" reflects the limitations of current analyses of skill and bodies of practical lore in the arts, then that too can be conceded. If "something more" means other kinds of explanation —those concerning motivation, tradition, and so on—then that is surely allowable and perhaps required. But if "something more" means that there is something else the person *does* (or his mind or body does) to behave inventively, then this is a logical contradiction. Whatever that supposed "something more" might be, skill as here flexibly construed would already include it, because such explanation would necessarily take the form of portable slow-changing units of behavior. If "something more" notes that even the gifted achieve occasional peaks of performance hard to account for in light of their routine practice, then it is also true that all repeated performances vary by chance around their mean, and occasional peaks as well as lapses need no more explanation than that. And finally, if "something more" becomes simply an article of faith that the heights of genius will forever evade any significant analytical prying, then others—the contributors to this book among them—hold an opposite faith, and the answer rests with their efforts.

Nothing would fit so well here as a thorough and profound division of artistic activities into a multitude of component skills. Unfortunately, these articles offer no fundamental exception to the argument above that analysis in terms of skills remains much closer to its beginnings than its ends. This invites the reader to view the offerings in a double light, both as significant investigations in their own right and as harbingers of the sorts of themes and tactics, issues and conceptions that may prove provocative and yield progress.

Howard Gardner's essay exemplifies analysis from the top down. Most typically, scholarship deals with particular issues and phenomena and perhaps toward the end relates them to the broader dominion of interest. But a discussion can begin with the whole range and by introducing distinctions work down toward more focused questions. Gardner's article adopts this tactic. It presents a simple taxonomy of human symbol-processing activities, aesthetic activities in particular, based on whether symbolic operations remain within or cut across sensory modalities, remain within or cut across symbol systems, and preserve or radically transform the materials operated upon. As all such efforts hope to do, Gardner's viewpoint offers a new way of construing the world it addresses—here the world of human cognition.

Analysis from the bottom up defers the general in favor of the particular, hoping to recover the general in due course. Analysis from the top down seeks the general first, hoping to work down to the particulars. All the essays in this book are hopeful in those senses. A mature theory—modern physics, for instance—negotiates a happy meeting; at the top stand general principles which in suitable combination explain a wide range of detailed phenomena at the bottom. Behaviorism is the obvious example of an attempt to do the same thing in psychology. But as is so often the case, the richness of particular phenomena seems to outstrip the explanatory power of the general scheme, which, while accounting for some points, remains manifestly and disconcertingly incomplete. Such lessons seem mostly tactical. Imperative are efforts to build from both top and bottom lest the virtues of either be forgotten, a continued push for meeting between the two, and severe standards of adequacy in the explanation of more specialized phenomena by more general principles.

John Kennedy's offering addresses a particular issue: can the blind interpret raised line drawings? His surprising affirmative, contradicting general if informal expectations, underscores how precarious this meeting between principle and particular is. How easily one presumes that information of certain kinds is limited to certain sensory channels—spatial layout to the eyes, pitch and rhythm to the ears, and so on. Though Kennedy sifts the particulars of vision and touch, his conclusions not only unsettle established findings in those fields but threaten to dislodge a cherished habit of analysis, that of binary classification.

The dichotomy in particular—the polar opposition—emerges as one of man's most frequent and dangerous conceptual playthings. The dichotomy is generalization in its most simple form. Its compelling trimness promotes credibility. The arts seem especially plagued by dubious dichotomies: creativity versus analyticity, Dionysian versus Apollonian, abstract versus concrete, form versus content, verbal versus visual, and on and on. Dichotomies pose a triple hazard. First, as perhaps with creativity versus analyticity, they may simply be wrong—products of faulty observation and thought. Second, as with the verbal-visual distinction, rescued by Nelson Goodman as linguistic versus dense symbol systems, they may bury some sort of insight in a conceptual muddle. But third and perhaps most important, a dichotomy cannot explain very much. Theoretical constructs become more powerful as they involve more distinctions than two, and also as they become generative or combinatorial, the basic distinctions combining in different ways to deal with different cases.

The article by Paul Kolers echoes all these issues. Dealing with the false opposition of visual versus verbal by comparing the reading of text and the reading of pictures, he isolates several striking parallels which complement the contrasts Nelson Goodman emphasizes in his analysis of symbol systems. As much as Kennedy's article, that of Kolers underscores the point that simple distinctions bloom into complexity under the least scrutiny.

His article also reminds us that the roots of artistic activity lie in a broad facility with varied symbol systems. Most obviously, if a man cannot read, he cannot read a poem or a novel. But more than that, examination of symbolic skills in general exposes patterns of behavior which mold the nature of aesthetic experience in particular. Kolers notes, for instance, that as reading skill increases, the scanning of text more and more adopts information-gathering strategies and less and less pursues a dogged word-by-word procedure. He argues that reading is selective—the person seeks what he wants to know or is in the habit of looking for and ignores the rest. He stresses how much reading is reconstructive—the reader interpolating information unspecified in the text or, as skill increases, interpolating information rather than attending in detail to the text. Confronting a work of art is not usually conceived of as an activity of selectively sampling a stimulus, decoding its messages, reconstructing its lacunae. Yet works of art are symbols, and in large part this is what reading them must involve.

Certainly the arts have their special natures and problems, but right now the kinship between artistic and other symbols often teaches more than examination of specific problems within the arts. In this sense, all the treatments here work "from the top down."

4 Senses, Symbols, Operations: An Organization of Artistry
Howard Gardner

1. A plethora of skills in search of an organizer

Imagine an attentive listener at a poetry reading. At sundry moments he may note the poet's rolling voice, special accents on crucial words like "love" or "admonition," a regular metric pattern or a lengthy run of unaccentuated syllables. He may focus on the sounds of the words, their literal meanings, their connotations. He may note relations among words in different stanzas, respond to an unusual metaphoric or metonymic figure, ponder the influence of a classical tongue upon the poet's syntax. His thoughts may leap to other works by the same poet or to related works by different poets. He may read along with the poet, or he may close his eyes and visualize a scene from childhood, recall a melody he has not heard in years, or tap his fingers in time with the dominant accents in each line.

An even more extensive set of activities may be undertaken by the poet at his writing table. In addition to attending and criticizing, the poet is deeply involved in the generation of ideas, images, rhyme schemes, stanza arrangements, and figures of speech as well as in the selection of particular words and phrases which best meet the requirements of the work. If one amplifies this list with the numerous additional capacities required of creators, performers, and perceivers in other art forms, it become apparent that full participation in the arts draws upon a dizzying complex of perceptual and cognitive processes.

There has been no dearth of attempts to describe what the creative artist or the competent audience member must do and how he can best do it. Indeed, the literature may even offer too many intuitions (some of them quite convincing) about the skills needed for participation in the artistic process. Notably lacking, however, are attempts to organize in a coherent manner the vast array of skills, capacities, and methods possessed by artistic practitioners. In the absence of such organizing frameworks the skills of the artist threaten to overwhelm our efforts at understanding: so much is going on, often simultaneously or in rapid succession, that the component parts and the critical factors elude the observer. Attempts to train artistic skills are also thwarted; without cogent notions about the constituents of a complex skill and the relations among skills, a systematic educational regimen cannot be set forth. Finally, efforts to frame a psychological model of the partly contrasting capacities of artists, performers, audience members, and critics would benefit from an analytic taxonomy in the light of which specific skills and clusters of skills can be assayed.

Achievement of a taxonomy of artistry is as yet a remote goal, one which would require the energy of an army of thinkers (or several committed geniuses). Knowledge must be brought to bear from a variety of disciplines; tentative frameworks need to be devised and then revised in the light of logical considerations and empirical observations. Possible pitfalls of such a program must also be confronted. The categories of analysis should not be so broad that they swallow up widely divergent activities, nor should they be so numerous or narrow that they merely describe (in different words) the often conflicting intuitions of earlier researchers. Consistent with the goal of classification and clarification, the taxonomy must pinpoint what is unique to the arts while at the same time highlighting links to other areas of study. Despite these and other potential difficulties, efforts toward such an organizational framework seem worthwhile if only to encourage other efforts toward the same goal and to call attention to the possible theoretical and pedagogical fruits of an effective taxonomy.

In this article I attempt to achieve a small portion of this goal, to formulate a set of categories which can order the variety of activities in which the *artistic perceiver* or *audience member* engages. It should be stressed that this taxonomy did not arise from an a priori analysis of the audience member's role; nor, on the other hand, is it an organizing principle which was virtually dictated by a compelling set of data. Rather, as is often the case in such undertakings, this taxonomy has slowly emerged from some thinking and some data-collection, and as these activities continue the framework will undoubtedly undergo further revision and lend itself increasingly to empirical investigation.

The ultimate uses of the framework are also open. The taxonomy's purpose is, in part, to organize existing findings: to suggest the central factors underlying diverse perceptual activities, to stimulate research by suggesting questions in need of study and by postulating certain outcomes. Though an individual line of research is most unlikely to confirm (or disprove) the framework, a series of studies should indicate whether it is useful in its present form, whether it requires modest or major reworking, or whether it is better abandoned as irrelevant to the questions at hand.

The plan of this essay is threefold. In the first pages the categories or building blocks of the framework are introduced. Then some psychological research with children and with brain-damaged patients is drawn upon in support of the "psychological reality" of *one portion* of the framework. These subject groups prove particularly informative for the investigation of skills, since capacities are more easily identified and dissected in the behavior of a brain-injured individual or of a child still learning and developing than in the versatile, consummate artistic practitioner. Finally, some applications and implications of this framework in the psychology and pedagogy of the arts are proposed. Clearly this is a working paper and draws on such evidence as exists without pretending that it is at all conclusive. And, though the emphasis falls on the skills of the perceiver contemplating a finished work, the framework should potentially be applicable to other participants, problems, and objects in the arts.

2. Senses, symbols, operations: The building blocks

That hypothetical auditor at a poetry reading will introduce the major components of the framework. The first dimension involves the *sensory modalities* which participate in the activity. In general, art objects arouse the sensory systems of sight, touch, audition, and/or kinesthesis, though in rare circumstances other senses (e.g., taste or smell) may also be involved. A listener who is content with (or intent upon) monitoring the aural input is utilizing but one sense modality; the one who hears the words but also watches the poet's actions, or examines a visual image in his mind's eye, can be said to be employing more than one sense modality. The identity and the number of participating sensory modalities constitute one means of classifying a task, the dimension designated as A in figure 4:1.

The second dimension denotes the number and type of *symbol systems* involved in the activity. As explicated in other essays in this volume, a symbol system is a set of elements which have certain syntactic relations among themselves and which relate in specifiable ways to a field of reference.[1] Such a system may be relatively linguistic (digital) or relatively nonlinguistic (analog), depending on the extent to which its individual elements are disjointed and the manner in which they are mapped onto a field of reference. A relatively pure example of a linguistic symbol system is musical notation, while a paradigmatic instance of a nonlinguistic system is representational painting. Should the hypothetical listener attend only to the sound patterns of the poem (if, say, he did not speak the language) and correlate these sounds with an international phonetic alphabet, he would be dealing with *linguistic* symbol systems. If, on the other hand, he pondered the various allusions in an appealing phrase and dwelled on its pictorial

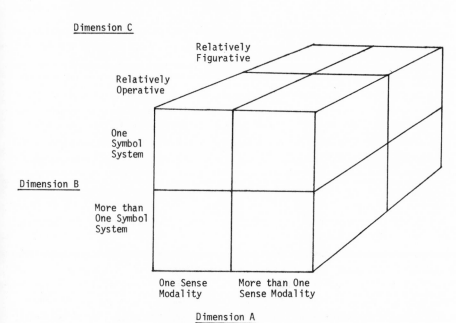

Figure 4:1. A schematic representation of the taxonomic framework. This figure does not designate particular sense modalities or symbol systems. Naturally, a more complex visual representation would be necessary if such detailed information were to be included.

properties, he would be utilizing a number of symbol systems of a *nonlinguistic* sort (visual representation, semantically dense metaphor). The identity and number of symbol systems entailed in a perceptual act constitute the second dimension, designated as B on figure 4:1.

Finally, consider the listener as he contemplates the words of the poem. He may elect simply to listen to them attentively, to savor every sound, perhaps to remember the verses in a faithful form. In so doing he is focusing on the auditory configuration, taking in all details, retaining them with little distortions, hence engaging in what is termed *figurative cognition.* If, on the other hand, he attends to the meaning of the words, then relates the poem to another favorite of his, or rephrases the themes of the poem using a different vocabulary, or translates it into another language, he has abandoned a concentration on the auditory configuration in favor of an active, transforming, or *operative* approach to the work. Whenever the original perception occasions such active cognitive steps (e.g., a more or less radical transformation into another symbol system, sensory modality, or classificatory system, or a concentration on intent, meaning, contradiction, or implication rather than surface manifestations), then an *operative* approach has been invoked. The relative *figurativity* or *operativity* of an individual's cognitive stance becomes the third dimension for assessing a task, that designated as C on figure 4:1.

Our first dimension, that of sensory systems, is a familiar category of psychological analysis. Much excellent research has been done on audition, visual perception, and haptic perception and on the relations among these domains.[2] As a result it will not be necessary to dwell on this dimension. The second dimension, that of symbol systems, is less familiar and, as it cuts across the sensory division, is somewhat less intuitive. A particular sensory modality like vision can be used with a linguistic symbol system (as in reading text) or with a nonlinguistic system (as in studying a painting); conversely, a particular symbol system (like natural language) may be perceived through a number of sensory modalities. It would be desirable to elaborate on the dimension of symbol systems, but the empirical literature on them is still scant.

The third dimension, that of figurativity/operativity, is probably the classificatory mode most in need of explication. Moreover, this dimension appears to be crucial in much artistic activity and of special consequence in differentiating artistic from scientific pursuits. A convergence of recent evidence in developmental psychology and neuropsychology helps to define and pinpoint the significance of this dimension. For these reasons this essay will focus on operativity and figurativity in an effort to draw out their psychological and pedagogical significance.

3. Figurativity and operativity: Some preliminaries

An initial description of figurative and operative cognition can be found in the writings of the developmental psychologist Jean Piaget.[3] Piaget wished to distinguish between certain acts of knowing which retain a stimulus configuration in its original, pristine form and other acts, far more crucial in the elaboration of intelligence, which alter that configuration more or less radically, with knowledge consequent upon the subject's actions and his reflections upon his actions. (The usage in this essay began with and was inspired by Piaget but has evolved in various ways that will be reflected throughout this discussion.)

For Piaget, the figurative modes of cognition constitute a necessary skill in the individual's repertory but hold scant intrinsic interest and limited value for intellectual growth. In figurative perception, one focuses on the stimulus in its most accessible and evident form, ignores nonsurface facets, and remains for the most part within the single sensory system originally stimulated by the external object. Since, for Piaget, knowledge derives from the organism's operations (or actions) upon the environment, such figurative modes as imagery, imitation, dreams, and language cannot of themselves yield knowledge. Devoid of logical structure, they merely reflect the operational level of the individual which is actually the product of his actions upon the world of physical (and social) objects. For Piaget the figurative achieves the status of knowledge only to the extent that it becomes an aliment upon which physical and logical operations can be performend.

This is no place to offer a critique of Piaget's distinction, since it is not a critical facet of his theory and has been reviewed extensively in the developmental literature. What must be noted is that Piaget's evaluation reflects his exclusive interest in the modes of cognition instrumental in scientific knowing. In his view, scientific thinking entails actions, relations between actions, and actions on the structures derived from actions; the specific figurative features of elements and objects in the world are at most a necessary point of departure. Moreover, the entire realm of language is played down in this formulation. Thought is generated independently of linguistic capacities; language is but a symbolic tool which reflects, without materially affecting, the logical thought of the user.

Whatever the validity of Piaget's claims in the scientific realm, they clearly have unsettling implications for the arts.[4] The very processes which Piaget discounts or minimizes are central in artistic activity: the ability to perceive details within a sensory modality, to retain sensory impressions, to value a sound *qua* sound or a color *qua* color, to be alert like our hypothetical auditor to the multiple aspects of language as well as to other forms of imagery. Certainly within a domain like language, there are certain processes—e.g., attending to qualities of voice—which are largely figurative; yet others—e.g., detecting irony—are distinctly operative in flavor. And, as will be suggested below, any developed participation in the arts necessarily involves a subtle interaction between figurative and operative processes. But all that need be established for the present is that aspects of cognition which are nonoperative (in Piaget's sense) nonetheless play an important part in many human activities and may assume special importance within the aesthetic domain.

The taxonomic framework introduced in the above discussion holds up a trio of yardsticks to any behavioral activity. One can assess the type and number of sensory modalities involved; the type and number of symbol systems entailed; and the cognitive stance (relatively faithful and figurative, or relatively transforming and operative) taken by the perceiver. If for the moment the identities of particular senses, symbols, and operations are ignored, there should logically be eight possible forms of cognition, each designated by one of the cubes in figure 4:1 p. 91. For instance, there are processes in which a single sensory modality or symbol system is involved and there is little transformation; the faithful memory involved in eidetic imagery or echoic memory is an example. There are processes in which more than one sensory modality or symbol system is involved but there is nonetheless little transformation, e.g., viewing and listening to a movie in a foreign language or relating a sound to a flash of light by means of classical conditioning. There are processes within a single modality or kind of symbol system that are marked by considerable transformation, e.g., translation from one spoken language to another, manipulation of a visual form into its numerous topological equivalents, and transforming a fugal subject. There are processes involving multiple sensory modalities and/or symbol systems in which considerable transformation is involved, e.g., the conception, scoring, and criticism of an opera. Various hybrids are also envisionable; for example, there may be a figurative use of two symbol systems while at the same time considerable operative activity is occurring in a single sensory modality. And of course, once one includes the specific properties of a particular symbol, sense modality, or operation, the number of variables to be monitored becomes enormous.

There will be no attempt here to decompose into its component tasks an integrated artistic activity (e.g., perceiving a poem or making a painting.) Such an activity is undoubtedly useful, yet it would venture too far from the goal of adducing evidence relevant to the taxonomic framework. Similarly, while it would be desirable to view the evidence concerning particular sense modalities and symbol systems, this too must be postponed for the present. In view of their significant psychological and educational ramifications, however, there must be a pause to consider what happens in these dimensions in the course of development.

As a general rule, as a child develops he acquires increasing capacity to deal with more than one symbol system. He becomes acquainted with new ones (musical notation, Morse code, diagrams, sketches); he learns to "read" and to "symbolize" in these systems; he gains facility at switching among them and at using each in the optimal way. By the same token, the ability to monitor several sensory channels, to combine information from two or more sensory systems, and to "transfer" information presented to one modality into a form accessible to others also increases until at least the time of adolescence. One may summarize a vast amount of literature by stating that fluency within and between symbol systems and sensory systems increases, for the most part, throughout the years of childhood.

In the case of figurativity and operativity, however, the situation appears more complex. In part this is because of a possible tension between these approaches to stimuli, objects, or works. The figurative ability to attend carefully to the properties of a stimulus and to retain them faithfully is not necessarily consonant with the operative proclivity to actively code, classify, and otherwise transform this kind of information. If, as has been suggested; figurative cognition is of crucial import in the arts, and if, as is also implied, figurative and operative capacities do not necessarily prosper together, then an increase in one form may be at the expense of the other.

Here, finally, appears the central issue of this paper: the development of these two principal cognitive modes and their respective roles in artistic activity.

4. Figurativity and operativity: The developmental evidence

There is little doubt that the capacity to operate upon materials in diverse and ever more complex ways increases during the course of childhood.[5] At first the child possesses but a limited set of schemes which he must employ with reference to every object and material. Over time, however, he develops a wide variety of actions and operations, including higher-order ones that can use previously perfected schemes as simple components. Given a group of rocks, the toddler will throw or try to eat them; but the older person can count them, arrange them in different arrays, make them stand for persons, objects or ideas, study their physical and geological properties, or use them as a point of departure for a drawing, a piece of sculpture, even a poem.

Ascertaining developmental trends in the realm of figurative knowledge is a more challenging task. As children in our culture grow older they become increasingly conversant with the giving and taking of tests. For this reason nearly all developmental studies document an improvement with age even when this upward curve may reflect not genuine enhancement of an ability but merely enhanced sophistication in test taking. Despite these factors, which tend to obscure any diminution of skill, there appear to be capacities which peak at an early age and begin to decline in the latter years of childhood or adolescence. These findings are very instructive for the developmental psychologist, and it is significant that they almost invariably involve figurative capacities.

A few apparent declines are frequently mentioned in educational writings, though there is relatively little documentary evidence bearing on them. Most notable is the ability to learn a second language, and, in particular, to imitate its sound patterns and rhythmic features. Whereas the preadolescent can master a new tongue in a short time, the adult more typically requires extensive tutelage and will never pick up certain subtleties.[6] Another area often cited is the acquisition of manual skills ranging from piano playing to water skiing or tennis. The capacity to attend carefully to a model, to imitate relevant aspects of it, to monitor the details of one's own performance, and to make suitable adjustment seems to be heightened in the preadolescent child, as noted by Pritchett:[7]

> That eager period between ten and fourteen is the one in which one can learn anything. Even in the times when most children had no schooling at all, they

could be experts in a trade; the children who went up chimneys, worked in cotton mills, packed coster barrows may have been sick, exhausted, ill-fed, but they were at a temporary height of their intelligence and power.

In addition to these putative declines, there is also some documentary evidence of regression at the time of adolescence in certain specific skills. Of special note is the capacity of certain young school children to retain in great and faithful detail a pictorial configuration they have seen. Such eidetic imagery is found in approximately 8 percent of the school population but almost never in normal adults (except, interestingly enough, in certain artists).[8] Hogarth relates how he strove valiantly to call images to mind with photographic accuracy. Artur Rubinstein can hear an entire piece "in his head," including the technical modulations and flaws found in the recording he is recalling. Indeed, the most carefully documented case of eidetic imagery occurred in an intelligent woman in her twenties who was a painter and a graduate student in foreign languages.

Another decline with age affects the ability termed incidental learning.[9] Incidental learning involves a spontaneous tendency to attend to aspects of a display other than those to which explicit attention has been called. Children aged nine through twelve exhibit a greater capacity to process and recall incidental facets of situations and scenes than do younger or older subjects. Presumably the older subjects have learned to focus primarily on those elements to which they are explicitly directed, consequently becoming less able to take in aspects which, while interesting, are not relevant to the task at hand. Perceptual attention appears to evolve from incomplete surveying in early childhood to partial sampling in maturity; during middle childhood there seems to be a time of complete immersion that does not hamper the performance of the focal task. Finally, there is a whole range of tasks which begin to decline as early as the fourth decade of life: ability to acquire new facts, names, dates, stories, many of these being primarily figurative in nature.[10]

To these well-established trends in the psychological literature should be added some recent findings in the perception and processing of various art forms. Studies I have conducted during the past few years suggest that preadolescents are at least as skilled as (and sometimes more skilled than) matched groups of adolescent subjects at recognizing which musical passages come from the same composition, at composing original endings for stories told them, at remembering details from these stories.[11] The approaches taken by preadolescents and adolescents also differ to some extent. The preadolescents seem immersed in the details and the elements of the works of art per se, founding their responses largely on the way these works of art affect them and on their momentary impressions of the work. Adolescents are more likely to relate their perceptions to facts they know, to the general structures of works of art, to explicit comparisons between works. The preadolescent commences with the actual musical or literary event; the adolescent is more likely to use his prior knowledge of aesthetics as a point of departure, fitting a particular work of art into his preexisting analytic framework.

In an effort to pinpoint further the nature of changes taking place at the time of adolescence and to compare the fate of figurative and operative capacities, a large group of tasks was recently administered to matched groups of eleven- and fourteen-year-olds, and a number of these tasks were given to younger subjects as well. Many but not all of the tasks utilized materials drawn from the arts.

Space does not permit a detailed account of methods for each of these studies, but a brief characterization of the general procedure is in order. Children representing several age groups (modal ages: seven, nine, eleven, and fourteen) drawn primarily from the middle class were seen individually in half-hour sessions over a number of weeks. The seven- and nine-year-olds participated in twelve tasks, while the preadolescents and adolescents—the subjects of special interest—participated in thirty-nine tasks administered in a randomized order.

As can be seen in table 4:1, a wide variety of perceptual, motor, and cognitive capacities was probed. Given the aim of identifying skills which might decline in adolescence, sampling was deliberately broad. A special effort was made to contrast tasks which were highly operative with tasks which were largely figurative, while keeping the materials and procedures relatively constant.

Some details on a representative task may provide a fuller clarification of the general scope of the study. In an effort to capture certain activities involved in apprehending linguistic or literary materials, twelve sentences spoken in twelve different voices were recorded and then played twice for subjects aged seven, nine, eleven, and fourteen. The only instructions were to listen carefully to the tape. Following their hearing of the tape, subjects were asked a variety of questions. They were required to supply factual information about the sentences (who did what) and to indicate whether sentences heard before had been worded in the same way or slightly differently. In the event that they could not remember the facts, they were given a multiple choice; in the event that they discerned a difference from the original sentence, they were required to formulate it in words. Finally, the subjects heard a set of twelve voices and were asked to indicate which of these voices they had heard before. They were also asked for a judgment about the confidence they had in their decision about each of these voices.

The study indicated that the youngest subjects performed as well as the adolescents in remembering which sentences had been heard before and in recognizing from multiple choice the factual content of the original senten-

Table 4:1   Performance of Adolescents and Preadolescents
on Operative and Figurative Tasks

No Improvement with Age (27 Tasks)

Recognition memory for fragments of classical music
Music style sensitivity
Recall of information in a visual display
Recognition memory for details of a visual display
Recognition memory for paintings
Digit recall
Three imitations of nonrepresentational motor gestures
Learning to identify types of birds
Spelling backwards[1]
Recognition of changes in syntax of linguistic materials
Recognition memory for details of a literary narrative
Originality of ending for a literary narrative (trend for younger subjects to excel)
Recognition memory for voices heard before
Three puzzles to be taken apart and put together[1] (trend for younger subjects to excel on one task)
Ability to learn a new motor sequence (using hands)
Ability to learn a new dance step
Originality of names for abstract designs
Two measures of ability to recite overlearned series in a new way (e.g., counting to 20 by 2's)
Ability to learn a tongue twister
Recall of facts in linguistic materials
Recognition memory for facts in linguistic materials

Improvement with Age[2] (p < .05 F Test) (10 Tasks)

Two tests of "formal operations" (Burt's test of verbal abstraction)[1] (Inhelder and Piaget's billiard game)[1]
Mirror writing (writing backwards so that script is legible in a mirror)[1]
Three "brain-teasers" (thought problems requiring abstracting ability)[1]
Singing backwards (reversing the phrases in a song)[1]
Recall for details of literary narrative
Code game (substituting letters for numbers)[1]
Operation upon a visual image ("mentally" folding a paper)[1]

Decline with Age (p < .05 F Test) (2 Tasks)

Incidental learning (memory for details irrelevant to the stated task)
Clerical task (accuracy of counting dots)

1. Denotes those tasks which are highly operative.
2. Older subjects generally performed more rapidly than younger ones. These improvements in speed have not been considered in listing the tasks.

ces. In matching an original stimulus with a new stimulus by comparing configurations there was little change across ages. Similarly, except for the youngest subjects, who appeared not to understand the instructions, all subjects recollected with equal skill which voices had been heard before. On the other hand, there was distinct improvement with age in the capacity to recall facts of the sentences on one's own and to relate these items to the experimenter; in specifying the way in which the original sentence had been syntactically changed; and in evaluating the accuracy with which voices had been judged as new and old. These latter tasks, it will be noted, required the subject to synthesize a response on his own, to make an evaluative judgment of his own behavior, or to formulate in verbal terms a perceived difference between two stimuli. Such tasks are distinguished by the demands made upon the subject to express explicit knowledge of his perceptions and to emit information and judgments spontaneously.

The findings of this language perception study are reflected in the overall results of the larger study undertaken with preadolescents and adolescents. When subjects were merely required to register an initial configuration and recognize whether it had been changed there were seldom differences across ages. But when a more active kind of comparison or evaluation between stimuli, or a recoding into another symbol system or modality, was required, age differences were frequently discernible. A list of all the tasks, with an indication of the performance of each age group, is found in table 4:1.

By far the largest group of tasks failed to reveal differences between subjects averaging eleven and fourteen years of age. Included were the following tasks, largely figurative in nature: remembering which pieces of classical music had been heard before; judging which bits of music came from the same musical composition; remembering the contents of an intricate photograph and recognizing finer details from multiple choice; remembering a large set of paintings shown the week before and indicating which paintings had been slightly modified; remembering a string of digits; imitating gestures made by the hand; learning a new dance step; learning to recognize and remember from week to week a dozen birds; spelling a word backwards.

On a smaller set of tasks, older subjects displayed a tendency to perform better, with some differences attaining a level of significance ($p<0.05$). These included a number of tasks which were explicitly operational, including the billiards problem used by Piaget as a measure of formal operational thought, a test of mirror writing, and a few "brain teasers"—e.g., would there be a sound if a tree fell and no one is present, and how might airplane hijacking be prevented. Older subjects were also better able to spell a word by converting each letter into a number, to sing the phrases in a song backwards, and to recall the details of one story. They tended to respond more rapidly to tasks, also adopting more efficient response strategies.

Contrary to expectations (founded on the earlier studies of artistic skills) there was no group of tasks at which younger children were strikingly better. The only tasks revealing a tendency toward superior performance on the part of the eleven-year-olds were solving one puzzle which involved disconnecting two metal triangles; production of an original ending for a fairy tale; memory for some incidental events of the previous week (an outfit worn by an experimenter, a histrionic gesture made by the experimenter at one point during the previous session); accuracy at counting the number of dots arranged in a geometric configuration on an index card. Only the latter two tasks yielded significant differences between the age groups. It is not apparent whether these four disparate tasks have a common thread. One could hypothesize that the first task involved departure from a "set" toward solving puzzles in a certain way; the second involved the avoidance of a stereotyped completion of a familiar plot structure; the third entailed incidental memory for features to which the subject's attention had not explicitly been drawn; the last required a meticulousness and attention to detail which older subjects did not exert on so trivial a task. Findings in the literature support these interpretations of a skill at which older children are relatively deficient. Yet in the absence of further testing it is difficult to assess the import of these preliminary results. Similarly, while it is tempting to speculate that such declines might have been magnified with somewhat older subjects or with adults remote from an academic setting, the data base is too slim to permit meaningful extrapolation.

Findings on this collection of tasks indicate relatively little improvement with age in tasks where the subject remains within a single sensory modality or where the amount of transformation required on the initial stimulus presentation is relatively modest. In contrast, on those tasks demanding considerable encoding and transformation of stimulus materials, use of intricate symbolic codes, or application of a complex set of rules, older subjects tend to perform better. This interpretation is reinforced by the findings that even younger subjects (ages seven and nine) are able to remember with considerable accuracy details of linguistic, musical, and pictorial presentations and that where they differ from older subjects is in the ability to re-create and report information on their own (i.e., not from multiple choice), the capacity to give informed reasons for their answers, the accuracy with which they evaluate their own performance, and the ability to manipulate information in a systematic way.

The trends in the experimental literature, as well as these personal studies, suggest a tentative account of the development of figurative and operative capacities. Without doubt individuals in our own society display a steady and continued improvement in operative tasks. Whenever recoding and reclassification are demanded, and particularly when more than one sensory modality or symbol system is utilized, the older child excels. On the other hand, it is more difficult to document analogous improvements in those tasks where little reclassifying or active transformation is demanded or on those tasks in which processing is restricted to a single sensory system or symbol system. Indeed, given the inevitable improvement in *task performance* over age, the insubstantial rise in figurative performances is noteworthy.

There is no firm evidence that figurative capacities decline at adolescence. Yet scattered findings on eidetic imagery, language learning, incidental learning, and sensitivity to artistic style raise the possibility that the ages of eleven and twelve may represent a high point in figurative sensitivity, with a slow but steady decline following. It is as likely, however, that there is merely an early asymptote in figurative capacity.

The early leveling and possible decline of figurative capacity may be a universal feature of development, tied to the maturation of the biological organism. Should this be the case, attempts to heighten figurative capacities are destined to fail. On the other hand, scattered evidence that artists have successfully maintained (and perhaps enhanced) these capacities at least raises the possibility that figurative capacities (like operative ones) continue to improve with age until at least adulthood. Since such an efflorescence of figurativity so rarely occurs in our society, we must ask whether a cultural emphasis on operative thinking has had, as an unintended consequence, a deleterious effect upon figurative capacities. Again there is no convincing documentation on this question. Yet various findings in the literature—the decline of incidental learning, the waning of interest in the arts which is so characteristic of adolescence,[12] and contrasting strategies of adolescents and preadolescents in the style discrimination tasks—at least hint at the possibility that operative progress occurs at the expense of figurative mastery. One possible scenario for this conflict has been penned by Charles Darwin, who in a famous passage lamented the loss of his aesthetic faculties:

> Even as a schoolboy I took tremendous delight in Shakespeare, especially the historical plays. I have also said that formerly pictures gave me considerable and music very great delight. But now for many years I cannot ensure to read a line of poetry. I have tried lately to read Shakespeare and found it so intolerably dull that it nauseated me. I have also lost my taste for pictures and music. . . . My mind seems to have become a kind of machine for grinding general laws out of large collections of facts but why this should have caused the atrophy of that part of the brain alone, on which the higher states depend, I cannot conceive.[13]

5. Figurativity and operativity: The neuropsychological evidence

This review of the literature on child development has raised the possibility that capacities of significance in the arts may be a casualty of the developmental process, especially in a scientifically oriented, highly operative culture. The developmental approach is one means of illuminating complex skills whose components are more readily teased out in the growing child. Another less familiar approach, which focuses on the organization of the brain and on the psychological consequences of brain damage, can also enrich our understanding of the crucial factors of artistry.

A word is in order on the place of neuroanatomical and neuropsychological research in the study of cognitive capacities. In no way is such a treatment intended as the sole explanation of artistry or, indeed, anything else; explanations on one level of scientific inquiry can never supplant explanations on another level. Numerous studies over the past decades have documented, however, that the organization of human skills can be uniquely elucidated by a consideration of how these capacities develop on a neural level and, more especially, how they break down when different areas of the brain are damaged.[14] Hence we turn now in this essay to some anatomical considerations which may place upon a firmer biological footing the building blocks of the taxonomy. This in turn will allow discussion of the fate of various artistic capacities under conditions of brain damage.

According to the neuropsychologist A. R. Luria, each sensory modality is represented in the brain by a primary or central processing area.[15] Brain stimulation studies suggest that particular elements or qualities of a sense modality are there represented; that is, the basic elements of a stimulus are there perceived and differentiated. There is also a secondary processing field or area wherein more complex elements (combinations of elements) and the relationships among components of perceived objects are apprehended. The primary processing area records the isolated sights or sounds of objects—colors, lines, vertexes; the secondary processing area must be intact if the *meaning* of the object (a round configuration having a sweet taste and a hard surface is construed as an apple, the ordered set of phonemes is heard as a word) is to be realized. Neuroanatomical development proceeds from the primary to the secondary processing areas; the newborn infant has intact sensory receiving areas that allow registration of simple elements like edges or vertexes, but the development of the secondary areas takes a few months. Secondary fields functionally integrate the individual stimuli differentiated by the primary zones of sensory modalities. These centers also orient the stimuli with reference to a concrete spatio-temporal matrix; thus they feature at least modest transformation of the initial stimulation.

Full appreciation of the meanings, implications, and connections among objects, however, as well as thorough integration of visual, auditory, and cutaneous-kinesthetic percepts depends upon the maturation of *cross-modal sensory areas*, tertiary neurological regions in which overlapping zones of the endings of the cortical sensory areas are found. Only when disparate cortical sensory zones have completely overlapped in these tertiary zones can percepts and operations based upon integration of several senses be established. Only then can capacities and skills dependent upon the integration of different modalities, such as calculations, understanding of language, writing, and spatial perception, be realized.

The young child differs from the adult in part because he is largely dependent upon his primary and secondary association areas while the adult relies more frequently on tertiary, cross-modal association areas in performing activities important in his life. The primary and secondary zones are concerned primarily with relaying information from the environment, and the tertiary zone is the site of integration among and action upon these data. This situation has important implications for neurological organization. If a child's cross-modal association areas are injured, his mundane activities are not much affected. These areas have not as yet assumed a critical role in his activities, and his primary and secondary sensory areas are able to operate independently of the connective areas. If the child receives an injury in a primary sensory area, however, his situation becomes very serious. Not only can he no longer make discriminations in that sensory mode, but the subsequent development of the cross-modal area is impeded because of its initial reliance on the input from the primary sensory areas. Fortunately, however, the child's brain is quite resilient. Other critical areas may compensate for the damage. Thus there remains an appreciable possibility that he will again be able to perceive via the injured sensory modality.

Trauma has a different effect on the adult brain. Injury of the primary sensory area may not be so damaging because considerable supplementary information can still be gleaned from other sensory areas. More importantly, the higher centers which permit the integration and interpretation of perceptions now dominate the primary zones in many activities. So long as information can reach these centers from any sensory modality, adequate functioning may be possible. If, however, one of the higher centers is damaged, the adult will be reduced to the level of the child. His sophisticated conceptual attitude is undermined, and he is thrown back on his primary sensory areas. But these have in turn receded in importance in view of the rise to domination of the cross-modal centers and are therefore ill equipped to return to a primary perceptual function. To complicate matters, the brain of the adult is less plastic than that of the preadolescent; accordingly the chances of regaining a premorbid level of intellectual competence are not high.

These general neurological considerations bear on the taxonomic framework. To begin with, the young child perceives sense data in one or more sensory modalities, but each of these is relatively independent because connections between sensory modalities have not yet matured. In a given task the child is restricted to working with material within a single sensory modality. Moreover, the child's use of symbols is in general quite primitive, and so the interaction or integration of a number of symbol systems does not occur in the young brain. In terms of the present discussion, the young child is most skilled at and dependent upon centers which are primarily *figurative* in nature—those primary and secondary cortical regions which register stimuli faithfully and retain them in their original form relatively bereft of complex associations or involvement in radical transformations. Those centers which connect several sensory modalities and which mediate more abstract operations and manipulations only become a factor during the middle years of childhood.

Information about brain development provides an organic underpinning to three important trends in childhood: an increased ability to use several sensory modalities in conjunction, an improved capacity to operate upon information within each sensory modality, and a heightened skill in employing abstract operations not tied to any particular modality. As the adult becomes increasingly dependent upon the "operational centers" he relies upon "amodal" mental operations and pays correspondingly less heed to incoming sensory information. Whether his figurative centers necessarily decline as a consequence is not known. Yet it is clear that injury to the figurative centers is devastating to the child but that the operative centers are more vital (and more vulnerable) to the adult. The adult's figurative centers are, at least individually, somewhat expendable.

Other information about brain organization also bears on the taxonomy. Although the gross appearance of the two cerebral hemispheres is similar, they control (or are "dominant" for) quite different psychological capacities. In particular, the left hemisphere plays a crucial role (in most individuals) in all linguistic activities while the right hemisphere, unimportant in language activity, is central in certain visual-spatial processes.[16] A convincing characterization of the right hemisphere's capacities is not yet at hand. And yet it has been established that the right hemisphere is important for making fine, highly modulated discriminations within a sensory realm; for controlling and integrating an individual's orientation in his spatial environment; for organizing parts of a display or object into a whole; and for the perception and production of nonlinguistic auditory materials, such as pitch, timbre, and texture. Moreover, there are recent hints that the right hemisphere is crucial for metaphoric thought and for the control of emotional response. This list of activities has struck more than one observer as a suitable description of major artistic activities. While the recent characterization of the right hemisphere as the "artistic hemisphere" is clearly too fanciful, the intuition that it plays a crucial role in artistic activity may be justified. In terms of the taxonomy, it is intriguing to consider that the right hemisphere is involved primarily in such figurative capacities as attending to the details of stimuli and making fine discriminations and comparisons. When a stimulus becomes familiar and hence codable, classifiable, or manipulable, its interest to the right hemisphere diminishes and it enters the domain of the more operative left hemisphere.

It appears, then, that those aspects of perception and conception which explore an external configuration are more implicated in right hemisphere activities while those which highlight codification, classification, and active transformation (as in mathematical reasoning) seem to belong more to the left. Put differently, the right hemisphere highlights the process of the primary sensory zones, the left hemisphere those of the tertiary cross-modal area. It is well known that in the young child the right and left hemispheres compete for dominance over his perceptual and motor activities and that in most children the left hemisphere gains increasing control after the opening years of life. The alleged decline in figurative capacities may conceivably be linked to the parallel decline in the dominance of the right hemisphere. There is insufficient evidence, however, to do more than raise this suggestive point.

While such knowledge of brain function comes in part from studies with normal persons and in part from research with animals, by far the major source is the examination of individuals known to have suffered injury to the brain. The literature on brain damage in individuals involved in the arts, though not extensive, is relevant and illuminating to the present inquiry.

In general, individuals whose left hemispheres are damaged suffer severe impairment of their language abilities. In many cases their performance on various kinds of conceptual tasks (e.g., sorting into categories) is also diminished. On the other hand, these individuals are well oriented in time and space, remain keenly aware of fine perceptual differences, and can engage in nonverbal artistic activities. Persons whose right hemispheres are damaged, however, continue to speak and to understand at normal or near normal levels. Their performances on verbal categorizing tasks are also unremarkable. Yet these same persons seem oblivious to the visual-spatial world about them, often getting lost, even failing to recognize other persons or to dress themselves. Moreover, their performance at tasks of artistic capacity, such as musical perception or drawing ability, is usually more seriously impaired than that of individuals with left hemisphere disease.[17]

There also appear to be qualitative differences in the way in which the two hemispheres handle information. For example, when an individual with right hemisphere disease draws figures, he includes all the constituent parts but grossly distorts the overall shape, or gestalt, and the relations of the parts to the whole. This result suggests that an intact right hemisphere is necessary for an appreciation of the general form of a configuration as well as for integration of parts into a whole. Conversely, the individual with left hemisphere disease will capture accurately the overall form of a problem or model and will relate parts to the whole. He may omit some of the parts, however, and simplify those that he does include. His difficulty stems from an incapacity to integrate each and every specific element and, sometimes, from an incomplete understanding of its function. The left hemisphere, then, contributes to the analytic, conceptual portion of such a task and the right to the perceptual, synthesizing aspects.

The scattered studies of artists with left hemisphere damage indicate that literary creativity is vitiated but that high-level performance in the visual and musical arts is possible, even usual, despite massive involvement of the hemisphere. Luria, for example, documents the case of an aphasic musician who remained able to compose at a premorbid level.[18] A number of neuropsychologists have gone so far as to claim that painters may actually improve their output in the wake of a stroke in the left hemisphere. The literature on artists with damage to the right hemisphere is even more meager. An informed guess is that literary achievement is impaired but not destroyed, that musical capacities are seriously impaired, and that performance in the visual arts is temporarily impaired or altered but not necessarily destroyed.

It appears, then, that the left hemisphere is more important in language-like and in operative capacities whereas the right hemisphere plays a dominant role in nonlinguistic and in figurative capacities. The question arises about the extent to which language activities are necessarily operative and nonlanguage activities necessarily figurative. From a logical point of view, of course, it is clear that these dimensions are separable: there may be both figurative (attending to sound) and operative (translating, attending to metaphor) language functions as well as figurative (attention to fine visual detail) and operative (orientation in a spatial matrix) nonlanguage activities. Yet the extent to which these conceptually separate dimensions may be confounded in our psychological apparatus is yet unknown.[19] It may be that the two dimensions can be neatly separated. But it is also conceivable that the linguistic hemisphere has a bias toward operative activity while the nonlinguistic hemisphere is more oriented toward figurative capacity. Precisely these issues are raised by the taxonomy, and there is every reason to believe that empirical studies can settle them. Indeed, it is difficult to envision how the functions of the two hemispheres can ever be convincingly sorted out unless attempts are made to describe alternative classifications and to test them experimentally.

The taxonomy aids in explicating other phenomena of brain damage. For instance, when individuals receive an injury in the primary sensory areas they will have unimodal figurative impairments. Thus an individual injured in the primary auditory cortex cannot process information he hears but is able to handle the same information given him through another modality, for example, through written language. Proof that operative capacities have been spared can be secured when the individual is tested in analogous tasks which employ other sensory modalities. When the cross-modal areas are themselves impaired, however, a breakdown occurs irrespective of the realm of presentation. An individual with a lesion at the intersection of the several sensory modalities suffers from what has been called semantic aphasia; he fails at operational activities of all sorts, including the capacities to orient himself in space, to carry out mathematical calculations, and to understand logical-grammatical commands (e.g., to put the X underneath the Y). Such a case offers a selected impairment of operational capacities against a background in which unimodal figurative perception may be spared.

Two other forms of brain pathology should be noted. In the case of dementias, where there is widespread cortical atrophy, both figurative and operative capacities usually decline. Operative capacities are generally the more brittle, perhaps because they are learned later and thus require the intact functioning of more specialized regions of the brain. For example, a senile patient no longer able to perform formal operations may still execute concrete logical operations and exhibit relatively well-preserved figurative functions such as repetition of spoken language, memory for objects, or ability to copy a line configuration. In contrast, in the case of disconnection syndromes, two processing regions of the brain are themselves intact but the pathways connecting them have been destroyed.[20] Here the subject is able to perform tasks that involve either one of these centers but fails at anything that requires the synergic combination of the centers or the transmission of information from one region to another. So long as the cross-modal areas are intact and some stimulus information can reach these areas, operational capacities may be preserved; but a relatively figurative mode of cognition that depends on a discrete connection between two specific centers (e.g., color naming) may be impaired.

On the basis of evidence in child development one might hypothesize that operative capacities are generally more brittle than figurative capacities. But judging from studies of brain damage the state of affairs is more complex. There are conditions in which figurativity is fragile but others in which operativity is vulnerable. In addition, and somewhat confusingly, the concept of operativity can be approached in another way, that is, through the extent to which cognizance of an object depends upon involvement of more than one sense modality and through the potential for active manipulation of the object. Application of this approach has recently shown that the kinds of multiple connections involved in operative cognition may be beneficial in certain tasks[21]—e.g., it is easier for an aphasic to name elements which can be embedded in a variety of actions (such as a ball) and to recognize a symbol which is rich in intersensory association (such as a dollar sign). Perhaps, other things being equal, the relative operativity of an element—its susceptibility to numerous actions and transformations—makes it more robust in the face of brain damage.

In sum, while (from the perspective of the present framework) trends of child development are relatively clear, neuropsychological studies present a highly complex picture. The early maturation of sensory zones leads to a dependence upon figurative modes of cognition and to extensive use of individual sensory modalities in early childhood. As the tertiary, cross-modal associations mature, there is an increased trend toward combining sensory modalities and engaging in more operative activity. The brain is less neatly organized along the lines of separate symbol systems, but the left hemisphere seems to play a more prominent role in the use of linguistic, discrete symbol systems and the right in nonlinguistic, dense symbol systems. The divisions of labor between the hemispheres are far from a simple matter, since the left also appears to be more crucial for operative activities while the right displays a special capacity for figurative activities. Unfortunately the extent to which the dimensions of operativity and linguisticness are confounded cannot be determined from the present data. Finally, studies of brain-damaged artists indicate that the right hemisphere plays a preeminent role in artistic activity except in the language arts, where the left hemisphere is understandably central. It was hypothesized that the increasing dominance of the left hemisphere in most individuals may occur at a price: a decline in the acuity of those functions for which the right hemisphere is dominant, including perhaps that figurative sensitivity of great moment in artistic activities.

6. Concluding remarks

The purpose here has been to introduce a taxonomy which may prove useful for analyzing activities involved in artistic practice as well as other human endeavors. Though it has not been possible to develop all facets of this taxonomy nor to test its application in any detail, these pages have sought to offer enough of its flavor and bring to bear sufficient developmental and neuropsychological evidence so that its potential applications (and limitations) in the study of artistry might be manifest. This concluding section will comment on the highlights of the survey and suggest certain implications.

Perhaps the chief impetus for this project has been the desire to develop some kind of language, or categorical system, which can provide an initial organization of the myriad activities involved in the arts. Of the numerous dimensions along which these activities can be considered, three have been isolated which seemed both pervasive and significant. And of these three, the dimension of *figurativity/operativity* has received special attention through a review of fresh evidence concerning its development and an argument for its salience in illuminating the relationship between artistic and scientific achievement.

The hope is to create an analytic language which can speak to workers in different investigative fields: to philosophers interested in taxonomies of skills and the logical relationships among tasks, to psychologists interested in building models of performance and production, to neuropsychologists interested in the biological bases of behavior, and to educators interested in the relations among diverse skills and the best means of fostering them. Because of a conviction that the component skills are most likely to be recognized when they are observed in the course of development or as the result of neurological breakdown, the present inquiry has focused on the evidence from developmental psychology and from the study of brain damage. The analytic categories introduced here, and particularly the contrast between figurativity and operativity, have served as a means of discerning parallels between these two contrasting processes without, however, implying that development and breakdown are simply duplicates (or total reversals) of one another. But obviously such an investigation is just beginning.

At present this taxonomy is useful chiefly as a framework for discussing artistic activities and as a source of hypotheses and experiments in cognitive psychology. As one instance, our survey has already indicated that the psychological independence of the various dimensions can be tested by ascertaining the nature of the division of labor between the hemispheres. Empirical investigations should indicate whether figurativity tends to be correlated with nonlinguistic and operativity with linguistic symbol systems. Moreover there is at least the possibility, suggested by recent experiments on short-term memory, that the auditory sensory modality may have a correlation with the left hemisphere and the visual sensory modality with the right.[22] Should this prove to be the case, one would then encounter a triple confounding among the principal dimensions: a correlation between figurativity, nonlinguisticness, and the visual (simultaneous, spatial) modality, and a corresponding correlation between operativity, linguisticness, and the auditory (temporal, successive) modality. Such a correlation might be deplorable on theoretical grounds, since the logical independence of these dimensions would not be honored by nature. Yet it is through a wedding of philosophical analysis and experimental testing that our understanding of human functioning is likely to grow.

It may be appropriate to mention a rather different application of this conceptual framework. As has been indicated certain tertiary association areas in the brain are particularly concerned with operations independent of sensory modality, while others are occupied with figurative perception and not at all with operations within or across sensory modalities. This leads to certain predictions concerning the effects of brain damage. If, in the adult, tertiary operational areas are destroyed, this should impair the individual's ability to perform logical operations independent of the modality of sensory input. (The same lesion would have little effect in the young child, since his tertiary areas do not yet play a significant role in mentation.) If a figurative area of an adult brain should be injured while the more operative areas remain intact, then the individual should remain able to perform operations so long as an alternative figurative-sensory channel feeds into the operative area. Other sequelae can also be mentioned. If operative functioning is impaired on information received from a certain figurative channel but that channel independently can be shown to be relatively intact, it follows logically that the operations under consideration will be impaired irrespective of the condition of other sensory modalities. In other words, if an individual can perceive adequately in one sensory modality yet cannot perform operations on materials presented in that modality, presumably he should not be able to perform these cognitive operations on materials presented in any modality. In addition to their academic interest, such considerations have implications for diagnosing the extent and locus of brain injury and for the kinds of rehabilitation likely to be effective.

In view of the goals of the present volume, one of the most significant challenges confronting the taxonomic system is to highlight those activities which may distinguish the artist from other practitioners. Even at the risk of exaggeration and oversimplification we must seek to characterize the activities of the scientist and the artist in terms of the analytic framework.

It is commonplace to note that artists discern connections between disparate entities and are sensitive to recondite but appropriate patterns. Sometimes these connections will obtain across sensory modalities, as when a tone expresses a certain color, mood, or verbal concept. At other times these associations will be within a sensory modality or a symbol system, as when two unlikely words are united, two contrasting chords are juxtaposed, or an object is depicted through an unaccustomed set of lines, forms, or colors.

Fluidity at this sort of pattern generation clearly demands skill at using particular symbolic media as well as alertness to specific aspects of the configurations or objects involved. It seems essential for the fluent artist to be keenly aware of the manifest aspects of objects, sounds, and sights with which he is concerned and equally vital that he succeed in relating these patterns to ones at some distance and in effecting a convincing translation and communication. His skill cannot remain entirely within the medium since he is always attempting to express aspects of his perceptions and feeling. The continuous feedback and interplay between the symbolic artistic object and the world of living experience is the lifeblood of meaningful artistry.

All this is no more than to insist that prominent facets of the artist's repertoire require developed operative as well as figurative skills. The artist must be exquisitely sensitive to the perceptual realms in which he works, and he must be equally able to transform radically what he perceives and to express it expertly in a symbolic medium. The perceiver of the work must also attend to the manifold aspects of the perceived stimulus, even as he relates it to other facets of a symbol system and other forms of experience.

Given this need for developed figurative and operative competence, one must ask what differences, if any, obtain between the practicing scientist and artist. To be sure, no absolute gulf divides them, and yet the emphasis in goals and methods is strikingly different. The scientist, as I argue else-where,[23] has as a principal goal the resolution of disputes about the laws governing the physical and biological universe; the artist has as a principal goal the communication in a symbolic medium of those ideas, feelings, and experiences he considers important and interesting. Both practitioners encounter problems which must be solved in their work, but the relevant facts of their problems differ. The scientist *must conceptualize the factors* relevant to a solution of the problem. Once the factors have been carefully isolated he has partially solved the problem and can perhaps collaborate with or convey the problem to a colleague.[24] The artist, on the other hand, emphasizes a specific execution within a given symbolic medium. Conceptu-alization plays only a preliminary phase in his work: the final product reflects preeminently an intensive and extensive experimentation with the given properties of a sensory modality and an artistic medium—words in literature, pitches and rhythmic units in music, and colors, forms, and textures in the visual art.

This analysis suggests that, for the scientist, the particular medium used is of less moment. Factors entailed, say, in a chemical experiment may be equivalently conceptualized in a variety of symbol systems, and once they are correctly formulated, a solution can again arise from a variety of media and modes. Such flexibility is less plausible in the arts, where the particular means of expression is a specific symbolic medium addressed to a particular sensory modality, and the plausible alternatives are constrained and deter-mined by that medium. There is a certain amodal quality to the logical steps of the scientist's theorem. So long as the logic is preserved, the medium in which it is expressed is immaterial. The artist's "points" themes, or motifs, however, rest upon his particular medium and resist translation into an equivalent medium or mode. For this reason it may be less crucial for the artist to step outside of, or reflect upon, his customary symbols, sense modalities, and mental processes.

These portraits of the artist and scientist can be expressed in terms of operativity and figurativity. The emphasis in the scientist's work falls on relating elements of a problem to one another in a new way, with the symbol system in which the particular elements are formulated not of major concern. For the artist the emphasis falls on the particular elements chosen and their sensual appeal, both treated alone and placed into a new context and configuration. Analogously, the individual who perceives an artistic work must focus on the particular sensory configurations as well as on the ways they are manipulated. The perceiver of scientific works must attend less to a particular configuration in a specific sensory modality but more to the operations obtaining among them and performed upon them. Thus the realm of figurative perception plays a more crucial role in artistic practice than in the activities of most scientific practitioners. More specifically, it is the figurative and operative activity *within a specific sensory modality and symbol system* which constitutes the crucial part of sustained artistry. On the other hand, it is operative activity independent of a particular sensory modality or symbol system which proves paradigmatic for the scientist. In sum, then, the artist continues to depend equally on figurative and operative capacities within particular media and sensory systems while the scientist increasingly emphasizes operative capacities without particular regard to the sensory modality and with relatively little premium on the particular symbol system used.

One can sketch a plausible though hypothetical account of how these cognitive modes develop. In the early years of life, figurative perception within the principal sensory modalities and a preliminary mastery of certain central symbol systems dominate. With age there is an increasing amount of operating upon the input in these sensory modalities and symbol systems; in addition the child becomes capable of *generalized concrete and formal operations*[25] which can be utilized independent of sensory modality or symbol system. For a while, between the ages of six and eleven, increased operativity goes in hand with sustained figurativity. Yet a growing body of evidence suggests that the developing individual relinquishes a certain sensitivity to particular configurations by the time of adolescence. It is also conceivable that continued concentration on figurative aspects may result in a lessened interest in the radical transformation of these elements, particularly operations extending across symbol systems and sensory modalities. The former trajectory—increased operativity, decreased figurativity—seems to characterize the incipient scientist, while the later course—deemphasis of operativity, continued heightening of figurativity—may be more characteristic of the budding artist.

A number of educational considerations follow from this analysis. Given the unmistakable trends (at least in our culture) toward increased emphasis on operational thinking, the positive as well as the deleterious implications of this cognitive mode must be directly confronted. The present analysis has suggested that this trend redounds to the benefit of scientific practice, possibly at the expense of developing facility within an aesthetic medium and at the cost of sensitivity to detailed, noncategorical features of artistic patterns. Accordingly, avenues to bolster figurative thinking by giving children and adults practice in it and by rewarding the kind of keen attention to particulars it entails should be designed and encouraged.

The putative division of labor between the cerebral hemispheres described above gives rise to other pedagogical suggestions. If the right hemisphere is indeed more crucial in figurative and the left in operative modes of thought, then the right hemisphere's function should be highlighted. It has been proposed that the left hemisphere is engaged primarily in handling information which is codable or has already been coded while the right hemisphere is particularly suited for coping with unfamiliar patterns, information not yet coded, or input which does not as readily lend itself to linguistic coding (for example, visual-spatial data). Continued exposure to unexpected configurations and patterns and treatment of them in terms of their own features rather than as something to be translated immediately into more familiar terms would seem to be a means of accentuating right hemisphere functions and preventing undue dominance by left hemisphere linguistic and operative functions. Perhaps, indeed, it is only through exposure to novel, unexpected experiences that the right hemisphere continues to be exploited. A further area for investigation and application is the interaction between the hemispheres. If each is dominant for different activities, it is important to determine the manner of their integration when an action (for example, describing a spatial layout, scoring a musical composition) calls for cooperation between them. Recent studies by Kinsbourne indicate that certain activities engender cooperation and others conflict or competition between the hemispheres.[26] Detailed understanding of these diverse relations would be highly useful.

Certain heuristic and analytic procedures serviceable in dealing with scientific problems are of dubious value in artistic practice. For example, speed reading, the writing of abstracts, and the use of textbooks are all valid, even valuable, accoutrements to scientific practice. The application of speed reading, abstracts, or "trots" in the domains of poetry or paintings, on the other hand, is evidently absurd. Yet if the emphasis on these short cuts and efficiency methods is allowed to proceed unchecked and unchallenged, it is highly probable that individuals will become less prone to attend at length to the configurations and sensory elements crucial for effective perception and production in the arts. In particular, a willingness to explore within a medium, to avoid premature translation, encoding or rethinking, and to consider alternatives in terms of their sensory effectiveness are important for artistic achievement.

I referred earlier to Charles Darwin's characterization of a mind so involved in operational thought that it had lost its ability to take in the aesthetic facets of experience, to utilize figurative modes of knowledge. Obviously such an overemphasis on operational-scientific thinking, on connections between modes, and on a radical transformation of input exacts its costs. It is also possible for someone to be overwhelmed by figurative experience. One such person was the mnemonist studied by Luria, who had so rich a set of sensory associations connected with experience and so keen a memory for all sensory experience that he was unable to retreat at all from his configurations. Thus he was unable to reformulate, encode, or otherwise translate his sensory experience into other forms such as symbolic codes. On an intuitive basis one might think that a person thus overwhelmed with sensory experience and having total recall of literature and works of art would be the ideal aesthetic perceiver and creator. In fact the mnemonist proves totally unable to appreciate the arts. Poetry, for example, was wholly lost on him, for he could never effect the transition from the specific images of poetry to the relations and allusions described at a somewhat less superficial level. Nor could he undertake his own transformations within a sensory mode. Luria indicates that:

> To understand a poem, we must be able to grasp the . . . meaning suggested by an image. . . . S [the mnemonist] found that when he tried to read poetry the obstacles to his understanding were overwhelming; each expression gave rise to an image; this in turn would conflict with another image that had been evoked.[27]

When confronted with a single verse, S. would generate so many concrete associations, some contradicting others, that a synthesis of meaning never occurred. As he complained to Luria after being overwhelmed by one such passage: "I'd have to read it through more quickly to get it, so that images won't appear. Otherwise I see every word."[28]

The cases of Darwin and the mnemonist serve to remind us, then, that an exclusive concentration on operativity or figurativity is counterproductive in artistic processes. (Whether it is productive for scientific thinking is also debatable, *pace* Darwin.) Rather, what seems optimally desirable is some sort of meaningful balance between operative and figurative modes: the capacity to dwell on the elements, symbols, and sensory experiences, indeed to revel in them, but also to suspend these and to focus as well on connections between them and operations upon them. The trend in development toward increased operativity and the possible breakdown of figurative capacities must be counteracted by a valuing of figurative modes or conceptions and an appreciation of the purposes for which they are uniquely suited. It should also be acknowledged that as development continues, realms of knowledge which at first were strongly operative, demanding considerable transformation and manipulation of elements, may gradually achieve a figurative status. As they become better known they are incorporated into routinized patterns and eventually themselves constitute the elements of new, higher-level operations.

The same kind of developmental principle plausibly extends to one's experience with a significant work of art. The elements discerned and the operations performed in an initial reaction to the work only foreshadow the extent of one's potential involvement with it. As the configurations and relations initially perceived are fully assimilated and fade into the background, new constellations and connections appear. The work may be appreciated more fully both in terms of the interrelations among its parts and in terms of its connections to other realms of experience. Just as the nervous system facilitates an ever richer pool of figurative and operative processes during the course of development, so too the individual's deepening experience with a work of art permits a continual expansion of the elements which can be appreciated and the modes of cognition which can be brought to bear.

Catching a final glimpse of that hypothetical audience member at a poetry reading, let us attempt to characterize his diverse acts in the light of the taxonomic framework. When savoring the sounds of the poet's voice or the phonological components of the poetic message, the listener remains within a sense modality and engaged in figurative cognition. When he explores the relationship among these sounds he is still operating with a single sensory modality but has begun to undertake a series of cognitive operations. When he focuses on a printed text he is dealing with but a single, linguistic symbol system; but when he relates the literary work to the pictorial or musical realm and when he cultivates the semantic richness and density of poetic allusion, he is entering other, nonlinguistic symbol systems. Similarly, when he becomes involved bodily in the perception of the poem or generates visual images or focuses on the physical appearance of the poet, he is also drawing on a variety of sensory modalities.

While there is considerable potential for the deployment of multiple symbol systems and sensory modalities, the audience member's behavior largely falls into a single mode and involves a single symbol system. The extent to which he highlights figurative aspects or concentrates upon operations would doubtless depend on his own interests and background, the circumstances of the moment, and the events taking place in the literary work. Were he, like Luria's mnemonist, overwhelmed by the sensory allusions in the poem, he might prove unable to operate upon the literary material and thus fail to encompass its deeper layers of meaning, its references to particular ideas and concepts. Were he, on the other hand, so intent upon extracting the factual information or the literary allusions embodied in the poem, he might sacrifice appreciation of the particular combinations of sounds and images and, like Darwin's compulsive fact collector, prove insensitive to the sensuous, figurative aspects of the poem. An education geared too insistently toward classification and coding might produce the complete computer; a training too consistently restructured toward savoring configurations and wholly deficient in the tools of analysis might yield the noncomprehending, overly figurative mirror. The challenge of education in general, and of art education in particular, is to facilitate a comfortable, flexible, and suitable balance between these modes of knowing.[29]

Notes

1. For further explication of the principal types of symbol systems, see Nelson Goodman, *Languages of Art* (Indianapolis and New York: Bobbs-Merrill, 1968); Howard Gardner, Vernon Howard, and David Perkins, "Symbol Systems: A Philosophical, Psychological, and Educational Investigation," *Media and Symbols*, ed. David Olson (Chicago: University of Chicago Press, 1974) 27–55.

2. See, for instance, the review by Herbert Pick, "Sensory and Perceptual Development," in *Carmichael's Manual of Child Psychology*, ed. Paul Mussen (New York: Wiley, 1970) 1: 773–848.

3. An introduction to his system is found in Jean Piaget, "Piaget's Theory," in *Carmichael's Manual* 1: 703–32. See also Howard Gardner, *The Quest for Mind* (New York: Knopf, 1973).

4. The implications of Piaget's theory for the arts are discussed in detail in Howard Gardner, *The Arts and Human Development* (New York: Wiley, 1973), chap. 7.

5. A useful review of developmental research germane to this point is found in Heinz Werner, *Comparative Psychology of Mental Development* (New York: Science Books, 1961).

6. On the difficulties of adults in learning second languages and on the possibility of a critical period for language learning, see Eric Lenneberg, *Biological Foundations of Language* (New York: Wiley, 1967).

7. V. S. Pritchett, *A Cab at the Door* (London: Chatto & Windus, 1968), p. 102.

8. On eidetic imagery, see Ralph N. Haber and Ruth B. Haber, "Eidetic Imagery: I. Frequency," *Perceptual and Motor Skills* 19 (1964): 131–38; also their "Eidetic Imagery in Children," *Psychonomic Monograph Supplements* 3 (1969): 25–48. For a review, see Alan Richardson, *Mental Imagery* (London: Routledge & Kegan Paul, 1969).

9. The literature on incidental learning is reviewed by Harold Stevenson, "Learning in Children," in Mussen, *Carmichael's Manual* 1: 909–11.

10. On the decline of mental ability with age, see Richard H. Williams, Clark Tibbits, and Wilma Donahue, eds., *Processes of Aging* (New York: Ahterton Press, 1963), vol. 1.

11. See Howard Gardner, "Style Sensitivity in Children," *Human Development* 15 (1972): 325–38.

12. On the waning of artistic interest in adolescence, see Herbert Read, *Education Through Art* (New York: Pantheon, 1945); Gardner, *Arts and Human Development*, chap. 6; Susanna Millar, *The Psychology of Play* (London: Penguin, 1968).

13. Darwin is quoted in Read, *Education through Art*, p. 253.

14. Howard Gardner, *The Shattered Mind* (New York: Knopf, 1975).

15. Alexander Luria's views are expounded in detail in *The Higher Cortical Functions in Man* (New York: Basic Books, 1966).

16. An introduction to cerebral lateralization and to the areas of neuropsychology in general can be found in Gardner, *Shattered Mind.*

17. On artists and brain damage see Gardner, *Shattered Mind*, chap. 8; also Th. Alajouanine, "Aphasia and Artistic Realization," *Brain* 71 (1948): 229–41.

18. Luria's case report is "Aphasia in a Composer," *Journal of the Neurological Sciences* 2 (1965): 288–92.

19. A discussion of this question can be found in Howard Gardner, "A Psychological Investigation of Nelson Goodman's Theory of Symbols," *The Monist* 58 (1974): 219–26.

20. See Norman Geschwind, "Disconnexion Syndromes in Animals and Man," *Brain* 88 (1965): 585–644.

21. Howard Gardner, "The Contribution of Operativity to Naming in Aphasic Patients," *Neuropsychologia* 11 (1973): 213–20.

22. Ina Samuels, Nelson Butters, and Paul Fedio, "Short-Term Memory Disorders Following Temporal Lobe Removals in Humans," *Cortex* 8 (1972): 283–98.

23. See Gardner, *The Arts and Human Development*, chap. 7; "Problem-Solving in the Arts," *Journal of Aesthetic Education* 5 (1971): 93–114.

24. It is instructive in this context to consider what the great physicist Helmholtz recalled about his own schooling. He reported a severe memory disorder for sheer rote learning,

which in our terms would be a figurative task. "I consider the difficulty, which I still clearly remember, in discriminating between right and left, as a first example of this; later, in language classes in school, it was more difficult for me than for others to remember words, irregular grammatical forms, and idiosyncratic expressions. Finally I could scarcely master history as it was then taught to us. To learn prose passages by heart was a torture to me. Naturally this deficit only grew and became a plague of my adult years." This quotation is found in Arthur L. Benton, *Right-Left Discrimination and Finger Localization* (New York: Hoeber, 1959), p. 58.

25. For an explication of concrete and formal operations see the reference works cited in n. 3 above.

26. Marcel Kinsbourne, "Cognitive Deficit: Experimental Analysis," in *Psychobiology*, ed. J. McGaugh (New York: Academic Press, 1971), pp. 285–342.

27. A. R. Luria, *The Mind of a Mnemonist* (New York: Basic Books, 1968), p. 120.

28. Ibid., p. 124.

29. The research reported in this paper was supported principally by the Spencer Foundation through a grant administered by Dean Arthur Powell, Harvard Graduate School of Education. The preparation of the paper was supported by Harvard Project Zero through National Science Foundation grant number GB 31064 and National Institute of Education grant number NE-G-00-3-0169 and by NINDS grant number 11408-03 through a grant to the Boston University School of Medicine. I am grateful to Drs. Judith Gardner, Norman Geschwind, and Richard Strub for their helpful comments on earlier drafts. Mary Kircher, Karl Kovacs, and Judy Levinson skillfully administered the tasks described in the paper, and Mary Kircher also analyzed much of the data. I gratefully acknowledge the cooperation of the Newton and Brookline, Massachusetts, school systems and wish to thank in particular Ms. Mary Winslow, Mr. Al Hurwitz, and Mr. Vincent Silluzio of the former and Ms. Babette Raphel and Ms. Ann MacDonald of the latter.

5

Pictures to See and
Pictures to Touch
John M. Kennedy and Nathan Fox

Where is the part of us that understands outline drawing? Is
it in the eye? In the visual nerves? *Or is it in vision at all?* This
article will describe some ideas about the foundations
of outline depiction. The evidence will suggest that outline drawings command entrance to levels of cognition lying beyond any one of our senses.

That outline depiction is not restricted to one sense modality is argued
in detail by some research on blind and blindfolded subjects. These subjects
were presented with "haptic pictures" (raised line drawings which they could
explore by hand), and even though they had never encountered outline
drawings before in their lives they understood them and recognized their
contents.

Compared to the blind, sighted people not only have the advantage of
another sensory channel, vision; they enjoy access to an extra method for
showing things, pictures. The blind usually make either a simple direct
contact with their world through touching or hearing or tasting real things,
or they make an extremely indirect contact by means of words. Sighted
people can make use of pictures, devices that are neither as direct as contact
nor as indirect as words.

At first thought, pictures seem inherently visual. One would think that
pictures must remain as alien to the blind as colors. But reflection suggests
three links between pictures and the abilities of the blind.

First, there is a very general point about representations, a point that
applies to both normal and blind subjects. Images, signs, language, and the
like do not correspond in any simple way to the different sensory channels.
We not only hear words; they can as easily appear in writing, in semaphore,
in Morse code, or, for touch, in Braille. We can receive the same message in
many ways, just as we can know someone has departed by finding that his
belongings have gone or by noticing the pall of silence in the house. Some

118

facts are not inherently tied to one sensory channel.[1] Some media (vehicles for discovering facts) are not tied to any one sensory channel.

Second, blind people are quite capable of dealing with at least some forms of representation, and so pictorial representation need not be confusing simply by virtue of being representational. The blind routinely deal with words, recordings, samples, and perfumes, for example. A general concept of representation is not difficult for them. Indeed, it should be fairly familiar to any adult blind person and provide him with a foundation for an attempt to figure out what a pictorial display is. Blind individuals from our culture should not be like those apocryphal untutored natives from isolated tribes who find the whole idea of a picture quite impossible to grasp.

Third, not all the facts we learn from pictures are inherently visual. Colors may be restricted to vision; but shape may be learned through many senses, and pictures are concerned with shape, be it the streamlining of a car in an advertisement or the symmetry of a vase in a still life. Pictures also deal with the locations of objects in space. We can discover location or form through vision but also through other means, as when we can hear and feel what parts of an engine are vibrating or that a loose nut is moving around in it. If many of the things we depict are not inherently visual, perhaps they can be apprehended through haptic pictures.

1. Evidence on tactile skills

Does psychological research support such reasoning? Strangely, the major, early work on blind subjects and their tactile skills runs counter to these arguments. Von Senden[2] reviewed a number of studies on people who had been blind since birth, studies made by psychologists, surgeons, and educators. His evidence ranged from informal tests made by physicians to accounts by the blind about their daily life. In his view, now widely accepted, the world of touch was quite different for blind people and sighted people. Von Senden's conclusions can be divided into five categories.

Perception on a geographical scale—a set of times? To the congenitally blind, von Senden claims, travel over long distances is not experienced as movement through space, but rather as time spent in a particular activity. The blind man does not feel he is moving from place to place. Instead, he senses that he is being jogged up and down for half an hour until his destination "appears." (Many sighted people may have a similar impression in plane flights.)

Perception on a domestic scale—habitual locomotions? To the sighted, a room is a space filled with furniture which one can walk around in freely. To a blind person, von Senden thinks a room is a place where he must walk and reach in certain ways. The room is "five steps from the door to the stove." To reach the sink from the table, one has to turn and stretch out in a particular way. When one is at the sink the window is located where one bends forward in a particular way to touch it. The room is a set of objects in a unified space for sighted people, but for the blind man is a set of objects glued together by special movements.

Perception of the space around the body—a set of movements? According to von Senden, the space around the blind man's body is apprehended as a limited set of movements and postures. A sighted person can pick up a nearby object with any of an endless variety of different movements—a slow reach or a quick grab, using the left hand or the right hand, taking the object from above or the side, and so on. But the blind man knows only one way to locate the object, for instance the movement he used to set the object down in the first place. Ask him to make a different movement and he will be at a loss.

Perception of the arrangement of object parts—a sum of features? The blind person does not have an impression of the overall shape of an object. Instead he notices individual features and counts them. A blind man may know the object has six corners because he has counted them. He may feel that the object is smooth, heavy, and wet. He may notice that some parts are soft. But the distribution of the features in one overall shape, with some parts near others, and other parts at opposite ends—this information escapes him. Two balls are felt as entirely different, even though they are both round, if they are made of different materials. Knowing that one of the balls can roll does not help the blind person know that the other can roll. Texture, temperature, and weight are differentiated in the blind man's world, but shape is not.

Perception of the size of object parts—movements and durations? Since the blind person cannot tell the relative location of the parts of an object, correlatively he does not directly apprehend the length of a part of an object like the pull chain on a lamp. He discovers the sizes of things by indirect methods, not by simply grasping the object and noticing its size. He has to rub his hand along the object at a controlled, steady rate and pay attention to the length of time the movement takes. In his world a longer object is one which requires a longer rub. Size is "movement in time," not a direct impression of the extension of an object, von Senden believed.

The basic conclusion von Senden reached is that anyone who has been blind since birth usually deals with his environment in terms of number of features, body movements, and the duration of activities. Von Senden went so far as to say that a capacity for form perception may be absent in touch unless sight is given an opportunity to train touch. Temperature, texture, hardness—these are evident to the blind man. He can tell X is wet without having to slip on it first, but he cannot tell how long X is without executing a particular movement on it and then thinking about how long it takes him to execute the movement. A strange world!

Von Senden's opinions are shared by English and American educators of the blind consulted in the past few years. If these opinions are correct, touch is not a suitable modality for outline depiction. Outline depictions present the shapes of different objects but ignore the different textures, temperatures, hardnesses, and weights. If blind subjects rely on these alone, then outline drawings are meaningless to them, for to understand an outline picture one has to use the very properties von Senden suggests are largely irrelevant to the blind—properties like straightness, curvature, nearness of one feature to another, and so on. If the present study finds that blind subjects *are* sensitive to form, it will also need to explain why von Senden came to the opposite conclusion.

Von Senden's work, last published in 1960, is not the last word, and recently remarkable evidence has emerged from a series of studies attempting to use the skin of the back as a kind of "screen" for projected images.

White and his colleagues made a television apparatus that converts light patterns into large, vibrating tactile patterns, which were pressed onto the skin on the backs of their subjects. After a little practice, subjects could identify the shapes of the objects at which the television camera was directed. Thus the skin was a suitable surface for shape perception.[3] Of course, the ability shown by some of White's subjects need not have been pictorial, for sometimes it might have made little difference whether an actual object was applying the pressure or an almost identical silhouette was obtained by means of the television apparatus. But some of White's findings suggests that truly pictorial skills were involved. For example, if the pattern on the skin expanded while keeping the same shape, subjects had the impression that a distant object was approaching them. Instead of expansion being understood as increase in size, it was understood as meaning decrease in distance, as it often does in vision. So some of White's subjects were not simply reporting impressions of pictures the same way that they would probably report impressions from contact with real objects.

Other recent research points to a quite primitive link between vision and touch in man. Infants a few months old expect visible objects to have tactile consequences. It has been found by Bower that an infant who reaches for a nearby object will shape his hand appropriately to grasp the object before actually touching it. If the object is really only an optical image, visible but not substantial, the infant will be distressed when his grasp fails to make solid contact with it.[4]

2. *Elements of outline drawings*

One would not expect colors, highlights, or reflections—purely optical phenomena—to mean much to the blind. The research mentioned above, however, and our own experience if we are sighted, suggests that some aspects of shape are not purely optical and are common to touch and vision. Then consider the variables of shape that commonly are depicted in outline drawings: with which can touch be expected to deal?

Objects may be taken as material bounded by surfaces. The surfaces are planar or curved and in various combinations make up the shapes of objects. The combinations include *concave corners*: two plane surfaces meet to form a corner like that of a room, where the air enclosed by the surfaces is less than 180 degrees; *convex corners*: two plane surfaces meet to form a corner like that of a building, where the air around the surface spans more than 180 degrees; *occluding edges*: convex corners display only one surface to the observer from his point of view, the other surface being behind the visible surface; *occluding bounds*: a curved surface bends gradually away from the observer until some of the surface is not visible from his point of view (the horizon is an occluding bound, and so are the visible limits of a ball); *parallel pairs* of corners, edges, or occluding bounds make thin, elongated features like wires, cracks, and the like.

Each of these five arrangements of surfaces are apparent to sight and are often depicted in outline drawings (e.g., figure 5:1).[5] Intuitively, it seems

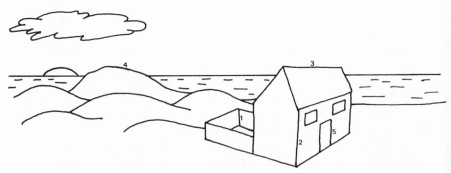

Figure 5:1. Five meanings for a line: (1) a concave corner; (2) a convex corner; (3) an occluding edge; (4) an occluding bound; (5) a crack.

obvious that four of the arrangements are readily identifiable by touch as well as vision. The concave corner of a room feels quite different from a building's convex corner or an occluding edge; either type of corner feels quite different from a wire, and wires, in turn, feel quite different from cracks. Here, then, are some variables in common to touch and vision.

But there are some reasons for debating whether an occluding bound is a tactile concept. A ball is rounded and also sharply silhouetted to vision. Visually, a ball has distinct occluding bounds. To the touch it may be rounded, but maybe to the touch there is no clear division between a perceptible front and a concealed back, a definite near side and a definite far side. So occluding bounds may be difficult for a blind person to identify in both actual objects and pictures of objects.

In sum, von Senden's research predicts that outline depiction would be a mystery to the blind. On the other hand, more recent research by White et al. finds that a few hours of training allows blind subjects to identify objects whose silhouette is pressed onto their backs. Bower's research also shows that even in very young infants vision and touch are interrelated. Even so, the relation between vision and touch is surely not simple, for occluding bounds may be very indistinct in touch but are impressively clear in vision.

Thus far the approach has been general. Now concrete examples may help to distinguish precisely how pictorial vision and touch are intertwined and where the most complex connections may be. For one thing, depth has a very different status in vision and touch. Consider how depth may create problems for outline pictures and touch.

3. Depth in outline pictures

The outline drawings of a table and a cup in figure 5:2 exhibit aspects which could be misleading to touch. The top surface of the table is projected as a figure in which some angles are quite acute and some quite obtuse. Nevertheless we perceive the depicted top as having four equal angles, not two acute and two obtuse angles.

The top of the cup is projected as an ellipse, but we perceive it as circular. One of the puzzles of pictures is that the depicted object has features that are different from the features of the arrangement of lines on paper. From that point of view, pictures are "distorted" versions of objects. But in our everyday use of pictures the projective "distortions" are not misleading or even noticed.

Because of overlap, features of objects that are quite separate are projected onto the picture surface and are represented by lines that are adjacent. That is, parts of an object that are distant from one another may be depicted by parts of the picture that are contiguous. In the picture of the

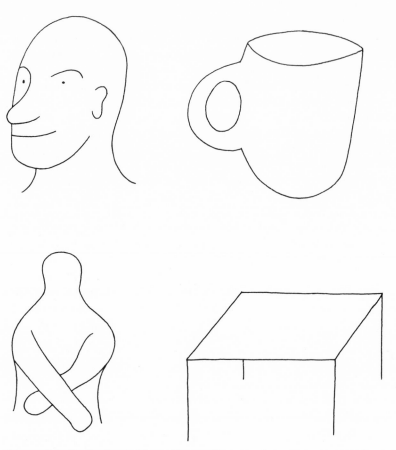

Figure 5:2. Projections. These flat outline drawings depict depth by using overlap and projective transformations of shape.

table, a line depicting the back leg of the table has a junction with a line that is depicting the front edge of the table. In the cup figure, the line for the nearest part of the brim is, of course, no nearer the eye than the surface immediately above it, but the surface above the line depicts an area on the object some inches behind the brim.

How could touch cope with these foibles of outline depiction? Consider a few simple predictions. It will turn out that the predictions are wide of the mark, but the surprising nature of the findings will be most evident if the simplest and most obvious theory is stated here, before the results are revealed. First of all, one might suppose that any drawings involving projective transformation of shape and problems of overlap would be misleading to the touch because to the touch an angle is the same angle irrespective of orientation and widely separated objects are not sensed by means of features that are adjacent.

This can be made more precise. Some objects have a silhouette or front surface whose shape clearly identifies them. Such objects could be pressed onto a waxy surface and leave a recognizable imprint. An object like a hand can leave a clear imprint on a flat surface. Drawing around the margins of the imprint would leave an outline drawing of the hand, a drawing free of projective transformations and overlap problems. A similar print of a cup would fail to give an outline; only a few points on the cup would make contact with the printing surface, and the result would not resemble a picture of a cup at all. Thus, one kind of drawing can be called an "imprint", but another kind requires projective geometry, and will be called "a projection." A simple theory would presume that imprints could be understood by blind subjects more easily than projections.

Some imprints are a hand, a fork, a flag and flagpole, and a man standing with one arm raised and the other arm down by his side (figure 5:3). Two of these are objects about hand-sized and two are much larger. One might expect that the larger objects would be more difficult to identify in manual exploration of a small drawing. The flag and the flagpole might be well-nigh impossible for congenitally blind subjects, for these objects would be almost entirely out of their experience. The subjects will, however, at least have heard of such things and perhaps have heard descriptions of the shapes of flags. If verbally supplied information is at all useful they might yet be able to identify the flag and flagpole.

Just as some of the objects that are imprinted are much larger than a hand, so are some of the objects to be depicted in projections. The table is one such object, and another (to compare to the imprint man) is a man with arms overlapped in front of his body. Projections of roughly hand-size objects include a face in semiprofile, where the nose overlaps the face, and the cup. Surely a simple theory would forecast the hand-sized objects should be easier to identify in manual exploration of small drawings.

Then these are the predictions: (1) Imprints should be easier to identify than projections. (2) Hand-sized objects should be easier to identify than larger objects. (3) Objects familiar to touch (like cups) should be easier to identify than objects foreign to touch (like a flying flag). (4) Lines depicting occluding bounds should not be identifiable to touch.

If the predictions are convincing—as they certainly seemed at the beginning of this investigation—then some of the results will come as a shock. The findings suggest that blind persons have a much better awareness of form than anyone has yet supposed and much more skill in dealing with lines than anyone has yet tried to use in their education.

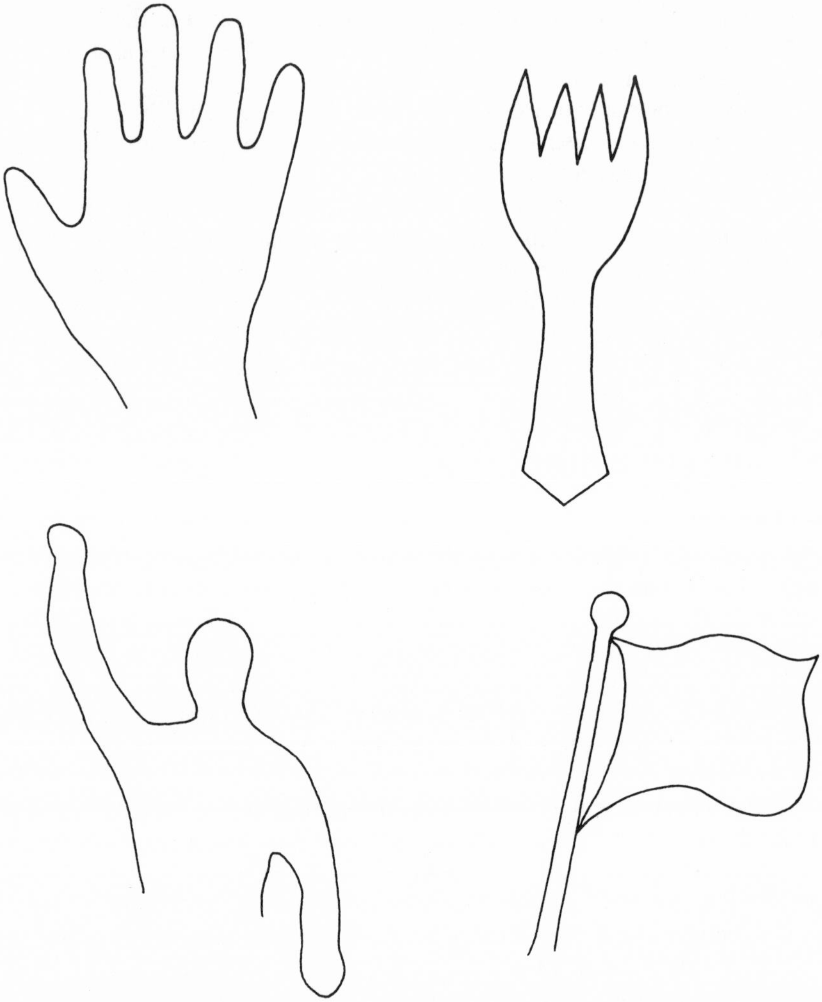

Figure 5:3. Imprints. These outline drawings do not involve overlap or projective transformation of shape.

4. Experimentation and findings

Consider first the research methods. Raised line drawings were made using a specific kind of plastic sheet available from the American Foundation for the Blind. These sheets are designed for use with a clipboard whose face has a layer of rubber. When a stylus draws a line or dot on the plastic sheet, the sheet blisters, producing raised lines or dots. The dots and lines are raised on the side on which the stylus was applied. A variety of different displays was prepared, including the geometrical shapes in figure 5:4 and the figures shown in figures 5:2 and 5:3.

Subjects examined one display at a time. The tests were administered to each subject individually, so there were opportunities to observe the ways a subject touched the displays and to question the subject after the tests were completed. Each display was taped to a sheet of cardboard and was surrounded by a cardboard window. Before being asked to identify the

Figure 5:4. Geometric shapes used in pretesting.

haptic pictures of objects, the subjects were given a set of pretests (on geometrical shapes) to ensure they understood the instructions and had some familiarity with the materials and to establish whether the subjects possessed some basic skills of form perception.

The pretests were always given before the haptic pictures, but the order of the haptic pictures was varied; half the subjects examined the imprint set first and half received the projections first. The maximum time allowed for any display was two minutes. The subjects were told to guess if they were not sure and were asked for guesses if they fell silent. They were told whether they were correct or not. When correct, they were asked to identify individual features of the display. Subjects were allowed to use either or both of their hands to explore the displays, and they were told that the displays were oriented with bottoms toward them.

Before investigating the reactions of truly blind people to the displays, the researcher tested the displays on blindfolded subjects.[6] For example, thirty-four blindfolded, sighted students from Harvard and Radcliffe all correctly identified the outline drawings of geometrical shapes. Evidently they had through touch a good basic sensitivity to line shape. The same sensitivity was found with dot shapes, for almost all of these blindfolded subjects identified almost all of the dot figures—with one notable exception. Only ten subjects (six male and four female) correctly identified the circle made of widely spaced dots. Twelve of the subjects found all the dots but called the shape an ellipse, a polygon, or a diamond. The rest of the subjects failed to locate all the dots, a source of trouble which was responsible for almost all the (infrequent) errors on the other dot figures.

How did the blind fare on these dot and line figures? In rank contrast to von Senden's views, they did well, just as well as the blindfolded subjects. Eight college students tested in Boston, seven blind from birth and one since the age of six, identified all the line figures, and the only failures on the dot shapes were provided by two subjects who did not identify the circle made of widely spaced dots. Clearly, outline and dot shapes were as detectable by the blind as by the blindfolded; and interestingly, the one shape that created difficulty was a problem to both groups.

Since almost all the subjects identified one of the circles—the one with closely spaced dots—the problematic figure was not difficult simply because it is a circle. And since figures with more widely spaced dots, like the square, were readily identified, the difficulty did not lie in dot spacing. It seemed to be a joint product of dot spacing and curved form that created problems. What is usually a dot circle for the eye may be ambiguous to touch.

When given the unfamiliar line figures, all the blind subjects accurately described their parts and angles, and only two of the blindfolded subjects failed. On the unfamiliar dot figure, once again all the blind subjects were accurate while four of the blindfolded subjects failed to locate all the dots.

The blind subjects often described the dot figure as connected by imaginary straight lines, in a "zigzag"; most of the blindfolded subjects did the same, but occasionally they remarked on a "curving" pattern or a "bowl" shape.

If anything, the blind proved slightly better than the blindfolded in these tests.[7] But could they "read" forms as representations, as well as pick out parts? Did lines "make pictures" for them? How would they compare to blindfolded subjects on pictures? Table 5:1 summarizes the answers.

The mean number of correct identifications per blindfolded subject was 2.4, or 30 percent. Only one blindfolded subject failed to identify any of the pictures, and the highest number of correct identifications was seven. Discussion with the subjects failed to uncover any reason (such as previous familiarity with the task or special haptic skills or problems) that would account for extreme scores. Upon completion of the test, all thirty-four blindfolded subjects were allowed to look at the pictures one by one, and immediately they correctly identified each picture on their first response.[8]

The blind subjects made ten correct identifications, including five imprints and five projections—a more even split than was the case for the blindfolded subjects, who made forty-six correct identifications of imprints and only thirty-six of projections. Three of the pictures—the flag-and-flagpole and the two depictions of torsos—were not identified by any of the blind subjects.

Table 5:1 Identifications of Pictures by Blind and
         Blindfolded Subjects (Ss)

	Picture	Blindfolded Ss (N=34)	Blind Ss (N=8)
Imprints	Hand	28	3
	Fork	8	2
	Man/arm up	1	0
	Flag	9	0
	Subtotal	46	5
Projections	Face	10	1
	Cup	11	2
	Man/arms crossed	1	0
	Table	14	2
	Subtotal	36	5
	Grand total	82	10
	Percentage correct	30	12.5
	Range	0–7	0–4

The range of correct identifications was almost as great among the blind subjects as among the blindfolded. Two blind subjects identified four pictures each—two imprints and two projections in one case, one imprint and three projections in the other. Only four of the thirty-four blindfolded subjects made four or more correct identifications.

Seven Toronto high school students who were legally blind were also tested.[9] These formed both a younger and a more diverse group of subjects, some intending to go to college, some expecting to have difficulty finishing high school. A few had had a small percentage of sight for almost ten years, some still had some sensitivity to large bright or dark objects, some had vague color vision, some were totally without sight. Possibly the main use to which their results can be put is in comparing the different kinds of outline pictures, and it would be unwise to assume that they lack visual familiarity with line and outline to the same extent as the Boston subjects. Thus the key question in mind when testing them was whether there would be a clear difference between the difficulty of imprints and projections. The answer is evident in table 5:2. Blindfolded subjects performed slightly better with imprints (forty-six compared to thirty-six projections) but the difference was not statistically significant, and blind subjects in both Toronto and Boston identified just as many projections as imprints.

With only a small sample of blind subjects and only a few displays being tested, these results should be interpreted cautiously. But certainly some pictorial outline representations were meaningful to blind subjects without prior training. A careful analysis of the errors made by the blind supported this conclusion, for they show that reasonable guesses were being made.

For example, the elongated fork with prongs several subjects guessed to be "an arm and a hand," "a flower on a thick stem," "an ice cream cone

Table 5:2 Identifications of Pictures by Blind Subjects (Ss)

Toronto Ss				Boston Ss			
Age	*I*	*P*	*Pictures*	*Age*	*I*	*P*	*Pictures*
13	2	1	hand, fork, face	18	0	0	
14	1	1	hand, face	19	0	0	
17	1	1	hand, table	20	1	0	fork
17	1	0	fork	20	2	2	hand, fork, cup, table
18	0	0	.	20	0	0	
18	1	1	fork, table	21	1	0	hand
18	0	2	man/arms crossed, table	22*	1	3	hand, face, cup, table
				23	0	0	
Totals	6	6			5	5	

*Boston S, aged 22, blind since age 6. All other Boston Ss were blind since birth.

with a funny bottom," or "a kind of bell." The man with his arm up was called a teapot! These are errors *that make sense to vision.* In addition, more than one subject indicated that the failure to identify the cup resulted from the absence of a line to depict the joint of the handle with the bowl of the cup. So the subjects were able to *correct* the drawings!

Further, when the subjects were told the correct identification of the displays, they thought these labels were meaningful. Most subjects could then proceed to pick out the parts without further help. In fact, one blind subject said the drawing technique was the reason for his failure and the shoulders on the man were too rounded, a fact often overlooked by sighted subjects but an obvious one once this subject pointed it out. Finally, some of the difficulties subjects expressed were trivial; for example, the prongs of the fork were said to be too close together to be distinct. In summary, comments from subjects supported the numerical data, showing that outline depiction of corners, rounded forms, surfaces, and background was meaningful to touch.

The results were not extensive enough to allow the variables of size and familiarity to be understood in detail. The findings suggest that direct tactile experience assisted in interpreting haptic line depictions, but this suggestion should be taken cautiously. Perhaps the results were stronger for the blind subjects than the blindfolded. For the blind subjects, objects that could be grasped as a whole were easier to identify. Out of ten correct identifications, only one was larger than hand-sized—a result which is significant at the 0.01 level on a binomial test. Nevertheless, benefits from verbal descriptions and general acquaintance with large objects cannot be disregarded. Large shapes and shapes known only by verbal description are not foreign to touch pictures, for the blind subjects found drawings of such shapes meaningful once a label was given.

The face, hand, and cup pictures all employed lines depicting occluding bounds. The last hypothesis ventured that occluding bounds were less definite in touch than in vision and that, as a consequence, figures like the face, hand, and cup would be troublesome to the blind. The conjecture fell wide of the mark, since these were comparatively easy figures to identify for both blind and blindfolded subjects. They were quite the equal of the table and the fork.

5. A common ground between vision and touch

Von Senden's evidence suggested that blind subjects would have considerable difficulty with form perception. His evidence now seems to have been misleading, and an alternative theory is called for. Perhaps the explanation lies in the complexity of the tasks his subjects faced. It may be that his subjects could solve problems of perception of location and shape through any of a number of cues. If so, his evidence suggests what blind people may normally do but not what they can do if pressed. That is, perhaps blind subjects normally can rely on the textures, smells, weights, and temperatures of objects to make identifications and so rarely need to notice overall shape. In going about their daily business, blind people may use time and movement to orient themselves. But the present evidence suggests that when called upon to use shape they can do so.

Another factor may be the length of time subjects are given on a task. At the outset of testing, subjects for this study (including blindfolded subjects) often said that they couldn't make sense out of the lines; they couldn't tell where one line was with respect to another; sometimes they couldn't be sure where one hand was with respect to the other, just as von Senden found. But subjects were pressed into guessing and persisting, and often the subjects were finally able to make correct identifications.

If this reinterpretation of von Senden is correct, then it seems that a blind person's tactile sense may have two modes. The dominant mode is one based on immediate qualities of warmth, texture, and momentary contact, together with expectations of the results of possible movements. In this mode, the person is closely aware of the feeling of his surroundings and the network of movements he might make. The secondary mode is one in which three-dimensional shapes and distances—the Euclidean and Cartesian environment—are important. This mode can be used by a blind person but may be less commonly used than among sighted people. Special tasks may be required to call it forth.

What do the findings suggest about this possibly secondary mode of tactile sensing that understands projection pictures? For a moment, reflect on the early origins of pictures. One of the striking facts about parietal art ("cave" or "rock" art) is the common use of overlap in depicting parts within one single object, and overlap of one detached object by another detached object is usually neglected.[10] From the success of the blind subjects with haptic projections of individual objects, and the prevalence of within-objects overlap in early art, one might conjecture that an essential part of the brain's internal representation of many individual objects in both vision and touch is the relative location of parts as conceived from possible points of view that entail overlap. Indeed, forms of overlap are not entirely foreign to touch; an exploring hand can find part of a table *covered* by a book, just as an exploring eye will see overlap.

This analogy should not be taken too far. The parallel between vision and touch breaks down when the distance between overlapping objects increases. To the eye, a back leg of a table can be projected adjacent to a front surface, but adjacency like that is unknown to touch. Some of the blind subjects said that the short fourth leg of the table figure was "less satisfactory" or "more difficult" or "something they had to guess at."

Evidently there are some *partial* parallels between vision and touch and some important common skills. Are these partial parallels and commonalities more than mere similarities? Does the common ground physically exist as a common channel in the brain? Turn now to the comparison between projections and imprints.

Simple theorizing predicted that imprints would be more readily identified than projections. The contrary finding is important, and just as striking as the finding that line depiction was spontaneously meaningful at all to blind subjects. The "language" of lines appears common to both vision and touch, and problems of outlining depth relationships appear treated in like fashion by both senses. The fact that a tactilely flat distribution of lines represents an object in depth confronts subjects with no more difficulty than the fact that a visually flat surface pictures an object in depth.

At this point it is worth noting what the subjects said about their methods for analyzing the displays. Blindfolded subjects were expected to convert the tactilely acquired information to a "visual image." Presumably no recognition of projections would occur until the subject had created a visual image, and perhaps the same might hold for imprints. The reasoning was that line representation was probably a purely visual phenomenon, and projections involved features of a purely visual geometry. So the subjects would have to convert the figures into a visual mode before analyzing them.

In keeping with expectations, some blindfolded subjects reported using a visual image strategy. But not all did. Some did not mention visual imagery. They described impressions of shape and distribution of parts, but no strategy of converting impressions from one mode to another. These subjects seemed to be operating with features of objects without referring their impressions to one modality or another. Taken literally, these reports suggest an amodal awareness of shape and location, perhaps an amodal knowledge that is similar in blind and blindfolded subjects. If these reports are treated seriously and taken together with the numerical results, this leads to the speculative view that the language of outlines is common to both vision and touch and that the different senses feed into an amodal awareness of form.

To add to this evidence, consider a comment made by several blind subjects. When told the identity of the cup figure, they said they understood why they had failed to identify the figure. They said they had taken the elliptical line depicting the space enclosed by the handle as a depiction of a flat elliptical surface, not a hole. This is precisely what figure-ground laws of vision would have predicted, for Rubin showed that often one can see shape on only one side of a dividing line or contour and that recognition of the line or contour depends, in many cases, on seeing the shape on the correct side.[11] Since figure-ground is an important part of the perception of pictures, these indications of figure-ground effects in touch underscore the common ground between vision and touch.

But surely at least the occluding bound of the side of a cup is a visual concept, not a tactile one? Inexorably the subjects' performances undermined this common-sense expectation. In its place perhaps the amodal theory should be pursued. One possible line of argument is this: Precisely because a distinct occluding bound is an important part of one sensory system, namely visual experience, a geometry available to all the senses incorporates the occluding bound concept. Vision has put the occluding bound concept into the amodal store. If so, although it is because of vision that one understands occluding bounds tactilely, lines can stand for occluding bounds in either vision or touch; both modalities feed into the amodal stores.

This, of course, is speculation. While the discussion began by testing ideas cautiously, it ends aloft in the winds of imagination. A critic, patient enough to follow this progress, would not forgive pushing yet further on the basis of interesting but slender evidence. A retreat to safer ground is in order.

This much seems clear. The aspects of shapes of objects often depicted in outline drawings for vision can be recognized when presented to touch via raised line drawings. Further, blindfolded and blind persons alike make comparable kinds of identifications of outline drawings of common objects. Thus the "language of outline" means to the touch of the blind what it means to the vision and the touch of blindfolded subjects. Outline representations, not restricted to vision, may depict *form*, a product of perception that lies beyond any particular sensory system.

Notes

1. We do not discuss relationships between facts and sensory channels in detail here because we have just one particular relationship to consider. The general issue is raised in a number of recent essays, one of the most effective and pertinent being Zenon W. Pylyshyn, "What the Mind's Eye Tells the Mind's Brain," *Psychological Bulletin* 80 (1973): 1–24.

2. Max von Senden, *Space and Sight: The Perception of Space and Shape in the Congenitally Blind Before and After Operation*, trans. P. Heath (London: 1960). A number of recent studies, reviewed by David H. Warren in "Early versus Late Blindness," presented at Society for Research in Child Development Conference, April, 1973, point to the same conclusions as von Senden's.

3. Benjamin W. White et al., "Seeing with the Skin," *Perception and Psychophysics* 7 (1970): 23–27. See also Paul Bach-y-rita, *Brain Mechanisms in Sensory Substitution* (New York: Academic Press, 1972) and Leonard Scadden, "A Tactual Substitute for Sight," *New Scientist* 19 (1969): 677–78.

4. Thomas G. R. Bower, "Object Perception in Infants," *Perception* 1 (1972): 15–30.

5. From John Kennedy, *A Psychology of Picture Perception: Images and Information* (San Francisco: Jossey-Bass, 1974).

6. Pilot testing, with the assistance of Judy Silver, Lochlan Magee, and Kathy O'Grady, has been undertaken with more than 100 blindfolded subjects of many kinds, including both children and adults ranging from five to sixty-six years in age, obtained as volunteers by notices

around Harvard and Toronto Universities. In this pilot testing, subjects were given various instructions about procedures, sometimes being told to use particular hand movements, rather than being left free to explore like the thirty-four subjects reported in detail. Nevertheless, it is still useful to note: (*a*) subjects as young as five identified the haptic pictures, and (*b*) the displays frequently identified by the forty-one subjects younger than thirteen are the displays frequently identified by older subjects in both the pilot testing and the group of thirty-four reported here.

7. Across the tests, the difference is significant at the 0.05 level on a binomial test, the blind being superior on more tests.

8. These uniform identifications act as an operational definition, attesting to the fact that these simple outline patterns are legitimate pictures.

9. The assistance of the North York Board of Education and Frances Paling in particular was invaluable in meeting with the Toronto high school students.

10. John Kennedy and Judy Silver, "The Surrogate Functions of Lines in Visual Perception: Evidence from Antipodal Rock and Cave Artwork," *Perception* 3 (1974): 313–22.

11. Edgar Rubin, *Synsoplevede Figurer* (Copenhagen: Glydendals, 1915). The remarkable affinity between Rubin's findings and touch in blind subjects emphasizes the possible role of a process in common to both visual and tactile senses. See Kennedy, *Picture Perception,* for a discussion of the relation between figure-ground and pictures, and Kennedy, "Misunderstandings of Figure and Ground," *Scandinavian Journal of Psychology* 14 (1973): 207–9 for a clarification of Rubin's legacy.

6 Reading Pictures and Reading Text
Paul A. Kolers

1. Verbal and visual

Popular discourse supposes a contrast between the verbal and the visual, between the serial, arbitrary, and conventional mode of language and the intuitive, immediate, and holistic experience vision seemingly permit us. Although nonverbal skills are often overlooked or neglected in our educational systems, the dichotomy between verbal and visual actually misses the distinction that it most seeks to make, for it is a misfounded dichotomy. That this is so is seen readily when we realize that one prominent activity—reading—falls into both categories. Obviously concerned with language, reading also depends, typically, upon scanning and discriminations of the most delicate sort by the visual apparatus.

Rather than use this misfounded dichotomy, one may speak instead of the contrast between the linguistic and the pictorial, in Nelson Goodman's terminology, or between displays that communicate by means of the marks that make them up and displays that communicate by means of the messages the marks embody. In *Languages of Art* Goodman pointed out some formal differences in the way the symbol systems employed in picturing and in language communicate, and he identified some notable similarities.[1] The present article, in discussing reading, complements that viewpoint by examining ways in which aspects of the perceptual processes involved in language and picturing run remarkably parallel. The contrast between reading text and reading pictures offers a natural testing ground for the purpose, one where again popular belief offers some presuppositions. Reading text is generally conceived of as a sequential process of word-by-word or even letter-by-letter decoding, in contrast with the holistic and virtually instantaneous apprehension of pictorial displays. Whatever the other differences between reading text and pictures, how well these contrasts survive a critical examination will emerge in the following pages.

2. Reading text

The study of reading was one of the major topics of research among the first and second generation of experimental psychologists. In the bibliography of E. B. Huey's masterwork, first published in 1908, one finds the names of many men such as Dodge, Cattell, and Woodworth who are still familiar to students of experimental psychology.[2] Indeed, Dodge devised the workhorse apparatus of the perception laboratory, the mirror tachistoscope, and apparatus for measuring the eyes' motion, as a means of studying problems in visual perception related to reading. But within about ten years after Huey's work appeared, that is, soon after the onset of the "Behaviorist Revolution," only a few experimental psychologists were still working on the topic. Not that the problems had been solved or deep understanding gained; rather, the climate of opinion regarding the proper course of experimental psychology had shifted. Sixty years later it shifted again, partly because of the influence of developments in the study of language and language use and partly, without doubt, because of a pressing social need. Literacy is necessary for successful living in a technological society, and many of our citizens are functionally illiterate.

Variously motivated, the recent increase of interest among experimental psychologists in the study of literacy shows promise of further payoff. Reading is an incredibly complicated activity, requiring for its successful performance the coordination of many special skills. Perhaps, indeed, its very complexity was a reason for its earlier loss of regard among experimental psychologists, for under the influence of the "radical behaviorists" other psychologists often sought fairly straightforward and simple laws of behavior, causal connections between stimulus and response, doing so in analogy to their perception of the early development of physics. Reading does not readily lend itself to such description; indeed, perhaps little in psychology does.[3] As the contemporary psychologist G. A. Miller has noted: "The dream of a single philosophical principle that explains everything it touches seems to be fading before the realization that man is vastly curious and complicated, and that we need a lot more information about him before we can formulate and test even the simplest psychological laws."[4] The idea here is that the performance of intricately organized living systems cannot readily be simulated or understood solely by extrapolation from simpler laws.

Conditioning of simple responses follows one such law, and twenty years ago a slogan such as "reading involves the activation of conditioned meanings" was thought to explain something about how people read text. Today's climate, however, requires more detail, more specific information, and a description which, even if it cannot yet predict how a particular student will read, at least makes plausible guesses about the major constituent activities of reading.

What is meant by "constituent activities"? Some of them concern the way the sensory apparatus integrates information over space and time; others concern the role of linguistic variables in the perception of discourse and the interaction of linguistic and nonlinguistic symbols in perception. There is a rich promise in such work, as Huey notes: "To completely analyze what we do when we read would almost be the acme of the psychologist's achievements, for it would be to describe very many of the most intricate workings of the human mind."[5]

No article can yet hope to fill that great a promise. The purpose here is to describe some aspects of reading skill that have been identified by experiment or analysis and to describe some overlooked similarities between the reading of linguistic and pictorial symbols.

3. Temporal aspects of reading

One of the more firmly held presumptions regarding reading is that our eyes move smoothly and continuously along a line of text; that we begin at the left margin and proceed regularly along the line of print to the right margin, and then step down a line to repeat the process. So overwhelming is this implicit assumption that it was not until about one hundred years ago that the ophthalmologist Emile Javal noticed and first formally described the fact that people's eyes actually jump about when they read.[6] These jumps, or saccades as they are called technically, have since been thoroughly studied. In normal reading they occur about three or four times per second, and each takes about 30–40 msec. (thousandths of a second). Thus a typical sequence is made up of pauses that last about a quarter of a second each plus travel times lasting about 30–40 msec. each.

It is a common observation that the eye's movements interfere with perception; we do not see as clearly while the eye is moving as we do when it is stationary. By means of a clever technique, Volkmann, Schick, and Riggs found that this impairment results partly from a smearing of visual impressions created by the eye's rapid movement and partly from the occurrence of the movement itself. The latter was shown by the finding that the ability to see a single word presented very briefly to the center of the eye was less when the eye was moving than when it was stationary.[7] This and related studies imply that most of what we perceive of the physical attributes of a stimulus display is based on what comes into the eye in the brief pause *between* movements rather than *during* movements. Javal's discovery therefore creates a major problem for research that has still not been resolved satisfactorily: what mechanisms in the visual system transform the discontinuous input created by eye movements into the continuous quality of perceptual experience? Our awareness of our reading tends to reflect the sequential regularity of the printed language, but the input we receive via our eyes from the printed page does not preserve this regularity, as will be shown below.

A number of notions have been put forth to explain the continuity and regularity of perception despite the irregularity of its input. Some people insist that, however the physical eye moves, they read sequentially letter by letter and word by word. Others have granted the relevance of saccadic motions and then have assumed that segments of words or even whole phrases are perceived simultaneously with each fixation and then are somehow combined. Some experiments, however, suggest that both of these notions create more problems for understanding than they solve.

4. Serial presentation of letters

Suppose that reading did proceed on a letter-by-letter basis. What would be the consequences for reading? To test this question, Kolers and Katzman carried out an experiment. College students, tested individually, sat in front of a screen on which the letters of familiar English words appeared. Their mode of appearance was unfamiliar, however, for they were presented one letter at a time, and each letter in the sequence was made to fall on approximately the same part of the viewing screen as every other one. The words used were all six letters long, and the typical sequence was for each of the letters to be presented and then for a pause to intervene during which the subject reported his perceptions. The duration of the letters' exposure varied; furthermore, the subjects in one test were required to spell the letters that they saw and in another to name the word the letters spelled. The main finding in both tests was that individual letters had to be exposed for about one-quarter to one-third of a second if the students were to attain about 90 percent accuracy of report.[8] As the average length of words in English is five to six letters, this finding means that if people did read letter by letter, they would read at the most about one word every two seconds, or about thirty words per minute. This rate is actually about one-tenth that of the average college freshman.[9] Hence a strict and straightforward interpretation of the notion of letter-by-letter reading is inconsistent with observed facts.

5. Grouping of letters

The notion of letter-by-letter reading can be interpreted more loosely to mean that one sees not single letters with each fixation but groups of letters. The problem raised by this interpretation depends upon how one defines "group of letters." Are groups to be thought of as fixed in size, say three or four letters per group, with the eye still thought of as moving in regular steps along the line of print? Should two letters ending one word and two letters beginning the next be thought of as a single group?

Another experiment carried out on college students modified the previous procedure to test these questions. In this study six-letter words were again presented to college students by means of a motion picture projector, but now their spatial arrangement was varied. In one test all six letters appeared on a line, as in normal print; in another test the arrays were two words of three letters each; and in a third test the individual six-letter words were arrayed in a triangle. Moreover, in some tests the whole word was followed by blank film, while in other tests the word was followed by arrays of superimposed x's and o's in a manner that masked or interfered with the perception of the word.

Four kinds of arrays are shown in figure 6:1. Each was presented for 167 msec. and was followed either by blank film or by a masking pattern for 167 msec. (and then blank film). Performance in three of these tests was nearly perfect. The unfamiliar geometrical arrangement of the letters in the triangular array, and its being masked, induce a slightly lower performance in one condition. These arrays, moreover, were so constructed that six letters in a row filled the centermost portion of the eye, occupying about four degrees of visual angle laterally. The triangular array extended about the same distance vertically. Hence these tests showed that the visual system seems to process all of the letters of a single word simultaneously, "in parallel," at least through spatial extents of about four degrees of visual angle, even when the duration of the flashes is markedly less than the normal fixation duration.[10] This finding encourages the notion of successive processing of groups of letters. But further experimentation revealed some problems.

6. Perceiving two words at a time

Another test studied the reader's ability to identify *two* words when their letters fell individually one on top of the other. The earlier experiment showed that letters had to be presented for about one-third of a second each if all six letters were to be identified correctly. In the present experiment two six-letter words were presented in neighboring temporal columns (figure 6:2). The letters appeared in pairs, each pair for 250 msec., which is the duration of a typical reading pause. In contrast to the first test, here performance fell almost to zero. Although college students could identify all the letters of a word in a single temporal column at these speeds of presentation,[11] and although the eyes can process words in unfamiliar

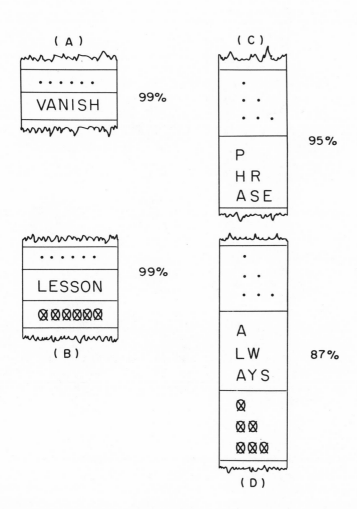

Figure 6:1. A variable-frequency motion picture projector displayed words in different spatial and temporal configurations. Here each frame appeared for 167 msec. Lateral extent of A and B and vertical extent of C and D about 4 degrees of visual angle. Not to scale.

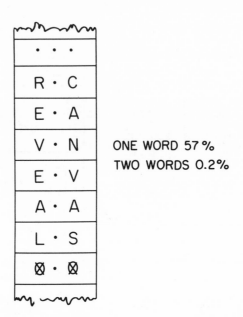

ONE WORD 57%
TWO WORDS 0.2%

Figure 6:2. Single letters or pairs of letters were exposed in a temporal column that spelled a common word. When presented for 250 msec. each, the letters in a single column were all perceived 57 percent of the time, but only 0.2 percent of both words were correctly reported.

geometrical arrangements even when they extend over four degrees of visual angle and at faster speeds of presentation, only one pair of words in 480 trials was identified correctly when they appeared, as in this test, in two temporal columns.

Why this impairment in recognizing two words at a time? Conjecture and test led to the assumption that the critical variable was not the way the array was extended in space or time but was the requirement placed on the subject to perceive two different words at approximately the same time. This conjecture led to two simple tests. In one, two three-letter words rather than a single six-letter word were exposed for 167 msec. as before and, again as before, were followed by flashes that masked or interfered with the words (figure 6:3). Although the words were shorter, more familiar and, one might think, easier to perceive, performance was actually poorer. Where 99 percent of the six-letter words were perceived (figure 6:1), only 60 percent of the pairs of three-letter words were perceived, a marked difference and a highly significant one statistically. In a second test, pairs of letters were again presented sequentially, but now the pairs of letters were part of a single word (figure 6:4). The students were again required to report the two words or, failing that, all the letters they saw. Only 7 percent of the time were both words reported correctly, but 42 percent of the time the first word was reported correctly. The readers were able to integrate sequences over time, that is, to perceive whole words from a presentation of the letters composing them, but they did so far more poorly when the letters were part of two different words than when they were part of a single word. Even a loose interpretation of the idea of sequential scanning therefore encounters difficulties when it must accommodate, as it must for normal reading, the fact that about one in three fixations would combine part of one word with part of another. Even skilled readers such as college students find it difficult to perceive two words at the same time.[12]

This is the case for words familiar as individuals but not related syntactically. Reading difficulty is reduced if the words are related syntactically, as E. B. Huey's review of the early evidence shows.[13] This finding moves the problem from the realm of visual processing to the area of psycholinguistics, but it does not explain anything. On the other hand, demonstrating an influence of syntax on perception helps to discredit the idea that we read passively, only apprehending what the eye delivers.

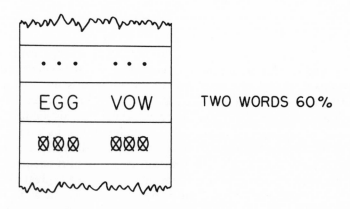

Figure 6:3. Two three-letter words exposed as in figure 6:1 were reported correctly only 60 percent of the time. In the tests the two words were separated by a single letter space.

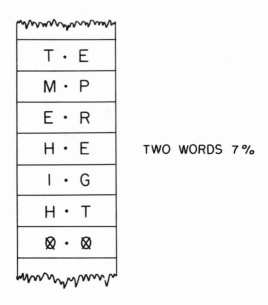

TWO WORDS 7%

Figure 6:4. The first three pairs of letters form one word, the second three pairs form another. The first word was identified 42 percent of the time, both words only 7 percent.

There are many other ways that the hypothesis of serial scanning might be formulated in addition to the two mentioned. But the evidence, although not definitive, strongly suggests that the hypothesis is not very useful in accounting for skilled reading. The limitations on performance seem not to reflect limitations in the visual system's ability to distinguish between objects, either spatially or temporally, or limitations in its complementary ability to synthesize or integrate into one perception the various components that extend in time or space. The eyes can see and report adequately single words extended in time or in space, but they seem to have great difficulty in doing so when more than one word is presented. Since the serial scanning hypothesis under even a loose interpretation would require the perception of different words (from different fixations) simultaneously, it is probably not the best hypothesis to entertain to explain reading. One should not conclude from this that motions of the eyes are irrelevant or play no important role in reading. To the contrary, motor skills can affect performance radically, as has been shown in many experiments.[14] Rather, the point is that mere sequential scanning is not by itself an adequate description of reading.

7. Scanning text

Fine control of eye movements is a characteristic of the skilled reader. His eyes must know where to go to find the signals on the page that are transformed into messages in his mind, so to speak. How this logistical task is accomplished is not yet known in detail; but it is easy to demonstrate that skilled scanning movements affect performance. In one experiment college students read aloud pages of text, all taken from a single source, that were prepared in various ways, as illustrated in figure 6:5.

The first sample there is normal English text. The second is also normal English but operated on as if by a Ferris wheel: it makes sense when read from right to left. In the third sample the order of words of normal text

```
If we wish to be certain that our indicant of anxiety is valid,

how should we proceed?  A direct approach is to ask people to

introspect on their anxiety, to report verbally how much anxiety they
```

```
ton seod sriaffa fo etats gniyfsitas eht taht edam eb nac esac gnorts A

eht tahw enimreted lliw rehtar tub ,nrael lliw lamina eht tahw enimreted

eriuqca lliw slamina taht deugra sah tsigolohcysp enO .od lliw lamina
```

```
Presented experimental the the order in the defense were to booklets

do in for the with witnesses and the had six prosecution the for

twelve which six manipulated.  Recent that were most followed favoring
```

```
Mgiikehhbr chupn ni Issseo sian rrm aip drt aehtoao he bwtr

asco aseoab r or coh ete erai fna slson iginls doe Emtu

adnee eoee.  Eneoh sap rooolef tc etahbg aaseki dh ds ssord
```

Figure 6:5. Four types of text that were read aloud both rightwards and leftwards. The first example is normal English; the second is normal English transformed as by a Ferris wheel. The third, scrambled text, contains all the words of a sentence but in scrambled order. Pseudowords in the fourth example were made by preserving word length and letter frequency of normal English but scrambling the actual display of letters.

was scrambled by a computer. In the fourth sample the lengths of words of the original text and the letters comprising it were preserved, but the letter sequences were scrambled. The pages contained, in each case, about 320 "words" in 26 lines of type. In some tests the subjects read the pages aloud as rapidly as they could from left to right, as English is normally read, and in other tests they read them from right to left. We insisted that the readers try to pronounce every "word" but accepted whatever pronunciation they gave. They differed in their pronunciation of the pseudowords, thereby expressing their individual knowledge of the rules of English pronunciation. (These variations are likely to be of greater interest to a phonologist than to a psychologist; the method seems to be a good one for studying phonological skills.) Time was measured with a stopwatch, commencing when the subject read the last word of the first line of a page. Average times are shown in table 6:1. The results as a whole were highly significant statistically for both direction of reading and types of text; that is to say, the individual scores differed from each other to a degree greater than would be expected by chance alone. This justifies considering some individual comparisons.

A well-known finding in psycholinguistic studies is that grammatical text is easier to hear and easier to learn and remember than is grammatically anomalous or syntactically distorted text. Conversely, nonsense words are read more rapidly and remembered better when they have grammatical suffixes than when they lack them.[15] The first comparison, between normal and scrambled text read aloud from left to right, extended this finding to the far simpler task of merely mouthing words. The difference between 1.28 and 1.76 minutes is small on an absolute scale but represented a fairly large percentage difference in performance. The same kinds of words were read in the two tests; their arrangement in familiar syntactic sequences in one case and in syntactically anomalous sequences in the other markedly affected speed of reading. This is an unusual aspect of an influence of perceptuo-motor skills on complex performance in that subjects were reading a familiar kind of passage and moving their eyes accordingly in one case, and an unfamiliar kind in the other.

More direct evidence of motor involvements is shown in other comparisons where several factors might play a part, in particular (1)

Table 6:1   Reading Time for Four Types of Text (Min.)

Type	Rightwards	Leftwards
Normal	1.28	9.96
"Ferris Wheel"	5.72	6.91
Scrambled	1.76	2.10
Pseudowords	5.54	9.44

whether the passage contained a message or not; (2) whether the passage was read rightwards or leftwards; (3) whether the passage was composed of familiar English words, or pseudowords, or "mirror images" of real words (the first example read leftwards and the second example read rightwards). Many other features can also be described, but consider only these three.

The influence of direction of reading was assessed by comparing performance on pseudowords read in the two directions. Subjects took about 70 percent more time on the average to read the pseudowords aloud leftwards than they did to read them rightwards. The same comparison was made with scrambled words which, read leftwards, preserved their "wordness": the subjects read "booklets to were defense the . . ." and doing so took about 20 percent more time than when reading rightwards. Hence, whether they were reading pseudowords, which had neither sense nor familiarity, or scrambled words, which lacked sense but were familiar, the subjects proceeded more rapidly in the rightward than the leftward direction. The contrast between familiarity or even a message, on the one hand, and a well-practiced motor skill on the other was brought out more clearly in the "Ferris wheel" transformation. Read leftwards, the second example is normal English prose, but in an unfamiliar arrangement; read rightwards it is a kind of pseudoword (orthographically the "mirror image" of real words and in this respect different from the pseudowords of the fourth example), but read in a familiar direction. The actual comparisons of time revealed a small but statistically reliable advantage to the familiar direction despite the absence of a message. Clearly, familiarity of grammatical sequences as well as familiarity of the words affect the speed with which words can be read aloud; in addition, both scanning movements of the eyes and efforts to speak familiar sequences affect performance markedly.

In these tests, then, performance proved faster when it required the exercise of skilled movements in a familiar direction. That a "program," or integrated set of skilled actions, was involved rather than a letter-by-letter or word-by-word analysis of text has already been illustrated with other tests.

The further question studied was whether the subject could transform a whole program, a set of skilled movements, in its entirety. For this test, subjects were required to name aloud letters that appeared in various geometric orientations, naming them sometimes from right to left and sometimes from left to right (figure 6:6). If results here followed exactly from what had gone before in reading words in the two directions, naming letters in the rightward direction should have proven always an easier and therefore faster task than naming them leftward. This was not, however, the case altogether (table 6:2): in two comparisons—normally oriented letters named rightwards or leftwards, and letters rotated around their horizontal axis named in the two directions—naming was faster in the rightward direction.

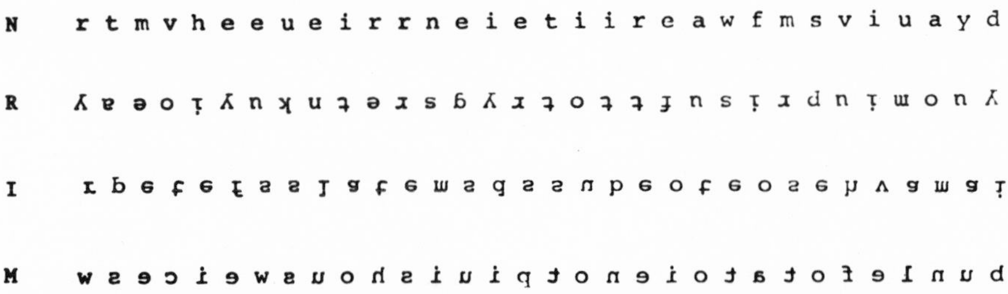

N   r t m v h e e u e i r r n e i e t i i r e a w f m s v i u a y d

R   ʎ ɐ ǝ o ʇ ʎ n ʞ u ʇ ǝ ɹ s б ʎ ɹ ʇ o ʇ ʇ ɟ n s ʇ ɹ d n ʇ ɯ o n ʎ

I   ɹ b ǝ ɟ ǝ ʇ ɐ ɐ ʇ ƃ ɟ ǝ ɯ ɐ q ɐ ɐ n p ǝ o ɟ ǝ o ɐ ǝ ɥ ʌ ƃ ɯ ƃ ʇ

M   w ɐ ǝ ɔ ʇ ǝ w ɐ u o ɐ i u i d ʇ o n ǝ i o ʇ ɐ ʇ o ʇ ǝ I u u d

Figure 6:6. Pages of letters, 832 to the page, appeared in normal form and in each of its three 180-degree rotations. They were named both rightwards and leftwards. The designations N, R, I, and M indicate normal, rotated in the plane, inverted, and mirror-reflected.

But in a third comparison—letters rotated around the vertical or y-axis—results were equivalent, and in the fourth case the advantage went to naming letters leftward.

To account for these results it was hypothesized that subjects examined not the whole letter but crucial features of letters and carried out this examination within the context of a skilled sampling sequence of looks and interpretations.[16] That is to say, it was supposed that the reader could mentally "turn around" the way he ordinarily sampled a text to perform the skilled sampling of features on a spatially transformed sample of letters. The conjecture held quite well for three of the four pairs of comparisons, failing only for the case of letters rotated around the y-axis, indicated by M in figure 6:6. The conjecture regarding mental rotation or transformability of perceptuo-motor sequences remains therefore as a hypothesis requiring further test.

8. Regressive motions of the eye

Skilled scanning movements of the eyes clearly were shown to play an important role in reading. Yet this fact is actually irrelevant to a description or understanding of reading at a certain level of analysis. The basis of this

Table 6:2   Naming Time for Transformed Letters (Min.)

Transformation	Rightwards	Leftwards
N	4.65	5.66
I	7.96	8.55
M	7.06	7.20
R	7.16	6.72

apparent contradiction is that while skilled scanning movements can affect performance, eye movements in reading do not normally proceed in a straightforward linear way. The eyes do not characteristically march stolidly across the line of print from linguistic segment to linguistic segment. For most readers the principal direction can indeed be described as rightwards and downwards, but both progressions are frequently interrupted. The nature of the interruptions can be appreciated somewhat by examining data collected by two of the small number of experimental psychologists who did continue research on reading during the 1920s and 1930s, G. T. Buswell and C. H. Judd.[17] Their chief strategy was to photograph the position of the eye as people read text or mathematical formulas or looked at pictures.

The first sample in figure 6:7 shows the eye fixations of a sixth-grade student reading a passage under instructions to "find out what it is about." The small vertical lines indicate the approximate point of fixation of the eye. The numbers above each line indicate the order in which the fixations occurred. The numbers below the line show the duration of the fixation in units of 40 msec.

The second, third, and fourth lines of the sample show regularity in the sequence of fixations: they proceed from left to right in straightforward

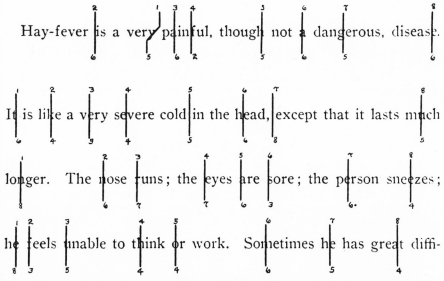

Figure 6:7. Eye fixations while reading text. The numbers above the vertical lines show the position in the sequence, the numbers below indicate the duration of fixation in units of 40 msec. This and the next two figures are from H. Judd and G. T. Buswell, "Silent Reading: A Study of the Various Types," *Supplementary Educational Monographs* no. 23 (1922).

order. The duration of the individual fixations varies somewhat, and even more variable is the distance between successive fixations. The first line of this sample, on the other hand, reveals a regressive movement: the second fixation is to the left of the first one.

A second sample (figure 6:8) shows even more irregularity. The passage, from a French grammar being "studied" rather than "read," reveals a large number of regressive motions, that is, returns of the eye to an earlier part of the sentence.

Regressive motions of the eye are interesting on at least two counts. Consider first the signal for the regressive motion. The visual system, as revealed by studies such as those of masking and metacontrast, requires about one-quarter to one-third of a second to transform a visual excitation into a perceptual experience;[18] moreover, each fixation lasts about that same interval of time. Therefore the next fixation—whether a regression or not—cannot be programmed according to the conscious experience of the current fixation. Rather, its location must depend primarily on preconscious or "automatic" processes in the visual system or on guidance from the conscious experience of prior fixations. The problem with guidance mediated through conscious perception is that the mind, choosing fixation c on the basis of its perception of fixation a, does not yet know what fixation b

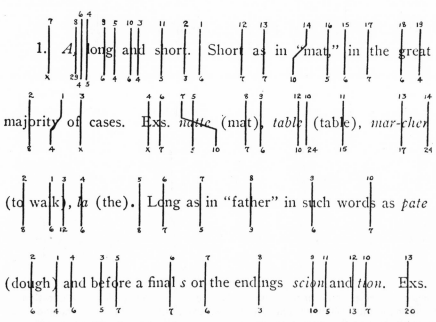

Figure 6:8. The fixations of a student studying a grammar. Note the irregularity of sequence and, as in figure 6:7, the variability of distance between fixations.

might reveal—indeed, *b* might acquire the very information sought. Though everyday experience assures us that conscious experience and conscious awareness of difficulty play some role in guiding fixations, the necessary time lag and consequent inefficiency argue that for the most part preconscious and automatic processes are the principal governors. It is not yet clear how to accommodate this implication in a more explicit theory.

The second implication of regressive eye motions is that if conscious experience accurately mirrored the input to the visual system, the conscious experience of text would be a word salad, a relatively incoherent, grammatically anomalous sequence of word fragments. This fact is brought out graphically in a third figure from Judd and Buswell (figure 6:9). They decided, somewhat arbitrarily, that the extent of a visual fixation was ten letter spaces and, on introspective grounds, that "one sees more clearly the letters at the right of a fixation than the letters at the left";[19] hence four letters to the left and six to the right of a fixation were taken as the span of visual input at a single fixation. Using these conventions, they illustrate in figure 6:9 the sequence of eye movements and the corresponding input of visual information for a subject "studying" a sentence with the requirement to paraphrase it. No matter how the successive fixations are calculated, however, a mixture of linguistically coherent and incoherent segments must assault the student's mind.

The reader's ability to achieve a coherent message from these radically incoherent samples must lay to rest any notion that reading proceeds as the result of simple linear scanning of a text. Sometimes reading may go forward in that way, but it need not, and the many instances in which it does not refute the allegation that it needs to. Many aspects of stimulus selection, editing, and supplementation intervene between what is on the retina and the text that is perceived. Moreover, the earlier finding of the difficulty of perceiving two different words simultaneously (figures 2 and 3) and the considerations regarding the timing of eye movements imply a further conclusion: while conscious testing of hypotheses and guesses about content may on occasion provide the signal for the eye's motions,[20] this is not a customary outcome.

The data of Judd and Buswell were obtained primarily from youngsters aged about twelve or thirteen years, skilled but not perfect readers. A curious fact about reading is that the frequency of regressive motions declines with skill. Taylor, on examining the records of about 5,000 readers, found that about 23 percent of the fixations of youngsters in the first grade were regressive and that this frequency fell off with skill; but the slope of the curve relating frequency of fixations to age was quite mild, for as many as 15 percent of college students' fixations were also regressive.[21] The small difference between 23 percent and 15 percent is hardly enough to explain the difference in overall level of reading performance in youngsters

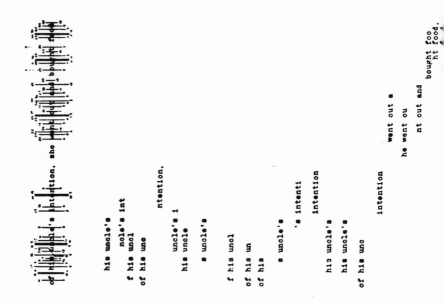

Figure 6:9. Part of sentence being studied in order to be paraphrased is shown at the top of the figure. The extent of each fixation, in units 10 letterspaces wide, is shown in successive rows.

out and b

ut and bou

went cut a

nd bought

ught food

's intenti

his uncle'

e went out

she went o

t out and b

out and bo

out and and

ent out and

ut and bou

e went out

out and b

bought foo
food

ought food

t food

food

bought foo

and bough

t and boug

bought fo

t food.

and adults. The numbers do suggest, however, that the linguistic characteristics of the text perceived by younger readers are even more perturbed than those received by older readers. To put it another way, the younger reader may have a more difficult job of unscrambling the linguistically disordered input, for his eyes present him with a still more scrambled message than the eyes of the more skilled reader present to him. But everyone gets disordered inputs, both from text and from pictures.

9. Reading pictures

Buswell, in a pioneering work, recorded eye motions not only when people read but also when they looked at pictures. His work challenged the common belief that pictures are seen whole and that only text is sampled, for it showed that pictures too are seen by means of a series of scanning, information-selecting movements of the eyes. For example, he displayed a photograph of Hokusai's *The Wave* (figure 6:10) to a number of subjects and recorded the sequence of fixations of their eyes while they looked at it.[22]

All of these fixations are shown superimposed on a low-contrast copy of the print (figure 6:11). There one may note that fixations are not distributed homogeneously across the whole picture, for some regions received none while other regions received many. This bias in fixations is brought out more clearly in a figure which illustrates the first three fixations made by forty different subjects (figure 6:12) while they examined the picture. Two additional features are noteworthy. One is the concentration of fixations upon a particular region of the picture—a region showing the greatest perturbation or irregularity of contour; the other is the wide variation in the sequence of looks made by different people. The observers' looks reveal great agreement on *what* is to be looked at but great individuality in the sequence of looks or manner of looking. This variability is even more marked in the sequences of the last few looks, made after some seconds of observing (figure 6:13). The subjects clearly read the picture in very different ways. What stands as a challenge to theory here is the manner by which so many different input sequences eventuate in a more or less common perception, for clearly the forty different people would have shown wide areas of agreement in describing what they saw.

This great variability in the sequence of looks can be also found in the reading of text, especially as it is carried out by more skilled readers. Judd and Buswell discuss the variability among youngsters,[23] and Taylor, in assessing the data from rapid readers, points out that regularity of input sequence cannot be found either in the way a single reader reads a number of pages or in the way different readers read the same page.[24] The input sequences therefore are highly variable, and yet the readers and lookers seem to agree quite well when they describe what they have seen or read. One example of the very marked variability found in the performance of a rapid reader is supplied in a paper by Llewellyn Thomas. His subject was the dean of a college, whose eyes he photographed while she read a popular book on science. He questioned her about the content of the book and received, he says, satisfactory answers, and she reported that she read the book as she normally would read. Llewellyn Thomas found that her eye movements across many pages followed a more or less counterclockwise pattern (figure 6:14), beginning at the top of the left-hand page and proceeding down it about two-thirds of the way, across, and up the right-hand page. The frequency and duration of her fixations were within normal range, but their nonnormal sequence illuminates markedly how far removed from a serial scanning of text may be rapid reading by the exceptionally skilled reader.[25]

10. Reading for comprehension

Although both convey messages, text and pictures differ in an important respect: text adheres to the formal syntactic regularities of language while pictures lack formal syntax.[26] The fact that text preserves linguistic syntax has been used by some to support the notion that reading, like listening, must proceed serially. What has been shown by studies of highly skilled readers is, to the contrary, that the skilled reading of text need not preserve, in the input that the eyes deliver, the syntax of the message on the page. Hence in this respect the reading of text and of pictures share an important characteristic: they can proceed without immediate regard to syntax but do have regard for the semantic or interpretable component. That is, people interpret or understand what they have looked at or read, but their means of achieving this interpretation or understanding can follow idiosyncratic or personal rather than formal rules. What it comes down to is that in reading and looking, people use many different inspection strategies, have many different options available, to achieve approximately the same end—an interpretation or comprehension of the object being examined. How similar or how different these understandings can be we know both from analysis[27] and from our own many experiences of misreading, misunderstanding, and misinterpretation, observed in our students, our colleagues, and ourselves.

None of this is to say that the order of words on a page or pages in a book has no relevance to reading. Textual material usually develops, to some extent; earlier material lays the groundwork for the comprehension of later material. Nor is attaining certain target information the sole purpose of reading; one reads the middle of a mystery novel, or a long poem, not simply to find out its outcome (a matter efficiently disclosed by a glance at the last

Figure 6:10. Hokusai's *The Wave* was presented in color and the locus of eye fixations made while examining it was recorded, as in figures 6:11–6:13. All four figures are from G. T. Buswell, *How People Look at Pictures* (Chicago: University of Chicago Press, 1935).

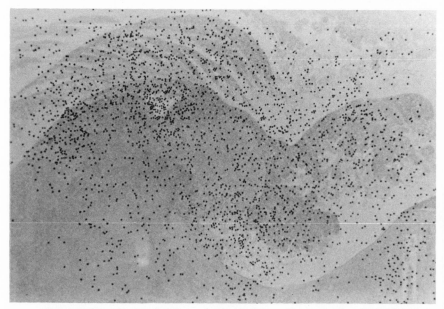

Figure 6:11. All the fixations made during a few seconds of viewing by a number of people are shown as black dots on this low-contrast copy of *The Wave.*

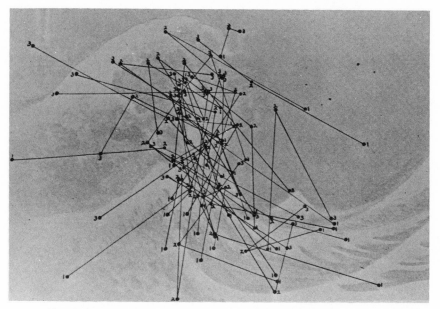

Figure 6:12. The first three fixations and the paths that connect them.

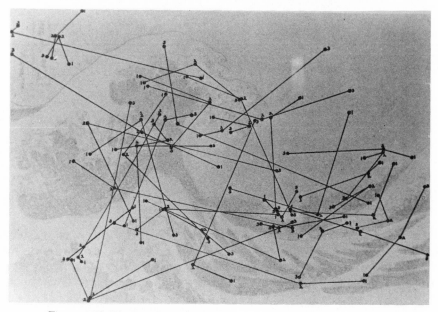

Figure 6:13. The last three fixations.

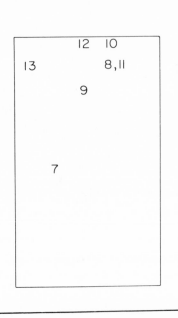

Figure 6:14. The sequence of fixations made by a very rapid reader while reading two pages of a book. This is only one of many patterns made by the reader, although all tended to follow a roughly counterclockwise direction. Adapted from E. Llewellyn Thomas, "Eye Movements in Speed Reading," in *Speed Reading: Practices and Procedures*, ed. R. G. Stauffer (Newark: University of Delaware, 1962), 10:104–14.

page) but rather to enjoy the experience of the unfolding. Nevertheless the central point remains. As skill develops, patterns of reading become more and more shaped by the informational and experiential goals of the reader and less and less constrained by conventional sequencing.

A fuller description of these facts must wait on the development of more adequate means of testing comprehension than are now available. Although there are many so-called tests of reading performance and comprehension, they are almost without exception imperfect tools. Indeed, I have taken many of them myself and have usually scored about 60 to 70 percent correct but without having read the passages on which the tests were based! A testing instrument that supplies that much information to the person tested clearly is not optimal; and the fact is that little is known concerning how best to test comprehension—or even how to define it—ex-except in a loose, intuitive way. This lack of a suitable testing instrument clearly limits the ability to study comprehension as a process and thereby to

identify its important constituents and their interplay. Such technical limitations allow at present only some plausible inferences regarding the
processing of pictures and text.

11. Analysis of reading errors

Again, a close look at reading offers some insight. One notion is that
the skilled reader creates an interpretation of text based on samples he
obtains from the physical array.[28] This sampling is usually directed more
toward the grammatical and interpretative aspects of words than toward
their physical representation as graphemes in a certain typeface that preserve
certain orthographic features of the language. This bias toward the linguistic
aspect of the textual material is shown by still other experiments in which
college students were required to read aloud, without regard to meaning or
interpretation and as rapidly as they could, English text that had been
transformed geometrically in various ways (figure 6:15). The transformations preserved all of the linguistic characteristics of English but rendered
unfamiliar its actual appearance on the page. In reading this material aloud,
students made a large number of errors, some of which they corrected. These
errors were examined for their linguistic appropriateness.

The analysis was done in two ways. The most common error was to
substitute another English word for the word that was printed. Suppose the
student was reading the preceding sentence and said, "The most common
error met. . . ." Here the substitution of *met* for *was* preserves the linguistic
coherence of the sentence up to the point at which the error was made but
clearly is inappropriate with respect to the whole sentence. Moreover, the
error could be corrected or not, and the word substituted for the printed
word could be one that "looks like" it or not. The upper left quadrant of
table 6:3 shows the percentage of errors that were corrected even when the
substituted word looked like the misread word. Eighty-eight percent of these
errors were syntactically and semantically acceptable at the place they were
made; that is, they were plausible readings of the text up to that point.
However, only 19 percent of them were acceptable with respect to the whole
clause, including the remainder of the sentence, and 60 percent were both
syntactically and semantically unsuitable with respect to the remainder of
the sentence.

This sort of analysis was carried through for other errors that were not
corrected and for both corrected and uncorrected errors that did not "look
like" the printed word. The findings were that about the same percentage
were acceptable in the place they occurred even when they were not
corrected (89 percent compared with 88 percent) but that among those that

N
*Expectations can also mislead us; the unexpected is always hard to
perceive clearly. Sometimes we fail to recognize an object because we

R
*Emerson once said that every man is as lazy as he dares to be. It was the
kind of mistake a New England Puritan might be expected to make. It is

I
*These are but a few of the reasons for believing that a person cannot
be conscious of all his mental processes. Many other reasons can be

M
*Several years ago a professor who teaches psychology at a large
university had to ask his assistant, a young man of great intelligence

r N
*On his first day in topsy-turvy land he was thoroughly disoriented.
His feet were above his head; he had to careen for his feet when he

r R
*A very young swab of decayed beef as it an object was merely a
visual image that serves and leaves the larb of Lew abstractly,

r I
*psychology became an experimental ecoenics during the during seades of
the nineteenth century, at a time when thought was detained by

r M
*Imagine two different pictures. One shows a bright red circle on a pale
yellow background, the other a bright green circle on a gray background.

Figure 6:15. Eight samples of text that have been altered geometrically. The asterisk shows for each pair of lines where to begin reading. On each of eight days, subjects read one page of each of the eight kinds of text.

were not corrected, 61 percent were acceptable with respect to the whole sentence and only 23 percent were nonsense. Analogous results were obtained among the "visually dissimilar" errors. The fact that 23 percent of inappropriate errors were not corrected speaks to the variability of acceptance criteria among readers. In some cases these college students were prepared to utter gibberish and still pretend that they had mastered the text.

The main finding, however, was that linguistic regularities, especially the syntax of the sentence, acted as a strong cue to the reader that he had misread a word. In this sense he was more sensitive to the syntax of the words he was reading than to their appearance on the page as graphemes or spelling patterns. In sampling text, therefore, the reader may, but need not,

Table 6:3   Grammatical Analysis of Errors (Percent)

| | *Visually Similar* | | | | | | |
| | *Corrected* | | | | *Uncorrected* | | |
	Antecedent Syn+	*Words* Syn–	*Whole* Syn+	*Clause* Syn–	*Antecedent* Syn+	*Words* Syn–	*Whole* Syn+	*Clause* Syn–
Sem +	88	1	19	1	89	4	61	2
Sem –	9	2	20	60	8	2	14	23
	Visually Dissimilar							
Sem +	98	2	48	5	100	0	89	0
Sem –	0	0	8	40	0	0	3	9

preserve the order of words on the page; he may, but need not, follow its orthographic or even its syntactic regularities; he may, but need not, note the typeface, color of the paper, size of the page, and the like. Indeed, counting the number of letters in the words misread and the number of letters in the words substituted for them revealed an impressive correspondence (figure 6:16). Of course it is implausible that in misreading a word the reader actually counted the letters in the text and in his substitution; rather, in substituting a word for what was read he "selected" from the words he knew a word that was similar to the original in many ways, one of them being linguistic appropriateness and another being length. To put it another way, the reader is sensitive to many features of the array that he is reading, sampling the array and constructing a representation of it in his own mind. This constructive act need not proceed serially, the eyes and the mind faithfully mirroring the text; rather, the inputs are highly variable and can be remarkably free from sequential constraints.[29]

12. Speed looking

This theme finds notable parallels in the reading of pictures. In an earlier section the variability that characterizes the movements of their eyes when people read rapidly was discussed and compared with the variability of eye movements in looking at pictures. It is not the eye movements themselves that are of the greatest importance, however; they are only performing a logistical task in getting the eye to where it needs to go in order to see what it needs to know. The fact that it is sequences of semantic information that are important is illustrated with films made a few years ago for the Smothers Brothers show by the talented film maker Charles

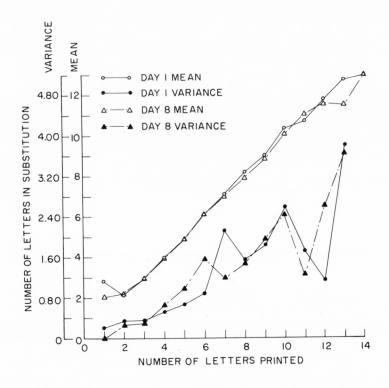

Figure 6:16. A frequent error in misreading the transformed texts illustrated in figure 6:15 was to substitute another English word for what was printed. The length of the substituted word matched the length of the printed word quite well. It is assumed that subjects did not count letters while reading, but syntax and word length were nevertheless important features of their substitutions.

Braverman. In these films, semantically or thematically related pictures are flashed in rapid sequence. In one film the pictures illustrated part of the history of the United States, in another some world events of 1968. If the viewer has some background in the subject matter, the films are remarkably evocative; lacking the background, the looker sees only a quick jumble of pictorial displays, some of whose features stand out sharply. The analogy to reading text on matters that are familiar or unfamiliar is quite marked. In both cases, knowledge or stored information is used to order and interpret the aspects of a complex stimulus sequence sampled over time. What makes the similarity especially interesting is that text is linguistic and pictures are not,[30] yet the mechanisms of reading the two share many characteristics. A detailed examination of how people read and interpret pictures—objects rich in semantic but deficient in orthographic and syntactic regularities—may, paradoxically, increase our understanding of how they read text.[31]

Notes

1. Nelson Goodman, *Languages of Art: An Approach to a Theory of Symbols* (Indianapolis and New York: Bobbs-Merrill, 1968).

2. Edmund B. Huey, *The Psychology and Pedagogy of Reading* (New York: Macmillan, 1908; reprinted Cambridge, Mass.: MIT Press, 1968).

3. J. Robert Oppenheimer, "Analogy in Science," *American Psychologist* 11 (1956): 127–35.

4. George A. Miller, *Psychology: The Science of Mental Life* (New York: Harper & Row, 1962), p. 345.

5. Huey, *Psychology of Reading*, p. 6.

6. Émile Javal, eight articles in *Annales d'oculistique* for 1878 and 1879.

7. Frances C. Volkmann, Amy M. L. Schick, and Lorrin A. Riggs, "Time Course of Visual Inhibition During Voluntary Saccades," *Journal of the Optical Society of America* 58 (1968): 562–69. A review of some of the issues appears in Ethel Matin, "Saccadic Suppression: A Review and an Analysis," *Psychological Bulletin*, 81 (1974): 899–917.

8. Paul A. Kolers and Martin T. Katzman, "Naming Sequentially Presented Letters and Words," *Language and Speech* 9 (1966): 84–95.

9. Miles A. Tinker, "Recent Studies of Eye Movements in Reading," *Psychological Bulletin* 55 (1958): 215–31.

10. Paul A. Kolers and Clayton L. Lewis, "Bounding of Letter Sequences and the Integration of Visually Presented Words," *Acta Psychologica* 36 (1972): 112–24.

11. Kolers and Katzman, "Naming Sequentially Presented Letters and Words."

12. Kolers and Lewis, "Bounding of Sequences."

13. Huey, *Psychology of Reading*.

14. Ian P. Howard and William B. Templeton, *Human Spatial Orientation* (New York: John Wiley & Sons, 1966).

15. William Epstein, "A Further Study of the Influence of Syntactical Structure on Learning," *American Journal of Psychology* 75 (1962): 121–26; Daniel C. O'Connell, "Facilitation of Recall by Linguistic Structure in Nonsense Strings," *Psychological Bulletin* 74 (1970): 441–52.

16. Paul A. Kolers and David N. Perkins, "Orientation of Letters and Errors in Their Recognition," *Perception & Psychophysics* 5 (1969): 265–69.

17. Charles H. Judd and Guy T. Buswell, "Silent Reading: A Study of the Various Types," *Supplementary Educational Monographs* 23 (1922).

18. David H. Rabb, "Backward Masking," *Psychological Bulletin* 60 (1963): 118–29; Lester A. Lefton, "Metacontrast: A Review," *Perception & Psychophysics* 13, no. 1B (1973): 161–71.

19. Judd and Buswell, "Silent Reading," p. 55.

20. Julian Hochberg, "Components of Literacy: Speculations and Exploratory Research," in *Basic Studies on Reading*, ed. H. Levin and J. Williams (New York: Basic Books, 1970); Kenneth Goodman, "Reading: A Psycholinguistic Guessing Game," in *Theoretical Models and Processes of Reading*, ed. Harry Singer and Robert B. Ruddell (Newark, Del.: International Reading Association, 1970).

21. Earl A. Taylor, "The Spans: Perception, Apprehension, and Recognition," *American Journal of Ophthalmology* 44 (1957): 501–7.

22. Guy T. Buswell, *How People Look at Pictures* (Chicago: University of Chicago Press, 1935).

23. Judd and Buswell, "Silent Reading."

24. Taylor, "The Spans."

25. Edward Llewellyn Thomas, "Eye Movements in Speed Reading," in *Speed Reading: Practices and Procedures*, ed. Russell G. Staufer (Newark: University of Delaware, 1962), 10: 104–14.

26. Goodman, *Languages of Art.*

27. Willard V. Quine, *Word and Object* (Cambridge, Mass.: MIT Press, 1960).

28. Paul A. Kolers, "Three Stages of Reading," in *Basic Studies on Reading*, ed. H. Levin and J. Williams (New York: Basic Books, 1970).

29. Some additional details regarding the role of superficial features of text in their interpretation can be found in Paul A. Kolers, "Memorial Consequences of Automatized Encoding," *Journal of Experimental Psychology: Human Learning and Memory* 1 (1975): 689–701.

30. Goodman, *Languages of Art.*

31. This paper is based on an invited address presented to the 1971 meeting of the Canadian Psychological Association. Preparation of this paper was aided in part by a grant from the National Research Council of Canada (Grant A7655) and in part by a grant from the Ontario Mental Health Foundation (OMHF 382).

THREE Symbolic Growth:
Apprenticing in Craftsmanship
and Fluency

"For a poet is a light and winged thing, and holy, and never able to compose until he has become inspired, and is beside himself, and reason is no longer in him." In these words Socrates both acknowledges the power of the artist and simultaneously dismisses him as an intellectual hummingbird. The artist possesses neither wisdom nor skill; rather he is a creature possessed, a vessel into whom the gods from time to time breathe intoxicating truth. The great teacher, who thought so penetratingly about education, never inquired whether those whom the gods chose had perhaps prepared themselves to be chosen.

As an explanation of artistic prowess, inspiration explains nothing. It merely provides a name for processes as yet unanalyzed. Its counterpart, the notion of genius, locates the fountainhead of invention within, rather than external to, the artist. But except for this detail, flowering-of-genius theories prove to be no more than Socratic intoxication *réchauffé* and equally insufficient as explanation. At the same time the inverse of these views, the "perspiration" theory, explains too much. Sheer persistence, however relentless and compelling, never yet contrived a Ninth Symphony, a *King Lear*, or a *Pietà*.

These two models of aesthetic development, as Vernon Howard laments in "Artistic Practice and Skills" below, dominate popular attitudes. Dubbing them the Athena and Penelope fallacies, Howard assesses in rigorous detail the flaws of the latter. His treatment is a trenchant warning against oversimple notions about the genesis of aesthetic or any other abilities. The barest examination discloses a world of complexity lying behind any substantial achievement, and events on vastly different time scales demand consideration. Practice, the focus of Howard's treatment, aspires to relatively limited objectives over relatively short time spans. But the acquisition of aesthetic competence may also be viewed from the longest of perspectives. As Barbara Leondar reminds us in "Hatching Plots," every mature artist was once an impotent babe. The course of events which transforms infantile ineptitude into symbolic fluency and mature craftsmanship remains virtually unknown.

Detailed treatment of some long-term and short-term developmental processes is the province of the individual offerings in this section. But here several general points should be mentioned, points which both find examples in and set the stage for the articles to follow. The first matter demanding attention is the persistently active and constructive nature of learning or development even at its most superficially mundane. Vernon Howard's essay speaks to this. He argues that, insofar as exercises are directed toward some end, they cannot be mere mechanical repetition but necessarily summon forth an active, attentive, and critical striving. Indeed, practice must in some circumstances be closely allied to interpretation and may thus precipitate a conceptual restructuring of an entire performance.

Although song provides his illustrations, readers familiar with other arts will surely recognize significant parallels. Howard's article demonstrates, moreover, how the method of conceptual analysis can serve aesthetic psychology by challenging habitual assumptions and opening new problems to empirical investigation.

If mastery is achieved by constructive action, the tracing of that action illuminates the nature of mastery itself. To map a developmental sequence is to identify the critical events en route to a specified endpoint through which a representative individual (within a range of "normal" deviation) will progress. Clearly, what counts as a critical event can only be ascertained with reference to the specified endpoint. But it is less frequently recognized that the endpoint itself—the achieved mastery toward which development thrusts—becomes better understood in light of preceding events. The complex orchestration of sets of subordinate skills required for mature comprehension of a novel or for polished performance of a sonata will be revealed in progressively finer detail as more is learned about the primitive components and their interrelations.

Exploration can begin at any point along the developmental chain and can proceed in either direction. But wherever one enters he finds capacities and convictions already established. The child or adult learner never presents a blank slate. He has a set of beliefs, however naive, and a set of strategies, however inept, for deploying his knowledge toward the accomplishment of a task. Developmental progression thus is never merely additive; it requires displacement of the old in favor of the new, a principle which Diana Korzenik's essay, "Saying it with Pictures," illustrates with some force. The children whose attempts at pictorial communication she observed supplemented their drawings with verbal or gestural explanation. Isolated from these nonpictorial adjuncts, the drawings proved unintelligible. Before the children could produce comprehensible pictures they had to supplant word and gesture with pictorial detail, and this in turn necessitated a psychological decentering, a partial displacement of the participant's perspective by the observer's. The old was ejected, the new installed.

In this observation are united three clusters of issues central to the study of long-range aesthetic development: those concerned with the natural maturation of aesthetic capacities, those concerned with the relation between such capacities and other maturational advances, and those concerned with intervention in the maturational process—that is, with learning and teaching.

The maturational psychology of Jean Piaget, which informs both Korzenik's and Leondar's essays, provides the researcher interested in aesthetic growth with a useful jumping-off point. He can ask whether the processing of symbol systems will advance by stages; whether periods of relative stability during which earlier gains are consolidated and extended to new applications will be interrupted by abrupt and dramatic cognitive leaps. He will not be surprised to find in aesthetic just as in mathematical or moral reasoning the sudden displacement of one concept or mode of performance, long established and resistant to change, by another more fruitful and versatile one. Sometimes transitional phenomena will signal such an impending transformation (as in the harbingers of emergent plot organization recounted by Leondar); more often, promising discontinuities in the conceptualization of nonaesthetic symbols will presage the onset of artistic restructuring as well.

Working within this framework, the investigator needs to nurture a wariness regarding the casual use and abuse of the concept of stages of development. This term is employed in different ways to mean different things, all too often without awareness of the contrasts. Stages may represent an arbitrary dissection of a continuum into subjectively comfortable steps, a series of paradigmatic behaviors where one ebbs as the next flows to its fullness, or—most authentically—a sequence of developmental plateaus with abrupt jumps in between. None of these meanings need be excluded, but specifying which is meant is crucial. Further, evidence for one or another kind of stage may prove evasive. For example, natural variance in a population may smooth what are sharp jumps in individual performance, and abrupt shifts in the logic by which a task is handled may yield only gradual improvement in task performance as the new strategy becomes entrenched and facile.

Thus sequences which on the surface do not appear to advance stepwise may do so underneath. This point applies to short-term learning as well; as Howard notes, even the learning of motor tasks may involve plateauing with abrupt advances in between. But where problems of measurement and analysis may conceal stepwise development, human enthusiasm for the neatness of a stepwise scheme often ranges ahead of prudence. Many developmental advances, sometimes construed as all-at-once events, in fact spread over long periods. Thus Korzenik points out that though some problems of egocentricity need to be resolved for the child to make his pictures meaningful to others, the general problem of egocentricity constantly reappears in new guises to confound, in particular, the art of the mature practitioner.

Other variables also demand attention. A developmental sequence may be linked to physical maturity or not—as, in Leondar's analysis of the mastery of story production, some children achieve the primary story much earlier than the characteristic five or six years. Likewise, sequences may or may not permit stages to be skipped. And further, sequences may require all the behavior of an individual to fall within a given stage, or they may allow the individual's behavior to sprawl backward and forward provided it centers in one stage. Finally, stepwise progression may come about for very different reasons in different contexts, reflecting the switching on of "wired-in" stages, the sudden surrender of one stubbornly entrenched conceptual framework to another, the need for consolidating a body of strategies before proceeding to build upon them, the acquisition of key skills superficially unrelated to the performances under study, a spurt of energy and effort on the part of the learner, and other changes.

These complexities guarantee that close but passive observation is the investigator's *least* impressive tool. The primary difficulty in describing developmental stages lies in determining the very units of development, in identifying the perceptual and conceptual structures by means of which the child renders his world intelligible. When, for example, a child understands a story, what is it that he understands? An accidental concatenation of events? An orderly progression? A causally linked sequence? When he looks at a picture, does he see a patchwork of shapes? An ordered arrangement? A logically related array of shape and color? Much of this primitive terrain has already been mapped in the development of scientific and mathematical reasoning, but in aesthetic maturation virtually everything remains to be explored.

Leondar's essay, which scouts this unknown continent, underscores another developmental trend that demands recognition. Her material on children's story production reminds us how far production lags behind comprehension. This is so in adults as much as in children. The child understands sentences he could not have invented; the adult recognizes Rembrandts he will never be able to paint. Thus, at whatever age, production tasks provide a less-than-satisfactory index of powers of comprehension and discrimination. Only recently has this point been recognized in the study of children's drawings, where for years what a child could draw was taken as a measure of what he understood about the shape of things in the world. Research methods need to be found which will tap discriminative skills, especially in the very young, where they are most difficult to assess.

These problems concerning the natural maturation of abilities constitute one major cluster of aesthetic-developmental issues awaiting investigation. A second cluster consists of issues concerning the interplay between aesthetic and other aspects of growth. Again, Korzenik's essay illustrates the sort of answer which a well-honed question can elicit. She found that the ability to decontextualize a pictorial communication depends upon a prior diminishing of egocentricity. Such a causal chain has come to be recognized as a commonplace element of growth, though the relevant aesthetic links must still be identified. Some of these links may emerge from a careful reading of the literature on other aspects of development. Piaget, for example, has reconstructed the cognitive chain which leads through mastery of complex mathematical concepts to a comprehension of temporal ordering. Such a reconstruction can be immensely suggestive, since temporal order must surely be implicated in the perception of rhythm, the recounting of narrative, the performance of dance, and a multitude of related aesthetic events. These seemingly effortless and spontaneous forms of childhood expression apparently arise only on a foundation of profound intellectual achievement. Investigation of the full spectrum of maturational prerequisites to aesthetic competence must, in light of this evidence, stand high on the research agenda.

Such investigation seems, moreover, a desirable and perhaps necessary antecedent to exploration of the third cluster of issues, those concerning intervention in the developmental sequence. In Korzenik's study, children aged seven or older found the task too simple to be interesting; those children had already decentered sufficiently to communicate with ease, and had done so without benefit of instruction. Indeed, instruction might well have proved futile. Often enough the tasks which an older child masters easily the younger one finds not only impossible but unintelligible. It is not simply that the younger child lacks know-how but rather that he cannot comprehend what is being asked of him. In these circumstances even the most ingenious intervention will be wasted; the child cannot exceed his developmental limit. Again in the shorter-term learning examined by Howard, steps build on other steps, and premature attention to advanced techniques is pointless.

Yet how to distinguish developmental incapacity from learning failure is by no means obvious. The child who grows up in a musical family may exhibit a lively musical sophistication at an early age and the child of a painter an alert visual intelligence. To discern in the texture of such performances the separate threads of imitation, instruction, and maturation (not to mention motive and reward) will require far more detailed knowledge than is now available. Still, conceding Nature her due and granting a lucky environment (although the meaning of "lucky" in this context remains obscure), some explicit instruction in skills of comprehension and production seem to be required for optimal aesthetic growth.

Perhaps the example of reading—the prototypical symbolic skill—can provide a suggestive parallel. Children who read before entering school are sometimes thought to have "taught themselves" or to have acquired the skill "spontaneously." Inquiry often reveals, however, the guidance of an older sibling or companion whose teaching wore the guise of play. It would not be unreasonable to hypothesize that similarly concealed instruction, coupled with much extemporaneous practice, underlies early aesthetic virtuosity. Likewise, aesthetic deprivation may signal the absence of appropriate instruction at critical moments in the developmental sequence. None of this is to say that Mozarts can be manufactured by suitable early encouragement but simply that even a major gift cannot reinvent the accumulated lore of an art form and needs exposure and exercise.

These pages, then, sketch a monumental task. Mature artistic achievement appears as the fortunate culmination of complex but by no means unfathomable processes. The three essays here can treat only a few aspects of these processes, tracing how children develop narrative competence, mapping the achievement of pictures at least minimally meaningful to others, and rectifying some careless notions concerning practice. Whatever the enterprise that remains to be accomplished, these offerings most forcefully suggest that the Muse can be summoned only when her temple has been made ready.

7

Hatching Plots:
Genesis of Storymaking
Barbara Leondar

Once there was a tiny babe, unremarkable in every way. Yet as Chance would have it, the Muses smiled upon him, and he became a master storymaker, a fabricator of extravaganzas so dazzling but at the same time so pulsatingly real that they "holdeth children from play and old men from the chimney corner." The infant was named Charles Dickens (or perhaps Honoré de Balzac, or even Fyodor Mikhailovich Dostoevsky) and for a long time he could not even speak a word. . . .

The preceding passage renders the trappings of fiction transparent. Its opening words announce to every reader the onset of an invented tale; soon thereafter the promise of a happy ending, following upon the benign intervention of fortune, echoes this announcement and at the same time establishes a set of expectations about what is to follow. Even the most pedestrian imagination could now take up the thread of the tale, spin it out for a paragraph or two, and wind it down to a satisfying conclusion. The more gifted, or the more verbose, might embroider for twenty pages, and a Proust might make a novel of it. A mere three sentences have sufficed to erect the scaffolding of an entire text.

Such economy is not the result of authorial magic. The author, in fact, is innocent; rather it is the reader who, in the ordinary exercise of a mature literary intelligence, acts upon familiar textual clues and extrapolates from them to a fully formed narrative in much the same way as the eye completes a partial circle. The literate reader, as Dewey has convincingly demonstrated, is never passive.[1] Prediction and anticipation guide his pursuit as he constructs anew the imagined world of the story. The judgments at which he arrives—that a plot succeeds, that a character is consistent, that an ending satisfies or surprises—can issue only from an active reconstruction. How such literacy develops is the concern of this essay.

That concern shows another aspect as well, one hinted at in the tale itself. The tale's final sentence frames an issue around which the story's subsequent episodes must pivot: how will the lucky—but, alas, speechless —babe come at last to be a master storymaker? In the emergence of literary craftsmanship this study finds another focus. But if Dewey's assessment of the reader's participatory role is a fair one, comprehension and craftsmanship entail similar skills. The constructive powers of the author and the reconstructive ones of the reader may be assumed to spring from a common source. On both counts, then, the development of narrative competence in early childhood invites examination.

1. Methodological hazards

Such an investigation can begin with only the most fragmentary and informal lore about children's narrative skills. For example, at an early age children appear to distinguish clearly between narratives and other forms of prose. Offered a laundry list, an advertisement, or a stock market report in lieu of a bedtime story, even the tiniest toddler will demur. But nothing is known about the criteria which provoke his rejection. What distinctions is he making? What properties has he detected and what found lacking? What features define the notion of a story as he applies it? These and similar questions demand resolution almost before systematic investigation can begin.

Because the questions themselves are indeterminate and imprecise, they invite a correspondingly open-ended mode of inquiry. Analysis of children's stories, spontaneously produced, would seem to offer a promising attack, since their salient features could be permitted to emerge from the stories themselves. But this tactic at once muddies the valuable distinction between competence and performance. Competence, in its most common usage, encompasses the entire repertoire of knowledge, skills, and strategies ideally available to a subject, whereas performance represents an extemporaneous activation of only some of those abilities, selected and combined in response to the demands of a specific occasion. En route to realization in a particular performance, underlying competence will necessarily encounter a variety of restrictions, some invariant (as when short-term memory imposes upon the length of an utterance) and some accidental (as when irrelevant happenings distract attention). Almost inevitably, then, a single performance can be counted on to marshal a skewed sample of available skills.

Thus performance provides at best an imperfect measure of competence, and that will certainly hold true for storymaking. Children, it may be assumed, know more about narrative structure than their stories display. But without the information extracted from these stories—without, that is, some preliminary assessment of the structures which children can command at the level of performance—further investigation would be stymied. At the risk of circularity, then, the analyses which follow are offered as a rough but nonetheless utilitarian gauge of emerging narrative competence in the expectation that their logical impurities can be purged by future studies.

A more substantial hazard concerns the very definition of competence in the present setting. Developmental studies commonly imply a *terminus ad quem*, a mature ideal toward which growth proceeds. Such a prototype defines the nature of competence in its adult form and thus provides a standard against which maturational advances can be measured. Much of Piaget's work, for example, assumes as a prototype the operations of the mature mathematical or scientific intellect. The sorts of skills such a mind possesses and the sorts of operations it commands can be formally described by the logical calculus, by analyses of inductive and deductive reasoning, and by the conventions of scientific method. In these well-established descriptions Piaget's studies found both support and guidance. Similarly, fruitful investigations of language acquisition waited on the appearance of acceptable accounts of mature linguistic competence and have flourished as those accounts have expanded in breadth and detail. Empirical prejudice to the contrary, such teleological assumptions provide a valuable and perhaps vital support for developmental research.

To reveal the uses of the adult prototype, however, is to admit an embarrassment into the study of literary growth. The cognitive skills entailed in an appreciation of literature and, even more, in its production remain a puzzle. Although everyone can tell a story and all can understand one, no adequate account exists of the modes of reasoning, the types of discriminations, the styles of planning, and the structures of perception and memory which must underlie these achievements. The study of literary competence has scarcely begun. To attempt to explain how children acquire such competence when the thing to be acquired cannot be described is surely risky and probably premature.

Still, a newly burgeoning literature on the structure of narrative suggests both a possible point of departure and a direction. These recent studies have sought to enumerate the elements common to all narrative literature and the principles governing their combination and recombination. More exactly, they have aimed at a grammar of fictional narration.[2] Regrettably, these accounts have not advanced cumulatively. The result is a gaggle of competing theories, all suggestive and sometimes brilliantly illuminating but none as yet sufficiently elaborated to stand alone. Nonetheless, substantial overlaps occur, and from these an outline of story structure has hesitantly begun to emerge.

The possibility of such a grammar of fiction arrives as an alien and sometimes unwelcome intruder in the domain traditionally occupied by literary scholarship. Although the conception is as old as Aristotle, its current manifestations descend less directly from classical aesthetics than from contemporary linguistics. From this source derives the most fundamental tenet of narrative grammarians, the conviction that literature, like language, is a system, an orderly arrangement of abstract elements governed by combinatorial laws. These rules, like those of language, determine coherence and intelligibility. Hence ignorance of the literary code condemns the reader to illiteracy; he will find its texts as opaque as the sentences of an unfamiliar tongue. To understand a story is to perceive its ordered structure, and to compose a story is to set into rule-governed motion a selected set of abstract elements. Although this theory has sometimes been accused of denigrating originality or devaluing imagination, neither accusation is just. A system of rules never dictates individual moves but merely delimits the range of options. Thus language speakers, chess players, baseball pitchers, and symphonic composers, all of whom are guided, like readers and writers, by complex codes, may still be honored for inventiveness and craft.

A possible grammar of narrative, then, will represent not only the structure of stories but also some portion of the tacit knowledge—the competence—which author and audience deploy in the acts of making and understanding literature. Just as a grammar of English provides a formal account of a prototypical speaker's linguistic competence, so a narrative grammar, insofar as it captures accurately the underlying organization of fiction, will provide a similarly abstract account of ideal literary competence. The beginnings of such a grammar, still admittedly primitive, permit at least some tentative observations of the manner and degree to which children's conceptions of fiction approach the mature paradigm.

2. Narrative theory new and old

Before proceeding to the stories themselves, a review of the elements of fiction as construed in narrative theory can provide a preliminary guide. Contemporary narratologists, although claiming descent from Saussure[3] and Propp,[4] share a conviction first advanced by Aristotle: that the "fable" or plot is the governing element of narrative.[5] Although Todorov, for example, conceives of a literary grammar as requiring three interrelated systems (a semantics, concerned with content; a syntax, concerned with structural elements and their organization; and a rhetoric, concerned with diction and style), his major efforts have addressed the second of these, the analysis of plot.[6] Plot must, of course, be distinguished from the experience or the history which provides its raw materials. Plot prunes experience of its irrelevancies and contingencies; it selects from the flow of events those perceived as significant. But in addition to selecting, plots organize. Raw experience, following time's arrow, advances in one direction only, whereas plot, though it must finally adhere to a temporal principle is less enslaved by chronology. It may alter both course and velocity by leaping or lingering, exploiting flashback or foreshadowing, omitting or replaying to achieve its effects. Plot thus artfully rearranges temporal sequence to disclose or highlight the relations among events.

The event itself is the basic unit of narrative discourse,[7] and the selection and ordering of events is the basic task of plot construction. What principles inform that selection and ordering? Once again, Aristotle proves instructive: a narrative plot "should have for its subject a single action, whole and complete, with a beginning, a middle, and an end."[8] This formulation reverberates in many subsequent analyses of the sources of coherence in plotting. The Russian critic Victor Shklovsky, for instance, seeking to explicate the notion of completeness, observes that plot move-ment is circular, the end linked to the beginning by resolution of an opposition or revelation of a similarity; that is, by contrast or comparison.[9] Todorov extends this analysis further by distinguishing five "indispensable" elements of narrative: a state of equilibrium at the outset; a disruption of that equilibrium; a recognition of the disruption; an action aimed at repairing the disruption; and a reinstatement of the initial equilibrium.[10] One can imagine a tale, he remarks, lacking the first two elements and thus starting from disequilibrium, or lacking the last two, thus ending in tragedy. But these would be felt as two hemicycles, each in its way incomplete. Narrative requires the full cycle.

The relation among these units is, first of all, one of temporal succession. But it is not merely that; another, more intricate pattern emerges. The fifth element will be seen to repeat the first, while the third is the inverse of these; and the second and fourth elements constitute a symmetrical and inverse pair. Thus a principle of transformation as well as one of succession binds the parts of a plot and permits a simple formula $(A,B,\overline{A},\overline{B},A)$ to describe them.

Todorov does not insist, as do others, upon a causal link in plot construction. In *A Grammar of Stories*, Gerald Prince defines a "minimal story" as consisting of three chronologically ordered events in which the second causes the third.[11] And of course, Aristotle had long since noted in his description of a proper ending as one that follows "by causal necessity" from preceding events, "It makes all the difference whether any given event is a case of *propter hoc* or *post hoc*."[12] A narrative grammar which aims at comprehensiveness cannot ignore the evidence supporting this injunction. If "necessity" imposes too strict a requirement upon the concluding element of narrative, it must still be admitted to the grammar as an option.

If plot is the soul of narrative, it is nonetheless supported by, and inseparable from, other aspects of fiction. Characters there must be even if, as Aristotle insisted, they exist only for the sake of the action.[13] Greimas prefers the term "actants" in order to emphasize this subordination of characters to plot.[14] (This should not, of course, be regarded as an aesthetic judgment, but merely as an observation. Greimas does not wish to disvalue characterization in assessing literary worth. Analysis only, and not evaluation, is at issue here.) Beyond this, literary grammarians agree upon little other than the classic injunction that characters should be "probable"; that is, their thought and expression (a modern critic might prefer "motivation") should be consistent with the actions required of them by the plot. Consistency is also the chief requirement for the setting. Locale and era are plot modifiers, "adjectives" which render events more specific, and so must be appropriate to the action.

Strictly construed, the author's attitudes toward his materials and his readers cannot be included in a narrative syntax. Ordinarily they would be assigned to rhetorical or stylistic analysis and thus ought properly to fall outside the ambitions of this essay. To disregard them, however, would be to neglect a revealing aspect of early narrative development and one which will prove intimately related to plot construction. For that reason they require some attention here.

The storyteller's stance vis-à-vis events of a narrative can be usefully comprehended under the rubric of point of view. Any tale implies a teller (not, of course, to be identified with the author), a fictional persona who perceives, selects, recounts, and sometimes comments upon the events of the plot. Hence the characteristic past tense of most fictional narration; the implied teller stands at a distance from his story and relates events already completed. He knows how the story will turn out, and this privileged knowledge allows him to vary the chronology, to foreshadow, and to interject.

The choice of an implied narrator and of his angle of vision may vary along several dimensions.[15] A narrator, for example, may or may not be present in the story itself and, if present, may or may not participate in the action. He may assume omniscience and peer into the minds and motives of characters, or he may be embodied in an individualized character whose perceptions have been distorted by his own idiosyncracies. These and more subtle variations will be familiar to every reader. But whatever the narrative perspective, it determines what information will be available to the reader. If the narrator's point of view denies him knowledge of an event, that event will not be recounted. If his situation requires that he learn of an incident long after its occurrence, that incident will not appear in chronological sequence. As a mediator between the reader and the raw material of the story and as a consciousness through which events are filtered, the narrator represents an additional principle of selectivity operating upon the construction of the plot.

Viewed in this way, narrative point of view also encompasses the storyteller's relation to his audience. Implicit in the angle of vision is an invitation to share it. A narrator who adopts, for example, an attitude of amused irony toward the events of his tale encourages in the reader a similar distancing and disengagement. In this sense, a tale manipulates its readers and creates for itself its appropriate audience. Or to reverse the point, a tale contains within it a characterization of its ideal reader. But the extent to which a story is elaborated may indicate another dimension of the author-reader relation. No story—indeed, no text of any kind—can include within itself all the information requisite to its understanding. The simplest telling of an event (e.g., "John threw the ball") assumes that the reader possesses and will appropriately apply certain relevant knowledge (e.g., that John is a masculine name, that throwing a ball is a certain sort of activity, and so forth). Thus information excluded from the narrative further defines the anticipated audience as those who can be expected to possess such background knowledge. According to Todorov, for instance, the initial situation of a tale will contain both general laws and specific details, but the general laws may represent prevailing value systems which need not be expressly articulated because they can be assumed to be part of the reader's acculturation.[16] Sometimes information apparently omitted will be indirectly present by logical implication. "John threw the ball," for instance, presupposes that John had a ball to throw and that he intended to throw it, that his behavior was not accidental. An accomplished storyteller may manipulate presuppositions with astonishing skill, even to the extent of omitting crucial incidents which the reader must then reconstruct from later occurrences.[17] The elaboration of context and detail, the texture of inclusion and exclusion, thus constitute an index of authorial expectations with regard to audience which will, of course, influence plot construction.

Parenthetically, these observations announce another complication in the assessment of children's narrative development. Since the decision to omit information from a tale may derive from cultural assumptions or from logical ones, both cultural acquisition and logical acquisition are implicated in the growth of narrative competence. While it is no surprise to discover an intimate connection among developing cognitive systems, the discovery adds a convolution which an exploratory study must ignore. What remains pertinent in the preceding account, however, are its literary conclusions.

One final literary issue remains to be addressed, that of fictionality itself. Narrative structure does not, of course, belong exclusively to literature, or even to those media like drama, television, comic strips, and cinema in which fiction predominates. Narrative elements also characterize history, journalism, anecdote, biography, and other nonfictional genres. What, then, distinguishes fiction from its opposite? In a Wittgensteinian analysis of the uses of the term "fiction," Thomas Roberts argues that "A book is fiction . . . if its writer has knowingly made it factually untrue but also warned his readers he has done this."[18] These "warnings," signals of fictionality, are incorporated into the text itself and should be discernible there. Of these, aesthetic form is surely the most powerful signal. A tale whose episodes are paired and balanced, in which an ordering principle dominates, and from which irrelevancies and digressions have been banished is clearly not a reproduction of life. Its artificiality and artfulness stamp it as man made. Another signal is the independence, even remoteness, of the text from the immediate practical concerns of teller and audience, a quality which aestheticians have called "disinterestedness" or "distance."[19] Neither the tale nor the act of telling it appears in any way instrumental to purposes extraneous to itself. The exclusion from the story of direct reference to author or reader as living individuals (rather than as personae or roles created by the text itself) underscores this quality of disinterestedness. But perhaps the most familiar signal is the "frame" or boundary marker, an earmark shared by a variety of other artifacts. Aesthetic representations are commonly set apart from the ordinary environment by a temporal or spatial frame. Paintings provide the readiest example, but the proscenium arch which encloses a drama and the pedestal which marks off a sculptural space exemplify the same principle. In many societies, stories are bracketed by ritual beginnings and endings, as they are in ours by "once upon a time" and "happily ever after." With this formula the storyteller assures his audience that the fictional world about to be entered, remote in time and place from the present, should not be mistaken for fact.

3. Primary narrative

The tales which follow are selections from a corpus gathered informally over a period of three years. The collection now numbers more than three hundred stories composed in the main by children between the ages of five and fifteen but including a sampling from children as young as two. The present exposition addresses chiefly the products of this younger group but from time to time invokes later developments to indicate a general tendency or a critical advance. Conclusions and generalizations concerning narrative characteristics are based upon the entire collection; the stories cited herein are illustrative only.

The experience of collecting these tales suggests that any child of normal endowment who is old enough to speak a few consecutive sentences has some conception of narrative fiction. No toddler past his second birthday appeared dismayed or perplexed by the request to tell a story.[20] Since these tales were collected in nurseries, kindergartens, and schools, no doubt the familiarity of story time bolstered the children's savoir-faire. But imitative and dramatic activity begin even earlier than speech,[21] and these, when joined with language and physical mobility, prepare the child to abstract from the tales he hears a model on which to pattern his own storymaking.

Initial efforts at narration, however truncated or awkward, invariably show recognizable literary properties. But mastery of basic story structure first shows itself in what may be called the primary narrative form, as exemplified by the following samples.

1. *Once there was a car and it broke. It went up a hill and got broke. Then a different car came. The other car made the other car go. And it went right home.* (Age: 2:10)

2. *Once there was a funny bird. He lived in a tree. And he fell down. The mommy bird came and made him fly. Then he went back in the tree.* (Age: 3:6)

3. *There was a bad boy. He went into the woods all by himself. A lion tried to eat him up. Then he shooted the lion and he ran all the way home. That's all.* (Age: 4:3)

4. *Once upon a time there was a cowboy with a big horse. He was a sheriff. And one day he was riding his horse and just riding along. And he met a robber. And he had a big hat and he had a big horse and he had a gun. And he shot the cowboy. And the cowboy said, "Oh no you don't!" and he tied him up. He tied his hands in back. Then he took him to the jail and he said, "Good night."* (Age: 4:11)

5. *Once a kitty was playing with another kitty. They were friends. And they came to a house and they went in. They had milk. Then they played with the toys. They purred and purred. Then the doggie came home and chased them out and scratched them. But the kitty said, "We won't scratch you. We like to play with toys." Then they played with the doggie. They all played together in the house. The end.* (Age: 5:8).

These stories represent narrative fiction stripped to its skeleton. Yet each is demonstrably "whole and complete, with a beginning, a middle, and an end." As the age tags indicate, a few children master the primary narrative before the age of three; most, however, begin to construct coherent tales some time between the fourth and fifth birthdays. In a classroom of five- and six-year-olds, most stories will incorporate primary narrative form, and some will show substantial elaboration of the basic elements.

If plot is the critical element of fiction, these primary narratives acknowledge that imperative; they are all plot and not much besides. But the plots will prove to be intricately organized. To begin with, they share a common plot structure which moves through four predictable phases. Phase I introduces a state of affairs described as continuous or prevailing, one which by implication represents the ordinary condition of things. Phase I is thus descriptive or, to use Prince's term, "stative" rather than active.[22] Phase II presents a misfortune, a malign event which disrupts the prevailing state of affairs. If the initial condition described in Phase I was already regrettable (as in the third story), in Phase II it worsens. In Phase III a counteraction occurs which reverses the misfortune of the prior phase. And finally Phase IV reports an event which restores the normal state of affairs. The primary narrative, then, contains an initial description succeeded by three events or actions.

This arrangement recalls Todorov's five "indispensable" elements of narrative. But the primary stories contain only four. What is missing is the Aristotelian moment of recognition, the third stage in Todorov's scheme. Reflection at once suggests that such an occurrence differs in kind from the other events of a story. It is less an action than a mental event, a pause in the action during which the narrative agent assesses his circumstances, reconnoiters, and plans. This sort of development exemplifies what Todorov calls a "gnoseological transformation," a change of knowledge or of motive.[23] Of the utmost significance in mature literature, the gnoseological transformation does not appear in children's stories before the age of eight or nine. Attributes of thought, feeling, or motive are entirely absent from primary narratives. Even the formulaic "*happily* ever after" ordinarily marks the transition to a more advanced competence.

In still another way the act of recognition differs from other events. Although such a moment may be accompanied by actions (slapping the forehead, stamping the foot), these are expressive and intransitive. They are, in fact, activities rather than actions; they extend but do not alter the preceding circumstances. Characteristically (though exceptions occur) primary narratives do not admit events of this sort once Phase II has begun. Each event of the second and succeeding phases transforms an immediately prior state of affairs. Only in the first phase (as in story 5) are events reported which do not change an earlier condition. This is merely another way of saying that plots of primary narratives are bare and unelaborated and that when children start to elaborate (as, again, in story 5) they begin at the beginning with Phase I.

But these observations also suggest that the arrangement of events in the primary narrative is less simple than it first appears. The chronological sequence is so straightforward as to seem to be the dominant ordering principle. Time's arrow moves guilelessly ahead without interruption or deviation. Closer inspection, however, reveals that each temporal advance is wedded to a movement through space, to a change of location or of spatial array. So closely are the two linked that it is impossible to estimate from the evidence of the stories alone which is the governing principle. Both Piaget and his associates, however, have reported that children organize their worlds spatially first and temporally only after the age of seven or eight.[24] Their demonstration shows that a younger child recounting a succession of events will report their positional rather than their chronological ordering. Although no such distinction can be detected in primary narratives, the storymaking efforts which precede this first complete form, as well as those which follow and amplify it, seem to confirm Piaget's observations. For example, manipulation of temporal relations—as, for instance, in the use of simultaneity—does not appear in children's stories before the age of nine or ten, and then only rarely. The next section of this essay, a description of the narrative antecedents of the primary form, will suggest additional support and will indicate as well the significance of spatial mobility in the growth of narrative competence.

A principle of selection, in addition to one of succession, also orders the plots of primary narratives. The relevance of events to one another—that is, their participation as components of a single continuing action—is apparent. Yet other imaginable occurrences, equally relevant, might have been included. Story 2, for example, might have noted that the bird was too young to fly, or that the bird attempted to fly, or that the bird's wing was injured, and so forth. Their exclusion evidences a selectional rule at work. These events, although not direct attributions of thought, feeling, or motive (thus not members of the class of "gnoseological transformations" which elude young storymakers), resemble that class in two particulars: they do not alter the prior state of affairs and, equally important, they are in a sense invisible. A bird's size can be seen, but not its age; a flapping wing can be seen, but not its pain. In short, to report such occurrences would require the storyteller to infer from perceptible properties the existence of imperceptible states. Primary narratives, however, report only events accessible to immediate observation. The principle of selection, then, dictates inclusion only of perceptible actions and, of these, only such actions as effect a change in the preceding circumstances.

This is not to suggest that young children are incapable of causal reasoning or that this form of logic is banished from their stories. In fact, an elementary causal link appears to join Phases III and IV of the primary narrative. If the end point of an action is rest and a return to equilibrium, Phase III can be seen as removing an obstacle to equilibrium and thus permitting its restoration. Had the condition established by Phase II continued, no restoration could occur. Phase III, then, represents an enabling action, a prerequisite to completion of the temporal/spatial trajectory. It is in this sense that Phase IV does not merely follow after but follows from Phase III. This elementary logic of action imposes a final ordering principle upon primary narrative plots.

To recapitulate, then, the plots of primary narrative consist of four phases, the first stative and the rest active. Each active phase consists of a single observable event. Events are chronologically and spatially sequential and, in addition, are logically related such that the third is the inverse of the second and the fourth a consequent of the third. These relations assure that all events represent components of a single action and that every event requisite to that action is included; hence, primary narratives are experienced as "whole and complete."

As noted earlier, however, a story is more than a structure of events. In primary narratives, although other elements remain subsidiary to the plot, they contrive to support it and thus to reinforce the unity of parts characteristic of such products. These subordinate elements deserve at least a brief review.

To speak of "characters" in children's stories may be an anthropocentric indulgence. Every sort of creature or mechanical contrivance—virtually anything to which motion can be imputed—may appear as an "actant." If characters are explicitly described at all, it is only to assign them the most conventional features ("a big hat . . . a big horse and . . . a gun"). More often, specific characteristics, even those relevant to events, are ignored and, where needed, must be inferred (as the bird's age can be inferred from the arrival of the "mommy"). The action of primary narratives provides two roles into which agents must be fitted. Announced in Phase I, the focal role is predominantly passive and reactive. Events act upon or happen to this character, who in Phase III (or perhaps as late as Phase IV, as in stories 1 and 2) reacts to them. The second role, emerging in Phase II or Phase III, contrasts with the first and requires an agent who is an active initiator, one who impels events in a new direction. Because it attaches to two sorts of action, this contrastive role may be subdivided into two aspects, malign and benign. If the contrastive slot is filled by a villain, it first appears in Phase II; if by a protector, in Phase III. But it appears nonetheless to be a single role, since its two aspects will ordinarily be mutually exclusive. Only rarely does a primary narrative include both a villain and a protector. Occasionally, however, the role is pluralized; its malign aspect may be assumed by a pack, a gang, or a swarm, its benign form by family or friends. Because both roles select their occupants and because roles are adjuncts to actions, the appropriateness of character to event is guaranteed.

Setting, an important component of mature literature, appears in primary narratives as an afterthought if at all. Although temporal sequence is respected by events, time as duration (as era or occasion or delay) is ignored. Details of locale are more frequently included, but only as mandated by plot requirements; place is treated as a component of action. That the car climbed a hill, for example, is connected (though one hesitates to say causally connected) to its breakdown. But if descriptive detail is minimal, an awareness of setting is always present by implication as the events of the plot move through space. Setting thus remains intrinsic to the story; it is not, as in second-rate novels, pasted on as ornament. Its potential, however, for advancing or inhibiting action and for explaining or motivating character waits to be discovered.

By contrast with the negligible exploitation of personae and setting, point of view appears to be as complexly ordered as plot structure. And, indeed, the close interaction between plot and point of view conduces to this outcome. In plot construction, one principle of inclusion, as earlier noted, requires that occurrences be visible; its reciprocal, a principle of exclusion, prohibits description of internal events and thus of thoughts, feelings, and motives. These complementary rules lead to what is customarily called an "objective" or "impersonal" point of view. The implied narrator reports only what a camera's lens might have seen; although events are reported retrospectively, the teller exercises no foreknowledge, nor does he claim privileged access to information not apparent in the action itself. But the camera is a mobile one; it pursues its quarry wherever events require. The observer thereby maintains a uniform distance from the action and avoids the distortions inherent in partial vision or awkward angle of view. Much experience must intervene before the storymaker can choose to vary the distance between observer and event in order to achieve a desired effect. Nonetheless, by virtue of the mobility of its implied narrator, the primary narrative represents a substantial increase in competence over earlier storymaking efforts, as will be shown.

That a narrator *is* implied is evidenced by the fact that the storyteller declines to speak *in propria persona*. The child says "There was a cowboy," not "I saw" one. In so doing he removes himself from the scene of events and eschews the privilege of commenting on them. Rather he invents the role of impersonal observer and recounts events from that perspective. Such an assertion of imagination represents a difficult and uncertain attainment for a child who has not yet fully differentiated self from surroundings. It is therefore scarcely surprising to encounter frequent lapses of point of view, even among accomplished storymakers. Five- and six-year-olds will still interrupt a narrative to assure the hearer that "it's just a story." And smaller children often revert briefly to the familiar dramatic form, entering into and miming the actions of the tale.

These lapses that inject the storymaker into his tale should not be mistaken for first person narration. Genuine first person point of view is a later achievement and one closely correlated with the appearance of psychological motive in characterization. Around the tenth birthday children begin to produce stories told, as it were, from inside a character who speaks in his own person. Such a character is frequently an inanimate object or nonhuman creature, and his story, except for its first person pronouns, differs little from an objective report:

If I were a piece of bubble gum, I would start out in a bag with my ten sisters, ten brothers, Mom and Dad, my three aunts, five uncles, and eight cousins. One day we all fell off the shelf and the bag got a tiny little hole in it. Every day it got a little bit bigger. One day I fell out! Then somebody picked me up and put me in their pocket. When we got home, the boy put me in a box and kept me there for a month. When the day the month was over, the boy came and took me out of the box and took off my wrapper and took a tiny bite of me. Ouch! That hurt! Each day the boy took a tiny bite until I was all gone.

The End

Once having discovered this interior psychological space, the child soon learns how to furnish it, and the first person speaker announces to himself and others his feelings, intentions, and hopes. If the storymaker of the primary narrative has learned to distance himself from outward events, by the time he masters the psychological tale he will have learned to distance himself from, and thus to observe, internal processes of mind.

At the primary narrative stage the storymaker's blindness to mental events extends to his audience as well as to his characters. In this respect his narrative output resembles his other linguistic productions; neither pays much heed to the requirements of an audience. His characteristic egocentricity, so fully described by Piaget, leads the child to assume a fully shared universe which renders explanation superfluous. Thus he provides little context, few descriptions, and, except for the temporal marker "then," no elaboration of relationships. Pronoun reference in particular can be monumentally perplexing. (In story 4, who is it that has a big hat, a big horse, and a gun?) Presuppositions, both linguistic and cultural, of course fill in much of the absent context. Analyzing a tale similar to story 2, Sacks points out that "the mommy" would be perceived by most readers as *his* mommy, the mommy of that particular baby, and that, indeed, such an assumption was intended.[25] Primary narratives, like other childhood communications, rely heavily on implications of this sort. But these should not be confused with that artfully simulated egocentrism which, in mature literature, cozens the willing reader into accepting the author's viewpoint as his own.

Perhaps the clearest signal transmitted by the young storymaker to his audience is his announcement of the fictional status of his communiqué. So insistently is this quality reiterated that one is tempted to regard it as overdetermined. Scarcely a strand of the story fails to contribute to its reinforcement: the artifice of the plot; the distancing of events; the storymaker's absence from the tale, even as commentator; the removal of events, through use of the past tense, to some remote other time; and so on. Only one element remains to be noted, and that one no reader has overlooked: the story frame. Although occasional primary narratives produced by the youngest children omit the frame entirely, more commonly the frame appears well in advance of the full narrative, and its use persists often beyond the tenth birthday. Its introductory form allows little variation; "once," "one day," "there was," and "once upon a time" virtually exhaust the alternatives. The conclusion of the story, however, permits wider inventiveness. Written stories are almost invariably marked "The End," and spoken stories frequently conclude with "That's all." "Lived happily ever after" and its inverse, "were never seen again," make a late appearance, rarely occurring before the age of six or seven. Most often, stories are rounded off by an event which poses a natural temporal or spatial boundary, coming home or going to bed being the most frequent. But whatever the variant, its specific form is less remarkable than the regularity and persistence with which children insist on such boundary markers. The capacity to distinguish fiction from experience and playful from purposeful discourse is a substantial intellectual attainment which the frame both records and protects.

One variant of the primary narrative, which follows fast upon its heels, deserves a moment's attention.

6.   *Once upon a time there lived a witch. She was an ugly witch. And she had a green face. One day she was taking a walk. She fell in a pond. Then everyone lived happily ever after.* (Age: 7:9)

7.   *Once upon a time there was a little boy who never knew how to tell times. And one day he went to his grandfather's and his grandfather said, "What time is it?" and he said, "I don't know how to tell time." So the grandfather said, "Oh, you sit on my knee and I'll teach you." And when they were done, the grandfather said, "What time is it?" And he said, "Twelve o'clock." That's all.* (Age: 7:0)

These later tales have obvious affinities with the primary narrative. In fact, they differ from it in only one respect: Phases I and II have been collapsed into a single episode. In these stories, the initial situation represents not the ordinary state of affairs but one of threat or deprivation, a condition introduced into the earlier tales only in the second phase. Thereafter these later narratives fit the earlier template; two phases follow, one which reports a counteraction to the initial condition, and another which, by redressing the initial misfortune, creates a condition of equilibrium. These, then, resemble Todorov's "hemicycle," the narrative which begins in the middle, so to speak, and which occurs familiarly in mature literature. What renders this observation arresting is the unexpected developmental sequence. The secondary story form which emerges later in the child's development appears on inspection to be more primitive and less elaborated than the earlier primary narrative. But since no evidence has been found of three-phase stories preceding the appearance of the basic four-phase structure, the former must be assumed to be the derivative form. Acquisition of a deletion transformation might be postulated to explain such an odd-seeming sequence. The three-phase transform does not, of course, supplant the four-phase structure. Both continue in active use, and both undergo a similar elaboration of component elements.

4. Emerging narratives

The primary narrative does not, of course, spring forth fully realized. Its roots extend far downward into earlier attempts at narrative construction and earlier conceptions of story form. A detailed review of this period of apprenticeship must be postponed, but examination of one interesting feature can suggest how development proceeds. The following emerging narratives will illustrate.

8.   *Duckie swam in the water. Then a boat came. The boat has a big whistle. Toot, toot! See, I'm the boat. It went around. Then duckie swam around the boat. Daddy duck came. He gave him a big worm that got dead.* (Age: 3:4)

9.   *A witch has a big house. And a spider. The spider tore her dress and threw it out the window. He broke her bike. He broke her hat and threw it away. He broke her house. Then a police came and took the witch away.* (Age: 4:7)

10. *Once there was a boy who loved cookies. And he didn't have any, so he asked his mommy for a cookie. She said no. Then a cookie came. A great big cookie with a lot of legs. It went for a walk. Walk, walk, walk. Then the other cookies came. They jumped on the table and they had a big fight. Then mommy said go to bed.* (Age: 5:0)

If plot is the essence of narrative, these will not qualify. But as the primary narrative so forcefully demonstrates, a plot is a complex of relationships, and some of these relationships are already discernible here. These children recognize, for example, that a story is a sequence of events, temporally/spatially ordered, set in some unspecified past, and observed by a camera's lens. Occasional lapses in the application of these principles (as in the reversion to present tense or to dramatic form) indicate that they have yet to be firmly fixed. But the lapses *are* occasional, and the application, on the whole, so consistent as to suggest more than partial mastery.

Yet despite this high degree of organization the narratives strike the reader as incoherent. What they fail to capture is the story's necessary focus on a single action, whole and complete. In the primary narrative, singleness is guaranteed by the specific conditions governing each event as well as by the logical relations between events. By contrast, story 8 has neither beginning, middle, nor end; it is a catalog of occurrences upon which no principle of selection operates. Story 9 has a conclusion but no prior development. Story 10, however, begins to approach the primary narrative; it opens with the description of a continuous state upon which subsequent events can operate, then proceeds to an event which alters the condition in force at the outset. And ultimately it comes to a satisfactory conclusion. In effect, it tells a story without a middle, or at least without an appropriate middle. What it lacks is Phase III, that pivotal event which must satisfy logical conditions more severe than those of any other phase, since it must counteract Phase II and simultaneously establish a state of affairs from which Phase IV will follow. When this storymaker solves that problem he will have mastered the primary narrative.

The solution to his problem will not be found, however, until he can free the story's implied narrator. The point of observation in story 10—indeed, in each of the emerging narratives—is immobile. Events are recounted as if the narrator were rooted to the spot and able to report only what passes before him. He rivets his attention to a restricted field of action and describes the changing state of affairs within that field. Personae may arrive or vanish, but they are observed only while within imaginary spatial bounds. Interestingly enough, stories 1 and 2 of the primary narratives—those produced by the youngest children—also satisfy this description. One may justly wonder, then, if their coherence signals a genuine mastery of narrative form or merely a lucky imaginative accident. Pitcher and Prelinger suggest that confinement within a limited fantasy space characteristically declines with age, at least during the preschool years.[26] Certainly the common experience of the child would seem to support such a development; as he grows older the boundaries of his play space ordinarily expand. A concomitant imaginative expansion might well follow naturally.

Whatever the explanation, immobility of narrative perspective appears generally incapacitating. It constricts imagination within a space too limited to allow the variety of actions from which the storymaker must be able to choose if he is to meet the logical conditions imposed upon him. When the child can free his narrator to move through space and thus to pursue events wherever they may lead, he will be able to complete the trajectory described by the primary narrative. Mobility of perspective appears to be a precondition to, although not an assurance of, coherent storymaking.

The emerging narrative awaits much more exploration. The foregoing illustration, however, highlights the growing points of narrative development. Increased skill in the manipulation of a single narrative element simultaneously increases combinatorial freedom and thus leads to changed relations among several elements. As in any complex system, a change in one of the parts reverberates throughout the whole. The effect may be slight, as when Phases I and II are collapsed to form a hemicyclic narrative; or it may be dramatic, as when "I" replaces "he" in the focal character's role. What triggers such an increase in skill remains uncertain. Cognitive maturation is surely a contributor, as exemplified in the decentration which permits the child to endow his personae with feelings and motives. But if cognitive maturation were its sole source, every child would grow into a Flaubert. Other determinants in the storymaker's environment or experience must still be sought.

5. Epilogue

This essay began with a tale which must remain incomplete. How the lucky babe will come into possession of his promised literary attainments remains a mystery. But a first installment has been drafted. The evidence of the primary narratives urges the conclusion that literary competence is neither haphazard in its growth nor accidental in its form. That most children by the age of five or six, and some children much earlier, have attained the degree of skill represented by these stories attests to the systematic character of growth. And that degree of skill is by no means negligible. Although the primary narrative is a skeletal form, it utilizes all the elements of mature literature and thus contains within itself the possibility of richer and subtler transformations. Like the child's physical skeleton, however, its approximation to the mature prototype shows internal variation. Plotting and point of view already obey sophisticated rules of combination, whereas characterization remains primitive and must be expected to catch up later.

If the correlation of attainment with age is one indicator of systematicity, the organization of the stories is an even stronger one. No principle of logic requires that, because six-year-olds can generally tell a good story, their stories must be of the same kind. One child might have produced a seven-phase tale, another a narrative of character and motive, and still another a story with an omniscient narrator. But the stories are strikingly consistent in their basic organization. Whatever the variations of content, style, and diction—and these often seem to range widely—the underlying plot structure evinces a shared set of logical and spatiotemporal relations.

Although only minimal information could be included concerning developments preceding and subsequent to the primary narrative, that evidence, too, tends to confirm the systematic character of literary growth. The emerging narratives make visible the thrust toward a complete story. In particular, the patterned interaction between plot development and mobility of point of view in those early efforts emphasizes the orderly unfolding of increasingly complex skills. The same can be said for the first person tale and its relation to psychological motivation of character, although those details were hastily sketched.

This study, then, offers justification for the hypothesis that narrative competence advances in a predictable fashion that is amenable to analysis and description. No doubt the direction of its advance will resemble, in a general way, that of other developing systems. One might therefore anticipate increasingly complex integration of increasingly differentiated and elaborated parts. To give those abstract terms a concrete literary content is the task of future investigations.

Such investigations, however, may find themselves, if not stymied, at least hampered by the slow development of narrative theory. That clear theoretical formulations provide an invaluable guide for developmental studies was evidenced in the analysis of primary narrative plots. There the availability of a convincing description of the logical relations obtaining in a mature prototype encouraged fruitful comparison. By contrast the examination of characterization, lacking theoretical guidance, was more hesitant and less revealing.

But of course, even frustrations may prove instructive. If developmental research gains from advances in narrative theory, the reverse may also be true. Developmental studies will not only call attention to gaps in theory but may well suggest new and fruitful ways to span those gaps. In fact, research into literary competence might wrench familiar problems of theory out of their familiar contexts, with salutary effects. The process of defamiliarization can disrupt and disorient but, when it frees thought from the bonds of habit, can invigorate as well. Developmental research, then, might hope to advance in symbiosis with narrative theory.

If that hope should materialize, the interrupted tale of the fortunate babe could conclude happily, for then its teller could recount not only how the child won his gift but what the gift was. But such plots are not hatched overnight.

Notes

1. John Dewey, *Art as Experience* (New York: Putnam, 1934).
2. Among the major landmarks are Claude Bremond, *Logique du récit* (Paris: Seuil, 1973); Gerard Genette, *Figures* (Paris: Seuil, 1966); A. J. Greimas, *Du sens* (Paris: Seuil, 1970); Claudio Guillén, *Literature as System* (Princeton: Princeton University Press, 1971); Gerald Prince, *A Grammar of Stories* (The Hague: Mouton, 1973); and Tzvetan Todorov, *Grammaire du Décaméron* (The Hague: Mouton, 1969). An excellent bibliography can be found in Robert Scholes, *Structuralism in Literature* (New Haven, Conn.: Yale University Press, 1974).
3. Ferdinand de Saussure, *Course in General Linguistics*, trans. Wade Baskin (New York: McGraw-Hill, 1966).
4. Vladimir I. Propp, *Morphology of the Folktale*, trans. Laurence Scott (Austin: University of Texas Press, 1968).
5. *Poetics* 6. 1450a. 39.
6. Todorov, *Grammaire du Décaméron*, pp. 16 ff.
7. Prince, *Grammar of Stories*, p. 17.

8. *Poetics* 23. 1459a. 20. The translation used throughout is that of S. H. Butcher, *Aristotle's Theory of Poetry and Fine Art*, 4th ed. (New York: Dover, 1955).

9. "On the Construction of the Short Story and the Novel," cited in Scholes, *Structuralism*, p. 85.

10. "The Two Principles of Narrative," *Diacritics*, Fall 1971, p. 39.

11. P. 24.

12. *Poetics* 10. 1452a. 21.

13. *Poetics* 6. 1450a. 23.

14. "Narrative Grammar: Units and Levels," *Modern Language Notes* 86 (1971): 799.

15. Wayne C. Booth, *The Rhetoric of Fiction* (Chicago: University of Chicago Press, 1961). See also Lubomír Doležel, "The Typology of the Narrator: Point of View in Fiction," in *To Honor Roman Jakobson* (The Hague: Mouton, 1967), 1:541–52, which claims to account for all possible narrative viewpoints by means of a distinctive feature matrix.

16. Todorov, *Grammaire du Décaméron*, p. 60.

17. Excellent examples are provided by Gerald Prince, "On Presupposition and Narrative Strategy," *Centrum* 1 (Spring 1973): 23–31. Elizabeth Bruss, "Models and Metaphors for Narrative Analysis," *Centrum* 2 (Spring 1974): 30, argues that "working backward in a narrative series, stating what each occurrence or its negation minimally presupposes, is thus a useful procedure for discovering its 'kernels' or minimal semantic units."

18. Thomas Roberts, *When Is Something Fiction?* (Carbondale: Southern Illinois University Press, 1972), p. 4.

19. The best known statement of this view is that of Edward Bullough, "Psychical Distance as a Factor in Art and an Aesthetic Principle," *British Journal of Psychology* 5 (1912–13): 87–118.

20. A similar experience is reported by Evelyn G. Pitcher and Ernst Prelinger, *Children Tell Stories: An Analysis of Fantasy* (New York: International Universities Press, 1963), pp. 27–28.

21. See Jean Piaget, *Play, Dreams, and Imitation in Childhood*, trans. C. Gattegno and F. M. Hodgson (New York: Norton, 1962).

22. Prince, *Grammar of Stories*, p. 29.

23. "The Two Principles of Narrative," p. 40.

24. Jean Piaget, *The Child's Conception of Time*, trans. A. J. Pomerans (New York: Ballantine, 1971). See also J. P. Bronckart and H. Sinclair, "Time, Tense, and Aspect," *Cognition* 2 (1973): 5–129.

25. Harvey Sacks, "On the Analyzability of Stories by Children," in *Directions in Sociolinguistics*, ed. John J. Gumperz and Dell Hymes (New York: Holt, Rinehart & Winston, 1972), p. 330.

26. Pitcher and Prelinger, *Children Tell Stories*, p. 154.

8 Saying It with Pictures
Diana Korzenik

1. What has to be learned

Contented and full after a big supper, Billy took out crayons and paper. Patting his stomach, he said, "Here's where my ice cream is," grasped a crayon, swung a full circle shape in the air, and landed a circular mark on the drawing paper. "See, I'm big and full," he said. Here's where the ice cream's melting." He formed a mark inside the circle. His speech and gesturing happened in time and space, but only the trailing end of his circular gesture actually left a trace on the paper. Because most of his representational behavior occurred outside the graphic medium of crayon and paper, only an observer present at that moment would know all the things he did to represent himself. His representation would be largely unavailable to a viewer absent from the context in which the picture was originally made.

People who make pictures have a problem to solve. Drawing is a more complicated process than it appears to be, but its familiarity often disguises the fact. Representational drawing is not, as is sometimes assumed, a mere photographic replica of the objective world, requiring only a knowledge of the chosen referent. This misconception pervades much of the research on children's drawings; it can perhaps be attributed to the habit of analyzing pictures in isolation, apart from the child and from the problem he attempted to solve. To correct for this, not only the final product but also all its accompanying observable behavior must be assessed. Billy's drawing and its context are, of course, a case in point.

Using this form of analysis, this essay argues for examination of how children understand the drawing process. If a child believes it important to attend to the "readability" of his picture, he will perform very differently from the way he will if he does not. But he will only be concerned with readability if he can *decontextualize* his work, if he can conceive of it apart from himself and from the time and place in which it was made. The study of children's drawing performances to be described below includes a number of instances like Billy's.

2. Decontextualization and drawing

Clearly, no single learning process leads to decontextualization. Rather it seems to be the outcome of feedback from earlier behaviors. As the child gets practice and gains interest in his own behavior, he shows a gradual sophistication—a detachment from his efforts—that permits him to evaluate what he is doing.

In general, decontextualization of picturing seems to be contingent upon three concepts. First, it demands an acceptance of the separateness of others from oneself and a recognition that they do not share one's context or motives. Secondly, it requires an awareness that the medium of representation is distinct from the object it serves to represent. And thirdly, it demands an understanding that pictures are likely to be looked at apart from the occasion on which they are drawn. In sum, decontextualization requires looking at one's behavior as others may see it; one must be able to conceive of a viewpoint different from one's own.

Such objectivity can be achieved only by a diminution of egocentrism, since it is this which determines whether an individual can put himself in the role of another person. Though characteristic of early childhood, egocentrism may survive into adulthood; to some degree everyone has difficulty acknowledging the inner life of others. Nevertheless a major change in the ability to take the point of view of others seems to occur around age seven and accounts for an increase in the child's effectiveness in many domains. He begins to learn how to explain and to supply information in a variety of media, and he thereby demonstrates his implicit recognition that his mind and experience are separate and different from those of others.[1]

Through their study of symbol formation, Werner and Kaplan analyze what seems to be the second prerequisite of decontextualization: the separation of the medium from what it represents. Their theoretical model of the maturation of symbolic communication processes proposes that, in infancy, a symbol is identified with its referent, whereas ultimately the symbol becomes a comment on the object. They show how the medium (in their case, language), referent, and audience are initially fused into one within the child's mind. Growth disentangles the separable elements. As the child becomes aware of his separation from the things around him, he also becomes aware that he can use words to represent these things. The medium then becomes a vehicle for consciously conveying thoughts about a referent. "Distancing"—Werner's and Kaplan's term for this disentangling of formerly fused elements—permits the child to evaluate the effects of his behavior because he can separate the medium from his intentions and can then compare his intentions with their actual effect. He can look at his work from outside the immediate context in which it was conceived. At the same time, he can recognize the discreteness of a mode of communication—a medium—available to represent information addressed to another's needs. Distancing, then, as a prerequisite for decontextualization, can be used effectively only if the child is also a role taker.[2]

The third prerequisite of decontextualization is an awareness that statements or actions are embedded in a context upon which their intelligibility depends. When a statement or action is disembedded from its originating context, it must be modified to account for that fact. Decontextualization thus requires learning that behavior, appropriately modified, can be understood independently of its initial invention.

The three kinds of understanding clustered together as prerequisites for decontextualization emerge in the course of development. This maturation in children's thinking might be expected to produce observable differences in their drawings, and their performances should reveal the sorts of problems they become increasingly capable of solving. Although many studies have monitored changes in the forms of graphic expression at different stages of development, information has been lacking about the child's changing conception of the problem of drawing. The thought and intention of the child are concealed by the simplification characteristic of his art; it is difficult to know when he is simply forming shapes and when he intends to represent something. And it is difficult to compare his intentions with his product without actually observing his effort. The experiment described here aimed to provide just this opportunity.

3. How children think about pictures: a study

A procedure was devised to reveal how children cope with the demands of picture making. It hypothesized that the ambiguity of a young child's drawings results from his egocentrism, his inability to decontextualize his work. The given task involved pairs of children of the same age and from the same classroom who were asked to serve as communicators. Each subject was told that he was going to play a "drawing game." The subject and the experimenter sat together at a low table upon which was a small drawing board with a drawing paper. The experimenter told the subject: "I am going to say three words to you. Listen to the words: bridge, sidewalk, jumping. Choose one. Then draw whatever comes to your mind when you think of that word." When the drawing was finished, the subject was asked, "Do you think one of your friends could look at this drawing and guess your word?"

If the subject said "Yes," he was asked to return to the classroom to get his friend. If he said "No," the experimenter asked "Why?" and then invited the subject to try again to depict the same word. Afterwards he was asked to summon his friend.

When the friend arrived, he was shown the drawing. He was permitted three guesses and was discouraged from further conversation. If none of the guesses was correct, the subject had the option of making additional drawings to assist his friend in guessing the word. The sequence of drawing followed by guessing was repeated until either the word was guessed or the children lost interest.

The procedure yielded two kinds of data: the children's pictures and a record of their actions. The first picture of each series was done *without* explicit knowledge of the communication task, but all subsequent drawings were made with such knowledge. The records of the child's actions included his movements, documented by the experimenter, and his speech, transcribed from tape recordings, as these occurred during drawing.

In the experiment the child was asked to transmit a chosen *word* by drawing. This was done so that the child would not have to verbalize his intention as he was drawing. Criteria for the selection of cue words required each word to represent the following:

> A concrete visible object, because our visual customs generally lead us to represent objects.
>
> An object familiar to the child, so that he could consider all the aspects of it with which he is familiar.
>
> An object not reducible to a pat formula, so that the child must develop his own strategy for representing it.
>
> A context-dependent object, so that the child must select and organize various parts in the right relationship with one another. (For example, a sidewalk cannot be depicted readily without inclusion of other elements that occur along with sidewalks like roads, cars, and stoplights. Yet prominence of these other elements may detract from the focal sidewalk itself. Organization and selectivity make all the difference.)

The two cue words *bridge* and *sidewalk* conform to these criteria. The third cue word, *jumping*, was selected to see what problems were presented by a cue word in the form of a verb, but otherwise in conformity with the criteria: familiar, not reducible to formula, and context-dependent.

Eighty-two boys and girls between the ages of 5 and 7 served as subjects. The age range had been determined in a pilot study which showed that only by age 5 were children able to sustain the task without becoming distracted, whereas after age 7 the task became too easy and no longer yielded fruitful results.[3] The subjects were pupils in two public elementary schools, both in the Boston metropolitan area. Teachers paired each subject with a friend of comparable maturity, and this friend served as the guesser. Of the eighty-two children, 57 percent were boys and 43 percent girls. The subjects comprised three groups: one of kindergarteners, ages 4:10 (4 years, 10 months) to 5, with a median age of 5:6; a second of first graders, ages 5:7 to 7:1, with a median age of 6:4; and a third of second graders, aged 7, with a median age of 7:5.

4. Strategies, premises, and maturation

The materials gathered in this experiment proved to require a two-stage analysis. First, the children's diverse performances had to be categorized, and then the materials in each category had to be studied in relation to age and thus to developmental changes in thinking. Three types of strategies or solutions emerged at once in the children's responses to the task. Thus each child's performance could be classified according to specific behavioral criteria.

The first class of strategies (type 1) indicated no reasoning about means or problems or conditions sufficient for communication. These strategies produced ambiguous drawings which were only minimally articulated. Among these strategies were verbal discriminations not incorporated into the drawing, gesturing rather than drawing, and shifting or altering the referent (cue word) as drawing progressed.

The type 2 strategies clearly demonstrated some reasoning about communication but nevertheless resulted in inefficient action. The resulting drawings were often less ambiguous than type 1 and included some graphic articulation of the referent. Although the child's objective was appropriate to the task, his action was inappropriate and tended not to serve his purpose. For example, in depicting *bridge*, one girl drew a square shape bisected by a long horizontal line. She said, "Now he'll guess it's a bridge, 'cuz he'll see this book [the square] that dropped on the bridge when the car went over it. He'll know it's him and he'll know where he is, so he'll know he's on the bridge and say bridge!"

By contrast, the type 3 strategies both demonstrated the intent to communicate and employed actions that served that end. The drawings produced by these strategies usually showed some articulation of the referent which actually facilitated guessing. The children tended to consider the medium and to talk about it. As they worked they also talked about the emerging drawing. Within the picture they included visible, graphic clues, and some children even tried to predict how the viewer would think when faced with the picture.

None of the strategies guaranteed that the drawing would be guessed. Even a type 3 strategy could not ensure identification of the cue word. Obviously, guessing was contingent upon both the execution of the drawing and the attentiveness of the guesser. Nevertheless the strategy employed appeared to be the critical factor in organizing the drawing. Inclusion and omission of elements based upon the child's interpretation of the task mattered far more than manual skill or lack thereof.

The drawing task, as indicated earlier, can be understood as a problem-solving situation, one which required the subject to define the problem for himself in such a way as to generate appropriate solutions. The children's solutions may thus be viewed as logical outcomes of particular premises. And if these premises can be made visible, they may explain some of the odd and apparently inappropriate solutions. For example, since some subjects blamed wrong guesses on the viewer's "stupidity," one can only conclude that these children regarded their own intentions as patently self-evident.

The children's implicit premises can be described in the following model which incorporates the three focuses of the initial problem: the medium, the self, and the others. The model presents two polarized sets of premises: the immature and the ideal. Each set is defined in terms of its attitudes toward the three focuses, but it should be understood that, though each set of premises may be adhered to in full, various permutations of the two are also possible. These two sets of premises are the keys to understanding how children cope with graphic representation.

Level	*Domain*	*Premise*
	the medium	"It does just what it should."
Immature	the self	"What I mean is always clear."
	the others	"People are stupid if they don't know what I mean."
	the medium	"I have to make the stuff show what I mean."
Ideal	the self	"I have to explain myself to be understood."
	the others	"People can't know what I mean unless I help."

First Level: The child believed that there was no communication problem. The child knew what he was drawing and he believed that all he thought, said, and drew was patently obvious. There was, thus, no need to exert effort to communicate. When a child adhering to the first premise drew only a minimal drawing and then was questioned as to whether the guesser could guess his word, the response was generally "Yes." He believed his intentions were self-evident.

Second level: The child believed that there was a communication problem to be solved. The child knew that it was by no means inevitable that the guesser would guess his cue word. When the child was asked whether the guesser would guess correctly, some of these children said "No" whereas others said "Yes." Sometimes one rejected the first drawing and asked to do a second. They were aware that they could modify their original ideas and do something differently. They believed that they might help the guesser, and they realized that they had to act to facilitate the guessing.

Consider now the three centers of concern. Regarding the *medium*, the immature premise gives no special attention to it; it simply does what it should. The ideal premise, by contrast, indicates the child's understanding that he must impose his will upon the medium, forming it to serve his purposes. Regarding the *self*, the immature premise posits, "I am always understood," whereas the ideal premise requires that "I must make myself understood. No one can read my mind." Regarding the *others* (and awareness of one's effect upon others), the immature premise holds that people are "stupid" if they fail to recognize the subject's intent. By contrast, the ideal premise shows acceptance of the separateness of other minds and of the need to help others to understand.

After these sets of strategies and their underlying assumptions had emerged from a study of the drawings and their accompanying behavior, examination of age relations could follow. Predictably, between the ages of five and seven a shift occurred in the types of strategies, and this marked a change in levels of competence. The immature strategies that predominated in kindergarten had declined in frequency by second grade, while new, more appropriate strategies dominated in the performances of the older children. Context-dependent, undifferentiated gestural-verbal-graphic representations, decipherable only because the observer was present to witness the entire act, yielded to more differentiated graphic representations which the child evaluated as if he did not know what had been depicted.

The strategies adopted by the children corresponded, in part at least, to differences in their understanding of the task as manifested in their speech. Those young children who indicated that there was no problem of communication tended to act out (by means of gestures) and to talk out their representations. Such a child might call his hand a car, move it along a line drawn on a paper, and say, "See, here's the car." Other children, realizing both that communication was problematic and that they were responsible for its success, tended to render their intentions explicit on paper. If drawing a car, such children would pencil in both the road line and the car shape.

The results thus indicated that the dominance or waning of children's egocentrism seemed to make the crucial difference in the children's choice of strategy. The egocentric child had trouble distinguishing his medium from himself and from his viewer; his picture served *him* perfectly well because he knew what he was doing, and he believed his intentions were perfectly evident. The child who no longer adhered to so egocentric a view of the world realized that he had to make the medium serve his purposes and that the viewer could understand only if he were helped to do so. Egocentrism thus seemed to blind the child to a realistic grasp of his relationship to the viewer so that he perceived no reason to question whether others understood what he did. As egocentrism diminished, the child began to be aware of the discrete perspective of the viewer and could adopt that perspective for the purpose of assessing his product. He could aim to affect his viewer with the means at his disposal within the boundaries of his picture.

5. Charley: a case study

Though one can talk about ideal types of strategies and premises, real circumstances reveal strategies and premises often intriguingly mixed. One such example will provide a more dramatic sense of the experiment and the behavior it revealed. Charley was a 5½-year-old kindergartener who chose to depict the cue word *jumping*. His strategies in approaching the problem can be described and interpreted according to their underlying premises in order to highlight the relation between thought and action.

Charley sat at a small table on which there was a drawing board and paper. He held the paper horizontally and drew a figure that was oriented toward the upper left corner of the page (figure 8:1).

As Charley said "He's off the ground!" he drew an almost vertical line near the right edge of the paper. By tipping the direction of the whole figure on a diagonal, Charley was able to show how high the figure was jumping. He cleverly "stretched" the paper and made the figure appear to be moving higher than the height of the paper would allow.

Charley's remark "He's off the ground," uttered while drawing the vertical line on the right, exemplifies how the minimal drawings of young children create an equivalence for the referent. Charley saw the ground line as a way of making the jumper "off," not as a way of representing the ground surface itself. He was not trying to expand his representation beyond the thing that jumps. But Charley also included the ground line within the boundaries of the paper. This strategy—however small and oblique the line itself—is more advanced than that of merely using the paper's edge as a ground line. Eighty-eight percent of the kindergarten children who depicted jumping did not include a ground line and used the bottom edge of the paper as its substitute. Charley's inclusion of the line demonstrated his awareness of the need to depict his referent more fully within the graphic medium, that is, to decontextualize it.

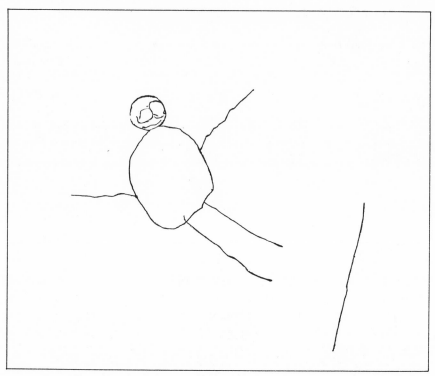

Figure 8:1. "You see he's jumping very high. That's one eye, there's another, there's a nose, a little too high—a nose should be in the middle between the two eyes. . . . He's off the ground!"

Moreover, even while drawing, Charley examined his product. Repeatedly he guided himself by talking about the things he was representing and their relative positions; for example, "It should be in the middle." His itemizing of "one eye," then "another," and then "a nose" was self-instructional speech. Rather than merely listing the items needed to depict a face, he told himself where to locate each in relation to the others. But self-instruction was not the only purpose served by his continuing monologue; it also provided him with a source of feedback. He treated his own observations as if they came from an external observer ("Nose, a little too high"); thus he could use them to correct distortions and to generate new ideas. Such an analysis of feedback is another strategy which promotes decontextualization.

After Charley had completed his drawing, he was asked, "Do you think that Nancy [the guesser], if she came in here and looked at your drawing, would be able to guess the word you had in your mind?" Charley answered, "Yes, she could see that he's up in the air because he's going that way. . . . I could make it easier to guess." In his response, Charley showed his mature (level 2) understanding of the problem. He was aware that the guesser guesses because of what he draws, and he realized that he could clarify his drawing further. He saw himself as the person who determined the success of the situation.

Though the parts were in the right relationship, Charley's drawing had some ambiguity in its orientation. He had placed the paper horizontally and put in the ground line as a small vertical, which was nevertheless "down" to him. In fact, his drawing was rotated ninety degrees. When he realized this, Charley turned the paper and thereby made the right side become the bottom. He seemed to vacillate as he did this. He was not completely sure which way it should go. Then he rejected this drawing and said, "I could make it easier [for Nancy to guess]." He never tried out this drawing to see if she could guess correctly. He wanted a new paper to start fresh.

Before beginning his second drawing (figure 8:2), Charley said, "Sometimes I don't do very well. Sometimes I erase." Here he described his own feelings about his skill, and he talked about his materials and what he does with them. He indicated that he would have to make the medium show what he meant. Like analysis of feedback, this strategy facilitates the distancing required for decontextualization.

In this segment of his self-initiated monologue, Charley guided himself again on how to draw. He told himself to make the person "straight." This comment may have been his response to his previous problem of orienting the figure. The body here was tilted again, though less obviously oriented toward the diagonal. This time the legs were almost perpendicular to the ground, which was now horizontal. When Charley said, "Look at what I did!" he was really calling his own attention to something he had done that surprised himself. Charley had drawn a semicircle over the head of the figure. Apparently it reminded him of a policeman's cap only after it was done.

Later, in the same drawing, he commented on his own skill and accuracy in positioning the nose. "There, I made the nose in the right place!" Here he referred back to the concern he had in drawing his first picture that the nose should be "in the middle between the two eyes." Charley continued to talk to himself, "I forgot to make the forehead," and did so by drawing an arc over the two eyes. When he said, "I forgot," Charley indicated that he was again analyzing the feedback from his own picture, as he had in his first drawing. He continued, saying, "What about his eyelashes and eyebrows?" Then he drew them. When asked if Nancy would guess from this drawing, he said, "Yes, because he's up in the air." Then he added, "I think I forgot his mouth," thereby telling himself to draw it in.

What is the observable difference between drawing 1 (the private drawing) and drawing 2 (the social drawing done for the sake of the guesser)? The most striking difference seems to be that the second evidenced

Figure 8:2. "This time I'm gonna make the person straight. He's jumping *that* way again. Here, look at what I did! Instead of drawing a person, I'm drawing a policeman."

more planning than the first. In the earlier drawing, the ground line had been almost an afterthought. The figure had been drawn almost horizontally and later turned so that it appeared in a vertical position. These ambiguities and discontinuities had been resolved in the first drawing and therefore no longer had to be worked out in the second. By then Charley had been through it all; he had integrated all the elements before. Thus he could guide himself by saying that he would make the figure "straight." The spatial orientation was ordered now in accord with the horizontal position of the page, and the elevation represented by the space beneath the feet was diminished. He apparently felt satisfied that he had mastered the "upness." What occupied him instead were details: eyelashes, eyebrows, and forehead. This change of focus from elevation to details of the figure might, of course, have been a consequence of his age and of his slight attention span. He no longer concentrated on rendering the idea of jumping. Having mastered the concept in drawing 1, he ceased to create again that same sense of elevation.

Charley wanted to test his second drawing. When Nancy guessed, "A boy!" Charley responded, "No, a policeman." The experimenter then intervened (as was the case in all uses of the word *jumping*, once the figure was guessed): "Yes, it is a person. Now can you guess the word that tells what he's doing?" Had this help not been offered, it is unlikely that the guesser would ever have thought to offer verbs. Nancy then guessed, "person stopping cars" and "person doing cartwheels," and Charley told her those were incorrect.

Both children were asked if they wanted to play some more. If so, Nancy would leave while Charley drew another picture, after which she would return to guess again. Both children agreed to continue. Charley was eager to go on to a third drawing.

The first sentence accompanying figure 8:3 was self-guiding, telling himself what to do. Then, examining his drawing, Charley saw that the figure lacked the crucial attribute of "upness," the space between the ground and the feet. He began then to imagine a justification, a clever fantasy, of the figure's appearance. He *was* off the ground, Charley insisted, but just didn't

Figure 8:3. "The ground and the person. He's so fat his leg is a little bit on the ground, his other leg went through the ground. [He erases where the leg "went through."] There we go. . . . What about his hair? I'm forgetting and his pants and his feet. . . . Oh! But he's on the ground—his feet are really in the air—he's so little in the air—but you'd think he's on the ground. . . . The floor is cracking—you know why? Because he's fat!"

look it. Here is a fascinating paradox in young children's drawings. Children are satisfied if *they* know that the feet are off the ground, even if the drawing indicates nothing of the kind. Many examples of this occurred in the children's performances. At the same time, a mature aspect of Charley's use of this apparent contradiction showed in his awareness that, to anyone else, his drawing would look as if the figure were *on* the ground. Nonetheless he was content with what he had drawn. He started to erase only the part where the feet passed through the ground line.

Again, he was asked, "Do you think Nancy will be able to guess your word from your drawing?" Charley had obviously lost track of the task, and the question about Nancy reminded him of what he was doing. Suddenly he recognized that Nancy would need to *see* that the man was off the ground. He answered, "Yes, I think because he's up in the air because he's so fat he's down on the ground. . . . I'll erase [erases to leave a space between the feet and the ground line]. There we go! Now he's up in the air! Now she'll guess!" This progression from verbal elaboration of a story about his figure to translation into the graphic medium exemplifies the shift in the use of a medium described earlier. Charley increasingly conveyed his intentions within the picture itself, relying less and less on verbal context.

When Nancy returned, Charley could not resist giving a verbal clue; he said, "These are pants." Perhaps he thought his drawing was ambiguous. He then said, "His legs are not touching this part," pointing to the ground line. The verbal clue called Nancy's attention to the space under the jumper's feet, that essential area, and she immediately guessed, "Jumping!"

Charley's series demonstrated a wide spectrum of strategies from both the first and second sets of premises. Among his immature strategies were fluctuating attention to the task and to the needs of the guesser. For a while he lost track of the task entirely and therefore was somewhat jolted when, having completed the third drawing, he was asked if Nancy would be able to guess. He also offered a justification of his drawing by inventing a story; in effect, he completed his picture by verbally amplifying what was on the paper. But these strategies did not articulate the referent in the drawing and therefore produced little that was available to a viewer.

Among Charley's mature strategies were his analysis of the visual feedback from his lines and his concern about handling the medium. He also analyzed the guesses and, after examining his second drawing, he said, "It *did* look like he was doing a cartwheel." Thinking about Nancy's previous guess, "person doing a cartwheel," he obviously felt that he had drawn something ambiguous and that he was responsible for the intelligibility of his drawing. These interrelationships among strategies, premises, and drawings demonstrate the mixture of both immature and mature thinking within a single child on a single occasion.

6. *What children's thinking teaches about adult art making*

This study showed that children shift in their understanding of the problem of picturing. Between the ages of five and eight their predominant attitudes shift from the first to the second set of premises. They change in how they understand their medium, their own role, and their relationship to the viewer. As they change, they learn that a picture cannot depend for its intelligibility upon any context outside the graphic medium; they must decontextualize their drawn representations. By the age of eight, when the child is able to judge what can serve his viewer best, he eliminates a great deal. He severs his representational motor activity from his graphic representation. He is less absorbed in re-creating the referent by inventing a form that is its equivalent, and instead he uses the pictorial medium to incorporate the necessary features that enable a viewer to read what he has drawn.

What is the relationship of this development in childhood to adult art making? Adults shape a form, in whatever medium, in order that it have meaning to others. Whether it be to soothe or to disturb, to clarify or to obscure, the effect of the work is anticipated. The image has its power, in fact, precisely because it exists in a community that can share in and react to its meaning. Whether a work challenges, distorts, or accepts the conventions of the culture, its relationship to the culture—to the viewer—is part of the artist's considerations. Picture making cannot be understood as other than a social act.

Just because people are alert to the impact of their work, it does not follow that all they create is conscious and premeditated. Like children, adults may use gesturing, rhythms, and other kinds of experimentation. These experiences may well be private and meaningful only to the artist; the acting out of motion and feeling may be distinct from any recognizable referent. Even in representational drawing, play with gestures and qualities of movement may have associations known only at the moment they are made. The artist may simply be enjoying lines and building up a repertoire of forms. No matter how private his work appears, however, as an adult he cannot but create a work that is influenced by all he knows and has experienced.

His private experimentation with the medium, with his own body movements, and within his own fantasy may well be the very substance of which the adult composes his work. But he can no longer be as totally immersed in these inner meanderings as is the egocentric child. He inevitably rejoins and maintains contact with his audience by internally anticipating his effect on a viewer, by seeking a way to salvage his private meanings so that they can become accessible to others. The artist thus must go where his audience is. Then he must carefully, with full knowledge of the vagaries and cares of his audience, lead them where *he* wants them to go. His awareness of his community and its visual conventions anticipates and orders his image so that it can participate in a dialogue with others. Through conceit or exclusiveness he may choose to communicate with some very select group, or even with some more appreciative future audience; yet to some degree he must be aware of the choice he is making. This is quite different from the child, who is unaware that there is any choice. Nevertheless, to some extent, the problem that the child faces remains a problem, in more sophisticated and enlightened form, for the mature artist.

In fact, the history of art is a history of the dialogue of artists with their viewers. By referring to, and then altering, stylistic conventions, artists have built upon the visual knowledge of their respective communities. This is as much true of the handling of paint as it is of the handling of subject matter. For example, Manet handled his paint loosely, creating effects of light that referred to and built upon the tradition of the Spanish artists of the seventeenth century. The impressionists then built upon and altered that effect further by breaking up paint units into even smaller globs. American abstract expressionists, in dialogue with these, played with color areas of different sizes to create virtual space even without object representation. The evolution and development of styles in art perpetually involve this dialogue through time.

What happens then to all that is no longer compatible with the adult's social use of pictorial communication? The early motor complement of graphic representation, the dynamic characterization of the referent, and the invention of form for the referent itself (without any contextual consideration for the sake of the viewer) all are inevitably excluded from social, comprehensible drawing. But they may yet be retained in the mind for private fantasy and logical problem solving. Private visual thinking may enable a person to address a problem in ways that are visual and yet beyond the pragmatic limits of the graphic medium's capability. Such thinking persists even in people who stopped drawing in childhood. Whether or not an adult continues to draw, he continues to explain problems to himself in visual terms.[4] This internalized process of visual thinking may also serve as a reserve from which people draw in their later creative work. In fact, the physiognomic gestural origins of forms, surviving in visual thinking, may be the impelling force for all artistic production. Artists throughout history certainly have not been enslaved by their awareness of the need for comprehensibility. Rather they have played with accepted forms and styles by exaggerating, simplifying, distorting, or even juxtaposing one against another.

Once the artist has internalized the requirement to decontextualize, ambiguous forms generated from his private visual thinking may influence his flexibility in handling comprehensible forms. An adult making pictures can then control the degree of deviation or distortion or even suspend comprehensibility because he is aware how his work will affect a viewer. When he can control the extrapictorial resources upon which children's art relies, he can increase the effectiveness of the graphic medium's inherent capacity.

Children's art, like other childhood behavior, inevitably must be shaped by the increasing awareness of the realistic components of each situation. Actually, it is through the shift in premises that children become liberated from a solipsistic world and can create within a social world in which they can expect to affect and respond to others. This shift in premises seems to be the dawning of participation in the world of art making. At this point the child's and the adult's way of thinking about picturing commence to converge.

Notes

1. Jean Piaget, *Play, Dreams, Imitation* (New York: W. W. Norton, 1962).
2. Heinz Werner and Bernard Kaplan, *Symbol Formation* (New York: John Wiley & Sons, 1963).
3. Diana Korzenik, "Visual Definitions: Communication in Children's Drawings" (doctoral diss., Graduate School of Education, Harvard University, 1971).
4. Rudolf Arnheim, *Visual Thinking* (Berkeley: University of California Press, 1969).

9

Artistic Practice and Skills
Vernon A. Howard

> Behind the music being created in his presence he sensed
> the world of Mind, the joy-giving harmony of law and
> freedom, of service and rule.
> —Hermann Hesse, *Magister Ludi*

This essay takes a critical overview as the desideratum of our vast practical understanding and growing experimental knowledge of artistic practice and skills.[1] As used herein, the phrase "artistic practice" refers to those repeatable patterns of thought and behavior considered essential to the development of various specific artistic skills. Practice thus encompasses everything from finger drills to dress rehearsals, while so-called artistic skills are distinguished less by anything inherently "aesthetic" than by their frequent or occasional use to produce works of art. Joinery and masonry as well as the more obvious examples of reading and writing can qualify under appropriate circumstances as artistic skills, along with the ability to execute a proper *plié* or musical phrase. Accordingly, mention of *artistic* practice and skills is intended more to underscore a point of view—that of the arts—on practice and skills than to suggest that they constitute a unique or exclusive category.

Just as no one skill or handful of skills is uniquely artistic, neither are there uniquely aesthetic emotions, pleasures, perceptions, and the like. Whatever the differences among the arts or between them and other human activities, artistic skills call upon the same general range of symbolic, cognitive, and manual capacities as such nonartistic efforts as reading a thermometer, swinging a tennis racket, or detecting the flaws in a cheap cigar.[2] It is a distortion to view the skills involved in both producing and perceiving art as confined to the most useless of all possible worlds and somehow all of a piece. Not every skill or product of skill, including acknowledged works of art, need be classified once and for all as art or nonart, aesthetic or nonaesthetic. Such classifications depend greatly upon one's viewpoint. Indeed, the category of the aesthetic will concern this treatment very little except as it relates to certain characteristics of works of art considered as symbolic end products.[3]

This essay falls into two parts, one mainly constructive criticism, the other mostly critical construction. Part I undertakes to correct certain common misconceptions of artistic practice (section 1) as well as to analyze the logic of repetition in practice (section 2) with an eye toward clarifying, among other things, how exercises are identified and utilized in artistic problem solving. Part II has three tasks: first, to analyze the deliberate drill and eventual routinization of skills, including the all-important roles of critical judgment and self-scrutiny in the practice process (section 3); second, to elaborate a rudimentary taxonomy of skills, facilities, habits, competencies, and attainments developed or presupposed by practice (section 4); and third, to view epistemological and experimental approaches to practice in reciprocal perspective (section 5).

As part of an initial effort to relate hard-won procedural insight to scientific investigation, an attempt will be made throughout to provide a modestly systematized account of practice lore, including the various deployment strategies, the obstacles and inhibitions to effective practice, and the evaluative thresholds characteristic of artistic practice in general.

Examples from the musical and dramatic arts receive somewhat more attention than other fields simply as a matter of convenient focus. In examining the practical development of skills, this essay proposes to view all the arts, not only the performing arts, from the perspective of performance at least to the extent that any work of art can be understood as the product of acquired skills.

I. ARTISTIC PRACTICE IN PHILOSOPHICAL PERSPECTIVE

1. Conceptions of practice

1.1 The work of artists. Among the more popular accounts of the artist at work are two to which it is useful to give descriptive names. The one here called the Athena Theory[4] usually emphasizes the artist's spontaneous imagination, inspiration, creativity, and the like. The other, labeled the Penelope Theory,[5] stresses more the honed skills and abilities that are also necessary for the making of mature works of art.[6] Though clearly representative of opposite sides of the productive coin, the two theories are not so incompatible as they might at first appear.

Under the Athena Theory, the inspiration for complex works of art is supposed to spring to the artist's mind in a flash of archetypal intuition, or perhaps in a series of such flashes. The artist is pictured as preparing himself for such moments by accumulating experiences which, under the direction of the holistic vision of his aesthetic daemon, may be transformed into art. What is more, he accomplishes all this without every really knowing what he is doing. Certainly the single most influential statement of this theory, the quotation from Plato opening the present section of this volume, bears repeating here: "For a poet is a light and winged thing, and holy, and never able to compose until he has become inspired, and is beside himself, and reason is no longer in him."[7] Thus Plato, not to mention his many modern imitators, goes so far as to make irrationality a necessary condition of artistic creation. By separating the sagacious skills of handicraft from those of art, Plato forged the familiar three-way link between creation, inspiration, and unreason characteristic of the Athena Theory.

But one need not go to such extremes when an argument from propriety will do as well. Even where the artist's training, skills, and special techniques are scrutable, it may yet be argued that: "It is better for people to know only the beautiful product as finished, and not in its conception, its conditions of origin. For knowledge of the sources from which the artist derives his inspiration would often confuse and alienate, and in this way detract from the effects of his mastery."[8] Just as realistic painting may be fallaciously reduced to seeing with an "innocent eye,"[9] artistic skill may be reduced by theory or propriety to creating with an innocent mind.

We are in fact accustomed for mostly good reasons to criticize a work of art independently of the artist's work habits and personality. We are also accustomed, more perhaps by the weight of Platonic tradition than good reasons, to consign the artist's skill to such shadowy sources as inspiration and idiosyncratic intuition. Whether intended to preserve works of art from genetic prejudice, aesthetic perception from distraction, or the wellsprings of talent from pseudoexplanation, the Athena Theory unnecessarily engenders understanding works of art at the expense of understanding the work of artists. Good critical habits require only that we distinguish the two, not that one be sacrificed for the sake of the other. The Athena Theory is at best a flimsy first-line defense against faulty accounts of artistic endeavor and at worst a last resort of aesthetic Platonists who would make of the artist a blind seer of his own works.

Unlike the Athena Theory, the Penelope Theory is less an inheritance from philosophy than a distillate from the artist's work experiences. It depicts the artist in his studio as a kind of devoted weaver of works, doggedly repeating the same sequence of motor acts, parts or wholes of works, or performances until he "gets it right." Getting it right, of course, may refer either to the artist's skilled activities such as his handling of a brush, metaphor, or bow, or to his final achievement in a finished novel, symphony, or performance. The theory chiefly concerns the activities and abilities of the artist as sometimes measured by his achievements. For example, a Penelopean interpretation of "practice makes perfect" would be something like "technique makes the artist," where technique is construed as voluntary control over those parts of one's body involved in making a work of art or, what amounts to the same thing, as manipulative facility in certain media.

More often than not, technique is related to practice by mechanical-causal analogy as being fully automatic, cue-determined behavior induced by mere serial repetition until, in the telling phrase, one can do it "without thinking." Since, on the Athena Theory, thinking is not a precondition of inspiration, it is possible to combine the notion of routine performance with that of spontaneous creativity or even intelligence generally where the latter is identified with *sagesse* or intuitive insight. In commenting on the views of the psychologist William James, Scheffler confirms that the arts and common sense are not the only places where this occurs: "Many thinkers have, in fact, supposed that performance is generally routine and habitual, while intelligence [add creativity] is, strictly speaking, spontaneous and innovative, the main function of education being to automatize performance so that the mind may be set free."[10] It is not unusual, therefore, to find the Athena and Penelope theories combined in a total view of the artist as a kind of inspired media mechanic extrapolating in rote fashion upon the literally "given" kernel of an artistic idea.

An underlying fallacy is, of course, synecdoche, the viewing of a complex process in terms of one of its aspects or stages. Thus whatever partial truth emerges from these familiar views of the artist at work taken separately or together, they inevitably encourage a general conception of the artist as endowed with a sort of mindless competence enhanced if not acquired by sheer repetitive exercise.

Beyond that is the reifying in explanation of such vague and over-worked notions as inspiration, intuition, creativity, and their kin, which themselves require explanation. Indeed it may be advisable to dispense as much as possible with such talk in favor of a vocabulary better suited to describing certain ubiquitous features of artistic practice. The rudiments of such a lexicon of practice will be set out in the course of the following discussion.

1.2 What practice is. Ordinarily, to practice an action involves repeating it, although we often repeat actions such as tapping a foot or finger in ways that could hardly be described as practicing them. As an ingredient of practice, repetition is guided by such specific aims as solving various sorts of problems and building skills and abilities. Moreover, to practice an action is not only to repeat it with an aim in view but to repeat it in accord with some developmental criteria of improvement, that is, criteria that would enable us to judge the stages of successive approximation to mastery of that action. Such criteria may be as specific as the elimination of note errors in a scale run or as recondite and pervasive as capturing the proper expressive mood of an entire symphony.

Besides aims and criteria of improvement, another cognitive feature of practice needs underscoring at the very outset. That is the fact that even effective, which is to say by some standard successful, practice is fraught with setbacks and failures, some of them instructive, some not, which figure as positive or negative reinforcement regarding how and what to practice.[11] In other words, aversive controls (for instance, pain or fatigue) are as crucial to consider as positive controls of practice behavior. Tentatively and generally, this would appear to be a more accurate account than either of those previously considered. Later sections will attempt to fill in some details of this rather more complicated picture, beginning with an examination of what effective practice cannot be, though it is often thought to be—*mere* repetition.

1.3 What practice is not. Many confusions engulf the notion of practice, none more perplexing than those relating to the nature and role of repetition, of repeating the "same thing" over and over. As noted before, it is a popular misconception that practice amounts to mere repetition of exercises or of whole pieces until, somehow, the performer "gets it right" and can "do it without thinking." In this context "getting it right" implies an achievement threshold—performing up to some preconceived standard —while "doing it without thinking" suggests the routinization of skills, which requires at least a modicum of critical judgment at some developmental stage along the way.

Thus while it is common to speak of practice as if it were merely repetition, more than that is implied from the start. Although repetition is an important, even crucial, aspect of practice, neither achievement thresholds nor routinized skills would seem to be characteristic of mere repetitive behavior such as nervous gestures, a peculiar gait, peristaltic movements, or a speech stammer. None of these serve any chosen aim and would hardly qualify as skills. Digestion and stuttering are not competencies in the usual sense of the term, and the former is not even a habit, whereas the purposive repetition of practice has a great deal to do with competencies and the cultivation or elimination of certain habits.

If one acknowledges that practice is purposeful, the characterization of practice as mere repetition is further misleading in suggesting both that practice reduces to drill and that the drill which is involved is thoughtless repetition. Routine tasks properly executed may require as much deliberate attention as novel ones which more obviously draw upon the full measure of an individual's awareness.

Consider the practice of advanced musical performers. Rarely is it repetition as a whole, for seldom is a piece repeated in its entirety again and again. Rather, troublesome passages are excerpted for special attention and may undergo considerable change in rhythm, dynamics, or expression while the performer concentrates on the aspect that is causing difficulty. Even then, when the performer does repeat, his efforts at improvement could hardly be described as mere repetition. Rather than mechanically duplicating a passage, he strives for particular goals of fluency, contrast, balance, and so forth. Successive repeats reflect his drive toward such goals rather than the passive absorption of a sequence of motor acts. To be sure, routinization of certain of those acts, for example manual dexterity at the keyboard, may be a requirement of higher levels of mastery. But that only shows that routinization is among the goals or achievements of practice, unlike repetition, which is more properly classed as a procedure of practice. Finally, as problems are solved, errors eliminated, and difficulties diminished, the dissected passages are reembedded in the original piece and previously ignored dimensions are restored for a run-through—all of which requires vigilance at every stage. Where vigilance may succeed without repetition (not everybody needs so much of it), repetition without vigilance is blind.

If it is a little clearer what besides repetition is involved in practice, repetition itself remains obscure. Some clarification of its role emerges from a comparison of intrinsic and extrinsic achievements (or aims) of practice. When practice is *of* a performance or parts of it, performing up to standard and with relative ease are intrinsic achievements of nonrote ways of repeating an action. Achieving something by practice in this sense is more like throwing smoothly or quickly than throwing and hitting a target. The success or failure is in the manner of the performance, not in any separate result or effect of the performance.[12] On the other hand, if a performance is improved through entirely separate (e.g., strength or facility-building) exercises or through exercises directed at particular aspects of the performance but abstracted and simplified, this is then an extrinsic achievement. The distinction is, of course, relative to how the behavior in question is to be evaluated—in terms of how it is done, or in terms of its proximate effects.

Among the cognitive aims of practice is knowledge not only that one has succeeded or failed to perform up to a given standard, but why. Even where achievement artifacts like a score, sketch, or print can be examined at leisure for the levels of skill they reveal, further scrutiny of certain intrinsic features of the skill activities themselves, such as fluency in the use of a notation or improper handling of a brush or chisel, may yield important insights into the causes of one's success or failure. In other words, development is gauged not only by results achieved, as in a standard test situation, but by how they are gotten.

Development as gauged and directed through repeated trials is a primary concern of education in the arts. Having a clear conception of practice and what is to be accomplished by it is therefore more important to the novice and the teacher of art than understanding mastery or "greatness" except as this understanding gives some indication of the direction practice should take. It is tempting in any case to speculate that the habit of treating performance standards as always extrinsic aims of practice (reinforced, perhaps, by the natural emphasis upon finished work or presentations) is at least partly responsible for the Penelopean view of practice as basically rote drill culminating as if by chance in some later success.

2. *The logic of repetition*

2.1 The ambiguity of repetition. Among other things, the foregoing discussion illustrates that the concept of practice is less vague than ambiguous. Scheffler, for one, notices the ambiguity between rote and critically repeated trials or performances.[13] There is an even more fundamental ambiguity in the conception of a repeated trial or, as we more commonly say, "doing the same thing over again." Simply to say that an artist repeats himself when he practices is as ambiguous as to say that the successive trials are similar without specifying the areas of similarity. Indeed, the ambiguity of repetition derives from that of similarity.

The reason is easy to see. Any two actions (or innumerable things in the universe, for that matter) are similar in *some* respect, so that any action could be said to be a repeat of any other.[14] Whether a given action does in fact repeat some other depends less upon the inherent nature of the action than upon the perspective from which we observe and describe it. In experimental situations, the task—sending and receiving telegraphic code, perhaps, or running a maze, or detecting pitch differences in a sequence of sounds—is limited and specified. Artistic tasks are much more various, and while it is common to describe the artist as "experimenting" in practice, the experimentation is loose, uncontrolled (in the scientific sense), seldom precisely circumscribed, and based on a body of lore that is peculiar to his art.

Some indication of what is to be repeated—e.g., pitches, dynamics, rhythm, or resonance—is normally supplied. But the specifications can be highly variable: more than one task may have the same purpose, and one task may serve multiple purposes. Consequently, what the artist may be explicitly instructed to do or described as doing will not always correspond to what he is implicitly expected or thought to be doing. For example, to say that someone is working on exercise A is not to say (though it may well be understood) that he is striving to produce a smooth sequence of pitches. Conversely, to say the latter is not necessarily to say or imply that his purpose need be served by exercise A. He may actually perform a number of different exercises and still be described as "doing the same thing"; or he may repeat the same exercise as identified by some criterion, for instance a score, while doing different things. This raises the logical question of how exercises, considered as repeated trials or performances of any kind, are identified.

2.2 Similarity and repetition. The preceding section claimed that an action judged similar to any other might also be judged to be a repeat of it. In practice some similarities count more than others, so that our judgments of repetition are more refined than that. There are many circumstances under which we should say that behavior B is similar to behavior A but not a replica or repeat of A. Betting on a horse is similar to but not the same as investing in stock. Or is it? The answer depends upon how one chooses to describe the two actions. A compulsive gambler, for instance, might well be described as repeating himself in both cases, namely as taking a risk, making a wager, or for that matter skinning a cat.

Given this variability it is worthwhile to take a brief closer look at how the description of behavior may change from "different" to "same." One would deny that A and B are behavior replica-pairs where they are taken to be entirely dissimilar. But there are many cases where one would deny that they are behavior replica-pairs even though they are similar in *some* way. Similarity in some respects is at least a necessary condition of repetition; but it further requires that some selection of those respects be taken as sufficient for B to be judged a behavior replica of A—that some shared property or set of shared properties serve as a criterion of behavior replicahood.

The selection of properties will vary with the context and generality of the description. That is to say, whether one behavior event is taken to repeat another depends upon the perspective from which it is being observed and described. Therefore to say that B is similar to A though not a repeat of A amounts to a denial of the sufficiency of the given labels common to A and B under the circumstances delimited by the perspective. The example above of the compulsive gambler illustrates the change from insufficiency to sufficiency with the shift from a lower to a higher level of descriptive generality. More simply put, specifically different actions may be generically the same.

Music provides rather more complicated examples of the identity and difference of practice behavior. Various stereotypical "exercises" are usually identified by a score, though they may be accompanied by supplementary verbal instructions relating to the aims of their performance. Where task identity is measured by a score, "doing the same thing over again" refers to a set of performances which, however different in other respects, are all compliants of a particular score. Under these conditions, task identity is but a subspecies of musical work identity.[15] In both instances, a score in standard notation serves to identify a compliant set of performances as being *of* such and such an exercise or work. Of course an actual score need not exist provided one could be written out. In fact, most verbal instructions incorporate descriptions of scores in lieu of an actual score or illustration; e.g., "Sing a five-and-nine scale on the vowel 'ah' in the key of C major."

It often happens that task identity is not measured by any one score but by a series of scores generated by a rule imbedded in the instructions, e.g., "Sing a series of five-and-nine scales on the vowel 'ah,' raising the tonic one half-step at the beginning of each successive scale." Here the overall task consists of a series of tasks corresponding to each separate score and vowel sound (where there is more than one). Hence what finally counts as the overall exercise depends upon whether one is speaking collectively or of a single subtask. The convenience of a notation ameliorates but does not eliminate this ambiguity.

Previously it was noted that tasks and their purposes can be variously correlated and described. It also makes a difference to what counts as behavior replicas (trials) in practice whether the behavior in question is identified by the task to be performed (e.g., running a C major scale) or by one or other of the purposes served by that task (e.g., improving manual dexterity). Even where a notation is available, as in dance or music, exercises may be identified in either of these alternative ways as well. In such cases, sameness of behavior varies with perspective as delimited by a notation, the tasks or achievements involved, or shifts in the level of specificity or generality within all three. Since any of these viewpoints can render true descriptions of what is being repeated in practice, the selection of one over another is a matter of knowledge, interests, and precision required. Thus an artist practicing may repeat himself in several ways even when he is said to repeat himself in only one way.

2.3 Ordering the lore. Before turning to some details of the epistemology and psychology of practice, a summary of what has gone before may help to pinpoint the sources of common perplexities and confusions about practice. Working backwards from the order of presentation: first, as perspective influences the identification of tasks, so, conversely, particular identifications shape the perspective one takes on what the artist repeats in practice. Second, not only can multiple tasks have the same purpose and the same task multiple purposes, but, third, the connection between them is always contingent and causal, not necessary and inevitable. Otherwise improvement would be automatic after the fashion of the Penelope Theory. Rather, practice presupposes at least a modicum of attention to tasks and their achievements plus the possibility of failure, and so it never makes perfect in *that* way.

A fourth observation not previously made concerns the relation between the identity and selection of practice tasks. Although prescribed exercises are often identified by the sort of task they constitute, they are selected according to what one can achieve by using them—by the contribution they are likely to make to the development of special skills and problem-solving strategies. This is not always clear to the novice, to whom exercises may appear as overwhelming *pre*-occupations prior to and only remotely related to their ultimate goals.

Many psychological studies demonstrate that informed intervention and knowledge of the aftereffects of an act being practiced have a significant influence on its future performance.[16] This common as well as scientific knowledge has consequences not only for the critical performance of stereotyped tasks (of the kind laid out in exercise books) but for the equally important business of learning how to select exercises and to construct new ones according to a wide range of demands, including those of particular styles or works or of one's own shortcomings. Failure at any stage to understand how practice conduces by degree to certain achievements or, vice versa, how special aims may require special preparation leads to a kind of "malpractice"—means without ends and dreams without means. Granting that, it is equally important to know *how* one is doing. Accordingly a crucial aspect of practice, especially in the performing arts, is cultivation of the secondary skills of self-observation and self-criticism (see Section 3.1 below). A precondition of these skills is having an answer to the question, "Why am I doing this?" A fully detailed answer is seldom the result of a single inspired effort. It is more likely to emerge gradually after careful pursuit, often with the help of others, and as the result of extended toil.

The foregoing remarks point up the dependence of any analysis of artistic activity upon our common stock of practice concepts as well as the established lore peculiar to the different arts. An understanding of artistic activity drawing only on those few aspects which have been experimentally investigated would be spotty indeed. By the same token we are forewarned that a mélange of conflicting precepts and techniques and the recondite successes of a few talented teachers, not to mention the cross-currents of novelty and tradition, do not by themselves comprise an orderly general view.

How, then, do our commonplace observations about habits, facilities, skills, practice, improvement, routinization, competency, and mastery map onto the distinctions and discoveries of the psychologist? A useful conceit is to regard informed accounts of skills expressed in the vernacular as collectively reflecting the outcome of a vast, natural trial-and-error experiment guided by highly refined aesthetic objectives. Some unified theory should therefore be possible, provided that sufficiently clear links are established between the common and technical languages of skills; provided, that is, that enough common ground can be found to accommodate procedural insight and experimental results within the same plot. Part II of this paper sketches the conceptual background against which such comparisons can be made, thereby delimiting a logical framework within which a general theory of practice and skills may evolve.

II. A CONCEPTUAL TOPOLOGY OF PRACTICE

3. The logic of awareness

3.1 Knowledge, awareness, and routinization. Having noted the dependency of an analysis of practice concepts in the arts on the established lore, and having suggested the possibility of cross-sectional comparisons at the interface of scientific and artistic perspectives, this essay now seeks to set out the rudiments of a comparative framework. It would be misleading to suggest that the framework, though somewhat prefabricated, is specially adapted to experimental purposes (it is too lacking in rigor for that) or that it captures every distinction recognized by ordinary and artistic experience (it is much too laundered for that). Rather its value lies in outlining the logical kinships among families of practice concepts that share a common ancestry though they have evolved in different conceptual environments.

The framework consists of two major parts: a strategic distinction between types of awareness involved in the control and routinization of behavior, and an epistemological sorting of ordinary practice concepts, including habits, facilities, skills, and the like. The distinction between types of awareness will be seen to cut across at ninety degrees, so to speak, to the epistemological schema so that, together, both parts of the framework constitute a conceptual topology on which bits and pieces of information from different sources can be located relative to the main features in the landscape of skills. Fortunately, previous analyses of several of the items contained in the framework assist in this task. A convenient beginning is with the relations among knowledge, awareness, and routinized behavior.

Post–World War II philosophers are accustomed to distinguishing propositional knowledge *that* from procedural knowledge *how*.[17] The difference is that between knowing that there are alternative fingerings for E-flat on the clarinet and knowing how to play an E-flat with different fingerings. Whereas historical, critical, philosophical, or psychological study of the arts all fall in the realm of propositional knowledge about art, performance competencies are more accurately classified as procedural know-how. Procedural knowledge thus encompasses skill acquisition, routinization, and the deployment of skills, all of which may involve but cannot be reduced to propositional judgment. Knowing how to ride a bicycle may be explained as adjusting the curvature of the bicycle's path in proportion to the ratio of the unbalance over the square of the speed;[18] but knowing that bit of information is clearly neither necessary nor sufficient to knowing how to ride. Propositional knowledge is embodied in statements adhering to logical standards of belief, truth, and evidence,[19] whereas procedural knowledge consists of skilled performances, activities which are the outcome of repeated trials involving given (or suggested) as well as newly discovered standards of achievement.

There is persistent confusion in the arts over the degree to which and in what respects one ought to be aware of skilled procedures both during their development and in their mature exercise. Novices at the dance, drama, or singing are enjoined to become more "aware" of what they are doing and in the same breath to "automatize" as much of their behavior as possible. Again, performers may be criticized for being unaware of some things and too aware of others. Aware in what sense, and of what, when?

The confusion lies less in the advice proffered than in the ordinary concept of awareness. Rather than the advice mixing quite different senses of the same term (simple ambiguity), the ordinary use of the word "aware" or "awareness" mingles one's intuitions willy-nilly. What are we to say, for instance, of the driver of a car who by reason of some distraction claims to have been unaware of the series of curves he has just negotiated? Was he or wasn't he? Of just such a commonplace situation involving both skill and some degree of awareness, D. C. Dennett observes: "Awareness sometimes seems to be a necessary condition for the successful direction of behaviour, and yet in another sense awareness is clearly detachable from behaviour (there are some limits on just how much of what one is doing one can be unaware of)."[20] Recognition of the "detachability" of awareness somewhat alleviates the problem of conflicting uses of the term and leads on to a useful distinction.

> When we say of the driver that he must have been aware of the curves under some description we are relying on the former [attached] sense of 'aware', and when the driver replies that he was conversing or daydreaming and unaware of the curves he is relying on the latter [detached] sense, and the crucial point is that we and the driver can be right at the same time. These two notions of awareness are entirely distinct in spite of their customary merger; what one can report directly, infallibly, and without speculation or inference is one thing, and what serves, or is relied upon, to direct behavioural responses is another.[21]

Dennett calls these awareness$_1$ and awareness$_2$ respectively. To simplify and somewhat modify his definitions: A is aware$_1$ that p[22] at time t if and only if A can state (or otherwise symbolize[23]) a perceptual report to the effect that p at time t. Dennett's example is "I am aware that there is an apple on the table," the principal clause of which could, of course, be either true or false; that is to say, the definition covers hallucinatory as well as real apples. A is aware$_2$ that p at time t if and only if p is the content of an event internal to A at time t that is effective in directing current behavior even though A is unable himself to describe that content. Thus the daydreaming driver is unaware$_1$ of the curves though clearly aware$_2$ of them.

A limitation on the distinction just drawn is that it applies only to the awareness of symbol-using animals; for it is a consequence of the foregoing definitions that a dog staring hungrily at a bone could only be said to be aware$_2$, not aware$_1$, of it *as* a bone inasmuch as the latter meaning depends upon capacities for symbolization not possessed by the dog. This lack of versatility derives from the fact that the distinction says nothing about the nature or mechanisms involved in either type of awareness that would allow us to deal with the nonsymbolic counterparts of awareness$_1$, if any. However, a theoretically useful line has been drawn, corresponding to our intuitions, between symbol-based and behavior-based awareness, a line not respected by the ordinary use of the word as applied to humans.

Both the above definitions are strategic attempts to distill from everyday notions of awareness just those aspects having to do with current consciousness and behavior control. Yet another extract of awareness refers to what is known independently of current consciousness or behavior.[24] As a partial synonym of "know," to be aware (of the fact) that Bruckner composed nine symphonies implies that it is true that he did. Such awareness is subject to truth conditions independent of any present consciousness or behavior. Certainly it is possible to be aware of something in all three ways; for instance, one is aware (knows) that it is three o'clock, is able to say so, and rushes off to an appointment. In this essay, truth-based awareness will be of little concern since it encompasses an individual's propositional knowledge about something as opposed to some skilled activity.

Symbol-based awareness$_1$ and behavior-based awareness$_2$ extend at right angles, so to speak, over the full range of procedural knowledge, but only when it is actually being exercised. The qualification is necessary since one could be said to know how to drive when not actually driving and quite lacking in awareness$_1$ of anything to do with driving. Thus the appropriate awareness is restricted to acts of driving, which is to say to particular bits of driving know-how as manifested on the road.[25]

Armed with this distinction, it is possible to give a relatively straightforward logical characterization of the routinization of skill. With respect to what one knows how to do, one may be aware$_1$ of something p that directs current behavior; become aware$_1$ of p by "paying attention" to what one is doing; or simply be aware$_2$ (without paying attention) sufficiently to direct complex behavior. From this viewpoint routinization is a matter of *ceasing* to be aware$_1$ and becoming aware$_2$ of a relevant bit of know-how. However crude, this classification helps to sort out an extremely wide range of skilled and unskilled behavior, as Dennett observes.

> It is not only simple reflexes that can apparently be controlled without the intervention of awareness$_1$. An accomplished pianist can play difficult music beautifully 'with his mind on something else', and need not be aware$_1$ of the notes on the page, the sounds of his playing or the motions of his hands and fingers. He must, of course, be aware$_2$ of these. . . . Experience suggests that although we can only be aware$_1$ of one thing at a time, the brain can control a number of complex activities at the same time.[26]

In emphasizing the role of perception without awareness$_1$, which is to say the brain's control of complex behavior below the threshold of awareness$_1$, Dennett indirectly throws light on the most puzzling feature of the Penelope Theory.

> As we say, we do many things without thinking about them, but surely we do not do these things without the brain's controlling them? It would be rare for a man to drive long distances without occasionally being aware$_1$ of his driving or the landmarks, and similarly the pianist would not long remain unaware$_1$ of the notes, the sounds or his finger motions. In particular, if he made a mistake, some sort of 'negative feedback' would no doubt shift him to awareness$_1$ of what he was doing.[27]

Clearly a good deal of what we learn to do never crosses the threshold of awareness$_1$. Controlled improvement, however, presupposes the effort to bring some things to the level of awareness$_1$ while pressing others down to awareness$_2$ for the sake of efficiency. But while effort is required to identify and solve particular problems, routinization occurs quite "naturally" since a performance problem, once solved, tends to gravitate to the level of awareness$_2$.

Drawing a distinction is one thing and applying it accurately is quite another. There is evidence to suggest that locating the line between awareness$_1$ and awareness$_2$ in any particular case is highly contingent upon the timing of a performing subject's reports. If not always the accuracy, certainly the detail of awareness$_1$ reports seems to decrease with increasing interval after performance. In "stream of consciousness" experiments on the thought processes of artists at work, David N. Perkins found that "one can elicit reports of complicated thought processes during thinking, and even more detailed reports by interrupting subjects and asking them to retrospect on the last few seconds. Subjects are surprised, saying in effect, 'I never knew I thought about that.' In general, the delay time in reporting is immensely important. The key point is that people are aware of much more than they ordinarily think they are."[28] This would seem to challenge Dennett's claim that "we can only be aware₁ of one thing at a time" and suggests that awareness₁ needs further refinements if it is to serve the purposes at hand. These are taken up in the next section.

Finally, to avoid misunderstanding it should be noted that this logical terracing of awareness states no more implies a psychological "quantum leap" from one disjoint state to another than crossing the Tropic of Capricorn implies a change in the weather. Stretching out on either side of the theoretical line between the two states are degrees of awareness not recognized by Dennett's distinction and having an important bearing on the guidance and development of skills.

3.2 *Focal and peripheral awareness.* To be aware₁ of what one is doing, to be able to describe or even to explain one's actions in a "detached" scientific manner, is not necessarily to know to what one ought primarily to attend—to be *focally* aware₁ of—in doing it. For example, one can say, "I am executing a *plié*," and be acquainted with the relevant physiological information, and still be unaware that kinesthetic concentration on an imaginary plumb line from head to floor enhances its proper execution. Such privileged information as that constitutes the elusive lore of any skilled performance. This aspect of knowing how might otherwise be labeled knowing *what* to think about, what precepts, percepts, images, or sensations to keep uppermost in consciousness at one or another stage of a skilled performance.[29] Whatever the focal center of attention at any given moment, one continues to be peripherally aware₁ of many other kinesthetic, muscular, visual, auditory, and tactile sensations grading into a penumbral awareness₂ of the fully routinized aspects of the performance. Many such background perceptions and sensations are irrelevant if unavoidable, while others contribute in an ancillary way to the guidance of behavior. Even the homely act of driving a nail requires both focal and peripheral attention to several factors, as M. Polanyi observes.

> When we use a hammer to drive in a nail, we attend to both nail and hammer, *but in a different way.* We *watch* the effect of our strokes on the nail and try to wield the hammer so as to hit the nail most effectively. . . . we are certainly alert to the feelings in our palm and the fingers that hold the hammer. They guide us in handling it effectively, and the degree of attention that we give to the nail is given to the same extent but in a different way to these feelings. . . . The latter are not, like the nail, objects of our attention but instruments of it. . . . I have a *subsidiary awareness* of the feeling in the palm of my hand which is merged into my *focal awareness* of my driving in the nail.[30]

In claiming that we attend to different areas of the perceptual field "to the same extent but in a different way," Polanyi is clearer about the difference in the ways (focal and subsidiary) than about the sameness of the extent. What sense is there to claim mutually exclusive focal awareness of some things and subsidiary or peripheral awareness of others, yet awareness "to the same extent" of both sets of things? Alternatively, does any sense attach to being aware of different things in the same way but to a different extent? It might be objected that this is making psychologically too much out of logically too little; but perhaps not, for in alluding to the "extent" of awareness, Polanyi inadvertently pinpoints what in fact is missing from his account of motor skills.

It will be recalled that Dennett draws a line between two types of awareness without any graded differences on either side of the line. Polanyi, on the other hand, recognizes graded differences without being able to say to what extent (on which side of the line) one is aware particularly of peripheral perceptual contents. Some clarification is won by combining both sets of descriptions in a single rubric, with Polanyi covering the "ways," so to speak, and Dennett the "extent." So, for example, driving a nail might be characterized as involving focal and peripheral awareness$_1$ respectively of the observed effects of the blow and certain sensations in the arm and hand. That is, someone performing this task can report all these contents, though the effects of the blow occupy the center of attention. Thus it makes sense to speak of being aware to the same extent (that is, aware$_1$) of contents of which one is aware in different ways (focally and peripherally). Similarly, to be aware of different things in the same way but to a different extent is more simply expressed as peripheral awareness$_1$ and peripheral awareness$_2$. (In the combined rubric one cannot, of course, be focally aware$_2$.) For example, one's peripheral awareness$_1$ of the feelings in the arm and hand merge into peripheral awareness$_2$ of the positions, say, of the shoulders, torso, legs, and feet. One is sufficiently aware of the latter to guide complex behavior, though not always to the extent of being able to issue a first person report of the contents of that awareness.[31]

Whether in driving a nail or a car, there may well have been—indeed, must have been—a learning stage that required focal awareness$_1$ of one or other of the routinized components of the skill. Consider the all-important stance and the placement of the feet in learning to use a sledge hammer. Often a lapse in efficiency, as measured by changes in the final effect, will precipitate a quick "cognitive review" of these supporting features of the action. However, while much of what one is peripherally aware of in performance can be observed in the first person, the performing subject is not always in the best position to survey all the relevant components of a complex skill. Therefore he may often require the aid of a therapeutic observer. Furthermore, many factors controlling behavior operate entirely below the threshold of awareness$_1$, as already noted, and necessarily require articulation by someone else before coming within the control of the performer. This underscores the crucial role of the performing arts teacher in alleviating problems of self-scrutiny and the "retrieval" of lost or yet unfound sensations and habits instrumental to proper performance.

3.3 *Knowing how and knowing what.*[32] Among the teacher's chief aids is a rich tradition of metaphoric language that passes with remarkably little change from one generation of performers to another. Despite altercations over terminology and meaning, every student of voice, for instance, will have some conception of what it is to "cover a tone," to "tuck the voice back in the throat," or to "place it forward in the mask." Such precepts and descriptions are suggestive not only of what to think about in performing but, equally important, of *what it is* to perform correctly. All that the teacher does by way of illustrating, ordering, and describing is designed to evince—with the intention to evoke—what it is to perform in the prescribed manner. This includes both simple and complex motor activities and their corresponding achievements.

There is a parallel here with the discussion of repetition in sections 2.1 and 2.2 above. There it was argued that being a repetition of *A* depends upon what are taken to be the essential features of *A*. Likewise, knowing what it is to perform properly also depends in part upon prior agreement on the salient features of correct performance. But only in part. Knowing what it is to experience something firsthand is idiosyncratic and irreducible to either propositional or procedural knowledge, though it is closely related to both. Some examples may help to sort out the relevant relations among knowing that, knowing how, and knowing what.

The first distinction to be made is between knowing what something is and knowing what it is to experience something. To know that something is red is not necessarily to know what it is to see red. A person blind from birth can understand the former without ever having had a visual experience of red. Similarly, one can know that there is a face in the trees in a picture puzzle or that the image of a staircase can be seen as from above or below, but one cannot know what it is to see the face or reverse the image before one actually does it, experiences it for oneself. By the same token, one can know what it is to see the face or reverse the image without ever knowing how one did it. Certainly there are many instances of direct experience for which no special training or procedures are required. One knows, for example, what it is to weep, to faint, to shudder, and to feel pain without knowing how to. Strictly, one never *knows how* to (come to) *know what it is* to experience something directly; which is just another way of saying that training is no guarantee of success. Nevertheless, insofar as a skilled performance is by definition one for which there are corresponding procedures of training and practice, such know-how is a necessary though not sufficient condition of knowing what it is to perform well.

"Knowing what it is to . . ." may also be contrasted with "knowing what it is *like* to . . ." where the latter indicates that one experience bears an analogous resemblance to another. One may not know what it is to be in the slums of Hong Kong, though one may know what it is like from having been in the slums of Rio de Janeiro or from reading about the adventures of Suzy Wong. Artistic instruction abounds in analogies, metaphors, and similes of endless variety, all intended to nudge the learner ever closer to the target experience. From a psychological viewpoint, such language functions as conditioned, secondary reinforcement in the shaping of skilled behavior by what Skinner calls "successive approximation" to a proper performance.[33] "Knowing what it is like to . . ." therefore typically refers to action-directed (as opposed to "scientific") explanatory knowledge *that* a likeness of some sort holds between a target state and an already familiar or imaginable experience. Thus the novice singer is enjoined to imagine his voice as "rising out of the top of his head" or "reaching out to encompass the farthest spaces of the room" not because that is what it is to project properly but because that is what it is like.

Another form of propositional knowing what, embedded in knowing how, is knowing what to think about (focally). Far from being a species of explanatory knowledge, however, it amounts to knowledge of a precept to the effect, "Think of that!" or "Do that!" It is a matter of knowing that such and such a strategy or "little piece of business" works under the appropriate circumstances. Knowing what it is to perform properly, on the other hand, is not in any way reducible to propositional *knowledge that*, since it requires direct acquaintance with the content of a person's awareness$_1$. Such content is, as has been mentioned, expressible in first person, nonevidential reports which may or may not succeed in evoking in somebody else what it is to perform properly.

For innumerable reasons one may never succeed in knowing what it is to perform properly despite trying to follow every precept of one's teacher, amassing volumes of scientific information, and listening carefully to the reports of those who do know what it is. Such a student stands in poignant contrast to the "natural" performer who grasps what it is to do something properly with relatively little guidance and drudged attention to subroutines. Such individuals mature in skill more quickly and, expending less effort on the stages of development, are often less aware$_1$ of the ingredients of their success than dedicated but less gifted persons. It is only mildly paradoxical to say (keeping in mind the difference between awareness$_1$ and awareness$_2$) that such fortunates know what it is to perform well without knowing how.

The knowledge by acquaintance associated with "knowing what it is to . . ." is perhaps most explicitly represented among psychologists by Piaget's "concrete operational" stage of thinking, with its emphasis upon manipulative encounters with the physical-sensory world.[34] This follows upon a "sensory-motor" stage of mere "figurative" acquaintance with the physical world limited to the sensory modalities and one's own direct actions. The transition from the preoperational to the concrete operational stage is characterized in terms of hierarchies of "operational schemes" which allow for increasingly complex interaction with one's environment so long as it continues to be within one's direct, perceptual purview. Through the gradual mediation of symbolic systems, the child of eleven to thirteen emerges into "formal operational" thinking, at which stage he learns to act on the world indirectly through various symbolic "representations": to make predictions, deductions, multiple classifications, and assessments of evidence having no direct perceptual counterparts.

It is worth emphasizing, however, that skilled motor activities learned after the achievement of logico-hypothetical thought, while indeed remaining concrete operations, must no longer be construed as mere stages en route to formal operations but rather as being among the analysanda, so to speak, of reflective thinking. That is to say, mature skills represent a higher level of integration, presumably through the complementary processes of "assimilation" and "accommodation," of "formal" thought with action in the category of concrete operations. In contrast with a child's slower development, an adult can quickly analyze and dissect his first, "figurative" experiences in elaborate and diverse ways designed to increase his sensory discrimination and control over the outcome of his efforts.[35] Knowing what it is to experience certain sensory cues as such thus combines with the lore in the common process known as "getting the feel of it."

4. Skill: the aim of practice

4.1 The constituents of skill. Among philosophers the concept of skill has been assimilated to habit at one extreme, as by Dewey, and to "intelligent performance" at the other by Ryle.[36] In fact, skill comprises at the very least both certain habits and their intelligent deployment in situations demanding continuous means-ends adjustments across a wide range of sensory-motor, symbolic, and evaluative parameters. The special habits, facilities, and strategies required for intelligent performance can be called the "constituents" of skill, whereas terms like "competency," "mastery," and "greatness" refer to evaluative stages of their development and use. Through procedures of training and drill, practice aims first at acquiring the constituents of skill and thereafter at developing competency in and mastery of them. It may seem odd to speak of competency in or mastery of habits, but contrary to Ryle, whether such epithets are appropriate depends less upon their status as habits than upon their relation to some skill. Again contrary to Ryle,[37] not even the lowliest of finger drills can safely be described as the mere "imposition of repetitions," since drill by no means excludes intelligent intervention, guidance, demonstrations, and painstaking care in the manner of execution. This fact is reflected in the different types and degrees of conscious control (see section 3.2 above) that are involved at one or another stage of the learning or mature exercise of a skill.

On the side of artistic lore and common sense, it remains to delimit the ranges (extensions) and relations among the principal aforementioned practice-skill concepts without committing undue violence to their standard uses. The program is to distinguish clearly different concepts to which ordinary terms are attached though with somewhat greater variability than the demarcations sketched herein would suggest.

In discussing the relations among cognitive and educational terms, Scheffler observes that the ranges of "learning" and "teaching" far outstrip "knowledge" altogether to include habits ("propensities") such as smoking or being punctual at one extreme and "attainments" like understanding or appreciation at the other.[38] To take Scheffler's example of punctuality, learning how to be punctual (the procedures that will ensure punctuality) is not equivalent to learning to be punctual (the habit); someone who knows how to be punctual may seldom or never exercise the procedures of punctuality, whereas someone who is in the habit of being punctual nearly always does. Of course one could say that the latter person knows what it is to be (habitually) punctual in the sense of section 3.3 above so long as that knowledge is understood not to be equivalent to any set of propositions or procedures.

Habits or propensities do often have "strictly associated" techniques. To be in the habit of smoking implies knowing how to smoke, though not conversely. Attainments, on the other hand, have no strictly associated techniques or procedures, nor, one might add, can they be withheld like skills. One can begin to understand or cease to understand a theory but not, except elliptically, refuse to understand it. Neither is understanding or appreciating a theory, poem, or painting reducible to some equivalent piece of "understanding know-how" or "appreciation know-how" as such. As Scheffler puts it: "Certainly there are techniques *embedded* in attainments: One who understands quantum theory knows how to read, and one who appreciates music knows how to listen. But these bits of know-how are not strictly associated; they are not equivalent to knowing how to *understand*, and knowing how to *appreciate*, respectively."[39]

The point seems to be that attainments are the nonequivalent achievements of the exercise of various kinds of know-how. Being punctual, understanding a theory, appreciating a poem, and the like *are* matters of knowing what it is to do or experience something, and as such they presuppose but are not guaranteed (implied) by bits of procedural know-how. We do speak, however, of teaching or learning such habits and attainments. This suggests not that attainments and habits should be excluded from the realm of knowledge but rather, perhaps, that not all knowledge should be considered a matter of only establishing a belief or procedure. But that is a separate issue outside the scope of this discussion.

Scheffler divides procedural knowledge, the notion of a trained capacity or skill in the broad sense, into "critical skills," which involve an irreducible element of critical judgment, and "facilities," which are relatively routinizable competencies such as typing or spelling. In general, the former would require both focal and peripheral awareness$_1$ and the latter peripheral awareness$_2$ only. Practice clearly applies to both critical skills and facilities, both being "typically built up through repeated trials or performances"; and though habits too are formed through repeated trials, Scheffler stops short of saying they are practiced.[40] The reason is that the concepts of proficiency, competency, and mastery are peculiarly applicable to skills (in the broad sense) but not to attainments (one does not become a master understander of a theory) nor to habits (one does not develop a competent habit of smoking or fingernail biting). In this way, ordinary discourse itself may be seen as corroborating the anti-Penelopean thesis of Section 1.3 that the concept of practice cannot be simply equated with that of repeated trials. As noted at the beginning of this section, not even drill, which always provides for intelligent intervention, can be safely equated with "the imposition of repetitions."

Such remarks notwithstanding, some habits at least do appear to be practiced, particularly those closely associated with skills. Does this not contradict Scheffler's view? Maybe not. There seems to be an ambiguity in his account between habit construed as a propensity or tendency of any sort, including facilities,[41] and habit as repeated behavior below the threshold of trained facilities.[42] (It is assumed that all the behavior in question is learned.) The reason perhaps is that in acquiring a skill, one strives to attain some habits while eliminating others. Certainly some attainment-like "habits," such as making a habit of success or playing beautifully as a habit, represent hyperbolic uses of the term. Other habits *of* competency, however, such as special breathing habits or posture, would include many of the routinized facilities required for competent performance.

The relation between practice and habits *of* competency becomes clearer when viewed in light of the most general aims of the former. Earlier, in Section 1.2, practice was said to involve not only repetition but repetition with an end in view. The ultimate aim of practice is mastery of or at least competence in a skill. The first aim of practice, however, is the acquisition of the requisite facilities and critical skills (in Scheffler's sense). Habits *of* competency would then encompass not only behavior judged generally conducive to the growth of skill, such as proper sleep, avoidance of conflicting stress, heeding others' performances, and so on, but also many of the constituents of the skill itself once they have been acquired and routinized. (But only then, since up to that point they could hardly be described as "habitual.") So, for example, facilities for phrasing or intonation in music or for gestural nuance in acting or the dance may become performance habits—ones which by their particular refinements often distinguish a performer from all others.

Naturally, many habits are either untrained (and therefore a-competent) or irrelevant; but relevance is relative by definition. It is common among actors, for instance, to speak of competency at certain everyday habits like smoking, walking with a peculiar gait, or even punctuality at picking up cues. This is because they are being considered in this context as acting skills—part of the actor's repertoire of "normal" behavior. A habitual off-stage smoker may be an on-stage fumbler, so aware$_1$ of what must seem to be and to a large extent must actually become "automatic" that he cannot be competent at it. Whether a common habit like smoking is to be assessed as a skill, as it were, depends on the viewpoint one takes of it—whether or not it qualifies under the circumstances as a facility to be learned and refined.

Still other habits become *merely* associated by "accidental conditioning" with particular skills and may eventually be deemed wrong or harmful because of their immediate or potential interference. Examples would be the tendency to stretch the neck upwards when singing at the upper limits of one's range or, at a more homely level, reading in a dim light. Practice therefore aims not only at the attainment of competency but at the acquisition of skill-constituent habits *of* competency as well as at the elimination (by extinction) of other interfering ones. What all habits have in common, be they skill-constituent or not, is their tendency to be regularly repeated and routinized under the aegis of awareness$_2$.

4.2 The attainments of skill. Competency, proficiency, and mastery can be listed along with understanding and appreciation as "attainments," as achievements of the exercise of skill. Accordingly, one does not repeat and hence does not practice competency or mastery. Rather, like understanding or appreciation, they are *shown* (exhibited, exemplified) in performances which can be repeated and practiced. The general category of "attainments" thus refers to the positive side of a sliding scale of evaluative, polar predicates characterizing the manner of something done: well or poorly, intelligently or stupidly, competently or incompetently. In other words, one practices *for* competency or mastery and may exhibit it in varying degrees or not at all.

How much, then, of a competent performance can be routinized by practice? Scheffler maintains that proficiency at a critical skill as opposed to a facility is not increased by routinization: "A critical skill such as chess is quite different from capacities in which increased proficiency does result from increased routinization."[43] Maybe not chess as such, but certainly many of the critical skills *of* chess, including aspects of strategy, would appear to be both routinizable and improved by routinization. Care must be taken, however, to distinguish the question whether critical skills are improved by routinization from whether they are improved by repetition and practice—by repeated exercise under different performance circumstances. "Critical skills," as Scheffler uses the term, apply only to situations offering some opportunity for intelligent, strategic choice and are therefore unroutinizable by definition, though yet repeatable and practiceable. Even strategic judgment, however, may be highly schematic and routinely adjusted to standard variable circumstances. Just as some habits may be skill-assessed, some critical skills may be enhanced by routinization, although the performer can never (safely) entirely relegate his critical capacities to "automatic" control.

Rather than restrict critical skills to whatever bit of strategy happens at the moment to be under the control of awareness$_1$, it seems preferable to maintain that *any given* critical skill—say, controlling the center in chess[44]—is likely to pass from deliberate, focal attention to routinized, reflexive status with increasing mastery of the game. Chess grandmasters and master musicians alike are conspicuous not only for their virtuosity but for the perspicacity of their play, an economy of means facilitated by the routinizing of vast areas of strategy. In short, it is not that critical skills as such resist routinization but rather that activities like chess and music allow for indefinite further development of critical skills as others are routinized. To that extent, neither chess nor music is routinizable; but such critical skills of chess or music as can be are no less judgmental for becoming routinized.

The latter point brings us to an essential feature of critical skills. Unlike, for example, a simple tracking task in a psychological experiment, a *critical* skill involves continuous, judgment-based adjustment of responses, usually of a highly complex nature, to changing contingencies. Judgments, like anything else, may fall into typical patterns, and to that degree they admit of routinization. But new contingencies will always arise to challenge the performer of complex tasks. Scheffler contrasts chess, as requiring strategy and choice from among permissible moves, with fully routinizable skills like typing or spelling, which lack any such "comparable occasion for choice."[45] Furthermore, principles of chess strategy, like rules of musical practice, are primarily heuristic, incomplete, and without any guarantees of success. The procedural judgment required for their proficient use indeed presupposes, though it is not itself *entirely* reducible to, previously mastered routines. Otherwise sheer Penelopean persistence at routines would make a grandmaster or master musician of anyone.

It is common enough to know how to play chess or the piano without playing well, where "playing well" may encompass anything from minimal to maximal critical competency (mastery). The notion of critical skill thus overlaps but does not coextend with that of know-how. Scheffler observes: "We may, in given contexts, wish to withhold the attribution of *know how* from the student until a certain level of intelligent play is attained. But such a decision is not forced on us, and we may well construe intelligent play as a further condition beyond the achievement of a minimal strategic know-how."[46] In other words, we may construe critical skills as exceeding the upper limits of know-how just as the ordinary notion of habit overlaps while extending below the lower limits of procedural knowledge.

Figure 9:1. Relative ranges of the major practice and skill concepts

Figure 9:1 shows the relative ranges of the major practice and skill concepts discussed thus far, including the kinds of awareness, whether focal (FA) or peripheral (PA), normally associated with them at maturity. Dotted lines between terms indicate graded, continuous differences, while the broken line of a brace indicates an area of variable application (vagueness) of a term.

4.3 The ambiguity of critical skill. It is clear from the context of his discussion that Scheffler is concerned with skilled performances of various kinds. However, the term "critical skills" is ambiguous between performative and evaluative skills, between the deployment of facilities and the assessment of results achieved by oneself or others. Depending upon the sort of performance one has in mind, evaluative skills, being essentially propositional, are detachable from some performances. If the performances themselves are propositional, as when we speak of "doing" science, philosophy, or history, the distinction between performative and evaluative skills loses significance (with the notable exception of the literary arts). It is as reasonable to argue that the best critical thinker in science *is* the best scientist as it would be absurd to argue that the best art critic is the best artist.

The reason critical skills of performance and evaluation are mutually detachable in the arts in ways unthinkable in the sciences is that they tend, on the whole, to be different skills, differently trained and having different aims. "Critical skill" in the performative sense is the meetingplace of propositional and procedural knowledge, with emphasis upon the latter. Art criticism, on the other hand, like science, deals in propositional knowledge; and although their respective standards of formulation and evidence differ drastically, they appear to be alike in that respect. Science too has its performative aspects in various laboratory, research, and field techniques, but they culminate in their contributions to some form of propositional knowledge. There are no duets for centrifuge and beam balance, and a musical performance would not normally be said to "confirm" its score.

In the end, the question is whether procedures are in the service of propositions or the reverse. So far as "doing" art is concerned, it is always the reverse, although the final product may itself be a set of propositions, indeed a novel full. Certainly an important ingredient of communicable know-how is knowing what (propositionally) to think about and to do; but it is not the primary aim of heuristic principles of performance to explain, justify, confirm, or disconfirm performance results but rather to achieve them. If the distinction between doing and criticizing science is somewhat gratuitous, it is yet a ubiquitous fact of art.

Among certain "intellectual" games like chess or bridge, criteria of criticism are largely drawn from constitutive rules and strategies of play. Knowing how to play (up to, say, the level of minimum critical skill) thus is both necessary and sufficient for making informed critical observations (if not to write critical reviews of matches, which requires additional skills). Here again, the difference in skills between doing and criticizing is less pronounced and therefore is somewhat misleading as a model for the arts. A possible exception is the literary arts, where writing skills are the common denominator of both literary art and criticism. But even here the difference between "creative" and "critical" abilities is widely recognized. As soon as one considers the nonlinguistic arts and the performing arts, some of which naturally involve language, it is clear that knowing how to produce such works is neither necessary nor sufficient for making informed critical comment. And conversely, one may succeed in becoming a competent critic without first being an artist. Perhaps as a cautionary note it should be said that detachable does not make desirable.

5. Questions practical, epistemological, and experimental

5.1 Finding the right response. These final two sections take a few tugs at a main connecting thread among the preceding ones, namely, the mutual bearing of practical know-how and the experimental study of skills and practice. Among the purposes of ordering the common language of skills in the arts is to make the procedural lore more accessible to experimental test while also indicating new areas of investigation of particular artistic skills.

Preceding sections stressed the continuum of propositional knowledge involved in skilled procedures, notwithstanding the irreducibility of the latter to the former, ranging from knowing what it is,[47] what it is like, and what to think about (direct experience, comparisons, and precepts) to testable, explanatory hypotheses about skills. While practitioners and teachers of art tend to be occupied with the different forms of knowing what, learning theorists are primarily concerned to answer such questions as these: What native capacities (sometimes called "abilities") are required for learned skills? How are particular skills learned? How do different skills interact; for example, how can the learning of new skills be helped or hindered by ones previously learned? How are skills "hierarchized"? Are there characteristics of practice behavior and development shared by most or all skills, for instance, the occurrence of "plateaus" or the effects of "distributed" versus "massed" practice?[48]

Complete and secure answers to these and kindred questions are not yet available, and those that are available are not always applicable to tasks differing in certain fundamental respects from those on which the answers were based. In studies of maze learning, for instance, Brogden and Schmidt[49] and Miller[50] found that increasing the number of alternatives at each choice point (assuming that the number of correct choices remains constant) increases both the time and the number of errors during learning but *not* the difficulty of remembering the correct response. That is, once the correct response is made, recollecting it appears to be uninfluenced by whether there are two, three, five, or ten alternatives per choice point.

One might expect a different result for tasks in which the disjunction between correct and incorrect responses was less clear. To take a common case from the arts: in learning to properly modulate a difficult vocal passage, it is likely that increasing the number of alternative interpretations would increase not only the number of errors and the time involved during learning but also the difficulty of remembering the correct response (assuming that there is one preferable to others). This is because the very notion of what *is* correct is (*a*) difficult to communicate (to know what it is like), and therefore the guidance to be obtained from such communication is comparatively limited, and (*b*) difficult to perceive (to know what it is first hand).

This expectation receives some distant support from studies of the influence of syntactic and semantic similarity on rote serial learning of adjective lists and paired-associate (stimulus-response) learning of adjectives.[51] Generally it was found that an increase in similarity resulted in an increase in the number of trials to criterion. Of course, things designated "similar" under one description (e.g., number of letters per word) may be quite dissimilar under another (e.g., sameness of meaning); hence it is vacuous to claim that "high stimulus similarity produces high stimulus generalization from one item to another."[52] That follows, if at all, in reverse, and simply from things being grouped under a common label. The significant claim is: "Since the stimulus items are less distinctive [in respect of one or other selected properties], they should be harder to discriminate. Likewise, if response items are highly similar, learners should have a harder time in finding and remembering their distinctive properties."[53]

Both difficulties are commonplace in the learning of artistic performance skills, particularly those requiring a high degree of "extrospection," so to speak—the ability to monitor the details of one's own performance. At the level of particular facilities, compensatory and pursuit tracking experiments on so-called "adjustive skills"[54] like tracing an outline, driving a car, or catching a ball are applicable to a wide range of artistic skills. These would include aspects of pitch and rhythm perception, classical dance movements, use of various notations—anything, in fact, requiring continuous adjustment of responses to an unambiguously "correct" target state.

Studies of adjustive skills involving kinesthetic, visual, and verbal "guidance" (information supplied prior to a response as contrasted with feedback, "knowledge after") seem to confirm the practice lore regarding the usefulness of juxtaposing errors and correct responses in the building of discriminatory facilities. Holding fairly summarizes the overall findings in this area:

> We began by considering how far reducing errors might contribute to learning. However, if this is done in such a way as to reduce the information available to the learner the learning will suffer. Knowledge of the correct response is incomplete if there is no opportunity to define it against the alternatives, just as we cannot be said to understand 'red' if we have never identified other colours.[55]

It is perhaps worth noting parenthetically that such comparisons by constant conjunction are an important step toward understanding the performing artist's refinements of jargon and metaphor. Holding continues:

> Kaess and Zeaman's experiment suggests that it is inefficient to present the learner with a number of possibilities without indicating which of them is correct [practicing one's mistakes?]. Giving both correct and incorrect alternatives while ensuring correct responses seems to be the best solution. . . . A learner practising alternatives is not learning errors if he knows which is the correct response.[56]

These remarks are particularly apropos of perceptual nuance but could equally apply to the discrimination of shades of meaning and expression in both the production and interpretation of works of art. In any event, such difficulty in learning to distinguish correct from incorrect responses after the fact is not one normally encountered by maze learners, typists, telegraphers, or spelling champions.

5.2 Beyond plateaus and inhibition. A majority of experimentally based studies of the arts deal with problems in the perception and interpretation of art: strategies of visual perception;[57] the expressive conventions of Western tonal music;[58] or the information-theoretic effects of style, mode, or medium.[59] Others focus on devising tests of artistic aptitude.[60] Relatively few studies tap the silent springs of artistic production—the work and practice habits of artists.[61]

Though the two are obviously conjoint, there is an emphatic difference between studying the development of skills and studying their mature exercise. The preceding discussion has ventured into both areas, but the emphasis throughout has been on tracing the anatomy of skill and practice concepts with a view toward understanding the procedures of the mature learner and user of skills. Although little research has been done on the search and practice strategies of artists at work, a large literature exists on general skill development centering around the questions rehearsed at the beginning of the previous section.

Some studies, as just explained, require cautious reinterpretation for artistic contexts while others are sufficiently general to require only the substitution of appropriate artistic skill-variables. Though somewhat inconclusive scientifically, studies of distributed versus massed practice and the related issues of "reminiscence," plateaus, reactive inhibition, and "hierarchization" contain many results readily adapted to the refinement and use of artistic skills. Conversely, the investigation of these phenomena in artistic settings may reveal new data and lines of inquiry, especially regarding how best to learn skills and what sort of changes take place during practice.

Bearing on the topic of how best to learn skills is the question whether learning is greater and quicker when practice is intermittent, interrupted by frequent rest periods ("distributed"), or when it is continuous and unremitting ("massed"). Since Lorge's classical experiments on mirror drawing and code substitution,[62] it has been repeatedly demonstrated over a wide range of psychomotor and verbal tasks that distributed practice is superior to massed practice, especially in the short run. In most instances, massed practice resulted in a marked temporary decrement and a lesser permanent one. In other words, distribution is likely to result in quicker though not necessarily greater improvement than massed practice.

Two notions relevant to artistic skill development have been adduced to account for this phenomenon: "reactive inhibition" and "reminiscence."[63] Reactive inhibition refers to a decrement in the rate or accuracy of response which accumulates under conditions of continuous responding and disappears with rest. Reminiscence, as the Platonic origin of the term suggests, refers to an apparently spontaneous improvement in response after rest from practice, as contrasted with the decrements of overresponding or forgetting. Reactive inhibition presumably accounts for the temporary decrement of massed practice and reminiscence for the gradual "evening out" over the long run of the difference between massed and distributed practice.

A secondary inhibitory state called "conditioned inhibition," wherein the subject *learns* not to respond well as a result of induced reactive inhibition, aims to account for any long-term decremental remainder between massed and distributed practice. Although conditioned inhibition seems not to have survived experimental testing—more accurately, a reliable test of it has yet to be devised[64]—it is intuitively useful for understanding a common practice phenomenon, namely, anticipatory fear of certain response decrements, or, as it might otherwise be put, habituation to failure. An example would be the difficulty a novice singer would experience while attempting to sing a high note at the end of a strenuous passage. Later on, when the singer's skill and endurance have improved to the point where he can perform with relative ease other passages of comparable difficulty, he may yet experience the same difficulty upon return to the original passage.

Referring indirectly to conditioned inhibitions, musicians, actors, and dancers often speak of "relearning" old works in order to bring them up to current standards. Such relearning can be more difficult than learning new material because of previously entrenched habits. Among other things, relearning requires unlearning old bad habits, which is to say, extinction of previously conditioned response inhibitions imposed by past limitations.

Experimental results and practice lore do not always agree. For example, it is commonly held that reminiscence does not occur in distributed practice, whereas the lore suggests that it often does. And again, while there is animal evidence to show that reminiscence is not an effect of mental rehearsal[65] ("thinking about it"), the opinion is widely held that it often is. In this instance, there is much to recommend the practical view that improvement frequently results from "silent rehearsal," especially where continued overt responding is likely to build up some reactive inhibition; in other words, where practice is deliberately distributed to avoid fatigue and frustration. Execution of difficult tasks is clearly made easier by reflection upon different aspects of the task, a shifting around of focal awareness$_1$ in the interest of corrective adjustment. Many of the "extrospective" judgments one makes during practice involve a degree of retrospection in the silent periods between trials. Finally, much training advice, indeed the language of instruction itself, requires mental rehearsal and presupposes on practical evidence that some improvement at least may result from it.

"Stream of consciousness" experiments of the sort mentioned in section 3.1 above wherein subjects record on tape their normally silent meditations may shed more light on the recondite grounds of reminiscence. Beyond that, investigation of the thought patterns of artists at work may provide insight into another widely recognized practice phenomenon: the occurrence of "plateaus," the flat areas of a learning curve where little or no improvement takes place. It is generally held that "the plateau occurs where the limit on the lower-order habits has been reached and where the higher-order habits have not yet begun to appear."[66] While it has been argued that plateaus are caused by a drop in motivation, it appears more likely that plateaus *cause* such a drop if, as seems true, plateaus occur at the points of transition between lower-order and higher-order habits.[67] One might expect a decline in motivation at those learning stages involving the struggle for a new ordering of the task and a corresponding leveling off in efficiency. If in fact plateaus are primarily cognitive rather than motivational in origin, an analysis of the artist's "logic," his problem-solving and associative strategies, may clarify how past gains are finally consolidated to produce new improvements.

Deese maintains that: "Something like this hierarchical structure must occur in all tasks in which there is opportunity to recode the material into larger and larger units. Thus, learning to typewrite, read music, and the basic skill of learning to read itself must involve something like hierarchies of habits."[68] "Recoding the material" hierarchically must inevitably involve changes in cognitive strategies and shifts of $awareness_1$, including routinization of previously focal tasks, not to mention the literal "recoding" of symbols in terms of how they are to be interpreted and used. An extensive investigation of symbol systems and the cognitive processes involved in their use emerges as a natural corollary and extension of the experimental work already done on the conditions of practice.[69]

5.3 A beginning. This discussion began by considering some popular half-truths and misconceptions concerning practice in the arts, beliefs rooted in confusions about the natures of and relations among practice, knowledge, repetition, and the identification of tasks and their purposes. Once sorted out, however, the distinctions of common sense and artistic lore reveal a complex structure of practical knowledge of skills that bears careful analysis and comparison to the experimental investigation of practice and skills. To those ends, the rudiments of a conceptual topology of practice-skill concepts were sketched, starting with an examination of the types of awareness involved in both the deliberate and routinized control of complex behavior and followed by brief analyses of skill constituents like habits, facilities, and critical judgment; the roles of training and drill; and competency and mastery as representing the attainments of skill. The discussion concluded with sample assessments of experimental findings and explanations of such practice phenomena as developing response discriminations, the virtues of distributed versus massed practice, inhibitory interferences, and plateaus. All this is only a beginning at the formidable task of ordering and integrating what is already known about practice and the development of skills. Yet even that warns against the practical consequences of misunderstanding and looks towards the leverage that organization of a complex matter may offer.

Notes

1. Several points and parts of sections were improved by the comments of Professors Nelson Goodman and Israel Scheffler, both of whom encouraged me in the philosophical pursuit of practice. The research for this paper was conducted under the auspices of Harvard Project Zero and supported in part by grants from the University of Western Ontario and the Canada Council.

2. See "Basic Abilities Required for Understanding and Creation in the Arts" (Harvard Project Zero Summary Report, 1972), p. 16.

3. For a thorough analysis of the symbolic status of art works, see Nelson Goodman, *Languages of Art: an Approach to a Theory of Symbols* (Indianapolis and New York: Bobbs-Merrill, 1968); also V. A. Howard, "The Convertibility of Symbols: A Reply to Goodman's Critics," *British Journal of Aesthetics* 15, Summer 1975, pp. 207–16.

4. After the Greek goddess of skills, and of wisdom and warfare as well, who sprang full-grown and clad in armor from the brow of Zeus.

5. After the faithful, weaving wife of Odysseus.

6. Though not alone sufficient, a point the theory conveniently overlooks.

7. From *Ion*, in the *Collected Dialogues of Plato*, ed. Edith Hamilton and Huntington Cairns (New York: Pantheon, 1961), p. 220.

8. A reflection of Aschenbach in Thomas Mann's *Death in Venice*.

9. Goodman, *Languages of Art*, pp. 6–10.

10. Israel Scheffler, *Conditions of Knowledge* (Glenview, Ill.: Scott, Foresman, 1965), p. 103. One is reminded in this connection of Thomas Edison's memorable epigram, "Genius is one percent inspiration and ninety-nine percent perspiration."

11. See, e.g., Frederic C. Bartlett, "Fatigue Following Highly Skilled Work," *Proceedings of the Royal Society* 131 (1943): 248–57, reprinted in *Skills*, ed. David Legge (Baltimore: Penguin Books, 1970).

12. Cf. Gilbert Ryle, *The Concept of Mind* (London: Hutchinson, 1949), pp. 149–53.

13. Scheffler, *Conditions of Knowledge*, p. 103.

14. For an excellent discussion of the vacuity of appeals to similarity, see Nelson Goodman, "Seven Strictures on Similarity," in *Problems and Projects* (Indianapolis and New York: Bobbs-Merrill, 1972), pp. 437–46.

15. On musical work identity see Goodman, *Languages of Art*, pp. 179–92.

16. See, e.g., Dennis H. Holding, "Knowledge of Results," in Legge, *Skills*; James Deese and Stewart H. Hulse, *The Psychology of Learning*, 3d ed. (London: McGraw-Hill, 1967), pp. 454–55.

17. See Ryle, *Concept of Mind*, chap. 2; Scheffler, *Conditions of Knowledge*, chap. 5.

18. The example is Michael Polanyi's in *Personal Knowledge: Towards a Post-Critical Philosophy* (London: Routledge & Kegan Paul, 1958), p. 50.

19. Cf. Scheffler, *Conditions of Knowledge*, p. 21.

20. Daniel C. Dennett, *Content and Consciousness* (London: Routledge & Kegan Paul, 1969), p. 117.

21. Ibid., pp. 117–18.

22. ". . . where p is a statement informing us about the 'object' of awareness." Ibid., p. 119.

23. Dennett ignores the artistically important consideration that perceptions can be variously symbolized.

24. Dennett, *Content and Consciousness*, p. 118.

25. Awareness$_1$ and awareness$_2$ are by no means restricted to the range of "knowledge" only. One can be aware$_1$ or aware$_2$ of physical sensations and emotions having little or nothing to do with propositional or procedural knowing.

26. Dennett, *Content and Consciousness*, p. 123.

27. Ibid.

28. David N. Perkins, personal communication.

29. Propositional and non-propositional types of "knowing what" are discussed in section 3.3 below.

30. Polanyi, *Personal Knowledge*, p. 55. I apply the term "peripheral" both to Polanyi's subsidiary (instrumental) and to accidental or irrelevant secondary perceptions and sensations.

31. For an excellent review of the psychological literature on "perception without awareness," see Norman F. Dixon, *Subliminal Perception: The Nature of a Controversy* (London: McGraw-Hill, 1971).

32. This section owes much to a conversation with Nelson Goodman at the Harvard Faculty Club on 13 May 1974.

33. James G. Holland and B. F. Skinner, *The Analysis of Behavior* (New York: McGraw-Hill, 1961), p. 98.

34. Jean Piaget, *The Construction of Reality in the Child*, trans. Margaret Cook (New York: Basic Books, 1954).

35. For an interesting discussion of different approaches to keyboard training, see David Barnett, *The Performance of Music: A Study in Terms of the Pianoforte* (London: Barrie & Jenkins, 1971), particularly chap. 2, "Performance as the Synthesis of the Categories of Method."

36. John Dewey, *Human Nature and Conduct* (New York: Modern Library, 1930), p. 71; Ryle, *Concept of Mind*, pp. 42–51.

37. Ryle, *Concept of Mind*, pp. 42–43.

38. Scheffler, *Conditions of Knowledge*, pp. 14–21.

39. Scheffler, *Conditions of Knowledge*, p. 19. Scheffler's sense of "embedded" is roughly synonymous with "implied by" as contrasted with the psychological embeddedness of awareness$_2$. Some logically embedded techniques may also, of course, be psychologically embedded.

40. Ibid., pp. 20, 100.

41. Implied by the assertion that "active propensities often have strictly associated techniques (e.g., a person who enjoys swimming and swims regularly knows how to swim)." Ibid., p. 19.

42. Implied by the fact that competency is denied to habits. Ibid., p. 21.

43. Ibid., p. 99.

44. I owe this example and the point it illustrates to David N. Perkins.

45. Scheffler, *Conditions of Knowledge*, p. 99.

46. Ibid., p. 98.

47. Which, though knowledge, is not strictly a species of propositional knowledge. See section 3.3 above.

48. See James Deese, *The Psychology of Learning* (New York: McGraw-Hill, 1958), pp. 181–212; Robert Borger and A. E. M. Seaborne, *The Psychology of Learning* (London: Penguin, 1966), pp. 11–12.

49. Wilfred J. Brogden and Robert E. Schmidt, "Effect of Number Choices per Unit of a Verbal Maze on Learning and Serial Position Errors," *Journal of Experimental Psychology* 47 (1954): 235–45; idem., "Acquisiton of a 24-Unit Verbal Maze as a Function of Number of Alternate Choices per Unit," *Journal of Experimental Psychology* 48 (1954): 335–38.

50. George A. Miller, "The Magic Number Seven; Plus or Minus Two: Some Limits on our Capacity for Processing Information," *Psychological Review* 63 (1956): 81–87.

51. Benton J. Underwood, "Studies of Distributed Practice: X. The Influence of Intralist Similarity on Learning and Retention of Serial Adjective Lists," *Journal of Experimental Psychology* 45 (1951): 253–59; Benton J. Underwood and David Goad, "Studies of Distributed Practice: I. The Influence of Intralist Similarity in Serial Learning," *Journal of Experimental Psychology* 42 (1951): 125–34; Richard S. Lazarus, James Deese, and Robert

Hamilton, "Anxiety and Stress in Learning: The Role of Intraserial Duplication," *Journal of Experimental Psychology* 47 (1954): 111–14.

52. Deese, *Psychology of Learning*, p. 208.

53. Ibid.

54. Dennis H. Holding, "Types of Guidance," from ch. 3 of his *Principles of Training* (New York: Pergamon, 1965), reprinted in Legge, *Skills*, p. 272.

55. Ibid., p. 272.

56. Ibid., p. 272, 274. Holding's reference is to Walter Kaess and David Zeaman, "Positive and Negative Knowledge of Results on a Pressey-Type Punchboard," *Journal of Experimental Psychology* 60 (1960): 12–17.

57. Rudolf Arnheim, *Art and Visual Perception* (Berkeley and Los Angeles: University of California Press, 1967).

58. Deryck Cooke, *The Language of Music* (London: Oxford, 1959).

59. Leonard B. Meyer, *Emotion and Meaning in Music* (Chicago: University of Chicago Press, 1956); Abraham A. Moles, *Information Theory and Esthetic Perception* (Urbana: University of Illinois Press, 1966); and, for a good general survey of the perceptual and interpretative literature, barring a few glaring omissions, Hans Kreitler and Shulamith Kreitler, *Psychology of the Arts* (Durham, N.C.: Duke University, 1972).

60. Carl E. Seashore, *Psychology of Music* (New York: McGraw-Hill, 1938); Edwin Gordon, *Musical Aptitude Profile* (Boston: Houghton Mifflin, 1965); Herbert D. Wing, *Musical Intelligence Tests* (Buckinghamshire, England: National Foundation for Educational Research, 1961).

61. For a survey of the available literature, canted toward education, see Margaret Gilchrist, *The Psychology of Creativity* (Melbourne: Melbourne University Press, 1972). In the area of children's artistic development, see Howard Gardner, *The Arts and Human Development* (New York: John Wiley & Sons, 1973).

62. I. Lorge, "Influence of Regularly Interpolated Time Intervals upon Subsequent Learning," *Teach. Coll. Contr. Educ.*, No. 438 (1930).

63. By Clark L. Hull, in *Principles of Behavior* (New York: Appleton-Century-Crofts, 1943).

64. Cf. Deese, *Psychology of Learning*, p. 195.

65. Glen A. Holland, "Simple Trial and Error Learning: Massed and Distributed Trials with Habits of Unequal Initial Strength," *Journal of Comparative and Physiological Psychology* 46 (1953): 90–94.

66. Deese, *Psychology of Learning*, p. 185.

67. Popular distinctions between lower-order and higher-order habits or simple and complex processes are misleading in suggesting atomic or noncomplex psychological processes. Such of these contrasts as are employed herein are intended merely to indicate the hierarchical inclusion of some processes within the relatively broader scope of others. For example, visual scanning is a prominent feature in the perception of whole objects.

68. Deese, *Psychology of Learning*, p. 186.

69. "Basic Abilities."

FOUR 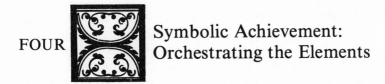 Symbolic Achievement:
Orchestrating the Elements

The accomplished theatrical director at work reveals with peculiar transparency the manifold functioning of the mature artist. He begins with a rich array of resources: a promising script, a talented company, a stage well designed. Although he may view them expansively, may perceive them as embodying infinite possibility, these primary materials might with equal fairness be seen as shackles. They impose upon the director a set of constraints so severe as to seem sometimes insurmountable. The script, though permitting interpretation, cannot be forced beyond its limits; the members of the company, though malleable, have habits of gait and gesture which no theatrical sorcery can undo; the stage, though versatile, is an enclosed terrain. The director's task, then, is to mobilize his materials for maximum effect within the limits of their intransigencies. When necessary, he will compensate by understatement or concealment; when possible, he will countervail by the deployment of alternative resources. And if these strategies succeed, he will probably achieve a satisfactory performance. If, however, he is able to push his materials to their very limits without violating their inherent constraints, he may approach brilliance. But again, if by some error of tact or intelligence he exceeds the capacity of his materials and exposes their limitations, he may achieve what is often called an interesting failure.

The resources and constraints which the director manipulates are plain to see; how these shape and ultimately determine his aesthetic effectiveness is similarly apparent. The web of decisions by which he orchestrates these elements can serve as a metaphor for any artist engaged in creation, interpretation, or performance and, indeed, for any informed and responsive audience as well. Most aesthetic producers and consumers work with resources and constraints less visible and less accessible to analysis than those of the director. The possibilities of their media aside, their resources consist for the most part of skills (in the enlarged sense expounded earlier in this volume) ranked in hierarchies, including those capacities for selection and organization which govern the smooth deployment of the rest. And their constraints, like the director's, consist of the limitations inherent in their resources.

In a sense, then, this section recapitulates issues discussed earlier. The nature, development, and organization of primitive components cannot, except by artifice, be separated from their selection and arrangement into larger units. Every part is itself a whole, capable of analysis into subsidiary units, and every whole may be a part of some subsuming entity. Moreover, the parts do not precede the whole but rather develop continuously with it. The child does not learn to represent first a nose, then an eye, then an ear, and finally assemble these to make a face. He learns to paint a face. Context everywhere exerts pressure upon detail, and detail reciprocally shapes, alters, and refines emerging context.

This section, then, differs from earlier ones in emphasis rather than in substance. Here the focus is upon the molar instead of the molecular and upon the relational skills of attending or noticing, of selecting, and of combining. The three essays gathered here illustrate with particular force the methodological problems entailed in investigating such issues. Perkins, for example, discusses specifically the difficulties of isolating and identifying intermediate-level relational skills and of rendering them observable. He notes as well the accusation frequently hurled at earlier investigations of this sort: that they mistake the part for the whole by treating an isolable skill as the sole or central one required by the artist. As a working poet, Perkins is unlikely to succumb to such reductionism. And he is especially favorably situated to assess the relation between word-selection strategies—the subject of his essay—and other pivotal components of the composing process.

Indeed, it appears to be no accident that each of the authors in this section practices the art he investigates—Perkins as a poet, Bamberger as a pianist, Dent as a producer. While that has been true of writers in earlier sections as well, there the reciprocity between symbolic research and symbolic practice has been a shade less intimate. Here the methodological solutions so much require both inventiveness and respect for the nuances of a particular medium as to demand a practitioner's familiarity and affection. One may wonder whether all research into the molar relations of art and intellect will call for a similar finesse.

The chief interest of Perkins's essay is, of course, other than methodological. It reveals two types of tactical inadequacy in the performance of student poets seeking an appropriate word to conclude a stanza of verse. One might be called a failure of coordination: where the simultaneous deployment of multiple discriminations was required, the poets frequently relied upon only one or, alternatively, upon a successive rather than a simultaneous application. The demand for simultaneity pervades in the arts and appears equally well in the dancer who must coordinate head, trunk, and limbs, or the instrumentalist who must attend to pitch, rhythm, tempo, and dynamics. Much evidence suggests that the poets' failures reflect a basic human constraint, a rigid limit on the number of elements which the mind, consciously at least, can process simultaneously.

But the nimble human intellect has devised two methods for exceeding its own limitations. One is to cluster items so that several together are processed as a single configuration (a face, rather than an assemblage of eyes, nose, and mouth). Bamberger's subjects illustrate this strategy; what they heard was a tune, not a sequence of pitches. A second tactic is to routinize, rendering a skill or set of skills habitual and thus subliminal, and thereby freeing consciousness to attend elsewhere. These are the skills Polanyi has called "tacit knowledge." Both strategems bring risk as well as advantage. On occasion it will be desirable to single out one item of a configuration or one element of a tacit routine in order to refine or recombine. But integration and routinization may work against such adjustment. Some evidence suggests that partially more than thoroughly practiced behavior may resist rearrangement. On the other hand, the latter may ultimately present more of a problem simply in being so taken for granted that adjustments are never considered.

The second tactical inadequacy disclosed in the poetry study was managerial. The subjects failed to marshal their considerable resources in effective and economical ways. The analysis takes some pains to sort out managerial lapses from attentional constraints, two matters not so easily distinguished. The conductor who attends exclusively to the strings while neglecting the rest of his orchestra may, on the one hand, be unable to process the multitude of sounds or may, on the other, be managerially inept.

Both these inadequacies surface anew in Dent's analysis of audience response. The bewilderment of audiences encountering a novel art form and the resistance often generated thereby stem in part from sensory and conceptual overload. As Dent points out, comprehension—that is, the discernment of configurations and of the relations among them—requires time, application, and practice. But further, audiences often neglect to mobilize effectively the resources for comprehension which they already possess, a failure which manifests itself in attitudes of passivity or acquiescence to authority. Dent seems to agree with Perkins, however, that some managerial lapses may be rather quickly remediable; techniques for the deployment of skills can be taught or brought inductively to birth by a rearrangement of the problem's context.

Bamberger's essay speaks to this latter theme. Her "music box" and "building blocks" created a context wherein her subjects could explore their repertoire of skills and means of combining them. Bamberger's essay thus returns to the issues of resource and constraint, part and whole. Her demonstration of the reciprocity of local and global design in the work of two naive musical composers illuminates surprising and satisfying parallels between the composing process and the achieved artifact. The musical building blocks that were given to the students supplied one set of resources and constraints; the conceptual model of melodic coherence that each had abstracted from his previous musical experience supplied another. Taken together, the two sets of possibilities appeared to dictate the logic of composition as well as the finished product.

What these essays do not purport to show—what no research can yet show—are the generative strategies and techniques of the greatly gifted. Analysis of a theme and its development, inversion, expansion, and elaboration in a Beethoven quartet, or explication in a similar vein of a symbolic motif in Shakespearean drama—these exercises hint at highly complex and delicate skills of selection and combination which orchestrate sets of richly elaborated components and subcomponents. Such subtleties will continue to outstrip the limited methods of inquiry now available. Equally inaccessible are the conceptual leaps which have permanently altered the nature of a symbol system. History records the moments when great craftsmen, unwillingly constrained by the recalcitrance of their materials, forced boundaries outward and expanded possibilities; hence, depth perspective, the flying buttress, atonal composition. Each of these concluding essays sparks currently unanswerable questions about such high achievements. Thus this section, more than any of the preceding, conveys the urgent thrust of an unfinished enterprise—indeed, of one just begun.

A Better Word:
Studies of Poetry Editing
David Perkins

> Without there was a cold moon up,
>> Of Winter radiance sheer and thin;
>> The hollow halo it was in
> Was like an ice-filled yea empty cup.

The last line of this stanza fails poetically. Inflated, metrically jarring, paradoxical in no illuminating way, it seems not just mediocre but bad. But no hasty blame attaches to the stanza's author. He never framed those final words. Indeed, his original phrasing seems fairly sound: *was like an icy crystal cup*.

One subject in an experiment in poetry editing offered the substitution above. His striking lack of success was not unique; very many of the substitutions which subjects devised proved equally unimpressive. In the special context of poetry writing, this observation raises a problem of enormous generality and relevance: why do people fail?

When the task involved is a creative one, some easy answers are current. The person has bad taste; if he cannot discriminate between better and worse options he can hardly construct an appropriate product. Or the person is influent; if he cannot conceive many options, his impoverished selection ensures an undistinguished final choice. Or the person displays "premature closure"; accepting the first remotely satisfactory idea he discovers, he never pushes on toward less accessible but maybe better options.

Explanation in another style also shows some promise. Good performance depends not just on having the relevant component skills of production and discrimination, but as much on organizing them effectively to achieve the objective at hand. Because a person can put one foot in front of another, because he can walk from one to the other end of any block in a city, does not mean he can find his way from his new office to the train station. Likewise, however facile a critic or coiner of phrases one might be, putting a whole poem together, or even repairing a single line, requires sensitively navigating a maze of alternatives. Here, as in any task, effective organization of personal resources bears powerfully on success.

Whatever the reasons, even moderately creative performances seem dismayingly rare. This specialized study on poetry writing reflects a malaise on an epidemic scale. Perhaps focused study of one task can yield at least some insights on the nature of effective performance there. And betting cautiously that the structure of any creative task partly mirrors the cosmos of them all, one can hope at least for some broader hints from any narrow focus. Then why, in the small context of this experiment, did people fail? What insights do the outlined explanations really offer? The answers require confronting human behavior in its most detailed manifestations.

1. Mechanics

"I don't like that [probably *icy crystal*] at all." Rereads. "Was like, that's uh . . . that's okay now. This is all pure image. White, the cold moon—" Rereads. "Was like, was like, uh, icy, or *shiny, white*," pause, "*very sheer, very fine*."

These lines report the first words of Amy, one subject beginning her assault on the experimental task. So detailed a record exists because Amy, like the others, spoke aloud in a "stream-of-consciousness" fashion as she worked through the problem posed. Amy's speech provided the data for a detailed probe into the structure of inventive performance. The appendix offers her complete transcript for this poem, together with another by Dora.

Amy, like the fifteen other subjects, had responded to advertisements placed around the Harvard community. The advertisements requested both amateur poets and persons who had no special interest in poetry but no special aversion to it either. Subjects would earn a small sum for participating in a study of poetry editing. Eight students took part in a first version of the experiment and eight more in a slightly revised version. In the first group, four were amateur poets. In the second, four considered themselves such, and a fifth who at first classified himself as a "nonpoet" had in fact written several poems. Amy, like the rest, had discussed the experiment in advance and knew in general terms about the verbal reporting and other requirements.

Five stanzas for use in the study were culled mostly from obscure sources, offered noncontroversial topics, possessed clear meanings, and exhibited regular patterns of rhyme and meter. Finally, each stanza, in the opinion of the experimenters, contained a flaw in the last line. For instance, in the quoted poem, *cup* jarred slightly with *crystal* because convention calls crystal vessels glasses, metal or porcelain being the material of cups. The five stanzas appear in the appendix. Half the subjects dealt with them in the given order and half in the reverse order.

The instructions challenged Amy to beat the author. She was to invent a phrase she judged, all things considered, superior to an underlined phrase in each original stanza. However, after making an effort, she could decide that the original remained sounder than anything she had devised. The design posed no time limit but encouraged everyone to proceed at his own pace. Amy completed the five poems to her satisfaction in less than an hour and a quarter, a typical period.

The experimenter, after explaining the task and answering any immediate questions, remained with Amy—as with each other subject—while she worked. The experimenter limited his role to three interactions. He would answer questions by repeating the gist of parts of the instructions. He would ask whether a subject who seemed to be making a half-hearted effort was sure he could find no suitable substitution. And he would prompt speech after a period of silence. He refrained from offering advice or opinions on substitutions, even if requested. At the end of the session, the experimenter asked a series of questions concerning each subject's writing and reading habits, courses of study, and feelings toward the experiment.

Experience with the first group of eight recommended some adjustments in the procedures. Subjects in the first group required several minutes to get the knack of the stream-of-consciousness reporting. Therefore for the second group the third poem in the appendix always came first and served primarily as a warm-up example. Here the experimenter placed little stress on reaching a final solution and proceeded to the next poem when he and the subject agreed that the reporting had become comfortable. The practice session was important. Reporting on the second poem almost always proved much more fluid.

No explicit criterion governed the pace of reporting in the first group of eight. The instructions urged subjects to talk continuously, and the experimenter prompted when he felt a subject was thinking to himself rather than experiencing a momentary block. The tapes commonly showed silences of ten to twenty seconds, and an appraisal of the transcripts from the first group disclosed that important information slipped by during these silences. So to Amy and Dora as members of the second group of eight, stricter standards applied. The experimenter prompted after any silence over five seconds long. Anyone who found himself thinking in circles or facing a blank was simply to say as much. Even this more rapid rate of reporting proved manageable. After the practice example, subjects required prompting only every nine minutes on the average, though the frequency ranged from about once every minute and a half to no prompting at all.

Finally, instructions to the second group encouraged them to view the tasks as a challenge, and the experimenter offered a bonus fee for any final choice judged superior to the original. These changes led participants in the second group to make longer and more serious efforts than the earlier subjects.

2. No windigo hunt

The windigo is that malignly shy beast of legend that retreats as the hunter advances, luring him ever deeper into a wilderness beyond hope. Popular conception would have it that human creativity is at least second cousin to the windigo. As inquiries press forward, the phenomenon subtly retreats, leaving only irrelevant traces of a prior passage. Certainly artists' and writers' numerous testimonials concerning their own working procedures offer no prescription for excellence or even for competence, despite their interest.[1] In the face of these omens, much of the thought and preparation for the present experiment strove to ensure that it would not be just another windigo hunt, that the experimental design would capture something of poetry writing.

An early concern was that the verbal reporting not scare off the literary and inventive powers of the subjects. Otherwise, patterns of thinking would prove ineffective and incoherent, bearing little relation to the strategies a subject might employ in more realistic contexts. But several factors argued compellingly that subjects could manage such reporting very well.

The subjects' own behavior offered the most direct encouragement. They neither curled up into a sullen ball, waiting for the experimenter to go away, nor did they ramble. Rather, the subjects proceeded straightforwardly, puzzling out approaches, inventing various options, and making final decisions for announced reasons. In other words, their behavior seemed not incoherent but well organized. A reading of the sample transcripts will support this.

Indeed, the subjects themselves judged that the verbal reporting proved no great imposition. When all five poems were completed, the experimenter questioned the subjects on the difficulties of reporting. Nine out of sixteen subjects maintained that the reporting helped them to organize their thoughts and procedures. Eight subjects said the reporting slowed down their progress but suggested no further impairment. Only two claimed that the reporting actively interfered with the quality of their thinking.

Furthermore, experiments with more scientifically oriented tasks have shown some advantage in talking aloud. In one such experiment subjects who were encouraged to speak solved a problem, on the average, in half the time required by subjects who were not asked to report.[2]

Finally, earlier studies in the arts argued that the experimental conditions were reasonable. Patrick[3] recorded in shorthand the spoken thoughts of thirty poets and painters of professional stature and of thirty nonpoets and thirty nonpainters, each undertaking whole works. The present experiment sought a level of detailed and rapid reporting and a fineness of later analysis going substantially beyond Patrick's data, which contained some three comments per minute, judging from the published samples. But she too was concerned with the intrusive influence of her method, and her checks on this problem were certainly supportive. She advanced four points: first, 80 percent of the poets and artists said their manner of working during the experiment was fairly representative of their usual procedures. Second, the works of the poets and artists were judged to be of higher quality than those of the nonpoets and nonartists. Third, several poems produced during the experiment later appeared in print and several artists volunteered to sign their works as legitimate examples of their craft. Fourth, clear stylistic parallels linked the poems and drawings produced and samples of the poets' and artists' usual work; indeed, expert judges assessing the quality of the poems with authorship concealed spontaneously identified several authors by style alone. Patrick concluded that protocols could fairly represent her subjects' usual working procedures, and her pioneering effort encourages the present study.

The thinking aloud aside, the poetry-editing task domesticated the authentic wild creature in other ways. Subjects had to adopt the style and content of the examples. Those that were poets would find their stylistically specialized repertoire of skills mismatching somewhat the experimental task's demands. And though a poet may sometimes resolve a difficulty at one spot by making a change in another, or both another and the one, here changes were limited to the underlined words. Would these concessions to methodology nevertheless leave a task significantly parallel to the natural one?

The mistake here is to hope for too much. If windigo eludes our net, perhaps rabbit will do. Of course the experimental conditions would yield behavior diverging somewhat from the actions a poet would take in editing. On the other hand, the experiment clearly involved skills and strategies relevant to poetry writing. Another glance at Amy's and Dora's transcripts underscores this point. It would be unreasonable to suggest that the kinds of searches they attempted, the considerations they raised, and the conclusions they reached had nothing to do with poetry editing. Critters both, windigo and rabbit would share many anatomical features. And with due caution observed, an imperfect match costs little when so little is known about the anatomy of inventive performance under any conditions.

3. *The nature of the task*

Here is the scene: the poet has already written, edited, and reedited most lines to his satisfaction. But a few trouble spots remain. The poet strives to improve these while preserving as much as possible the existent form of the poem and the investment of time and creative energy it represents. He knows this late editing phase is crucial. Those first few inspired and germinal lines would come to nothing without the polishing he now attempts. (Indeed, novices commonly fail right here: some subjects who were amateur poets provided samples of their usual work; many of their poems which offered some fine lines needed nothing so much as a sensitive editing.)

The poet knows he no longer enjoys the freedom of the blank page. Constraints are strong: rhyme and metric schemes, if any, are long since settled; the root metaphors, their meaning, and the diction are so far developed that any change in these would mark a substantial setback. The many entrenched considerations can make an editing problem a genuine conundrum, requiring dedicated effort and inspired invention to resolve. When this happens, editing becomes no less a creative challenge than achieving an initial conception, though it is a challenge with quite a different flavor.

Of all aspects of writing, the late editing phase matched best the needs of experimentation. Because the circumstances were highly constrained in somewhat specifiable ways, success or failure admitted a largely objective assessment. Again, in accommodating themselves to the problem as given, subjects were not free to follow their own fancies. Comparisons between subjects thus grew more meaningful.

Further, the editing task gained a significance beyond poetry in that it exemplified a special problem type in the universe of problematic situations. There was no algorithmic solution—no certain procedure, as for extracting square roots or making a long-distance phone call—that would surely win through to an appropriate solution. But at the same time the task did not lend itself to a *hill-climbing* strategy, where a solution is approached through a series of successive approximations or resolutions of sub-problems. Tasks on a larger scale—the whole endeavor of writing a poem, for instance, or of landing a man on the moon—typically accommodate such an approach.

This task instead required *constrained random search:* a subject needed to conceive several options satisfying initial "plausibility" requirements and screen these for their appropriateness in other respects. For the most part, there was little that could be done to build toward a final answer—one simply had to be found. The task resembled searching for a parking place in a crowded business area, where one can do little but look along the streets known to be most promising until a place appears.

Such a characterization makes the task seem a conventional "fluency" exercise, where a subject must generate as many options as he can that satisfy given requirements.[4] But this oversimplifies the circumstances. Here, subjects had to conceive their own "plausibility" requirements in terms of which to invent alternatives. Furthermore, they could not stop with a list of alternatives but had to make a final choice among them or explicitly choose to consider them all inadequate. Finally, though not permitting a steady progression toward a solution, the experimental task did offer certain opportunities for limited hill climbing, opportunities not always exercised.

If constrained random search is a special strategy, it is not an unusual one; just the contrary. The occasions that permit hill climbing and other strategies commonly exhibit episodes of constrained random search. The detective may comb the scene of the crime for clues, the chess master enumerate alternative moves, the mathematician experiment with alternative means of integrating a formula. In general, human problem-solving activities are replete with episodes of constrained random search. Though a weak strategy when hill-climbing methods apply (the proverbial monkeys typing at random until they produce *Hamlet* come to mind here), constrained random search serves at the level of detailed procedure and incremental progress where other means may not. How occasions of constrained random search are handled bears importantly on the whole success of many problem-solving efforts. Therefore, whatever generalizations this study may suggest speak to the larger range of human problem solving.

4. A catalog of lapses

In *Practical Criticism*, I. A. Richards examined a series of brief essays by college students that analyzed various poems whose authors had been concealed. His conclusions seem as dismaying now as then. The numerous misreadings and misevaluations stemmed not so much from recondite problems of obscure allusions or delicate discriminations as from relatively mundane difficulties with making out the plain sense of a poem, approaching it free of ideological prejudices, discerning conventional forms like the sonnet, and so forth.[5] Echoes of Richards's findings sound in the present study of poetry editing. Taken collectively, subjects' proposals demonstrated an unsettling number of mundane ways to go wrong. Another stanza used in the experiment, together with the one cited earlier, sets the context for some examples.

> A slumber did my spirit seal;
>   I had no human fears:
> She seemed a thing that could not feel
>   The touch of *earthly years.*

Straightforward technical matters of meter and rhyme occasionally caused trouble. The *ice-filled yea empty cup*, mentioned earlier, and *the touch of diurnal tears* for the above stanza broke the strictly established metric patterns. *The touch of earth nor air* violated the rhyme scheme of the above stanza. Several similar violations occurred with the other poems. Of course, here caution is due. A break in the pattern of meter or rhyme may contribute to a work if there are poetic reasons for it, for instance if there is an advantage of emphasis to be won. But these cases seemed simply arbitrary, jarring without compensation.

Problems with the accessibility of proposed substitutions' meanings ranged from the one pole of cliché and redundancy to the other of downright incomprehensibility. *The touch of bitter tears* seemed a cliché. In *was like an empty crystal cup* the *empty* echoed weakly the *hollow halo* image. Meaning rested obscurely in such phrases as *ice-filled yea empty cup*, the *touch of diurnal tears*, and *the touch of timely tears*. In each of these cases, examination of the transcripts showed that the subject had something in mind but failed to package his message effectively.

Entirely comprehensible substitutions sometimes clashed with the established tone or imagery of the given poem. Examples included such proposals as *was like a misty velvet cup, was like a smoke-filled cup*, or *was like a golden loving cup*. All three expressed a warmth and softness contrary to the frigid and brittle overtones of *cold moon* and *winter radiance sheer and thin*, supported by the hard tones of the *up* and *in* at the ends of the lines.

Whatever specific counts various proposals had against them, many also fell short simply in failing to offer any positive poetic values. The lines *was like an icy fragile cup* and *was like a frozen crystal cup* simply lacked potency, even though they did no violence to the established meter, rhyme, meaning, or overtones of the poems. They were substitutes that in their denotation and sound fell short of the original *icy crystal cup*, with its alliteration on the c's and the chilly play with s, i, and e sounds between icy and crystal.

Despite the generally grim picture, a few proposals seemed more or less on par with, sometimes better than, the authors' originals. *The touch of human tears* and *the touch of mortal tears* picked up the *human fears* from the second line with a feeling of reinforcement rather than repetition. The verb *touch* matched well the light size and weight of *tears*, and *tears* introduced an alliteration. Finally, *tears* made sense, although a sense somewhat changed from the original (the instructions explicitly permitted this). *Fragile frosted cup*, like *icy crystal cup*, offered an alliteration and picked up the icy brittleness established in earlier lines. But *fragile frosted cup* canceled the problem of cups not being crystal, moving to a porcelain cup image which fitted the context entirely comfortably. The price, of course, was the loss of that chilly sound play.

After this sampling, some numbers will sketch the vista. The five poems times sixteen subjects permitted a possible eighty substitutions. In twenty-three cases (29 percent) the subjects chose to make no choice, deciding that whatever alternatives they had conceived could not stand against the original. This left seventy-one proposed substitutions. I, in some consultation with assistants, judged seventeen of these (24 percent) to be on a par with or better than the original lines.

Such statistics based on a few persons' judgments merit the usual grain of salt. Nevertheless, the general situation they describe seemed quite clear. Worries before this experiment that assessing subjects' substitutions would require decisions of extreme delicacy came to nothing. Most proposals failed not from any subtle tangency to more suitable options but because of sharp divergence from good practice. Nor did an issue of contrary tastes between the experimenters and the subjects cloud the conclusions. As mentioned earlier, several subjects during a later visit judged some options proposed during the experiment, including options they themselves had conceived. On this occasion their critiques proved similar to and no less severe than the remarks above (more details will be offered later). In any case, the appendix offers a complete listing of the poems and proposed solutions for the reader's own assessment.

The findings underscored an important characteristic of the experimental task: many were the ways to go wrong. Chances for misstep included at least the various categories reviewed above: difficulties with rhyme and meter, cliches, redundancy, incomprehensibility, conflicting imagery. Even if these traps were avoided there remained the problem of producing something with positive poetic values. Thus the task demanded a comprehensive monitoring of varied problem sources. Such behavior claims no uniqueness. Bartlett, for instance, examined how subjects would complete patterns that had gaps in them. He found that when the partial information given established a systematic progression in more than one respect, subjects typically discovered one but missed the others.[6] The subjects of the present study also extrapolated to fill a gap, and they also commonly overlooked salient aspects of the multifaceted pattern the given stanza presented. Whatever isolated discriminations concerning meter, meaning, or other matters the subjects could make, getting it all together emerged as a further and perhaps severe challenge of the task.

5. *A terminology of search*

To the casual observer, invention rises like Neptune from the sea: all of a sudden there it is. But eventually the scientist comes along with his glass-bottomed boat, intent on surveying what happens under the surface. The transcripts disclosed that the subjects' final proposals were products of a concentrated and complex effort. They showed that whether or not a subject's choice was suitable, that choice surfaced as the selection of a highly organized search. But "organized" need not mean "effectively organized." Were patterns of search organization related to failure or success with the experimental task?

Two avenues of inquiry spoke to this question. On the one hand, perhaps subjects' failures originated in particular phases or levels of search within the subjects' overall efforts. On the other, perhaps any phase of search could misfire in different ways. The analysis became an attempt to define *where* subjects searched ineffectively and *in what ways* their searches were ineffective.

Sensible talk about search requires a small vocabulary which an example will introduce. Subjects' hunt for rhyme words often displayed very straightforward episodes of search. The stanza ending *earthly years* needed a rhyme. One subject mentioned in the course of his transcript *cares*, *sears*, *rears*, *cheers*, *dears*, *airs*, and other full or partial rhymes, at last coming to *tears* and accepting it as his final choice.

Items of a search are candidate solutions produced and examined, as with the rhyme words above.

Conditions govern the generation and screening of items in a search. *Preconditions* guide the generation and *postconditions* the screening. Rhyme appeared the sole precondition governing the string of words above; at least no other obvious property related the bulk of the words produced to the requirements of the stanza. The postconditions would include the many poetic considerations that prompted the rejection of all the items up to *tears* and the acceptance of *tears*.

Stop rules describe when search will terminate—either in success or failure—and how any final selection will be made. The stop rules for success involve the postconditions but would also reflect more complex factors: Are many suitable items located before a final selection (in the example the answer was no; the first suitable candidate was chosen)? Need all or only some postconditions be satisfied? Are one or many final solutions chosen (this context permitted only one final choice)? Will the selection standards ease if an extensive effort does not turn up anything wholly appropriate? And so forth. Stop rules for failure might consider how long a search had proceeded, how hard it was becoming to generate further items, whether the items produced so far had seemed encouraging or discouraging, whether abandoning the particular search meant failing on the whole problem or simply shifting to another approach. Finally, a bright idea may abort a search and send the thinker in a new direction; though "stop rules" sounds a little strange in this context, whether a search admits such interruption will be considered part of its stop rules.

This vocabulary provides a useful and illuminating way of describing searches only in some circumstances. The record of the search behavior must permit easy identification of items and allow plausible inferences concerning what pre- and postconditions and stop rules might operate. Fortunately, the transcripts did lend themselves to this approach. Some further terms prepare the way for analysis.

Options and *constraints* were two important building blocks for searches. Options were candidate substitutions for the stanzas, ultimately to be accepted, rejected, modified, or simply forgotten. In the earlier terms, options were the *items* in subjects' overall searching effort. All the options Amy announced are italicized in the transcript. The final choice, *fragile frosted*, represented a selection from many others—*fragile crystal, finely frosted*, and so forth. An option could be a single word, like *fragile*, that required a companion word or a phrase like *finely glowing* that completely filled the slot in the given poem. Likewise, a subject could later separately consider words initially paired.

Constraints were conditions subjects employed as relevant to the appropriateness or inappropriateness of options—for instance, conditions of meaning, meter, rhyme, connotation, sound play. A subject could employ constraints as *postconditions* while evaluating options. Thus in the first few lines of the transcript, Amy noted that *ceremonial* did not convey icy crystalness, *glistening* had an extra syllable, cups had no reason to be *finely glowing*, *christening cup* was a phrase of uncertain meaning. Constraints also appeared as *preconditions*, guiding the generating of options. Some-times a subject explicitly mentioned such constraints. On other occasions the constraints appeared implicitly in some family of options generated. For instance, in the first few lines of the transcript Amy mentioned *shiny, white, shining, glistening*; obviously Amy was conceiving options reinforcing the radiant moon and cup image, though she did not say so explicitly.

The *top-level search* refers to the entire process of seeking a solution. Its items were the options, its pre- and postconditions the constraints, as outlined above. Reading the italicized phrases (the options) in Amy's transcript gives a schematic overview of the top-level search, conveying something of the number and variety of alternatives explored, the way individual words were combined, the recurrence of and vacillation between options, and the final choosing. Even so cursory a survey shows important features: how many and what variety of options a search examines bears importantly on the search's likely degree of success. But treating the top-level search as compounded of types of subordinate searches yielded a more detailed picture.

Within the overall search for options, episodes often appeared where a subject concentrated on one particular constraint. The text above offered two examples: Amy at the beginning of her transcript sought words expressing luminescence, and another subject sought words rhyming with *fears*. As the examples suggest, such episodes typically arose from constraints concerning meaning, or rhyme in those cases where the slot to be filled required rhyming. Episodes of this sort in themselves qualified as searches. Their items were also items of the top-level search, and they shared the postconditions of the top-level search. Each subordinate search was guided by one or more preconditions among the many that operated at some point within the top-level search. Finally, and independent of the top-level search, subordinate episodes would have their own stop rules for failure, limiting the effort to be spent exploring a particular constraint of meaning or rhyme before moving on to other approaches.

The *evaluation* of options as much as their conception was a search process. Here, rather than seeking options satisfying a constraint, the subject sought constraints true of an option, constraints that also had a bearing on the option's appropriateness. These were called *pros* and *cons*. The importance of distinguishing between conditions and items on the one hand and constraints and options on the other here becomes clear. Contrary to the phases of search discussed earlier, the evaluation searches generated constraints, not options, as items. And no constraint, but the demand for constraints true of the option and relevant to evaluation, served as a precondition.

Finally, the constraints used to generate options were themselves the "output" of various search processes. Most obviously, subjects typically spent some time reading a stanza carefully, interpreting it, and so forming conceptions of the conditions their solutions needed to meet. Accordingly, and like evaluation, this phase of search generated constraints as items, stressing a motion from particulars—the given stanza—to general characterizations. Reciprocally, the top-level search and subordinate searches to meet conditions of meaning or rhyme stressed a motion from general characterizations to particular instances.

Whatever the phase of search concerned, how could the conduct of a search prove inappropriate relative to a problem's demands? Three ways a search might misfire complete this vocabulary.

A search could be *scanty*, inadequately exploring a range of items under a precondition; without sufficient persistence, solutions might never emerge. A search could be *biased*, restricted to or drawn toward a limited subset of the relevant items by some unnecessary and often unrecognized precondition. Third, a search could be *misdirected*, generating items satisfying preconditions which could have been judged unpromising at once; a large part of good strategy consists in looking mostly in the likely places and not the unlikely ones.

Such a brood of concepts had better earn its keep. It offered a potential instrument for appraising the patterns of subjects' searching behavior, locating the phases of search where difficulties arose, and classifying the particular kinds of difficulties. The following sections relate how this instrument meshed with the realities of the data.

6. *Symptoms of trouble*

The analysis of subjects' difficulties focused on the transcripts gathered from the second group of eight subjects, employing the finer-grained data encouraged by the five-second standard for reporting. The analysis excluded the practice poem and also the poem ending *a white and shapeless mass*, since this longer phrase confused cataloging of options explored to fill particular slots. The results proved striking. In a sentence, all three difficulties with search appeared in one level of search or another, and there were problems of some sort apparent at all levels of search.

Scanty searches occurred persistently. In the top-level search, subjects examined a mean of only 12 options. The figures excluded repetitions and single words which occurred later as one of a pair. Further, in exploring areas of meaning, subjects sampled a mean of only 1.4 options per area. This figure derived from grouping the options in each transcript into semantically related clusters. For instance, *misty*, *cloudy*, *foggy*, *steamy*, *vaporous* were related words in one subject's transcript.[7] As the mean of 1.4 reflected, any one option most commonly stood by itself rather than belonging to any larger group. Finally, subjects mentioned a mean of just 2.6 pros and cons concerning words in their final choices. (Only evaluations bearing on final choices should contribute to this statistic: since evaluations of rejected options typically terminated on finding a serious con, only evaluations of final choices would reflect the persistence of evaluation searches.)

These findings demanded initial caution. A search can be brief without being inappropriately brief. If the brevity meets the purpose, extended search simply wastes time. But in these cases, the searches seemed genuinely too cursory. First, the number of options judged adequate offered a basis for estimating the appropriate length of the top-level search. The second group of subjects working on the three stanzas under close analysis mentioned 10 options judged on a par with or superior to the original wordings. Four of these the subjects selected, and 6 the subjects passed over for other choices or for no choice at all. Then as a rough estimate, the chances of conceiving a suitable option were about 1 in 27. In these terms, what length of search would have yielded a reasonable probability of conceiving at least one suitable option? For a 50 percent chance of success, a search should explore 18 options; for 75 percent, 37 options; for 90 percent, 61 options. In sum, given the quality of options that subjects in fact produced, searches should have been substantially longer. The easy conclusion that subjects should simply have looked harder is premature. Rather, other helpful strategies might take more advantage of what hill-climbing opportunities the task offered. But the brevity of search remained a symptom of difficulties, a symptom requiring diagnosis of causes.

Searches of areas of meaning also seemed brief. But perhaps subjects pushed these searches as far as logically possible, few words in fact having the desired meaning. The data did not support this. Amy, for instance, conceived several words expressing luminescence: *shiny, white, shining, glistening, glowing, silver,* and perhaps *frosted,* which synthesizes both white and cold. Though these 7 options numbered substantially more than the overall mean of 1.4, one could readily proceed to list *luminescent, brilliant, dazzling, scintillating, bright, glossy, shimmering, glinting, pearly, opalescent, phosphorescent, gleaming, beaming, coruscating, blinding, sparkling,* and perhaps others. The same pattern held true generally: one could easily retrieve many more words from an area of meaning than subjects in fact did. Further support for this conclusion comes from the retesting described later, where the subjects themselves proved able to retrieve many more words than they had originally.

Accordingly, subjects' searches typically represented very partial samplings. Now some problems require only a small sample from an initially likely area to assess that area's potential: if one vacillates between the cupcakes and the cookies at a bake sale, a ten-cent sample from each will likely decide. But for poetic purposes, words in a given area of meaning do not taste alike as do cupcakes from the same batch. Nuances are so important that suitability varies drastically within a general area of roughly appropriate meaning. A glance at the above list of words signifying luminescence accents the point. A small sample does not explore adequately a likely area's potential.

Finally, were evaluation searches improperly brief? Here the argument is easy. As documented earlier, subjects in fact persistently overlooked major negative features of their final choices. Yet effective evaluation required a thorough effort to find major cons, since even one such would disqualify an option. Some problem situations call for a balancing of pros and cons against one another. But characteristic of poetry and the other arts is that pros do not easily balance a serious con. If a word breaks a formerly established rhyme scheme for no good reason, any perfect aptness of meaning will offer little reprieve. If a word carries undesirable connotations (*interrogate* rather than *inquire,* say), no perfect fit with metrical and phonological considerations will redeem it.

The evaluation search placed an unusual premium on exhaustiveness as the searches under consideration went. The top-level search and searches of areas of meaning needed merely to examine sufficient numbers to give good chances of success. Touching 70 or 80 percent of the possibilities could serve or much more than serve. Indeed, that last 20 or 30 percent could so resist retrieval that the time would be better spent on other approaches. Evaluation, however, was different. Overlooking even a last 20 or 30 percent of potentially disqualifying features simply invited disaster.

Besides scantiness, bias and misdirection caused problems. Biased searching surfaced most consistently during evaluations. Pros and cons concerning the semantic fit of the phrase with the poem—in respect to both literal meaning and connotation—occurred far more frequently than any concerning meter, cliché, redundancy, sound play, and so forth, even though the choices of many subjects fell short in these respects. A count of pros and cons mentioned in those transcripts closely analyzed showed only 34 percent concerned with other than semantic fit. Was this much attention in balance with the need? To answer this question, each final choice was judged against six categories: ametrical, stereotyped, unrhymed, redundant, incomprehensible, and clashing with the prevailing tone (as *velvet* clashed in the *icy crystal cup* example). Of these six, the latter two concerned whether the option and stanza fit one another comfortably in literal meaning and connotation. By this measure, some 65 percent of cons concerned difficulties other than semantic fit, suggesting that subjects' evaluations neglected these aspects.

Occasional biases in the top-level search also emerged, though not for all subjects. Sometimes subjects would unnecessarily limit the areas of meaning explored in their top-level searches, giving up the effort when viable approaches remained. For instance, Dora decided she liked the *crystal* in *icy crystal cup*, failed after some effort to find a new companion word, and then gave up without reviewing her initial decision to keep *crystal*.

Besides biases, the top-level searches also displayed occasional misdirection. Sometimes a subject would pursue a badly chosen area of meaning: the subject proposing *friendly autumn rebound* (see appendix) early seized on the misguided idea that the poem could end with summer looking forward to fall and pursued this for the remainder of his effort. Sometimes a subject would seek a companion word when the first word chosen was inappropriate beyond rescue: the subject who suggested *misty velvet cup* conducted an elaborate—and finally successful—search for a companion to *misty*, neither first nor last recognizing misty as fundamentally a misfit in the crisp context of the given stanza.

In review, most subjects working on most poems displayed several symptoms of ineffective search: their exploration of options (top-level search), or subordinate areas of meaning, and of cons in evaluation were scanty; their evaluations were biased toward appropriateness of meaning; and other problems of bias and misdirection intruded in particular cases. Inferior searching practices might indeed account for subjects' poor results.

7. *A logic of diagnosis*

To find scantiness, bias, and misdirection was not to diagnose the causes of such lapses. But the vocabulary developed during this study offered a handle on that problem, too. The model of search—the generation of items guided by preconditions until stop rules terminated in success or failure—permitted the blaming of difficulties on generation, on preconditions, or on stop rules.

How could scanty searches come about? First of all, the dynamics of generating items according to the established conditions could fall short—a person could conceive items slowly rather than rapidly, his production rate might quickly drop rather than endure. In other words, *influency* might prove a problem. Second, stop rules could cause a scanty search, for instance if the stop rules for failure "gave up" too easily or if those for success exercised inadequate standards. (Preconditions so restrictive that they admit few items could give the appearance of a scanty search, but such a search counts as biased, not scanty.)

Problems with stop rules recall two common explanations for failure described earlier—*premature closure* and *bad discrimination*. Bad discrimination suggests relevant postconditions that the searcher cannot effectively judge. Premature closure suggests that the searcher can judge the relevant postconditions but that he either does not insist on them strictly enough or does not recognize within his stop rules that an easily achieved but merely adequate solution signals the likelihood of a much better solution with a little more effort.

Biased and misdirected searches by definition must find their causes in the preconditions governing search. Both bias and misdirection involve the breadth and focus of these conditions and hence concern neither the fluency of generation nor the stop rules of the search under consideration. But in a roundabout way, bias and misdirection can derive from problems of fluency or stop rules.

This is so because the terminology applies recursively. The preconditions governing one search may themselves derive from another search. Problems with the preconditions could issue from scantiness, bias, or misdirection in that other search, difficulties in turn perhaps attributable to influency or stop rules there. Likewise, sparse generation of items at one level of analysis—the top-level search in the present study, for example —may partly reflect infertile subordinate searches, for instance explorations of semantic areas. And finally, what one level of analysis labels simply as "stop rules" may at a finer level prove an entire searching process in itself. Thus the stop rules of the top-level search in the present data involved the whole evaluation process, itself a kind of search. When that is so, difficulties assigned to stop rules at one level of analysis can translate to problems of scantiness, bias, or misdirection at a finer level.

This diagnostic viewpoint helped to account for the subjects' scanty, biased, and misdirected searches. First off, scanty performance marred at least the top-level searches, searches of semantic areas, and evaluation. This could derive from influency or from problems with stop rules. Unfortunately for the importance of the issue, the transcripts permitted no easy decision as to whether a subject could have conceived more options overall, more words in an area of meaning, more pros and cons than he in fact did.

8. Influency?

The resolution lay in a further experiment that focused on questions of fluency. Six of the eight subjects in the second group returned individually months later for a special series of tests. Each subject listed as many constraints as he could relevant to finding a substitution for the poem ending *earthly years;* the number he listed would be compared with the number mentioned in his transcript. Each subject conceived as many words or phrases as he could, satisfying conditions he himself seemed to have been employing at points in one of his transcripts. Thus one subject who had looked for "adjective phrases to describe a clown" was asked to do so again; another searched again for synonyms for *clown*. Each subject attempted two such tasks; the number of options he conceived was later compared with his original performance in the transcripts. In addition, all subjects addressed three searches not taken from any poem: list flowers, list synonyms for *street*, and list two-syllable rhymes for *ate*. Again, in each case subjects continued as long as they felt they could.

Revealing their evaluative powers, each subject offered pros and cons for two options they themselves had originally proposed. When possible, these options included the subject's final choice and a rejected choice for the same slot. In addition, subjects listed pros and cons for two new endings for *icy crystal cup: luminescent cup* and *milky chilled cup*. The number of pros and cons conceived was later compared with the average number conceived for final choices in the original performances.

Finally, each subject sought a substitute word for a new poem according to a prescribed procedure. Briefly, a subject had first to list as many relevant constraints as possible, next to list as many options as possible deriving from the constraints he thought most promising, and then to pick two favorites among the options and list as many pros and cons as possible. A later section will elaborate.

These tests consistently showed that subjects could conceive substantially more items than suggested by their original transcripts. Table 10:1

Table 10:1   Original Performance Versus Isolated Fluency Tasks

	Original Means	Retest Means		Original Means	Retest Means
Preconditions for *earthly years*	4	8	Searches of areas of meanings		
Evaluation:			Options satisfying some constraints originally used	4	14
Pros and cons for original options	3	6			
Pros and cons for new options	—	5	Options satisfying new constraints		
			flower names	—	32
			street synonyms	—	15
			rhymes for *ate*	—	11

summarizes the comparisons between subjects' original performances and the isolated tests of fluency. Table 10:2, in a later section, contrasts the original efforts with performances on the new poem.

In sum, the retesting forced an important conclusion: the scanty searching did not seem to result from a fundamental lack of fluency in the behavioral repertoires of the participants.

9. Why searches stopped

If fluency could not account for subjects' scanty searches, stop rules remained to do so. Defying any condensed description, the apparent reasons why subjects stopped prematurely ranged from general forces that influenced all or several subjects to idiosyncratic accidents of particular approaches to individual stanzas.

Motivation proved one factor. A number of poorly motivated efforts appeared. These transcripts exhibited few explicit options and a meandering exploration of various approaches rather than vigorous pursuit of any one. The subject would give up without any solution or would propose a weak one just to give an answer. For example, one subject offered *and cheer the world around* in place of *toiling clown*. His choice was the very first he conceived; he accepted it immediately, announcing that he could do better but did not feel so moved.

Judging from subjects' comments in the transcripts, low motivation largely related to a subject's personal reaction to a poem. A subject might find a particular poem so atrocious or so divergent from his style that he could not involve himself in improving it. Indeed, subject 5 in the first group of eight neatly deflated three of the poems with such endings as (try them in place!) *dog pound, bunk,* and *an Alka-Seltzer dissolving in water.* This certainly inventive behavior, in transgressing the boundaries of the task, falls outside the present analytical effort. Or a subject might like the original phrasing and see no hope of finding anything better. One subject struggled with *icy crystal cup*, localized the problem in *cup*, which he could not change, and despaired of resolving the difficulty by changing *icy crystal*.

A rough standard gave a count of the weak efforts in the second group of eight. A performance numbered among the poorly motivated when the resulting handwritten transcript spanned less than a page and half (corresponding roughly to five minutes of effort) and also the subject either reached no final choice or offered one with misgivings or an offhand attitude, as in the example mentioned above. This criterion would not downgrade efforts where a solution that genuinely satisfied a subject just happened to emerge early. By this measure, all subjects made a serious effort on at least two of the four poems (discounting the practice example). Of the thirty-two transcripts, eight counted as poorly motivated. These cases stood as artifacts of experimental design and choice of poems but carried little interest so far as the experiment probed the skills and strategies underlying effective poetic performance. The subjects did not even bring to bear whatever capacities they had.

There remained just three cases classified as serious efforts where the subjects failed to find a substitution. Dora's transcript represents one. The rest included the few concluding with suitable solutions and many with inadequate ones. Such poor solutions implicated stop rules for the top-level search with insufficiently severe standards. Dealing with the adequacy of options, the stop rules incorporated the whole process of evaluation and therefore insufficiently severe standards translated to a scanty and biased search for pros and cons.

The retesting results argued that not influency in evaluating but the stop rules of the evaluation searches accounted for their scantiness. Exactly why evaluation searches terminated early was a matter for plausible conjecture. A likely explanation lay in subjects' desires to complete the task. Once they found options with features that pleased them they were perhaps reluctant to discover other disqualifying features. So motivated at an unconscious level, they often ceased searching. Another influence could have been a psychological set toward brief episodes of evaluation established by the bulk of options considered. Most options met quick disqualification for glaring flaws, a trend which could have oriented the whole pattern of subjects' evaluations toward snap decisions. Whatever the case, the fact remains that the stop rules for evaluation stopped too soon, mismatching the actual demands of the task.

The retesting also recommended stop rules rather than influency to explain the sparse explorations of particular areas of meaning. Again, the reasons why subjects sampled such areas lightly rather than exploring them fully remain conjectural. Perhaps sometimes a subject treated a sample or two as a sufficient test of a likely area's potentials and passed on when his samples did not fully pass scrutiny. Often a subject probably did not recognize that he was searching an area of meaning. His essentially "associative" explorations touched on one or two representatives of an area only to shift away through the idiosyncratic accidents of memory. Compounding this, tangential ideas occurring spontaneously could divert even a deliberate effort under way to seek words from a certain area.

Even Amy's transcript, one of the best efforts, suggested some of these phenomena. As was described above, she intermittently concerned herself with words expressing the luminescence of the cup. Yet her efforts were fraught with byways. The first several lines of the transcript reflected a concern with luminescence interrupted but not diverted by *finely ceremonial*, and other options. In considering *finely glowing*, Amy found that the phrase suitably conveyed *delicate* and *fragile*. Thus tripping over the word *fragile*, she saw it as an option and, distracted from the issues of luminescence, spent the next several lines considering it. She returned to the luminescence problem later with *softly glistening, glistening silver*, and other options. Though luminescence remained an underlying concern, the match of adjectives to those substances cups are made of guided much of the thinking. In summary, Amy's transcript showed a recurrent concern with luminescence but no outright and persistent effort to explore the area of meaning fully at one time.

All in all, the stop rules defining why subjects abandoned areas of meaning apparently reflected more the seduction of thoughts external to the search than the progress of the search itself, when indeed the appearance of the search signaled more than just associative thinking. In any case, as with the evaluation search, subjects did not press their surveys of areas of meaning to their own best advantage.

10. Bias and misdirection

Of bias and misdirection, bias wielded the more insidious influence, preoccupying subjects with appropriateness of meaning at the expense of other considerations. As with scantiness and influency, a crucial issue arose: was this bias intrinsic to the subjects' capabilities? Perhaps considerations of meter, rhyme, assonance, diction, cliché, and so forth fell beyond the reach of their judgment. As with the question of fluency, the retesting suggested an answer.

Like the solutions subjects originally proposed, the options they evaluated during retesting were judged against the six categories ametrical, stereotyped, unrhymed, redundant, incomprehensible, and clashing with the prevailing tone. By this measure and for these options, some 44 percent of

cons concerned difficulties other than semantic fit. Of the subjects' evaluations, 45 percent dealt with matters other than semantic fit. Though surely
accident provided so close an agreement of the percentages, subjects'
performances on retesting seemed much better aligned with the full range of
poetic problems the substitutions exhibited.

In keeping with the more balanced and more extensive evaluations,
subjects generally pointed out fundamental flaws in the options they
considered. For instance, the inventor of *ice-filled yea empty cup* noted its
redundancy and lack of punch. Several observed that the overtones of liquid
and warm cows in *milky chilled cup* weakened the image.

However, the retest performances fell well short of perfection. One
subject proved generally imperceptive despite the pressure to produce pros
and cons; he missed the major flaws in three of the four retest options. The
other five proved more acute with one qualification. *Luminescent cup*, a
retest option offered to all six subjects, fit the *icy crystal cup* slot straightforwardly in meter, sound, and meaning, but it introduced a word length and a
technical tinge new to the stanza. Whether this intrusion jars or delights may
be debated, but in any case four of the six subjects (including the generally
imperceptive one) overlooked the issue entirely.

If outright insensitivity did not underlie the bias toward appropriate
meaning in the original performances, what forces might have caused this?
Possibly psychological set could have been active. Except when rhyme was a
consideration, almost all searching necessarily employed semantic
constraints. This heavy emphasis could have desensitized the subjects to
meter, sound play, and like factors. When freshly approaching a poem, as in
the retesting, they would prove more alert.

Though bias and misdirection often marred the top-level searches, no
single problem dominated all subjects or poems. In line with the recursive
diagnostic plan, bias in the top-level search suggested a scanty search for the
constraints which guided the search for options: the subjects did not seek out
sufficiently varied avenues of approach. Again, influency proved an unlikely
explanation since subjects conceived many more constraints on retesting.
Rather, the search for approaches terminated early.

One reason particularly prevailed: often there *was* no structured search
for alternative constraints to guide the generation of options. Subjects did
not conceptualize the search process at that level. Unaware of emerging
biases, they could not correct them. An example is the subject mentioned
earlier who became more and more firmly convinced that the problem with
icy crystal cup lay in the word *cup*, which could not be changed. Another
subject decided that *crystal* should be kept, then gave up after failing to find
a suitable accompanying word. These subjects seemed unaware that they
might revise their dead-end decisions.

Similar biases arose occasionally in evaluation searches. One subject
proposed the substitution *and cheer the heart's been downed* for *and cheer*

the toiling clown. Examination of the transcript revealed the intended meaning of his opaque phrase: *and cheer the heart that has been downed*. The subject had rendered the phrase incomprehensible by condensing it drastically for the sake of meter. Biased by his own closeness to the substitution, knowing its meaning because he had conceived it, he never noticed the problem.

Explanations were also sought for the scattered instances of misdirection. Such cases, involving useless persistence in a direction of search that could have been recognized as fruitless from the outset, arose from mistakenly evaluating—or simply failing to evaluate—the preconditions guiding the wasted search. Sometimes effective evaluation of preconditions fell beyond the ken of a subject. Several, for instance, seemed unacquainted with the meteorological phenomenon of a ring around the moon in the *icy crystal cup* stanza, and their efforts to cope with the image led in strange directions. Indeed, Amy failed for some time to realize how the image functioned, discovering its operation only after rereading the poem, when she remarked: "Oh, I get it. It's the halo, the hollow halo was like a—That makes sense."

More interesting cases of misdirection reflected poor judgment where the subject should have been able to judge. An earlier example mentioned the subject who for *icy crystal cup* conceived *misty* and after further effort the companion word *velvet*. He needed no special knowledge to realize that *misty* or like words stood at odds with the dominant imagery of the stanza. But he remained blind, pursuing his conception to the end. Similarly, another subject mentioned earlier pressed on with his strange notion that *cheer the toiling clown* could be changed to convey summer looking forward to fall. These cases as well as a few others show not just a misevaluation about the final substitution but an earlier misalignment of approach that ideally would have been nipped in the bud.

Of course, the test of making a likely constraint concrete in an option deserves no criticism per se. As noted earlier, particular options capturing a given constraint can vary drastically in appropriateness. But by the same token, options generated according to a constraint fundamentally inappropriate to the context will never prove out. The best strategy would require carefully considering the appropriateness of a constraint before any *extensive* pursuit. Quite the contrary, the overwhelming trend in the transcripts was to pursue any idea at once in terms of particular options. This behavior reflected not so much bad judgment about the appropriateness of constraints as a failure to evaluate them at all. The subjects did not structure their searches at that level of generality.

This problem and several others look back to the characterization of the poetry-editing task as requiring *constrained random search*. There the text warned that some limited opportunity for hill climbing did exist. Judging the aptness of a constraint prior to pursuit offered just such an opportunity, and one often not taken. Subjects seemed generally alert to another opportunity—modifying an option to fix a problem rather than dismissing it out of hand. Amy, for instance, conceived *finely glistening cup* and, noting a metrical problem, changed it to *finely glowing.* But other subjects mishandled other occasions. One, for instance, dealt mostly with two-word phrases rather than dealing first with substitutions for one word and then seeking a partner for his most promising choice. Again, probability recommended seeking items that would satisfy the most severe condition relevant and screening these items for further conditions. A rhyme requirement limited candidate words drastically, but although most subjects searched for rhyme words and screened for semantic appropriateness, occasionally a subject would seek words with appropriate meaning and never find one that also happened to fit the rhyme scheme. Finally, no subject attempted one potentially powerful strategy: considering several preconditions for the top-level search and choosing the more likely among them before seeking particular options. In summary, subjects' efforts often missed taking advantage of what hill-climbing opportunities the task offered.

11. The potentials of tuning

The analysis so far draws a fundamentally optimistic picture of subjects' problems. The subjects seemed better equipped with the basic skills for the task than their performances suggested. But this might not have been so. For instance, deGroot found little difference in the statistics of searches conducted by novice and advanced chess players.[8] Simon and Chase, extending his work, argued that skill seemed to reside largely in the rapid reflexive capacity of the experienced practitioner to notice salient patterns in the arrangements of the pieces.[9] Certainly reflexive perceptual capacities are important to poetry, too. But here, across the subjects and the varied tasks, important differences in manners of searching did emerge.

Gold, to make a metaphor, waited in the hills. And the citizens had the competencies to mine it: they could walk as far as they had to, dig as deeply as they needed, tell fool's gold from the real commodity. But pitfalls abounded. In the eagerness for a find, fool's gold and real could not be so readily distinguished. A mediocre find could arrest further exploration toward a better one. One fruitless trip could discourage additional effort. Time could be wasted in unsystematic meandering.

But none of these snares seemed pegged to any fundamental disability. Steps toward better performance appeared plausible. Since fluencies were not a problem, long-term training of fluencies seems to be a secondary concern. But subjects could learn the scope of searches that are likely to be adequate, and they could practice treating likely areas of meaning thoroughly rather than flitting from one to another. Adverse psychological sets could yield to deliberate elaboration of phases of search. A subject could, for instance, systematically assess sound, meter, redundancy, comprehensibility, and connotations to ensure that no feature had been overlooked. Rereading the whole poem with a substitution installed could resurrect neglected considerations (subjects often did not do this). A deliberate search for negative features could guard against rose-colored glasses. A deliberate search beyond a tempting option could guard against premature choice. None of this implies that problem solving should always involve an enormous consciousness of search tactics. Rather, deliberate practice of good tactics simply serves as a transition to spontaneous and fluent behavior.

However, features of an individual's working procedures might integrate closely with his whole personality and world view, therefore resisting change. Fortunately, some other research suggests a more tractable situation. A dimension called impulsive-reflective characterizes one aspect of individual working styles. Some people tend to make rapid and ill-considered decisions, others ponder long and painfully, and there are all degrees in between. Experiments have shown that training can guide students to become more or less impulsive.[10] Beittel's research on the process of painting provides another illustration. He characterized two procedural styles in painting called *spontaneous* and *divergent*. Surprisingly, he found that though a painter would typically follow one style or the other, the painter could change his style dramatically on the basis of a simple verbal description.[11]

Despite these encouraging findings, such steps as outlined above write no recipe for certain success. They may not be as easy to take as they seem. And they can hardly address the myriad possible ways of going awry in the experimental task, much less in the whole enterprise of writing a poem. The suggestions stand, therefore, as practices that seem likely to meet some of the problems unearthed but that nevertheless are untested. Since this world does not guarantee to package plausible solutions with all problems, in just this limited sense the results are indeed encouraging.

The steps cited and others like them would comprise an effort to "tune" the subjects' thinking processes. The basic flow pattern of their efforts —what they do first and next—would remain intact. But at various points in that pattern, behavior would become more persistent, or more structured.

12. Radically restructuring the task

No experiment probed the potentials of the "tuning" discussed above. But one phase of the retesting explored a drastic rearranging of the subjects' approaches. During the retesting, the six subjects again sought a substitute phrase bettering an underlined phrase in a stanza given them. But as was mentioned, they proceeded according to a prescribed pattern. First, subjects were to state many conditions the substitution might satisfy. Next, subjects were to employ conditions they judged promising in listing all the specific options they could. Finally, subjects were to choose the two options they liked best and the two they liked least, evaluating each with as many pros and cons as possible.

This procedure dramatically reorganized the subjects' behavior patterns as shown in the first experiment. Originally, subjects chose solutions by a "threshold" principle; they searched until finding a solution satisfactory to them, and then stopped. Simon has named such a strategy, common in human problem solving, *satisficing*.[12] Confirming its presence, the data showed the subject's final choices were the last new options conceived in 92 percent of the cases. But the prescribed procedure imposed selection by *maximizing*: subjects chose the best options from a pool they had established earlier.

Further, phases of conceiving constraints, options, and pros and cons originally interwove. Roughly, subjects employed each constraint as it was conceived and evaluated each option at once. But the prescribed procedure divided these phases into successive stages. In their initial performances, subjects ceased searching well before they could search no further, not only at the top level but in evaluating or exploring areas of meaning. But the prescribed procedure encouraged searching until production rates dropped near zero. The experimenter urged the subjects to continue as long as further ideas were forthcoming, and subjects proceeded to the next step only after "running dry."

The revised procedure would plausibly short-circuit a number of subjects' difficulties by imposing a plan of action where the difficulties rarely arose. Most obviously, the requirement to list as many constraints, options, and pros and cons as possible and the segregation of these phases from one another would discourage the trend toward early stopping and scanty searches. Furthermore, bias and misdirection could not so readily prevail when subjects surveyed alternative guiding constraints at the outset rather than pursuing each at once. To put this more positively, the prescribed procedure would lead subjects to take better advantage of the task's hill-climbing opportunities. Also, *comparative* evaluation of constraints and options would occur, since the procedure deferred selection until a range of choices had accumulated. Comparative judgment here, as in many areas of human perception, would probably prove more acute than assessing items in isolation from one another as each was first conceived.[13] Finally, requiring a final choice would forestall giving up.

The stanza employed reflected a changed philosophy. Rather than a stanza with an existing weakness, the experiment used a stanza altered to introduce a weakness. How would the subjects' proposals measure against the target of the original? The stanza, selected from a poem by Barry Spacks,[14] appears in its original form except for italics:

> The bolted benches seem to know
> their place. The pond's like safety glass.
> The days like bright policemen pass,
> and when at times a manic weed
> starts crawling at heroic speed,
> a jungle folded in its seed:
> it *smothers* in the close-ranked grass.

In the experimental version, the word *withers* replaced *smothers*. The subjects, not told that the stanza had been modified, were simply asked to improve the underlined (here italicized) word.

Withers presented a problem of consistency. Superficially, *withers* fits the slot well enough: as with *smothers*, the weed expires confronting the park's inimical orderliness. Yet it is overexposure—sunlight, deserts, a dry season, lack of shade—that withers, whereas here the weed develops buried in the grass, close-ranked grass at that. More deeply, the stanza evolves a covert theme of oppressive conventionalism and militarism, expressed through the *bolted benches*, the *safety glass*, the *policemen*, and *close-ranked*. *Smothers* reinforces this, but the overtones of exposure and openness in *withers* blunt the theme. It was to these dissonances that subjects might respond.

The results matched the emphasis the prescribed procedure placed on exhaustive searching. Subjects conceived many more constraints and options than originally, as tabulated below. The entries represent performances

Table 10:2   Original Performances Versus Performances on New Poem Following the Prescribed Procedure

	Original Means	*New Poem Means*		*Original Means*	*New Poem Means*
Preconditions:			Searches of areas of meaning:		
Constraints mentioned	4	9	number in area	1.4	2.8
Areas of meaning of size 2 or more	1.3	5	most options in areas of size	1	5 or greater
Top-level search:					
Total options	12	28	Evaluation:		
			pros and cons per final choice	2	2

of the retested subjects on the revised procedure and on the three original stanzas *earthly years, fragile frosted cup,* and *toiling clown* (that is, excluding the practice example and the stanza requiring a long substitution). But one entry broke the general trend in the data: in evaluation, subjects conceived no more pros and cons than originally. Also, the prescribed procedure proved no cure for bias in evaluation. Constraints concerning appropriate meaning still dominated the subjects' assessment, with only 15 percent focusing on different considerations. Yet the sort of rating used previously, with the addition of an "ungrammatical" category since several substitutions required this, yielded about 60 percent of cons concerned with other than semantic fit. A list of instances speaks better than any simple characterization. The pairs of best substitutions the six subjects chose were:

strangles, inhales	*suicides, smothers*
stifled, surrendering	*hungry, crushed*
suffocates, forcibly closes	*festers, fattens*

One point surfaces quickly: the subjects generally perceived something of the poem's demands. One subject proposed the poet's original choice, *smothers.* Three others offered near synonyms: *suffocates, stifled,* and *strangles.* A fourth mentioned *crushed,* a word more distant from *smothers* but reflecting the repressive theme of the stanza. Only one subject of the six offered no choice moving toward a meaning more apt than *withers.* As in the original experiment, one can ask whether subjects' proposals represented an improvement over the given option, here *withers. Smothers, stifled,* and *strangles* seem preferable to *withers,* all things considered, and *suffocates* might appear on a par with it, achieving better-placed meaning at the cost of jarring the meter.

Comes the crucial question: were subjects more likely to reach better solutions following the prescribed procedure than originally? Several points confound any easy answer. The prescribed procedure asked subjects to choose their *two* best answers. And with choices required, subjects' solutions could not necessarily be taken as better in their own judgment than *withers.* Requiring the substitution of one word rather than the two perhaps offered subjects less of a chance to go wrong. Finally, the retesting required work on only one stanza. Did it happen to pose a generally easier or harder challenge than the original five? No a priori argument can draw a final conclusion, although a more complicated "counterbalanced" experimental design could do so.

These caveats issued, the data did permit a simple contrast. Originally, subjects chose only one option; on retesting they chose two. Comparison requires some correction for this. Examination of the original transcripts showed that despite the flaws in the final choices, subjects usually selected the best among the options they had conceived. Presuming that parallel behavior would obtain here if one best option had been requested, four out of the six retested subjects, or 66 percent, could have located a choice on a par with or better than the poet's original. If one subject had chosen otherwise, 50 percent would be the figure. The first experiment yielded a success rate of 24 percent. The percentages differ sharply. Indeed, though based on just six subjects, the difference is large enough to be just barely significant in statistical terms with the 66 percent figure, though not with the 50 percent.

Clearly, though, the conclusion rests on a precarious tower of inferences and assumptions. Alone it would mean nothing. Taken in company with other considerations—that subjects did conceive many more items in most phases of a search, that many of their choices seemed directed at the problem the given stanza presented, that the subjects themselves termed the prescribed procedure much easier—the figures at least encourage an overall picture of somewhat more effective performance.

But there is no claim that the prescribed procedure defined the best way to deal with an editing task. More complex "hybrid" procedures lying between subjects' normal practices and the prescribed procedure offer obvious benefits of flexibility. Suppose a subject discovered a new and relevant approach while evaluating an option; in the revised experiment he had no opportunity to pursue it. Or suppose a subject found the best option he had conceived just not good enough. He had no chance to seek further options. But a realistic game plan of progressing from constraints to options to selection and evaluation need not insist on a strict one-way progression. Any manner of patterning search must remain responsive to the successes, failures, and opportunities of the evolving circumstances.

13. The limits of performance

Tuning and *radically restructuring* behavior seem hopeful approaches. But they should not disguise the genuine challenge of doing well on such tasks. Several considerations limit what one can reasonably expect. First of all, despite the several bad searching strategies common to most subjects, in many respects subjects' transcripts read as highly individual ventures, succeeding or failing for reasons idiosyncratic to each.

Amy's and Dora's transcripts illustrate this. Whereas Amy soon formed definite objectives of expressing fragility and luminance, Dora's efforts flitted from one approach to another, never vigorously pursuing any one. In part this reflected the general trend toward shallow searches of semantic areas. But granting that, most subjects who made serious efforts soon settled on a particular approach. Yet Dora did not take her dissatisfaction with several approaches as a signal that she might commit more energy to exploring the potentials of some one.

Another factor constrained Dora's performance. As noted before, Dora early decided to keep *crystal*, seeking substitute words only for *icy*. Most subjects, like Amy, chose to explore the much larger range of substitutions permitted by changing both words. Dora's infertile decision would count as an instance of bias. For one particular consequence, Dora's decision led her to reject *fragile*, a word that indeed paired weakly with *crystal* but could prove more viable with another partner like *frosted*.

Such observations warn that the several weak strategies common to almost all subjects—scanty sampling of areas of meaning, and so forth—account only in part for failure. As a basis for training, they therefore promise only limited improvement. The many other reasons why particular efforts turned awry could—and perhaps should—guide training. But their diversity and individual rarity of occurrence guarantee a reduced payoff for the same training effort.

The retest findings support these points, confirming that really superb performance does not come easily. As a trend, the retesting enticed stronger showings. But as noted earlier, one retested subject offered singularly unperceptive evaluations of the specified options; apparently an authentic lack of discriminatory powers limited his performance as much as any failure to exercise available resources. Furthermore, though on retesting all the subjects proved more fluent, some exhibited much more fluency than others. And though the prescribed procedure perhaps yielded better results, it did not yield superb results. Such proposals as *festers, fattens, inhales, surrendering, hungry* seemed entirely at odds with the tone of the given stanza. Stranger yet, many failed to fit the simple grammatical demands of the stanza's last line. Though the experiment imposed a "forced choice" —subjects had to select two best substitutions from their list of options —better alignment between choice and stanza, or at least more critical awareness of misalignments, would seem possible. Indeed, some subjects showed clearly elsewhere that they could make such judgments. This warns that the prescribed procedure, whatever its strengths, did not push subjects as far as they could go.

A further point renders this problem acute. Consistently effective performance would appear to depend not just on doing things right much of the time but on avoiding pitfall after pitfall. Amy's other transcripts speak to this. Throughout her efforts she proved perhaps the most impressive performer, as generally discerning and fluent as in the *icy crystal cup*. Yet in *earthly years*, the stereotyped nature of *bitter tears*, her final choice, slipped by her scrutiny. And in *toiling clown*, her *black-masked clown* offered little against the original; as with Dora on *icy crystal cup* her most obvious mistake was perhaps an early decision to keep *clown* and search only for an accompanying adjective. None of this is to say that creative endeavor demands continuous caution. Indeed, such would surely be countercreative.

It *is* to say that invention requires the sort of care and persistence that catches mistakes sooner or later, that sometimes avoids slips and sometimes corrects them afterwards but rarely lets them slide by altogether.

Too easily the situation can appear hopelessly grim. On the contrary, such strategic principles as can be defined provide a clear guide toward improved performance. Furthermore, a tremendously significant point is that many phases of behavior desired in the ultimate self-directed performance will emerge in response to isolated tasks or verbally prescribed procedures. When any means at all serve to evoke such phases, those means can plausibly serve as well to evoke them in combinations, building toward more integrated performance. In contrast, no short-term means whatever appear available for quickly evoking basic skills of discrimination or production, even in an isolated context. In this sense, the trend of the present findings recommends optimism. But for the many reasons cited above, and no doubt as many more, excellence remains a stiff uphill climb away.

14. The real thing

This study's narrowest objectives were to analyze performance on the experimental task and consider how training might improve such performance. But obviously no great interest lies in enticing laboratory subjects to perform better and better on laboratory exercises. Let it be granted that the analysis explains something about performance on the experimental task. Do the findings really bear on the normal problems of novice poets, and just how do they bear? Necessarily, the experimental conditions would transform the behavior of the participants. Would the conditions turn a Dr. Jekyll into Mr. Hyde? Were some subjects' bad habits, crude judgments, and rough and easy satisfactions parts of another self, not the sophisticated and sensitive self that would sit down in a secluded spot to write a poem?

An earlier section argued that the contrived experiment nevertheless preserved much of the natural phenomenon. Effective writing demands effective editing, guaranteeing the importance of the phase of writing under study. The subjects' own behavior, recent studies of scientific problem solving, and Patrick's original process-tracing studies with poets argued that participants could maintain organized and directed behavior despite the verbal reporting. Though subjects' special skills would match their own particular styles, clearly the stanzas elicited thinking concerned with poetic matters and attempts to cope with poetic problems.

Here a final point enters. No Dr. Jekyll on his own time, the novice poet typically does fail in effectively editing his first drafts into polished products. Yet if all novices did search for options as thoroughly as they could, did evaluate as discerningly and broadly as they could, and so forth, it is difficult to believe their poems would exhibit so many problems. Letting artificiality explain away all strategic difficulties the subjects exhibited here simply discards out of hand possible explanations for poor performance in real circumstances.

Where does this leave the findings? Several aspects of inadequate searching emerged: too few alternatives considered, a curtailed survey of options from particular areas of meaning, biased and brief evaluations, and others. In the light of the above reservations, no sure diagnosis or cure for novices' difficulties can be announced. But the impoverished searching practices found stand at least as plausible hypotheses explaining novices' difficulties in their normal work.

The analysis also explored possible reasons for inadequate searching. These reasons could apply as well to the normal problems of novices. For example, subjects looked more kindly than keenly at their own options. So human a problem surely afflicts the novice dealing with his own work. For another, some subjects, conceiving phrases with intended meanings, misjudged their meaningfulness for the reader. This exemplifies a commonplace problem: the artist's distance from his own work. Setting a work aside for days, weeks, or more is the partial solution. But getting anything done requires dealing to some extent with that problem of distance by anticipating what difficulties may arise: one cannot put aside every small decision for a week.

Then plausible hypotheses abide, plausible because they emerge from an experiment that, whatever its limitations, has some clear relation to poetry writing; because the hypotheses would logically account for inadequate performance; and because some, such as the problem of 'distance,' make good sense in terms of conventional difficulties with creating art. Plausible hypotheses cannot substitute for firm conclusions. But in an area of behavior as subtle as the writing of poetry, they represent a necessary step toward understanding failure and success.

15. Toward a science of search

This paper began with a mystery: why do people so often fail on tasks requiring creative and discerning effort? Some familiar reasons seemed plausible. A person might be unable to discriminate adequate from inadequate end products or intermediate products. He might be unable to conceive sufficiently many alternatives to provide a fruitful selection (influency). Or he might exhibit *premature closure*, accepting the first barely appropriate option rather than pushing on toward better ones.

But the experimental task disclosed some very different explanations. In part, subjects failed not from bad taste but through neglecting to discriminate as best they could, not through influency but through insufficiently employing their fluency. Premature closure did prove a problem. But its standard characterization—stopping early in the top-level search—only touched a complex situation. Premature closure in the top-level search reflected premature closure in subordinate phases of search, namely evaluation and the exploration of particular areas of meaning. If all this must be summarized in one phrase, subjects did not deploy the skills they possessed to their own best advantage.

These particular obstacles to effective performance apply most confidently to the experimental task. But relevant to almost any task are the analytical concepts marshaled—the general notion of search and such varieties as hill climbing and constrained random search; the preconditions and postconditions which guide search; the stop rules which terminate searches in failure or success and select solutions by satisficing, maximizing, or other strategies; evaluation as itself a process of search; flaws in search such as scantiness, bias, or misdirection; and finally the recursive way that search so often involves searches within searches, which provides the opportunity to trace flaws on one level to possibly different flaws on subordinate levels. To the extent that analysis in such terms illuminates any task, new directions toward better performance may follow, involving tuning or more radical revision of the way individuals manage their more specialized discriminatory and productive skills.

The emergent contrast between the two modes of explanation for failure—resource management versus the lower-level skills that are managed—maps more richly the obscure territory of human invention. Failure explained through influency or bad discrimination underscores the role of essential component skills, skills that often may be rather specific to the task. Thus, readily listing rhyme words or keenly differentiating roughly synonymous words contributes especially to poetry and other literary contexts. Explanations concerning personal resource management cling less to the task's specific demands. The problems found—premature closure in many phases of search, and so forth—would certainly occur in many contexts. Accordingly, the latter mode of explanation looks toward a very general account of human invention. The benefits of such an account would be tremendous.

But at the same time this approach introduces a whole new area of task-specific knowledge. As Newell and Simon have emphasized, any subject area limits and channels the procedures appropriate for goal-seeking activities in that domain.[15] But whatever rough shaping may take place, normal performance stands some distance from any optimal fit. Certainly the experimentation reflected this. In the number of options considered, in the brief sampling of areas of meaning, in the nonexhaustive searches for disqualifying cons, subjects exhibited patterns of performance which simply mismatched the realities of the task situation.

Then whatever general principles may emerge, pat formulas for all contexts, such as "look as long and as hard as you can," seem unlikely. Rather, each subject area not only defines its relevant generative and discriminatory skills and defines the rough paths along which search must proceed but also desginates a fine structure of trap and opportunity, a structure which usually seems to elude all but the expert. Thus the real promise lies in coupling general concepts of effective search with some analysis of the throughways, byways, and dead-end alleys a given terrain presents. Such an alliance pursues a simple purpose: to steer behavior out of the ruts of bare adequacy toward truly inventive performance.[16]

APPENDIX

1. The stanzas

A slumber did my spirit seal;
        I had no human fears:
She seemed a thing that could not feel
        The touch of *earthly years.*

Without, there was a cold moon up,
        Of Winter radiance sheer and thin;
        The hollow halo it was in
Was like a(n) *icy crystal* cup.

From soil somehow the poet's word
And from that word the spreading tree
Where swells all fruit, sings every bird,
Whose strong trunk is *philosophy.*

And like a dying lady, lean and pale,
Who totters forth wrapped in a gauzy veil,
Out of the chamber, led by the insane,
And feeble wanderings of her faded brain,
The moon arose up in the murky East,
A white and shapeless mass—

Now swarthy summer, by rude health embrowned,
        Precedence takes of rosy-fingered Spring;
And laughing joy, with wild flowers pranked and crowned,
        A wild and giddy thing,

And health robust, from every care unbound,
    Come on the zephyr's wing,
And cheer *the toiling clown*.

2. Word choices of subjects in the first group of eight.

Numbers correspond to the eight subjects. Subjects 1 through 4 were amateur poets.

Philosophy
  1. yet waving free
  2. life
  3. faith in man
  4. imagination
  5. bunk
  6. the thought made shape
  7. the gross absurd
  8. the sense of all we feel and see

Cup
  1. —
  2. smoke-filled cup
  3. Diana's icy cup

  4. frozen crystal cup
  5. golden loving cup
  6. —
  7. —
  8. —

Mass
  1. winking on the dark and vaprous trail
  2. a greying form
  3. a dimmed consciousness reigns
  4. wan and intangible
  5. an Alka-seltzer dissolving in water
  6. cloud-embroiled, doomed to set
  7. pausing to peer below
  8. —

Years
  1. earthly tears
  2. —
  3. timely tears
  4. —
  5. eroding years
  6. —
  7. earthly tears
  8. —

Clown
  1. cheer the rest that summer's found
  2. —
  3. cheer the gardener triumphant in his toil
  4. time
  5. the dog pound
  6. the growth explosion
  7. —
  8. —

3. Word choices of subjects in the second group of eight.

Numbers correspond to the eight subjects. Numbers 1 through 4 were amateur poets. Amy is 1, Dora is 2.

Philosophy
  1. —
  2. —

Years
  1. bitter tears
  2. —

3. —
4. humanity
5. emotionality
6. —
7. —
8. sweet melody

Cup
1. fragile frosted cup
2. —
3. —
4. empty crystal cup
5. misty velvet cup

6. —
7. icy fragile cup
8. ice-filled yea empty cup

Mass
1. an escaping breathless sigh
2. then sank just as your love ceased
3. like the shadowed soul of some rough beast
4. like light in an old woman's eyes failed
5. stumbled across the dusty sky and slumped into bed
6. a pale, dissolving form
7. a weak and shapeless beast
8. her endless drive and her insatiable feast

3. human tears
4. —
5. mortal tears
6. waking fears
7. mortal cares
8. diurnal tears

Clown
1. lonely painted clown
2. the world around
3. the heart's been downed
4. —
5. the sweat-stained herdsman on his rounds
6. gesturing clown
7. season's fling
8. friendly autumn rebound

4. *Amy's transcript for* icy crystal cup

First remark is: "I don't like that [probably *icy crystal*] at all." Rereads. "Was like, that's uh . . . that's OK now. This is all pure image. White, the cold moon—" Rereads. "Was like, was like, uh, icy, or, *shiny, white,*" pause, "*very sheer, very fine.*" Repeats "was like" several times. Rereads. Says it sounds like it doesn't scan but she guesses it does. Rereads to "was like a *shining,* was like a *ceremonial cup,*" repeats but says that doesn't convey icy crystalness. "Was like a—a *finely* da da cup, *glowing* cup, *glistening* cup." Rereads stanza; can't remember what she said; E tells her glistening. She rereads, inserting *glistening.* She notes she has an extra syllable while counting on fingers. Says *finely glowing* and says she likes *finely glowing,* especially *finely* because whole image is something very delicate and fragile—she tries *fragile,* "was like a *fragile christening cup,*" but says she doesn't know what a christening cup is. After brief pause, tries *fragile* with crystal cup. Rereads stanza with *fragile,* decides she likes fragile better than icy because the cold and icy are so very similar. Thinks crystal could be kept because it's in with the sheer and thin part of it. And *fragile* carries out the idea of delicacy or sort of not being quite all there—S laughs and says she didn't mean that; it came out funny. Rereads with *fragile crystal* but then decides she's changed her mind and should get away from crystal. Suggests *softly glistening.*

S confirms crystal is glass; then says it's funny because she never thinks of a cup as crystal, cup sounds very sort of earthenware cup, tin cup, so cup and crystal jar in her mind. Rereads last two lines, decides she could change to *silver—glistening silver cup*. Repeats *glistening silver*. Couldn't be *fragile silver* because silver's not too fragile. Rereads with *glistening silver* again. Says she personally never uses glistening. Rereads with *glowing silver cup*; this sounds like an ad, suggests *shining* but feels that sounds even worse, rereads and discovers: "Oh, I get it. It's the halo, the hollow halo was like a—That makes sense." S asks if halo would be fragile; decides it would. Rereads, then asks if she can change *an*. E notes she can make choice of "a" or "an." S says she keeps thinking of a fairy story by C. S. Lewis where there was a very special cup that was very thin, very fine—glistening and silver and just glowing, she keeps thinking of that and it is influencing her. Rereads. Says *frosty*, which goes back to cold moon. Changes to *frosted crystal cup*. Rereads; asks herself how many choices she has, which she has been writing down on paper while talking. Reads her previous choices. Rereads with *frosted crystal* cup and then *finely frosted*. Rereads, pauses and notes that she loses crystal and doesn't know whether with *finely frosted* she's keeping the idea of fragility—but says finely is the frosted, not the cup. S remarks that *finely frosted* scans. Rereads with *finely frosted*, then with *fragile*, questions *fragility*, goes back to *fragile*. Rereads with *fragile frosted cup*. S now trying to decide between *fragile frosted* and *finely frosted*, notes she has a lot of alliteration coming in but says crystal cup is also alliteration. She asks if she has to decide on just one choice. E asks if she has several she approves of equally. S says she goes through several versions. Over a period of months, she keeps going back and maybe changing one word so she has different versions, so what she is doing now would be the first stage in writing a poem when she has all these choices so she wouldn't naturally pick one out. S goes back to *fragile frosted* versus *finely frosted*. Says *fragile* modifies the cup whereas *finely* modifies the frosted and the whole idea of thinness, sheerness, is lost by use of *finely frosted*, although she likes phrase *finely frosted* in a vacuum by itself better than *fragile frosted*. But she'll keep *fragile frosted* because she thinks a modifier for cup is needed because when she thinks of cup she thinks of something very sturdy and in the original he's got crystal which takes care of the cup. So *fragile frosted*.

5.   *Dora's transcript for* icy crystal cup

Reads, thinks it's Keats or Coleridge, maybe "Ancient Mariner." Rereads, says she likes it, pause, says it's a little indefinite, she doesn't feel crystal cup has to be icy but icy adds to it and she thinks of a frosted marguerita glass. Repeats she likes it but says she's not sure she knows the kind of hollow halo he's talking about (or she) or whether icy describes that completely or precisely, but she likes the sound of it. S says she guesses she could get more exotic. Rereads, says she'd keep crystal and would get more precise, would replace icy with—would go to a thesaurus and start looking up marvelous words, has to be two syllables, *fragile's* no good, fragile would be good but it's not better than icy. *Ice chilled*, pause, says she's thinking of corny things like *milky* (?), *Milky Way*, and she can't get that far afield, has to stick to visual things.

Hollow, no not hollow, like a *thin*, got thin. Could use something like—to spread this thing out a little bit—like a *cosmic*—S says that's something like she would use but this person probably wouldn't. *Cosmic*, pause, E prompts, S says she's thinking *Irish crystal* cup, *Waterford crystal*, that's really getting specific. Says she likes *cosmic* or a *misted crystal* cup but that's too much of a mouthful. *Misted, frosted* (writing) decides icy is better. She says there are some really great words she can't think of which would suggest the brittleness, but *brittle crystal* is no good. *Liquid*, no, rereads *twisted*, no. Says there are other words she can't think of but wants to use. *Persistent*, says that's another poem, another poet. S feels she's too much influenced by this guy's type of words, like radiance and sheer. Says she'll stick with *icy* or *frosted*, pause, E prompts, S says she's thinking it's too bad that she can't think of a kind of word she wants, maybe she's inhibited, maybe she just needs to mouth lots and lots of words like *misted, twisted, frosted*, pause, *snowflake*, pause, says she thinks of its character like mysterious, spooky, none of which are—out of reach. Was like somebody's, pause, somebody, the *gods'*, the *astronauts'*, the *birds'*, pause. Was like a *milky crystal cup*, says she still has got the Milky Way in there. Decides she'll stick to icy, says she wants to but can't do better.

Notes

1. See, for instance, Brewster Ghiselin, ed., *The Creative Process* (Berkeley: University of California Press, 1952); Melville Cane, *Making a Poem: An Inquiry into the Creative Process* (New York: Harcourt, Brace, 1953); Rosalmond Harding, *An Anatomy of Inspiration* (New York: Barnes & Noble, 1967); I. A. Richards, "Poetic Process and Literary Analysis," in *Style in Language*, ed. Thomas Sebeok (Cambridge, Mass.: MIT Press, 1960); William Packard, ed., *The Craft of Poetry* (Garden City, N.Y.: Doubleday, 1974).

2. Robert M. Gagne and Ernest C. Smith, "A Study of the Effects of Verbalization on Problem Solving," *Journal of Experimental Psychology* 63 (1962): 12–18.

3. Catharine Patrick, "Creative Thought in Poets," *Archives of Psychology*, Vol. 26 Serial No. 178 (1935), pp. 1–74.

4. Michael Wallach, "Creativity," in *Carmichael's Manual of Child Psychology*, 3d ed., ed. Paul Mussen (New York: Wiley, 1970), 1: pp. 1211–1272, accomplishing an extensive and valuable review of the literature on creativity, concluded that so far as creativity is a concept independent of general IQ it should simply refer to fluently producing large numbers of unusual candidates. But whatever a person's creative capacity in that special sense, the results of this study warn that in real problem contexts people may not use the fluency they have.

5. I. A. Richards, *Practical Criticism: A Study of Literary Judgment* (1929, reprinted New York: Harcourt, Brace & World, 1968).

6. Sir Frederic Bartlett, *Thinking—An Experimental and Social Study* (New York: Basic Books, 1958).

7. The capacity to shift categories readily while generating is one of the three forms of fluency called "flexibility"; J. P. Guilford, "Intellectual Factors in Productive Thinking," in *Explorations in Creativity*, ed. Rose Mooney and Taher Razik (New York: Harper & Row, 1967). The contrast between the figures here and the retest results described later suggests that a person's apparent flexibility in real problem contexts is at least as much a question of the person's habits of search as it is of individual limits of capacity.

8. Adrianus D. deGroot, *Het Denken van den Schaker*, trans. as *Thought and Choice in Chess* (The Hague: Mouton, 1965).

9. Herbert A. Simon and William G. Chase, "Skill in Chess," *American Scientist* 61 (1973): 394–403.

10. Jerome Kagan and Nathan Kogan, "Individual Variation in Cognitive Processes," in Mussen, *Carmichael's Manual*, Vol. 1, 3rd edition, pp. 1273–1365.

11. Kenneth Beittel, *Mind and Context in the Art of Drawing* (New York: Holt, Rinehart & Winston, 1972).

12. Herbert Simon, *The Sciences of the Artificial* (Cambridge, Mass.: MIT Press, 1969).

13. Eleanor J. Gibson, *Principles of Perceptual Learning and Development* (New York: Appleton-Century-Crofts, 1969) reviews findings that discrimination is much finer when stimuli are presented in close succession and that reliable scaling or naming of a range of stimuli involves much cruder subdivisions of the range than can be discriminated in side-by-side or close sequential comparisons.

14. The stanza is the last from "My Dear, You're Like This Public Park," in Barry Spacks, *The Company of Children* (Garden City, N.Y.: Doubleday, 1969).

15. Allen Newell and Herbert Simon, *Human Problem Solving* (Englewood Cliffs, N.J.: Prentice-Hall, 1972), chap. 14.

16. This research was supported by the Spencer Foundation, National Science Foundation Grant GB-31064, and National Institute of Education Grant G-003-0169. The opinions expressed here do not necessarily reflect the position or policy of the National Institute of Education, and no official endorsement should be inferred. I would like to thank Sharon Randolph and Roy Rudenstine for their extensive and valuable assistance in carrying out this study.

11 In Search of a Tune
Jeanne Bamberger

Seated before a computer terminal, a student types, simply, G1. Instantly an electronic music box performs a brief, three-note motive, called a "tune block." These motives may be thought of as building blocks of various shapes, but the "shape" depends on the particular configuration of pitch and time which the prepared computer procedures describe. There are five such tune blocks; the student's task is to arrange them so that they produce a whole melody, one that makes

sense to him. Although the blocks are parts of an actual tune, the student is not trying to get a "right answer" but rather to invent his own reasonable tune within the limitations of these materials. He can, of course, play the blocks as often as he likes, individually or in any arrangement. If he wants to hear two or more blocks in succession, he simply types out their names in the order he chooses. The duration of the pitches remains exactly the same when blocks follow one another; that is, the computer processes the whole chain of blocks (e.g., G1G3G2) and then plays the whole chain "in time"

when the student indicates he is ready. In designing his tune, he is free to repeat blocks whenever he thinks it appropriate.

This student is participating in a study of musical intelligence which began with two fundamental assumptions. The first was that the perception of music, like the perception of a visual scene or a line of text, is an active process; it involves the individual in selecting, sorting, grouping, and interrelating the features of the phenomena before him. In this sense perception of even a simple tune is an intelligent process which requires the individual to reconstruct its features and relations. The second assumption held that individual differences in response to a potentially sensible melody (perceiving it to "make sense" or not) rest heavily on just which features the individual has access to or is able to focus on. In addition, flexibility of focus and the kinds of relations the individual can build among features strongly influence his response.

The task, then, was to capture the individual's particular representation of a melody—that is, how he represents it to himself, what features he seizes, what relations he finds. The second task was to observe how an individual's representation of a melody might change in the course of working with given melodic materials within a relatively controlled experimental environment.

Thus this study set for itself the following questions: What are the crucial features captured by an individual's representation of a melody? Will these be significantly different among individuals? As a corollary, do individuals differ in their internalized models of a sensible tune? And more specifically, what strategies will an individual invoke and on what bases will he make decisions in *building* a tune that makes sense to him? Finally, is there a describable relation between an individual's model of a tune, his mode of representation, his working strategies, and his completed tune?

The search for answers to these questions entailed observation of step-by-step progress of musically untrained college students as they built an original tune. The experiment was actually one small part in the development of a new learning environment where students of varying ages are actively and systematically exploring the bases of musical coherence.[1] Within this experimental environment students are encouraged to probe and question their own responses and to search within the relations of pitch and time for what makes sense, for what generates a new effect or a new structural meaning.

The gadgetry with which the student works is quite simple. He finds himself before a typewriter which is coupled on one side with a computer and on the other side with a "music box" about the size and shape of a lunch box. The music box can produce a five-octave range of pitches and can play up to four parts simultaneously. The box also plays two percussion sounds, one similar to a tom-tom and the other to a brushed cymbal. The student describes to the computer what he would like to hear by typing on his typewriter-terminal. The computer in turn causes the music box to produce the configurations indicated. The response is immediate. Thus in using the system the student need only be concerned with thinking out what he wants to happen. He can sit back and listen as often as he wishes to what he has invented, change it, and listen again to the result. The instant feedback of his ideas in sound and time tells him immediately the relation between his thinking, his description, and the resulting musical effect. He is thus learning how to influence and control musical relationships through designing a particular kind of musical process. If he can think it and describe it adequately, he can make it happen, and if he is surprised by what his description brings forth, that is often the moment of most productive learning.

Although the task seems obvious enough, it was astonishing to discover the varieties of strategies and levels of engagement of each student. There seemed to be as many procedures for playing this game as there were players. Indeed, of the eight students in this particular experiment, each invented a different tune, and each tune had its invididual effect or character. Interestingly, each student's "solution" was met with astonishment, even distaste, by the others. In fact, in order to understand each student's tune, the others had to "restructure" their thinking and to adjust their perceptions of the shared material. While this gives some inkling of the importance of context (since only the *arrangement* of the blocks varied among the tunes), the student's own discovery of the significance of context was of greatest importance. Students found that the "meaning" of a block changed as its position in the set changed. That is, as they played with various arrangements, embedding the blocks in different contexts, they gradually became aware of new and different features in each individual block. The notion of what constituted a significant feature or a significant structural "element" (e.g., a note, a particular pitch-time figure, a rhythm, a whole block) became of paramount importance, influencing the eventual form and affect of the completed tune.

Observations of the students give a glimmer of what learning might mean within this environment. At the same time, the observers themselves were catapulted into a reexamination of assumptions: models of structure, modes of description, categories of analysis, and theoretic "givens" were exposed for reassessment.

Most of the examples discussed here are taken from the work of only two students, but it should be emphasized that this project was merely a beginning for them and for their observers. The musical materials with which the students worked are limited; the blocks have built-in stylistic constraints which, in turn, suggest a limited set of possibilities for achieving structural coherence. But these very limitations permitted students and experimenters to explore the nature of these particular possibilities, which proved to be much richer than imagined. Further, the relative familiarity of the stylistic constraints permitted students to confront more easily those generative primitives from which larger and more complex musical structure derives. In subsequent projects involving the particular contents of tune blocks these primitives were more explicitly explored.[2] In addition, when students listened to significant works in a variety of musical styles, they discovered (sometimes dramatically) that these same generative primitives contributed to a musical coherence which had previously been inaccessible to them. Their affective response and musical taste was often quite transformed as their perception became more acute and more mobile.[3]

1. The two tunes and how they grew

The two students, Mark and Jorge, make a striking contrast. Mark "studied the violin a little in high school" but claimed to have forgotten all that he had learned. Jorge, from Peru, played the guitar a little "by ear" and enjoyed singing Peruvian folk songs, of which he knew a great many. Mark worked carefully and methodically often pausing in his work to "think." Jorge worked impulsively, quickly, and seemed to enjoy every bit of melody, every possibility that he caused the music box to play. Mark talked little; his comments were cryptic. To complete his tune he made only nineteen requests of the music box. Jorge talked a lot and expansively. He made a total of eighty-two requests to the music box to complete his tune. (The complete protocols for the two students can be found in the appendix).

Their strategies were also markedly different. Mark searched quickly for a beginning and ending for his tune and then systematically found material to fill the gap between. While he focused right away on particular features of blocks, especially similarities and differences among them, his perception of features and his selection of priorities changed dramatically in the course of his work. Jorge tried many, many combinations of blocks and often responded with some comment concerning their effect or their character. Only later did he become concerned with particular features which generated these effects, and still later with how his combinations of blocks might work together to form a whole tune. The shift in Jorge's reconstruction, in his perception of the blocks and their features, came suddenly and carried with it an equally sudden insight for the structure of his completed tune.

2. Beginnings:

Mark begins in his typically orderly way—he plays each block in order and notes what are, for him, cogent features:

| G1: | G2: | G3: | G4: | G5: |
| "oh-oh" | "the fast one" | "could be a closing" | | "similar to G1" |

Mark has been told that the blocks are jumbled—that is, that their numbering is arbitrary and has no particular significance to an arrangement that might eventually make sense to him. Considering each block as an individual entity is therefore inevitable at first, and yet whatever he hears first will also inevitably influence whatever follows it. Thus, G2 is "faster" as compared with G1. His comment notes a relatively local difference between G1 and G2: G2 includes more notes per unit of time. The comment is local because Mark is pointing to a single, particular feature, one that he spontaneously selects as differentiating G1 from G2.

In contrast, "could be a closing," his remark on G3, is a higher-level comment: it implies relationships among several local features. In addition, it is more global because it suggests that this aggregate of features generates a function which may be significant to the overall structure of the complete tune. The aggregate of features which generate the function. "closing" includes the following: G3 ends with a *low pitch of longer duration;* both these features create a point of structural articulation—an accent. Moreover, the motion to this final pitch is stepwise downward; the melodic motion is clearly directed toward the accented note. And finally, the block ends with the pitch that sounds most stable or at rest in relation to the other pitches; this pitch is usually called the *tonic.*

But this last feature results from other features not only of G3 but also of G1 and G2—which are, after all, already part of Mark's working context. For example, the sense of stability results both from the specific limitations of the pitch collection thus far (i.e., all those pitches included in blocks G1–G3) and the order in which these pitches havs occurred (particularly in G3). Note that it is not any single feature but rather the relations among the set which generate the higher-level feature, stable pitch, or tonic.

Listening to G5, Mark now compares it with G1, this time noting similarity rather than difference. His single word, "similar," suggests his access to the identical rhythm (set of durations) of G1 and G5 and to their pitch shape, which is also essentially the same. But it is important to observe that he has remembered G1 well enough to compare it with G5 even though three other blocks have intervened. Evidentily his access to these similar features and his means of representing them to himself are sufficient to allow him to hold the configuration in memory for future recall and comparison.

Indeed, all of Mark's comments serve him as mnemonic labels, as a means for representing the blocks to himself so he can retrieve them and manipulate them in his head. Except for his very first comment ("Ah-oh"—what can I do with that?) his labels make use of local features or aggregates of features as identifiers. In turn, these labels and the selective priorities they imply influence and guide his use of the blocks as he continues to develop his tune.

3. *Beginnings:*

Jorge begins quite differently. He plays the whole set of blocks as a single string, as if to ask what kind of a melody that would make. After that he quickly plays individual blocks beginning with G1, twice, but then jumps around in random order (see appendix). His comment at the end of these eleven requests is, "G2 and G4 are the main parts—but how to use them? I don't know what comes after G2. G5 may be an ending." Notice that none of Jorge's comments refer to specific features of the blocks. As if the blocks were characters or events in a story, he ponders what might come next, which blocks are the "main" ones, which block might end the tale. Jorge's initial notion that G2 and G4 are the "main parts" influences his work almost to the end. The problematic G2 will continue to trouble him for a long time, and his assertion that "G5 may be an ending" undergoes a surprising switch.

4. *Working out possibilities: Mark*

Taking off from his first observations, Mark tries pairs of blocks, testing his hunches. Playing his "similar" blocks, G1G5, he creates a new entity and gathers new information:

Juxtaposition of the three-note motives G1 and G5 defines (or perhaps confirms) the higher-level rhythmic grouping. Notice that it is only by playing the blocks in pairs that Mark can determine the duration of the last note of the first block in this pair. For example, G1G5 could have been

rather than

Juxtaposition determines that the new entity is an uninterrupted set of equal durations. In turn, juxtaposition reveals that the unit pulse generated by the uninterrupted set of equal durations is grouped into threes by the pitch shape which is shared by both blocks.

Thus, it is the *pitch* relations that generate the higher level *rhythmic* grouping. To explore this point, consider the following example: If the music box drum plays six hits all of equal duration and loudness, the listener can arbitrarily group these hits into twos or threes:

But once pitch is added, as in G1G5, the grouping is no longer arbitrary; the grouping is defined as two pairs of *three* notes each, at least until some additional information is introduced which conflicts with this grouping. Thus the pitch shapes in G1G5 generate a slower pulse with a ratio of 1:3 to the unit pulse. (This ratio of grouper pulse to unit pulse is called meter. G1G5 generates triple meter; a ratio of 1:2 would produce duple meter.)

Moving ahead now, Mark makes a ninth request (G4G2), which shifts his focus and leads him into new realms of inquiry:

"Sounds like an opening, but there's a change in time." Pause. "How long *is* this tune?" Pause. "I don't know how to match." What did Mark mean by "change in time"? At first we assumed that he was simply referring to the increase in number of notes per unit beat; "change" meant faster. Later, however, another student's comments suggested that Mark was responding to an implied shift in metric grouping. The last note of G2, with its relatively longer duration, contained or delimited the faster motion leading into it; thus this last note seemed to function as an accent or downbeat. The result was the suggestion of a duple grouping in contrast to the clear triple grouping in G4.

With this glimpse of a problematic beginning, Mark pauses, looks visibly uncertain, and then seems thrust into a search for the whole. ("How long *is* this tune?") But this leap towards global structure is too early for the current state of his representation. It goes beyond what he knows of the features of the blocks and the relations among them. He retreats to a more limited position: "I don't know how to match." What can he mean?

Part of the explanation lies in his earlier work in this session. He had been playing a different version of the tune blocks game which required him to listen to a complete tune and then simply to rebuild it. In this first game he *did* know how long the finished tune was going to be; he had only to "match" blocks with the original till his arrangement fit. While it is clear to him that he can now build his own tune, he is evidently uncomfortable in this new situation; design, including proportions, depends only on his decisions. What can he base his decisions on?

Mark's comments suggest his search for a strategy. Without the defined constraints of an actual tune, he is left to "match" the features of the tune blocks with the ill-defined features of his model of a sensible tune. He has found a beginning that tentatively works; on what basis can he make decisions for a continuation? For example, how can he build a destination, a goal for his beginning; how can he form groups of blocks to make larger structural elements; how can he form parts of a whole if the whole does not yet exist? Mark is grappling with crucial questions involving the interaction between local and global structure, between detail and larger design. Each level of the structure defines, even generates, the other.

With his next request (G1G3G5) he escapes from his momentary discomfort:

G1G3G5:

"Ah, cool—I could end the song with G3, a long note, but G5 would be a surprise ending. I have lots of endings." He still doesn't know how long the tune will be, but at least he knows where it's going. Like a lost traveler he has an idea what his destination is, and that should make it easier to find his way there.

What are the features of Mark's ending combination? Interestingly, his first pair, G1G5, is included in his closing combination, but it is now broken apart by the interpolation of G3. As a result of this new embedding, the sequential relation between G1 and G5 is obscured. Indeed, both G1 and G5 assume new meanings: G3 takes over the role of G5 as resolution or completion to G1; G5 takes on the new role of "surprise ending." But why is G5 a "surprise ending"? Note that G1G3 is self-contained, ending conclusively on the tonic and on a strong beat in the triple meter. But G5 continues on after the halt of G3; the action spills over. Again, after the rhythmically accented, longer duration of G3's tonic final note, the tonic but weak-beat ending of G5 generates a whimsical close. At the same time, G5 echoes G1 in pitch shape and rhythm but has a different function; G1 is a lead-in but G5 is another ending (and thus is a little like a pun).

Mark has constructed the outline of a complete tune; his tune is delimited, his problem-spaced defined. Now he has only to work out some means for getting from one end to the other. As often happens with real composers, the middle of the composition will be discovered last.

5. *Working out possibilities:*

Jorge's style for working out possibilities is again strikingly different from Mark's. Jorge quickly makes twenty-one requests of the music box, trying various pairs of blocks and occasionally a longer string (see appendix, requests 12–33). The problem "what comes after G2" is clearly worrying him; eight of his requests call for G2 followed by another block. His explorations lead to two discoveries that have significance for the future. He notes that G4G3 is "good, and maybe at the end after G2." Indeed, this pair

G4G3:

does end his completed tune, though it undergoes much manipulation before settling down. And juxtaposing the blocks with the most variety and the greatest density of events (G2G4) he responds, "It's a wild one, huh?"

G2G4:

Jorge enjoys the expressive potential of even this limited musical material. Later on, when he sang some Peruvian folk songs, it was clear that for him the music's primary purpose was to reinforce the quality of the words; you couldn't really "get" the song without understanding the words.

Now, tired of worrying about G2 and looking for a way to get on, he hits upon a useful strategy: immediate repetition of a block as a means for evading the restrictions of the material. He describes his strategy quite clearly: "I repeated blocks to make bigger things to work with. The blocks were too small alone. It was a way of stopping to use a new block each time. By repetition I relieved that restriction; I had more blocks to work with." Typical examples of the procedure are:

Out of his experiments with repetition of blocks another structural principle seems to emerge: a tune can be built up of cells or modules. The pairs of repeated blocks form the beginnings of these cells, which Jorge then expands into larger modules. These modules can then be pushed around and modified to form a sketch, a tune-in-progress. Once more he describes his strategy: "I was thinking in small blocks that were growing. Then I built a whole song that I could change to make it better."

Typical of this process are the following examples, built up from the smaller cells in the prior example.

Notice that the large modules which make up the two halves of each tune are kept intact. In request 51 Jorge simply reverses the two halves of request 50. In the process his ending combination (G4G3) comes up in the middle!

Listening to the result propels Jorge into new considerations. He focuses directly on the potential function of G3; more important, for the first time he focuses on a feature which generates that function: the "silence" at the end of G3 makes it a "link" and an "end." His representation of G3 is changing. He draws a picture of the tune:

Only G3 is a defined entity—the pillars in an otherwise amorphous whole. Questioned about the "silence" at the end of G3, he tries G3G1 and discovers the inaccuracy in his representation. "No, a long note so it must be an end." Contact with a level of greater detail leads him still further along this path; he draws a pitch-by-pitch picture of his "main" blocks, G2 and G4:

In the process Jorge's representation of G2 and G4 is transformed: it now includes more and different features. He comments: "Before I couldn't remember them so well. Now I can spend less time playing them." Starting from a tune-in-progress, he has worked down from his larger vista into its details. Like a camera zooming in, refocusing the lens, features of blurred shapes become clearer. Now, with access to sharp features, he grabs them and fixes them in his drawing—to remember.

Jorge has made fifty-five requests of the music box up to this point. His delight with the possibilities, the potential character of these possibilities, and with his evolving models has led him only now to consider particular features of individual blocks. Jorge said, on looking back at his work: "Drawing the blocks was important. You start out asking the computer to tell you. Later you can memorize them and do it in your head." To remember, then, means *to capture particular features, even to name the blocks through these features*.

Now he finds himself facing a problem: How should he proceed with this new and different information? How can he relate the kind of detailed features he has just discovered to his larger vista with its blurred but character-rich shapes? He is caught between two views of this small world. A question from the observer guides him back to his previous world: "What do you know so far?" He says: "G2 and G4 are complex, important. G3 is an ending, it goes perfectly after G4." The observer asks, "Does it [G3] go after G2?" Playing G2G3, Jorge bursts into a description of the problematic G2:

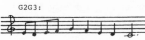

"I didn't like it (G2G3). The problem with G2 is it ends too fast; it goes up and should have something else before going down. The last note of G2 is too quick, it ends right on the border of the next one, so the next one needs more time in beginning. Maybe G1 [goes] after G2." Stepping back again he tries G1 after G2, inserting the pair into his previous tune-in-progress:

Jorge's analysis of the problematic G2 is quite remarkable. It points to very specific features of the music but in language which reflects his sense of qualitative character. He seems to have bridged the gap between asking the computer to "tell" him and seizing the relevant features for himself. Consider more closely what he says: noting that G2 "ends too fast," he is pointing to the same feature that Mark described as a "change in time." That is, the accent generated by the longer duration of the last note of G2 (relative to the preceding notes) implies a shift in metric grouping; the accent arrives too soon, before the expected downbeat. Jorge's remark "it goes up and should have something else before going down" points to the instability, both in rhythm and in pitch of this last note. The pitch G demands resolution, but first it should be extended, perhaps to fill out a second metric group (or bar) of two beats. Referring to G2G3, he says, "The last note is too quick, it ends right on the border of the next one." Thus while G3 does resolve the instability of the last pitch of G2 by returning to the tonic and to a downbeat, it does so too directly. The rapid movement through G2 needs to be slowed down, prolonged before descending to resolution. And finally, G2G1 is "better" because resolution is not achieved; the downward motion stops before reaching the tonic or a downbeat. However, there is still "no space" between G2 and G1. This evidently refers to the metric problem again; a rest following G2 might satisfy his need for "more time in beginning."

At last Jorge has a clear image of what he wants. The problems are defined. But how to resolve them?

In contrast to Jorge, Mark generated local mnemonic labels from the very beginning: "the fast one," "could be a closing," "similar to G1." With access to local features he could, in fact, "do it in his head." With his tenth request he delimited the boundaries of his whole tune.

At the same time, Mark's exploration of the material was more limited than Jorge's. He showed no interest in quality or character, and his ability to fix features also narrowed the possibilities he could foresee. It seems fair to describe Mark as solution-oriented or product-oriented, playing with the material only just enough to get an answer. For Jorge, playing seems more important than answering. The differences in approach have interesting consequences for what each student learns as well as for his final tune.

6. Endings:

His tune delimited by a beginning and an ending, Mark has now caught a glimpse of the whole. Trying his beginning combination again (G4G2), he now finds it "OK." Why? While he has focused previously on relatively local *differences* between G2 and G4 ("There's a change in time"), his shift in focus to the whole seems to direct his attention to features which both blocks share. Specifically, they share the same fundamental melodic skeleton: G4 and G2 are together a melodic embellishment or prolongation of the single pitch, G.

G4 begins on the pitch G, moves below it, and returns. The middle G is again extended by the short, upper neighboring tone and the return to G on a weak beat. The motion around G is comparable to that of a rubber band held still in the middle and stretched out on either side. Following G4, G2 becomes a further extension of this fulcrum pitch. Starting with the lower embellishing pitch E, G2 moves *to* the fulcrum pitch. The final G generates an accent, but one that seems to arrive (as Jorge said) too soon, out of phase. But embedded in the whole, G2G4 can work as a lively prolongation of the single skeleton pitch G. Thus G2 becomes a truncated and rhythmically animated version of G4. The relatively low-level rhythmic conflict, the shift in metric grouping, becomes a momentary ambiguity subsumed within higher-level relations; a detail in the larger structure assumes its appropriate role within Mark's new picture of a developing whole.

Moving into the final phases, he works rapidly now. His strategy is clear: take the last block of a constructed entity (G4G2, the opening) and use it in a trial combination with another block (G2G1), keeping in mind the ending combination, that is, the destination of the whole tune. Through this process he arrives, on his thirteenth request, at the following expansion and transformation of his initial opening pair:

The original opening (G4G2) is still present, but it no longer forms a structural group. G4 is now a low-level goal, the destination of the subgroup G2G4. G2 has become a beginning; twice it starts things off, first leading to G4 and then again leading to G1. In this context the motion *to* the accented G in G2 acts as a kind of kickoff. Mark's seventeenth request joins this

expanded opening with his ending combination. Satisfied that he has a possible tune, he writes a little computer procedure called "TO MARK" which defines his whole melody:

TO MARK

1. G2 G4 G2 G1 G1 G4 G1 G3 G5

END

Now when he types MARK, the electronic music box responds with his whole tune.

Mark is working now with the melody as a whole. Not satisfied with the middle of the melody, the joint between his beginning and ending structures, he deletes the repetition of the G1 block:

Still not satisfied, he tries another procedure which again only alters the same midpoint. This time he deletes G1 altogether and replaces it with G3:

Mark searches for an alternative; he tries G2G5 and then G1:

That's it! "G3 should end on the same note as G1." The following was played on the piano:

That was what he wanted:

At this point in Mark's work he is able to say explicitly what he wants to hear, something that isn't there but that he can now imagine and describe as a single precise pitch. He has begun to compose.

What is the source of his dissatisfaction with MARK? What are the structural features he is trying to match; what are the features of his model of a sensible tune? The problem is made explicit when he invents his own tune block: it's a question of higher-level structural rhythm. Mark is searching for a subgroup which will be equal in total duration to the opening subgroup, G2G4. His internal model of a sensible melody seems to demand higher-level structural symmetry. G2G4 includes three downbeats or measures, and G2G1G1 also includes three measures. This solves the balance problem. But the second subgroup includes three small *motivic attacks* while the first subgroup has only two:

MARK1 solves the problem of equalizing the number of motives in the two subgroups but spoils ths symmetry of the measures. The subgroup G2G1 includes only two measures:

Introducing G3 in MARK2 solves all the problems of symmetry but causes the first half of the tune to come to a full stop. Indeed, the first half now ends more conclusively than the second half, which has the "surprise ending" appended to it.

Mark's composed block solves the problems completely. He finds the necessary local features to generate a symmetrical higher-level (metric and motivic) rhythmic structure and an open-ended first half which can thus function as a beginning or large structural upbeat to his closing structure. In addition, his composed block is similar to G3, reinforcing the symmetry:

Moreover, on the highest level of structural rhythm—the relation between the two halves of the melody—Mark has also created symmetry: each half of the tune includes six measures. The surprise ending functions to balance the first half in total duration. On the lower level of subunits, the second half of the melody provides a nice variation in the rhythmic grouping. There are two groups of three measures in the first half, while the second half groups into two, three, and one:

7. Endings: Jorge

Jorge has just exploded into description of specific features necessary for a solution to his insistent problem: what comes after G2. His solution defined, he searches now for further constraints. Like Mark, he asks, "How long is this tune?" and receives the answer, "Twelve blocks in all." He replies, "Yes, I thought I was missing something in the middle." Actually this is very funny since Jorge's current tune-in-process is entirely different from the original tune from which the blocks were taken. Thus his "middle" is not the middle of the original tune at all. But like Mark, Jorge seems to assume that there is only one possible tune to build out of these blocks—one right answer. He believes he almost has it; if only he can extend *his* tune in the middle, he will arrive at the original.

It is interesting that this question occured at quite different moments in the course of each subject's work. For Mark, the question of length came at the moment when he had only a beginning; a beginning sent him in search of constraints on the whole. Jorge asks the same question only after a long period of exploration during which he has seized explicit features of some of the blocks and, through them, has come to a definition of the problem to be solved. And at this point he is also working with a sketch of the tune as a whole; only now does he look for constraints which will define its total length.

After a few more combinations, Jorge tries G4 following G2 (the very same pair that formed Mark's beginning combination). Anticipating the result, he says, "This will be a strange one." Asked why, he says:

G2G4:

"Because I never thought of mixing G2 and G4. I felt they were separate groups. I thought the complex ones would be surrounded by simple ones (like islands); but they sound not bad."

This is the decisive turning point in Jorge's work. In manipulating his modules, his initial assumptions about these "main" blocks had kept him from thinking of them as a possible pair. Earlier on (request 27) he had

actually tried the pair once; that was his "wild one." Still, not quite
convinced, he tries G2G4 again. He then performs his usual manipulation
—repetition and expansion: G2G2G4G3.

Asked to look again at his description of the problematic G2 in the
light of his discovery, Jòrge notes: "Yes, G4 doesn't go down immediately,
and it's slower." Indeed, the features of G4 do meet his explicit definition of
a possible subsequent to G2. But interestingly his constraints are met on the
level of global features rather than on the level of local features of the blocks.
G4 is, indeed, "slower" than G2, but on the local (note-to-note) level it is not
significantly slower than G1 or G3. However, G4 is longer in total duration
than G1 and includes more notes than G3. In fact, the combined effect of
these features is to make G4 effectively "slower" than G2 and also slower
than G3 or G1 when paired with G2. At the same time, on the local level
(note to note, again) G4 does, in fact, "go down immediately." On the more
global level, however, G4 goes nowhere. Embedded in the context
G2G2G4G3, G4 is simply a prolongation of the fulcrum pitch; it starts there
and ends there, as noted earlier. Once more, on the more global level, the
effect is one of "slower." Again, G4 does not take "more time in beginning" as
compared with G1 or G3, but more globally the repetition and prolongation
of G2's ending pitch throughout G4 functions to generate this very effect.
Where does G4 begin? The border of G2 is obscured by the beginning G of G4,
a continuation of the border pitch. And all these features together give G4 the
right function in relation to G2: G4 does not resolve G2 but extends it.

Jorge has found an unexpected solution to his very first problem, "I
don't know what comes after G2." Inherent in his solution is a genuine
restructuring. His initial description of surface quality is first transformed
into a description of explicit features of G2 and G4. These features in turn
form the basis for a description of constraints which define a possible
solution to the problem. Once defined, he recognizes the solution and
simultaneously breaks out of his previously binding assumptions.

Jorge's new insight takes place on his sixty-nineth request. Requests 75
and 77 produce sketches of the completed tune but noticeably excluding G2
and G4. The question now seems to be where to embed them.

Request 75:

Request 77:

Request 77 is a clear elaboration of request 75. Using his procedure of
expansion by repetition, Jorge creates, whole, the beginning of his tune.
Annoyed at the constraints imposed by "twelve blocks in all," he goes on
anyhow. Request 79 finds him flipping the two halves of his previous sketch
once again and adding to these modules his expanded G2G4G3 ending.

Request 79:

reverse of Req. 77   New   Ending - Combination
                           Beginning

And finally, switching the beginning modules back again but maintaining the second part, he arrives at:

Not yet completely satisfied, Jorge tries the beginning of his tune once more and then, like Mark, begins to compose: "I would like to have a G6 in place of the second G3." He sings what he wants G6 to be, and the block is built for him by the observer.

With this new block Jorge is satisfied; he has a tune that he likes.

What are the significant structural features of Jorge's tune? Its most distinctive characteristic is the cumulative drive to G4 as climax. The climax is achieved in three phases:

Opening   Sequential Expansion Begin again   Climax   End

Phase I is a relatively stable opening statement returning three times to the tonic C. (Notice that Jorge begins his tune with the block that he had originally described as "may be an ending.") Phase II is a sequential expansion of Phase I. Phase III starts again as in Phase I, moves forward quickly to the highest pitch and to a climax, and abruptly ends. The sequential relation of Phases I and II (i.e., two modules, the second the same as the first in pitch shape and durations, but shifted up one scale degree) generates a balanced and clearly articulated onward and upward impetus. The forward impetus is, in fact, achieved only by Jorge's composed block, G6. The penultimate version, made from the given blocks, failed exactly because it dropped the onward thrust and also created a stop; it was closed out.

The second part of the tune begins like the first with G5G5 and carries the upward thrust of part one to a climax (G2G2G4). The increase in activity which has been such a notable feature of G2 functions now to build to that climax. G4 establishes and prolongs the high point, achieving the anticipated climax followed by the closing block, G3, with which the tune abruptly ends. G2G4, the "wild one" of this small musical world, realizes its structural potential as climax. And the tune does include twelve blocks.

On the largest level, the tune is neatly symmetrical:

But the inner grouping of these two parts, together with the structural functions each generates, shows quite a different organization:

Part one includes two balanced modules: four bars plus four bars; three motivic attacks plus three motivic attacks. Part two is a single climactic gesture which moves forward in pairs of measures—two plus two plus four (or two plus two). In addition, part two includes an increase in activity, not only on the local level (more notes per beat) but also in the rate of events in the larger melodic line:

In part one, each phase embellishes but one fundamental pitch; in the first phrase it is E and the second F. In part two, E moves through F to G in four bars, G is prolonged for two bars and then moves back to C in the final two bars. Not only is the rate of events faster but, more important, the pitch distance covered is expanded, made larger; that is, more happens. Thus the high-level structural rhythm (eight plus eight) and the asymmetrical but proportional inner grouping (four plus four, then eight) provide a framework which contains the increasing rate of events generated by the skeletal melodic line.

Looking back now at Jorge's work, the evolution of his tune becomes clearer.

Through pairing and repetition he arrived at this initial tune-in-progress. Like a sketch of the completed tune, it included the ascending sequential relation between its two parts and also the ending combination. But it offered little sense of development and no climax. Then he switched tactics (requests 52–58). He limited his vista, moved in and sharpened his focus on detail, defined his immediate problems (especially what could follow G2), and finally defined the features of a possible solution. At that point a breakthrough occurred (requests 58–81). Jorge's initial assumptions about not pairing G2 and G4 were cast out when he juxtaposed them and recognized his solution. Next, building outward, he elaborated this pair through repetition on one side and the ender, G3, on the other (G2G2G4G3). He thus found the crucial climax and close. Continuing his search for a "middle" that would meet the constraints of twelve blocks in all, he tried G5G3G1G3—a skeleton of request 49 and also of the first modules in the completed tune (request 75). Fleshing out the skelton by repetition, he arrived at G5G5G3; G1G1G3. But now, returning again to the larger vista,

Request 75:

Request 77:

he freely pushed around modules before returning at last to the above arrangement to which he added his newly discovered climax and his ending. With this whole tune in hand, his final modification led him to composition. Like Mark, he dipped down once more to the level of precise pitch (singing rather than naming) to complete a tune that he liked.

8. *The tonesmiths compared*

The contrast between Mark's work and Jorge's work is striking. Three aspects of this contrast deserve examination: the differences in strategy, from which emerged differing results, implying in each case a different tacit model.

Strategies and modes of representation. Mark's work was cautious, methodical; his intention was often explicit. He had ready access to local features from the outset. His representation of local features served as a guide to more global relations into which the initially local features could be embedded. With a few trial combinations of blocks his representation of the same data was thus transformed. For example, in juxtaposing G4 and G2 he noted "a change in time" which on a more global level then became "OK." Later, influenced by the pair G2G1, he reversed his opening pair, making it G2G4. G2 thus assumed a structurally more consistent function, leading into G4 rather than extending it on as before.

Mark's first significant decisions generated the functions of beginning and ending. With the limits of his tune defined, the framework for his next steps and for the design of his tune was also defined. He had generated a context within which he could make choices, one in which particular features could assume particular functions. His process for completing the tune was to search for a series of events which would appropriately fill the gap between his defined limits. He joined the last block of his beginning pair with a possible next block. Continuing in this way, he built up a chain of blocks to which he could reasonably attach his ending combination. The gap filled, the tune was complete.

In contrast to Mark, Jorge worked impulsively, exploring many possibilities and responding often to the qualitative character of the results he generated. He seemed more interested in the process itself. What would a new combination bring forth? How could he make use of his repeated pairs and expanding modules?

Jorge did not focus on local features of the blocks until well along in his work. (Unlike Mark, who could work "in his head," Jorge had to wait for the music box to "tell" him.) Starting with an initially broad vista, he worked down into details and then back up again to a larger perspective which gradually changed as it included more and more explicit detail. In contrast to Mark's early definition of limits and subsequent directed chain building, Jorge worked outward (backwards and forwards) or just around wherever he happened to find himself. In addition, he worked with trial whole tunes and then modified his trials to make new wholes.

The possible structure of the tune emerged slowly in this process of moving in and out of the material. Exploring, testing, building up and taking down, Jorge added various features to his representation as he went along. In the process, the meaning of a block—i.e., its possible function in the whole—was often transformed. Each new representation created a new set of possible constraints and a new definition of problems. The most dramatic of these moments occurred when he was able to define the features of a solution to his gnawing problem. The problem defined, he recognized a solution which in turn shattered his previous assumptions. The initially rejected pair, G2G4, which he had originally described as a "wild one," was rediscovered as the key to his problem. With this breakthrough, his prebuilt modules quickly fell into place. His internal representation of the blocks was again restructured; he could now find appropriate relations among them and thus complete his tune.

While Mark worked more quickly, he did so at the cost of defining a single structure very early, thus limiting possibilities, playing less, and maybe learning less, too. Jorge's work was perhaps more like that of a real composer; immersing himself in the material and in his direct experience, he gradually discovered its potential for structural coherence.

Results: the tunes compared. Mark's tune is essentially a single, balanced antecedent-consequent statement. Phrase 1 starts at the high point establishes implications for resolution, but remains open-ended, incomplete, a structural up-beat to phrase 2. Phrase 2 realizes the harmonic and linear implications set up by phrase 1, closes them out, and balances phrase 1 rhythmically with a "surprise."

Jorge's tune is cumulative. It begins with a statement of a generative motive, continues with the development of this motive through ascending sequential elaboration, and concludes with a final longer gesture leading to a climax. Climax is generated by an increase in the rate of events and an ascent to the high point of the piece, followed by quick resolution and closure.

Do the results reflect the strategies invoked? The two completed tunes are certainly different in their structure and effect. It is tempting to make a correlation between Jorge's more impulsive, even flamboyant style and his tune with its dramatic build-up, its cumulative structure. In turn there appears to be a relation between Mark's careful and methodical strategy and his neatly balanced, relatively straightforward and constrained musical statements. But how much are these results influenced by strategy? What about other factors like tacit models of a sensible tune together with differences in ethnic and intellectual backgrounds and in the traditions implicit in these backgrounds? The relation between strategy and results must remain for the moment an open question, but it suggests the need for further research with more and different kinds of players. It is clear, for example, that tacit models did influence each player's decision making, his notion of what constitutes appropriate relations or logical structure.

Tacit models. What were the differences in the model for a sensible tune which guided each player's decisions? The last stages of Mark's work brought out certain structural features of his model, particularly the importance of higher-level rhythmic symmetry. Jorge's work was much more dramatic.

When Jorge had completed his composition, he listened to the tune from which the blocks had originally been taken, a French folk song:

Looking quite astonished, he whistled and said: "That's totally different! I never would have arrived at that." And on second hearing, "It's unbelievable that G4 begins the tune. I never heard a tune like that!" The context was so different that he didn't even notice the identical endings of both tunes.

Curious now to hear the tunes that Jorge did know, the body of music from which his model must derive, the experimenter asked him to sing some Peruvian songs. More extended and elaborate than Jorge's tune, their structure proved remarkably similar. Characteristically they were cumulative; they included repetition of small, melodic cells, each one clearly articulated. These cells were, in turn, developed sequentially, and led to a longer gesture which reached a climax and then quickly and abruptly closed. Rarely did the Peruvian songs include the characteristic balanced antecedent-consequent phrase structure so typical of familiar nursery-rhyme tunes, of the French song, and indeed of Mark's tune. At first they sounded as strange as the French song had to Jorge. When, for example, he finished the first song, Jorge was asked, "Is that the end?" and he replied, "You really have to know the words to get it."

By contrast, Mark's tune was, in basic structure, quite similar to the first part of the French song: a single, two-phrase "sentence." The first phrase, an antecedent, started with a lead-in to the high point, reached towards resolution, but remained open-ended; the second phrase, a consequent, started much like the first but reached resolution and closure. Not surprisingly, Mark was perfectly satisfied with the original tune; it was another, perhaps more successful, realization of his model. He commented, merely, "Oh, yeah."

Indeed, why is the original folk song more successful? Several features seem pertinent. In the first place, the implications of the initial motivic materials are further worked out; the tune is more complete. It includes a beginning, an elaboration of the opening material (middle), together with a return—A B+A¹. Moreover, motives appear embedded in new contexts which exploit their implications, thus providing both variation and unity. For example, G1 appears in three different contexts, each time with a different function. Indeed, G1 acts as a kind of pivot, each time sending the tune off in a different direction. In A, G1 hints at closure which is fulfilled only with the return to G4 followed this time by G3. In B, G1 is elaborated sequentially G1G5, and then prepares for return, G1G2. Indeed, the pair G1G2 appears in both A and B, but the context disguises this paired repetition. Finally, the return to G4G3 seems both fresh and familiar as a result of the elaboration and development which precedes it. All of the phrases are balanced, as are the two large sections of the melody, i.e., A and B+A¹. However, the second half of the tune generates two distinct structural functions, development, and return. Thus the second half, while equal in total duration to the first, includes a greater density of structural events.

Interestingly, experienced musicians who have played with this set of blocks frequently build a tune much like the original but often exclude the first statement of G1 and the second statement of G2, saving both G1 and G5 for the contrasting B section.

G4G2G4G3G1G5G1G5G4G3:

While Jorge's tune clearly derives from a different model, it does share with the original tune development of material and a sense of directed motion through the build-up of tension and its release. On the other hand, differences in the function, the meaning of various blocks in Jorge's tune as compared with the original are striking. Meaning in music is indeed dependent on context.

9. Some speculative conclusions

It should be clear now that both Jorge and Mark were involved, each in his own way, in active analysis of musical relations. The relations were perhaps primitive, but they were so in two senses. The materials with which they worked were limited and in this sense primitive; but the decisions they made and the problems they faced demanded a confrontation with the powerful primitives from which much larger and more complex musical structure derives. Observations of the students' procedures, comments, and decisions seem to demand analysis and reexamination of certain fundamentals of musical coherence and of learning.

The categories implicit in music notation and music theory tend to guide their users toward the selection of certain features and the exclusion of others. The students had to discover their own priorities, their own processes of selection. Since the students did not read music notation, they were not influenced by the particular selection of features captured by this mode of representation. Nor were they influenced by the categories implicit in traditional music theory.

As a result, those descriptions which trained musicians have come to take for granted were often burst open for reexamination. Features selected by the categories of traditional music theory, it appears, are not given; they must be generated by relations among a collection of features. The tonic or key center, for instance, results from an aggregate of features; even beat and certainly beat groups or meter results from a collection of features. For the students these were not givens, assumptions implicit in the notation, but rather relations which were generated by the data as the students gradually enriched their representation of that data.

Musical perception, like visual perception, is a processs of intelligent reconstruction. While the computer-driven music box always produces the same data, the human perceiver processes this information in various ways, depending on which features he gives priority to or even has access to—i.e., on just how he represents the data to himself. Focus is influenced by the particular context in which a particular figure is embedded, whether actually or only in the player's imagination. A new context suggests new priorities and reveals new features. Learning occurs when the student gains greater freedom in his ability to enrich his representation as he discovers new relations among these features.

For example, players tended to focus first on a particular characteristic of a single block, or perhaps on some feature which two blocks shared or by which one block might be distinguished from another. Later, new features became accessible, often resulting from new contextual embeddings, and often these features generated higher-level representations. In addition, as students gained a glimpse of a whole tune, more global features emerged, features that had to do with relations among the blocks. The most significant learning occurred in the dynamic interplay between local and global focus; local detail shed light on global possibilities, global structures revealed new details.

The whole process reflects that interaction between detail and larger design which is such a powerful factor in the vastly more complex world of, for example, a movement of a Haydn quartet. There, shifts in focus, new contextual embeddings, transformation and elaboration of a single detail or a brief motive are essential components in the logic and affect of the work itself. Without access to such processes within the work of a great composer, its very greatness often remains beyond the experience of the listener.

In fact, the learning which took place for Mark and Jorge bears certain similarities to the learning which occurs in the work of the creative musician as composer or performer. Arnold Schoenberg has written:

> One can comprehend only what one can keep in mind. Man's mental limitations prevent him from grasping anything which is too extended. Thus, appropriate subdivision facilitates understanding and determines *form*. A composer does not, of course, add bit by bit, as a child does in building with wood blocks. He conceives an entire composition as a spontaneous vision. Then he proceeds, like Michelangelo who chiselled his *Moses* out of the marble without sketches, complete in every detail, thus directly *forming* his material. No beginner is capable of envisaging a composition in its entirety; hence he must proceed gradually, from the simpler to the more complex. Simplified practice forms, which do not always correspond to art forms, help a student to acquire the sense of form and a knowledge of the essentials of construction. It will be useful to start by building musical blocks and connecting them intelligently. . . . These musical blocks (phrases, motives, etc.) will provide the material for building larger units of various kinds, according to the requirements of the structure. Thus the demands of logic, coherence and comprehensibility can be fulfilled, in relation to the need for contrast, variety and fluency of presentation.[4]

Schoenberg's design for the development of young composers seems close to the process observed in the work of the two students. But what about the role of tacit models for these players as well as for composers? It seems clear that such models functioned as constraints in the students' decisions, in their sense of logic and appropriateness. For Mark and Jorge the process of discovering implications in the given material necessarily remained within the constraints of that material, but also within the constraints of their tacit models. Mark introduced the term "match": "I don't know how to match." And both students at a dynamic moment in their work looked for the explicit constraints of a right answer, "How long is this tune?" Still, the solution emerged only after each player had sufficiently (for himself) explored the implications of the material. Only then could each make a particular product which reasonably matched his model.

For serious composers such models play a significant role, too, but in a more dynamic way. E. H. Gombrich uses the term "stylistic schemata" in discussing the role of models in the creative process. He speaks of "making" and "matching."[5] Leo Treitler, applying these notions to musical composition, suggests that the composer approaches the creation of a new work through the "mediation of an internalized vocabulary of forms and schemata . . . Invention is both a process of coding by means of such a vocabulary ('making') and a process of modification toward some goal-image ('matching') for the product."[6]

A study of Beethoven's sketchbooks reveals clear instances of this process in the composer's relentless modifications of motives, particularly beginnings. An initial, often banal idea (banal exactly because of its close "match" with stylistic norms or stylistic schemata (undergoes endless modifications. The normative constraints of the initial idea are restructured in the light of implications which Beethoven foresees, that is, in light of the motive's potential for assuming new functions and new character within his "goal-image." Transformations occur as Beethoven, in his head, embeds the motive in new contexts; simultaneously he seems to envisage the structure as a whole, a structure which is, itself, still evolving. Thus Beethoven's modifications of a single motive represent much more than explicit local changes. The process of transformation helps to define the unique constraints through which the particular whole evolves. Beethoven's workbooks suggest a more subtle meaning for Schoenberg's statement that a composer "conceives an entire composition as a spontaneous vision."

Thus it might be said that the serious composer, as compared with the two players, is more concerned with "matching" his "goal-image" than with "making" stylistic norms. His product reflects a dynamic interaction between the constraints of traditional models and the evolving constraints of his "goal-image" generated by the compositional process itself. For this reason, a new work may be on the fringe of comprehensibility for those listeners who are searching for good "matches" with traditional models. Levi-Strauss says in discussing twentieth century serial music:

> Either it will succeed in bridging the traditional gap between listener and composer and—by depriving the former of the possibility of referring unconsciously to a general system—will at the same time oblige him, if he is to understand the music he hears, to reproduce the individual act of creation on his own account. Through the power of an ever new, internal logic, each work will rouse the listener from his state of passivity and make him share in its impulse, so that there will no longer be a difference of kind, but only of degree, between inventing music and listening to it. . . .[7]

This may be an equally appropriate description of the truly musical listener even when the composition does allow the listener to refer "unconsciously to a general system," as, for example, with works of Beethoven or Haydn. Too often, though, the listener lets such works slip by, giving in solely to their familiar "stylistic schemata." Failing then, to be roused from this "state of passivity," the listener will also fail to discover the "ever new, internal logic," the unique process which distinguishes the great work, that which makes it more than just another instance of a style. It is precisely this confrontation with the demands on the listener which appears as one of the primary goals of the student's work.

And if the performer's process of learning a work is considered, the comparison with the students' learning is even more exact. The performer with a set of givens, a complete existing work, must also become involved in a continuous process of rehearing, of restructuring, of discovering the particular coherence in the work he studies. Concretely, this often involves a shift from local considerations (playing each note on the page with the right pitch and rhythm, overcoming technical difficulties, etc.) to global considerations like relations of harmonic direction, structural downbeats, grouping and articulation of motives and phrases, and the proportions of parts to a whole. As with Mark and Jorge, the "same" features assume new meanings; fast becomes slow, upbeat becomes downbeat. But in the end, of course, global considerations must dictate local decision; indeed, this may be one way of describing a *"musical"* performance.

Artur Schnabel is said to have described such a performance this way:

> In high tension—emotional and intellectual—the performer must anticipate the rendering in sound of the entire composition, as a total unit. Schnabel compared this with the intake of a deep breath—deep enough to make the entire performance appear as one slow exhalation. . . . Any preoccupation, at the moment of performance (and this is what differentiates performing from certain preliminary phases of practicing), with playing the right notes, memory, fingerings, or with thoughts on the "difficulty" of a section of a piece makes it impossible to concentrate fully in the way here described.[8]

Of course this development from local to global hearing is not a simple one-way path. As with Jorge, the inverse movement from larger vista to smaller detail may carry with it implications which also affect the larger conception. Again, Schnabel's view is revealing:

> The mature performer works for those rare inspirations when his conception of a score becomes one with its physical realization in performance. At such moments technique is more than just the disciplined functioning of the body at the command of the ear: it grows into a physical activity *which in turn may stimulate the imagination*. . . . Piano technique, as Schnabel used the term and taught it, is the faculty to establish channels between the sound heard inwardly and its realization in all individualized subtlety. . . . His method of

practicing was experiment rather than drill. . . . As Schnabel phrased it, "the conception materializes and the materialization redissolves into conception."[9]

The comparison of the student's work with that of great musicians may seem far-fetched. But one should not confuse the product with the process. This essay has been concerned with a way of learning which both reveals and shares in that other learning—by experiment rather than by drill—which seems so characteristic of creative activity. For it is through building up, taking down, and thus restructuring internal representations that new implications are born, new knowledge discovered. Most specifically, it is by discovering and playing with the constraints he himself has imposed on what does make sense or on what can be done that the learner cracks the boundaries of his perception, that he develops the capacity to appreciate and even to invent new constraints. Perhaps it is in just this interplay between constraints and invention, between the known, the unknown, and and knowing, that learning takes its biggest leaps.

M A R K - PROTOCOL

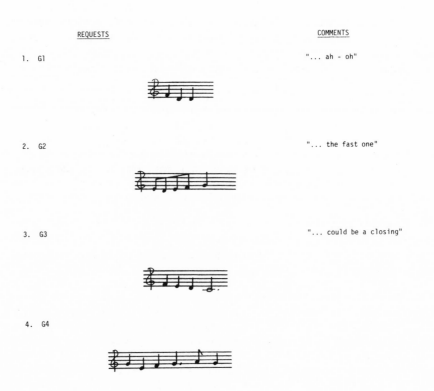

REQUESTS	COMMENTS
1. G1	"... ah - oh"
2. G2	"... the fast one"
3. G3	"... could be a closing"
4. G4	

5. G5   "... similar to G1"

6. G1 G5

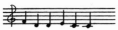

7. G3   "... can be related to G1 G5
                                                         or to G4"

8. G4   "... there has to be a flow
                                                         between two blocks, the
                                                         change can't be too great"

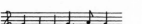

9. G4 G2   "... sounds like an opening, but
                                                         there's a change in time."
                                                              (pause)
                                                         "How long is this tune?"
                                                              (pause)
                                                         "I don't know how to match."

10. G1 G3 G5   "... Ah, cool - I could end the
                                                         song with G3 - a long note,
                                                         but G5 would be a surprise
                                                         ending."
                                                         "I have lots of endings."

11. G4 G2   "... A change in time, but still O.K."

12. G2 G1

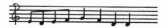

13. G2 G4 G2 G1

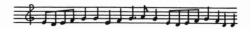

14. G2 G5

15. G1 G4

16. G1 G4 G1 G3 G5

17. TO MARK: G2 G4 G2 G1 G1 G4 G1 G3 G5

18. TO MARK1:

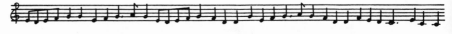

"Deleting one of the G1's...much better."

19. TO MARK2:

> "That wasn't right...G3 wasn't the right note; too low."
> "Wanted it to end on the same note as G1."

J O R G E - PROTOCOL

1. G1 G2 G3 G4 G5

2. G1 G1
3. G3
4. G2
5. G4
6. G2
7. G5
8. G1
9. G2
10. G3
11. G4

> "G2 and G4 are the main parts — but how to use them?
> I don't know what comes after G2."
> "G5 may be an ending."

12. G1 G1 G2 G2 G3 G1 G4 G3 G5
13. G1 G5
14. G2 G1
15. G1 G3
16. G2 G5
17. G1 G1 G2 G1 G3
18. G5 G2
19. G4
20. G2 G3
21. G4
22. G4 G5
23. G3

24. G4 G3

"... Good, and maybe at the end
after G2."

25. G2 G3

"... Not too good, not too bad."

26. G1 G1 G2 G2 G3

27. G2 G4

"... It's a wild one, huh?"

28. G2 G3

29. G2 G2

30. G5 G4

31. G1 G2 G3 G1 G4 G3

(... agreed that he was thinking of this grouping:
G1 G2 G3, G1 G4 G3,)

32. G2 G4

33. G4 G5

34. G5 G5 G2

35. G1 G1 G4

36. G3 G4
37. G5 G2
38. G3
39. G3 G5
40. G1 G1 G2 G5 G5 G4 G3
41. G5 G5 G2 G2

42. G1 G1 G4 G3

43. G4 G2
44. G2 G3
45. G1 G2
46. G5 G5 G2
47. G1 G1 G4
48. G5 G5 G2 G1 G1 G4 G3

49. G5 G5 G2 G3 G1 G1 G4 G3

50. G5 G5 G2 G3 G1 G1 G4 G3   (... beginning next session where
                                                    he left off.)
51. G1 G1 G4 G3 G5 G5 G2 G3

52. G2 G3

"... G3 has a silence at the end
so it must be a link, and at
the end."

THE OBSERVER: "a silence?"

53. G3 G1

"... No - a long note; so I think
it must be an ending."

54. G5 G5 G2 G3 G1 G1 G4 G3

55. G2 G4

(... he notates...)

G2:

G4:

"Before, I couldn't remember them
so well; now I can spend less time
playing them."

OBSERVER: "What do you know so far?"

"... G2 and G4 are complex, important."

"... G3 is an ending. It goes perfectly with G4."

OBSERVER: "Does it go after G2?"

56. G2 G3

"... I didn't like it. The problem
with G2 is it ends too fast --
it goes up and should have
something else before going down.
The last note of G2 is too quick,
it ends right on the border of
the next one, so the next one
needs more time in beginning."

"Maybe G1 after G2."

57. G5 G5 G2 G2 G1 G1 G4 G3

"... No, no space; but is better."

58. G2 G1

59. G5 G2

60. G1 G3

61. G2 G5

62. G1 G1 G3

"... How long is this tune?"

OBSERVER: "12 blocks."

"... Yes, I thought I was missing
something in the middle."

63. G5 G5 G2 G2 G1 G1 G3

64. G2 G3

65. G5 G5 G2 G4 G3   "... This will be a strange one."

               OBSERVER: "Why?"

                           "... Because I never thought of
                             mixing G2 and G4. I felt
                             they were separate groups.
                             I thought the complex ones
                             would be surrounded by simple
                             ones (like islands), but they
                             sound not bad."

66. G1 G2

67. G1 G2

68. G2 G4

69. G2 G2 G4 G3

                        (OBSERVER read Jorge's previous description
                           of G2.)

                             "... Yes, G4 doesn't go down immed-
                             iately, and it's slower."

70. G5 G5 G1 G1

71. G3 G3

72. G5 G5 G2 G2 G1 G1 G3 G3 G2 G2 G4 G3

73. G2 G2 G3 G3

74. G1 G1 G2 G2 G4 G3

75. G5 G3 G1 G3

76. G2 G4

77. G5 G5 G3 G1 G1 G3   "... You shouldn't have told me that
                                   there were 12 blocks."

               OBSERVER: "Just get your own tune logical, O.K.?"

78. G5 G5 G4

79.   G1 G1 G3 G5 G5 G3 G5 G5 G2 G2 G4 G3

80.   G5 G5 G3 G1 G1 G3 G5 G5 G2 G2 G4 G3   "... That's all right."

81.   G5 G5 G3 G1 G1 G3   "... I would like to have a G6 in the
                                           place of the second G3."

                                           (Sang 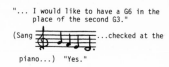 ...checked at the

                                           piano...) "Yes."

82.   G5 G5 G3 G1 G1 G6 G5 G5 G2 G2 G4 G3

FRENCH: G4 G1 G2 G4 G3 G1 G5 G1 G2 G4 G3

                 (Whistles) "... Wow, that's totally different! I never
                             would have arrived at it!"

FRENCH: G4 G1 G2 G4 G3 G1 G5 G1 G2 G4 G3   "... It's unbelievable that G4
                                                             begins the tune."

Notes

1. See Jeanne Bamberger, "Learning to Think Musically," *Music Educator's Journal* 59, No. 7 (March 1973); idem, "The Luxury of Necessity," *Bulletin of the National Association of Schools of Music* (1974).

3. See Jeanne Bamberger, *Progress Report,* LOGO Memorandum No. 13, MIT Artificial Intelligence Laboratory.

3. A written description of the students' work presents certain difficulties for the reader. The reader's experience in looking at a score of the musical examples can only partially capture the experience of those who play this game entirely by ear. Representing the tune blocks in

standard music notation introduces information which is biased by the assumptions inherent in the representation itself—and possibly quite different information from that available to the nonreading listener. Observations of the tune blocks game played by a small number of individuals suggest significant differences between those who read music and those who do not. Perhaps the most crucial asset for the nonreading listener is his ability to deal directly with the motive as the basic element of a tune, in contrast with the reader for whom the note tends to be the basic element. Thus the question becomes: On what level does one enter the world of a given melody, and with what sorts of tacit assumptions?

4. Arnold Schoenberg, *Fundamentals of Musical Composition* (New York: St. Martins Press, 1967), pp. 1–2.

5. E. H. Gombrich, *Art and Illusion* (Princeton, N.J.: Princeton University Press, 1960).

6. Leo Treitler, "Methods, Style, Analysis," in *Report of the Congress of the International Musicological Society* (Copenhagen, 1972). I am grateful to Professor Treitler for drawing my attention to Gombrich's book and for suggesting the association between the ideas found there and Beethoven's compositional processes.

7. Claude Lévi-Strauss, *The Raw and the Cooked* (New York: Harper & Row, 1969), p. 26.

8. Konrad Wolff, *The Teaching of Artur Schnabel* (New York: Praeger, 1972), p. 20.

9. Ibid., p. 22.

12 Initiating the Audience
Frank Lloyd Dent

Under the impact of modern communications and entertainment media each of us is almost continually part of an audience. Radio and television bombard the public constantly with
wanted and unwanted experiences. Books, magazines, films, performances,
exhibitions, and games compete for attention. As spectator, customer, and
listener, with varying degrees of anonymity and choice, human beings are
willy-nilly brought before some new spectacle they may or may not aspire to
understand. All the world seems less a stage than a "house" for the most
brazen shill and cleverest manager-promoter.

Certain elemental tactics assist in surviving this pressure. Primarily,
most of the invitations are ignored. Occasionally, when convenient and
cheap, a quick detour may be tolerated from regular habits into some
experience that has aroused curiosity. The odds that it will sustain interest
and gain a follower are functions of the usual variables that govern choices
for use of leisure time. For the most part, tastes develop under pressure of
peers, colleagues, and friends in the context of appraisals by experts and
critics. Individual leisure choices appear to change much as a river shifts its
channels and, more gradually, its course.

Such haphazard tactics in many ways thwart the possibility of creative
audiencehood and actually extend the domain of boredom. The danger in
ignoring most opportunities is that interesting new options are passed by
simply for failure to give them a chance. Art organizations' marketing
practice of numerous mailings to a large list of prospects testifies to the
difficulty of getting someone even to take a look. The problem with
relatively brief investigations of new audience experiences is that too much is
expected from too cursory a glance. Building a solid interest in a new subject
requires exposure with some depth and frequency and the suspension of
hasty judgment. But amateur and professional criticism as well as publicity
tend to skew appraisals in the direction of "winners" and "losers" rather

than assessment of various levels of meaning and value in a work. Such errors are primarily sins of omission—failures to look, to look hard, to withhold judgment, and so forth. They lead to what one arts manager tersely described as the main error of omission audiences make: "not coming."

But further errors abound even in the most willing and enthusiastic audiences. A useful catalogue is provided by the work of I. A. Richards, who in his *Practical Criticism* exposed and explored a number of errors readers make with respect to poetry. As relevant to audiences as to readers are: lack of broad exposure to the different modes of artistic expression, a "love for art" which is all too often coupled with an incapacity to understand the work, too many stock responses, too many preconceptions, too easy retreat into bewilderment, too much authority worship, and lack of sensitivity to physical variables that affect response such as fatigue. All these bear witness to a central problem Richards identified: the need for systematic training in constructing and comprehending multiple definitions of the same subject.[1]

Further audience error concerns well-entrenched conceptions of how works are made. All too often, works are imagined either to spring from the inspiration of the moment, or—particularly where physical skills are impor- tant—to mature gradually as the inevitable consequence of a regimen of routine practice. Neither view acknowledges the true role of the artist as an actively and extensively involved fashioner of the work, shaping it choice by choice toward its final presentation. Both views diminish the value of a work by trivializing its origins and treating the emergent work as fixed and inevitable rather than malleable according to the performance, presenta- tion, audience, and, of course, further revision by the maker.

1. A practical experiment in audience education

The lecture-performance and related programs show promise toward initiating audiences into a more fruitful perception of the arts. A dual objective seems possible: both to mature the attitudes of audiences already somewhat committed to a subject, and to attract and introduce novices. Though here the stress is on assisting the audience toward encounter, insight, and enjoyment, there are some data to suggest that lecture- performances might be successfully used for the very pragmatic aim of building subscription lists for specific arts organizations. That practical aspect, a simple consequence of guiding the audience through the hazards of first encounters and misconceptions concerning art forms, will be discussed further at the conclusion of this article in the context of the lecture- demonstration as part of a commercial engagement by professionals.

Whatever the potentials of the lecture-performance format, making those potentials actual is a precarious enterprise. The problems of audience education were explored through a series of lecture-demonstrations organized by Harvard Project Zero under the general title "Art in the Making." Over a period of three years, a dozen programs offered a variety of responses by recognized artists to problems of widening and deepening audience understanding.[2] An axiom of these lecture-performances was that each artist had to reveal something of his way of working rather than merely display the products. In the presence of an audience free to ask questions, each artist explored alternatives, exposed some constraints of the medium, compared various efforts, and searched for the desired effect choice by choice. This distinctive concentration on the process of creating revealed the final work as the product of innumerable decisions by the artist. Thus the "Art in the Making" series marked at least a beginning in awakening audiences to an understanding and enjoyment of the multiple potentials in a chosen subject.[3]

Five principles guided the planning of these presentations. (1) Reputable artists were commissioned to prepare the programs. Usually they were also experienced teachers who set out to inform as well as perform for their audience. (2) The presentations were neither exclusively performance and "amusement" nor instruction and "lecture." (3) A special segment of the public formed the nuclear or "target" audience for whom the artist was to key the presentation. In this case that audience was the faculty, staff, and students of the Harvard Graduate School of Education. This special audience was granted early admission and reserved seating in the hall before the general public was admitted. (4) Each program involved imaginative use of audiovisual hardware. (5) Pedagogical techniques included alternative approaches to the same subject, the discussion of unfinished works, and illustration of stages in the development of an art form or of a particular work as well as presentation of some successful works.

Alternative approaches to the same work or subject were intended to expose the audience to different modes of expression, thus challenging preconceptions about traditional interpretations and the blind worship of authority. To prevent such a program from becoming boring, the repetitions were brief and the differences clear. In presenting works in progress or reviewing the history of a work, it was hoped that the novelty of the artist's hesitation, mistakes, and caution would generate questions which would take the audience beyond stock responses into increased discrimination and sensitivity. Concluding such an analytic presentation with some successful works would recall the audience to a more traditional role, but with a heightened appreciation for the ways both artist and audience work.

A description of the programs will clarify how these principles work to correct audience errors. One of the more conceptually sophisticated presentations concerned poetry writing. "How does a Poem Protect Itself? Protect from What? From the Author, the Movement, Fashions, Critics, Biographers, Teachers . . ." was I. A. Richards's provocative title, suggesting the remarkable strategy with which he approached the task of exposing an audience to the labors of the poet. His presentation offered insight not only into the problems of writing poetry but also into the difficulties of exposing those problems. Showing 35-mm. slides of texts, complete with his alterations and inserts, he bent the program away from mere performance or "reading" in the direction of an open record of the poet's mind at work.

In confessing circumstances and feelings that generated each poem, Richards offered insights into his works and treated the impassioned critics' search for esoteric meaning with disdain. He displayed his conscious precision with respect to meter and theme, though he steadfastly disclaimed more than a few hints to the mysteries of the craft. "Poems," he commented at one point, "are like volcanoes. No matter how placid they appear, you can never tell when they are due for a new eruption." His slide record and comments about word and rhyme changes and about the appearances of new meanings easily supported the analogy.

In the field of photography, the series included "A Discussion on Film Making" and "Still Photography." The three artists, Eric Martin, Derek Lamb, and Alfred Guzzetti, were all teachers in various departments related to photography at Harvard University. Their primary goal was to reveal to the audience some of the decisions that build toward a finished film or exhibit. Martin and Lamb discussed the rejected footage for several films in progress. They also showed film clips in different sequences to demonstrate the work of an editor in generating excitement, suspense, and other effects.

Guzzetti presented lantern-slide enlargements of portions of his contact sheets, the first prints from a roll of exposed film where the images are the same size as the negatives. He sought to communicate a feeling for the factors that establish a mood in still photographs. The position of the frame, that of the subjects within the frame, the direction of light, and the action were all elements of composition that the uninitiated viewer as well as the photographer could recognize. For any given subject the viewers saw at least two slightly different treatments. First, the artist spoke briefly about the different shots, making explicit some of the differences. Then he asked the audience to contemplate them without his further comments. Gradually members of the audience began to discuss among themselves, to ask questions, and ultimately to point out considerations which the artist himself had overlooked.

The three programs on the subject of music were "From Sign to Sound" by Leon Kirchner, "Sculpting Sound" by Robert Ceely, and "Drums, Dances, and Voices of Africa" by Ladjie Camara. Similar strategies contributed to all of these. Music notation systems were illustrated by means of audiovisual aids when possible. Repetition of musical passages revealed how the artist's interpretation can change the effects of a given selection. Unfamiliar instruments and sound sources were discussed in terms of similarity to more familiar ones. For example, Ceely explained "white sound" by reference to radio static. Although each artist varied his approach to the problems behind a performance, all freely halted performers, repeated passages, and discussed the more and less successful elements of the work used as illustration. They also included some uninterrupted works, but only after the audience had been exposed to some important distinctions in interpretation.

Ceely's subject lent itself to a "historical" approach, an illustrated discussion of the development of electronic music in the last decades. Kirchner and Camara proceded more in the manner of an "open rehearsal" where musicians stop to work on selected passages. The novelty of Camara's work was not an unmixed advantage. Unlike the audiences for the traditional and contemporary Western music programs, his audience had had little previous exposure. Thus there was less emphasis on subtlety and variant interpretation than on the virtuoso's skill in producing a range of music. His exciting and unusual material served more to expose new art than to offer a developed insight.

Three programs related more closely to theatre. They were George Hamlin's "The Director Who Chooses," "How to Make the Proposition" by the Proposition Theatre Company, and "Anatomy of a Theatrical Production" by James Yannatos, Paul Cooper, Franco Colavecchia, and John Paul Russo. The first and last of these programs were built around recent productions at the Loeb Drama Center at Harvard. The first required extensive search for film and videotape versions of *Death of a Salesman*. Hamlin used two live and two film versions of a scene from that program to show how a director could shift the emphasis from one character to another or alter the relation between characters. For example, a few changes made the mother, Linda, a bitter rather than a reconciling figure. Another treatment offered Biff rather than his father, Willy, as the central character. Importantly, the presentation focused audience attention on the different interpretations a director can effect rather than on contrasts in acting. The contrast in skill between professional and student actors became irrelevant to the purpose of the presentation.

"Anatomy" was coupled with a seminar that met for several weeks, taught by the four artists collaborating on various aspects of the premier production of *The Rockets Red Blare*, a pop opera by Yannatos. Topics included problems of stage design and direction and consideration of how the various artists reached agreement in the final show. The evening lecture-demonstration was a concentrated version of the same effort. "How to Make the Proposition" by the nationally recognized improvisational theatre company of Cambridge had a much stronger emphasis on performance than most programs, though of course "performance" in this case meant improvisations on the basis of audience suggestions. The basic presuppositions of the actors and director Albert were thus exposed largely by illustration. A number of silent improvisations and exercises provided insight into the work of actors preparatory to performance. Special emphasis was placed on how they developed ease of interaction.

Four lecture-performances about dance and one about mime completed the series. The dance programs were "Dancers and Composers of the Ina Hahn Company discussing and illustrating their work in two lecture-performances," "The Ina Hahn Dance Company in *Theatre of Sound and Movement*," and "Dancemaking" by Anne Tolbert and the Dance Circle company. The sequence of programs by Hahn was an attempt to capture the complete process of choreographing and dancing for a particular performance. Hahn lectured in the early programs and asked dancers to illustrate various simple movements such as kicking. She demonstrated the way in which dance movements can be derived from such gestures of ordinary life. In addition, the rehearsals for these lecture-performances were open to the audiences.[4] The resulting final production of *Theatre of Sound and Movement* drew upon an audience which had participated in all stages of the works. Through the heavy attendance as well as the questions and comments directed at dancers, this sequence demonstrated the potential of the lecture-performance as an audience-building technique.

In "Dancemaking," Tolbert, the choreographer, deliberately stopped the creation of a dance at a point short of completion. The production involved a number of "movers"—so called because athletes, actors, and occasional members of the audience as well as dancers made up the cast. Each performer exercised freedom to interpret, improvise, and select from various alternatives given by the choreographer and rehearsed meticulously in advance. In cavernous Sanders Theatre at Harvard University, accompanied by special music and lighting effects, they explored the aisles, crawled along the balustrades and seat backs, shouted and sang. In the major work of the program, "Scale for Sanders: An Occupation," the movers drifted up from the audience onto the stage and used it for a time in more traditional modern dance patterns. Later, in another work, they abandoned the stage to a collaborating electronic musician, Alvin Lucier, who built a web of wires that sounded in various pitches when touched by passing movers. Another artist collaborator, Arthur Hoener, simultaneously began rotation of multiple slide projections across the audience and amphitheatre vault. As one critic described the piece: "Sometimes they look like dancers; sometimes they just look like bodies in motion. . . . Certain rules are imposed upon the performers; but within the context of these rules, they are free to make their own decisions as to which actions to take. . . . You are no longer in a theatre; you are in a gallery. You may choose the material you wish to enjoy rather than be forced into a fixed sequential pattern."[5]

"Mime Mask and Contramask" by Jacques Lecoq, director of his own school of mime and movement in Paris, proved an introduction to the world of mime as a less familiar mode of theatrical expression. His "conference-spectacle" demonstrated the language of movement organized around different kinds of masks. To direct attention to what he called a "dramatically neutral state," one with an absence of emotion, he wore the neutral mask. This expressionless carved face with openings only for eyes forced the wearer to use gesture to communicate feeling. Enacting hypothetical situations such as bidding a friend farewell, the wearer could demonstrate different moods through gestures at once broad and subtle. Departing from this technique, Lecoq then donned the different traditionally expressive masks of the commedia dell'arte to illustrate how body movement creates various characters. Changes in the wearer's movement could alter the meaning of a mask. One expression which appeared proud and strong gradually became weak and cowardly as Lecoq altered his posture by slow degrees. He further showed how a mask with a characteristic expression of joy might convey grief, all by means of changes in movement and gesture. Additional elements of the presentation were relations between sport and theatre movement, observations on how nationality and age affect gesticulation, and depictions of animals and plants. As one critic wrote: "Mime is a poor term to describe Lecoq's art. He has liberated it from ancient traditions and modern stylizations. Like Desarte he divides the body into emotional zones. Using every possible movement, gesture and attitude, he has made of it an expressive hieroglyphic instrument that can be adapted to theatre, ballet, opera, motion picture, or television."[6]

2. Audience error and the lecture-performance

This sketch of the programs in the "Art in the Making" series permits a quick survey of just how these presentations combatted the audience errors outlined earlier. Most obviously, an assault on ignorance of the artist's working processes was a major thrust of all the programs. The presentations exposed in one way or another the artist's activities in preparing a work for public presentation. No one attending several of the presentations in the series could long maintain a naive conception of the artist either as a magician pulling rabbits out of hats or as a methodical drudge practicing technical skills. Their elaborate and thought-laden dealings with ongoing works left little doubt of that.

Several of the programs also addressed that problem of initial contact with less familiar arts. Lecoq's presentation on mime, the Proposition's demonstration of improvisational theater, Ceely's account of electronic music, Camara's display of African drumming all drew audiences with little prior familiarity to these more unusual art forms. By coupling elements of lecture with elements of performance, they conveyed to their novice audiences the fundamental presuppositions and basic strategies of their respective art forms with a clarity and specificity that an outright performance could never hope to attain. Where conventional presentations risk confounding an audience with novelty, these assisted the viewers into a ready rapport.

Beyond the problems of misconceiving artists' working procedures and failing to make a good initial contact with genres, the introduction noted a general difficulty in achieving a sensitive and comprehensive insight into particular works. This difficulty was signaled by a number of audience misbehaviors which in effect displaced more sophisticated responses. In place of comprehension, all too often audience members fall back upon hasty and global value judgments, undiscriminating enthusiasm, conventional reactions to the broad features of a scene (comic, tragic, or whatever) which ignore the nuance of the artist's individual treatment, and acquiescence to the authority of an artist's reputation, a critic's opinion, or the consensus of peers, all in place of one's own best reading of the work. Underlying these hapless gestures is, on the one hand, a lack of experience in dealing with the manifold discriminations and multiple approaches that characterize the arts or even a particular genre and, on the other hand, a self-defeating willingness on the part of audiences to retreat into various forms of bewilderment or superficiality rather than requiring of themselves a more probing attitude.

The "Art in the Making" series spoke to these problems in several ways. The technique of alternative approaches to the same subject offered a quick if partial corrective for lack of broad exposure to different interpretations of the same work. The most obvious examples here were in the areas of theater and music. Hamlin and Kirchner contrasted different treatments of the same traditional material to demonstrate how much the theater director and the performing musician could do to change the emphasis, the feeling, the impact of a given dramatic or musical text. Thus the evening was an effective substitute for contrasting experiences an audience member would normally need to gather over several performances. Also, precisely because the different interpretations had contrasting if not, in some cases, contradictory effects, the easy error of stock responses to the gross features of an event was challenged.

Judged by the audience response to the programs, one of the main problems was the absence of much question and answer between audience and artist. Partly this was because most program time was spent in repetition of segments of the work chosen for illustration. Subsequent newspaper reports and audience remarks, however, suggested that the contrasting illustrations, though lengthy, fulfilled their purpose in increasing understanding of how the same work can be viewed and presented by the artist in different ways, with different emphases, to different purposes.

The technique of discussing and illustrating unfinished works, on the one hand exposing the artists' working processes, did double duty in pushing the audience toward a more acute perception and comprehension of works. In the program of Guzzetti (photography), Tolbert, and Hahn (both dance), for example, the audience heard artists speak openly about the various factors which governed their choices in selection of photographs or choreographic elements. Though the audience response began as one of uncertainty, by the end of the program viewers were more keenly aware and even enthusiastic about what they saw, judging from the increasing number of questions as well as audience participation in the exploration of the dance performance space through movement. The artists in charge, who were also experienced teachers, encouraged and willingly answered questions. They also took pains to discuss and in some cases agree with alternative choices and interpretations proposed from the audience. The rapport established was such that various audience strategies of retreat from the work were undermined, and audience joined artist in an insightful confrontation with the detailed problems of expression, meaning, and value.

With much the same ends in view, a broader panorama was sketched by the programs which illustrated the history of an art or the construction stages of various works. By presenting various phases in development and by showing the relationship between the art or the specific work to other arts and works, artists such as Ceely (electronic music), Lecoq (mime), and Richards (poetry) offered audiences reasoned insight and thoughtful analysis as well as examples of skilled performance. These programs purchased their breadth and organization through adopting a more traditional lecture format than many of the others, though elements of performance were still prominent. Nonetheless, the large audiences, the enthusiasm to question the artists, and the reviews of these presentations suggest that they were entirely effective—perhaps more effective than some programs emphasizing performance more—in providing fresh understanding and appreciation for both more and less conventional arts.

Although the impact of lecture-performances on the audience has been the mainstay of this treatment, some word concerning the reactions of the participating artists seems essential. All participating artists testified to a greater respect for the lecture-performance form as a result of their efforts. Generally they agreed that, however awkward its name, the lecture-demonstration was potentially a form of public presentation quite as important and creative as a normal performance.

In discussions with the series management, each artist was informed about program strategies effective in earlier lecture-performances. Since few of the programs concerned the same art, the burden of selecting useful experience from previous programs fell primarily on the artist. Even without the benefit of a summary of working principles such as this document, most artists were interested to know what strategies their colleagues had used and with what success.

After their presentations, most artists expressed surprise and satisfaction with the quality of questions and comments raised by the audience. Most engaged at some point in an interesting dialogue with audience members about the material illustrated. From the artists' viewpoint the programs were a welcome change from performances where rustling feet and rattling programs, coughs, and silences—sometimes awkward, sometimes attentive—are the only means of communication, salient though those are for professional performers and teachers.

3. Alternative directions

If a similar series were again to be launched, naturally certain elaborations and even shifts in direction would be promising in light of the experience to date. For one point, the informal observations reflected here could profitably give way to systematic investigation of audience reaction. Means could be devised to survey audience response both in terms of insight attained and in a more commercial context to measure support for performances and exhibitions. Questionnaires distributed at the lecture-performance events or mailed afterwards, recordings of the dialogue between artist and audience, and systematic interviews with a sampling of people in attendance are three possible tactics. Where a lecture-performance prepared for a later event, ticket buyers might simply be queried whether they had attended it and whether their experience encouraged them to view the actual performance.

Where the "Art in the Making" series took as its central theme the exposure of working process, another direction stems from the central difficulty which Richards noted in *Practical Criticism*: the need for systematic training in constructing and comprehending multiple definitions of the same subject. Of course, many of the presentations, dealing as they did with the artist displaying options and making choices, treated both themes at the same time. One could imagine another series either persisting in this synthesis of both themes at once or taking as its center Richards's theme.

Clearly, multiple perspectives on the same subject is a motif expressible through means other than display of working processes or even through lecture-performance per se. The museum technique of juxtaposing works for an illuminating contrast comes to mind here. Another example might be a program inspired in part by Lecoq's presentations. "Hockey Seen! A Nightmare in Three Periods and Sudden Death" was a dance built around different artist's responses to the tension, drama, and swift excitement of professional hockey. With regulation hockey masks from the pro supplier Ernie Higgins, choreography by Martha Gray, calligraphic line drawings of hockey action by Katherine Sturgis projected as background, and music by

John Adams utilizing hockey crowd noise, the event became a successful blend of different arts which demonstrated to enthusiastic youth audiences that the arts could relate to and offer a perspective on a domain where they felt a commitment.[7]

4. Audience building

Whatever the variety of audience errors, they all contribute ultimately to that single and most practical one noted by harassed arts managers: "not coming." Precisely because not coming is so very much a consequence of not understanding, a closing note on the lecture-performance's role as a mediator between potential audiences and half-empty theaters or galleries seems essential. Although that opportunity appears a very real and important one, certain contrasts prevail between the academic context of the "Art in the Making" series and the necessarily commercial context of lecture-performances as audience builders for the professional circuits.

First of all, a note on the success of the series itself in drawing and holding audiences and encouraging them to attend other, professional events. Attendance ranged widely, from 300 to 800, varying with everything from the fame of the artist and familiarity of the art form to the vagaries of Cambridge weather. In three years of programming, the management accumulated a regular mailing list of approximately 100 patrons outside the target audience and the university who came to the programs because they were part of the series rather than as a response to interest in a specific art. The comments of this group indicated growing awareness of and sympathy for the merits of this mixture of the didactic and the entertaining. Toward the end of the period favorable audience response was so dependable that a few successful workshops in mime and theatre presentation could be sponsored as adjuncts to the performances themselves.

At least with respect to one art, modern dance, some practical results of the series were encouraging. The performances of Ina Hahn's dance company were sold out at the Loeb Theatre. At their first such presentation there it is unlikely that this regional dance company could have filled the 500-seat theatre several times without the preparatory lecture-demonstrations and open rehearsals in the months preceding. Further, the hospitality for modern dance and mime increased at Harvard to the point that Lecoq was invited back to give an intensive mime course at the Loeb Theatre Summer Workshop, and a dance center is now open for teaching and performance every summer at Harvard's Agassiz Theatre under the sponsorship of Harvard Summer School. How directly this series led to these events is a matter for speculation, but it is certainly undeniable that before the series was offered little in those fields was available at Harvard, much less receiving strong audience support.

As a result of subsequent observations and applications by this author in a more commercial context, this form of arts presentation emerged as a special kind of inexpensive and informal entertainment that built community support for the various arts even as it contributed to understanding and appreciation of them. Among several events, lecture-performance presentations by the internationally recognized dance companies of Alvin Ailey and Paul Taylor are credited by the management of Houston's Society of the Performing Arts as having noticeably improved ticket sales for the performances, and this indeed encouraged the inclusion of modern dance as a regular part of the organization's program season.

A similar kind of programming, which might be called public relations as much as education, was developed by the Houston Grand Opera. The "opera preview" consists of excerpts from the current production by a few of the principals. The story of the opera is told, and a pianist accompanies the costumed singers as they perform a few scenes. A question period completes the hour-long program. The management of the opera company views as a permanent part of their program these now-popular presentations, which began as lunch-time diversion in the downtown Houston Public Library. Slightly more elaborate presentations of this sort are given in various public school auditoriums to the student bodies.

But various problems trouble such commercial contexts more than the "Art in the Making" series. Commercial programs generally feature professional performers rather than performer-teachers, who bring their insights into the needs of the novice. The age and experience range of the audiences for these events is much broader, especially since programs are often sponsored by nonprofit public arts organizations for the benefit of school children as well as adults. These organizations are usually required to sponsor some "educational" programs within the community in order to qualify for subsidy by the National Endowment for the Arts and many private foundations. Since such presentations are an additional burden for the visiting artist, whose main purpose is to perform rather than to teach, little time can be given to planning such programs. Most often they tend to be brief excerpts from the artist's repertory presented on a bare stage with perhaps some anecdotal commentary and some time for questions.

The abbreviated performance with explanation has more often been attempted for secondary school students than for adults. It is difficult to simplify explanations for such audiences or even for the wider range of people who attend a free public lecture-demonstration. Since that task is finally peripheral to the performer's main purpose, the educational and artistic potential of these programs is rarely explored by the artists or the arts organizations. There are exceptions, of course. Concerts for young people by various major U.S. symphony orchestras are an outstanding example. But if the lecture-performance is truly to come into its own, these difficulties must be faced and resolved one way or another. Motivation of the commercial and performing community seems a key factor. When it is realized how much problems of understanding divide artist from audience, lecture-performances and other means planned to effect a reconciliation will attract the attention they need and deserve.[8]

As an informal experiment in audience research, these examples of lecture-performances clearly display educational, artistic, and commercial potential. With closer consideration of audiences from the point of view of errors in understanding and appreciation, it should be possible to tailor such programs to deal with local audience problems. For example, exposure to broad varieties of modern dance was more important in Houston than in Cambridge, where the emphasis fell on the different responses of choreographers to various spaces and subjects. In short, if the educational potential of public media, particularly television, for any art is to be effectively utilized, the connections between teaching and entertaining processes, between classrooms and public support, must be continually examined. The study and practice of the lecture-performance as a teaching tool and, at best, as an art itself offer a primary and largely neglected asset in that enterprise.

Notes

1. I. A. Richards, *Practical Criticism: A Study of Literary Judgment* (1929, reprinted New York: Harcourt, Brace & World, 1968).

2. Funding for the "Art in the Making" series 1968–71 was provided by the Old Dominion Foundation. Director of the series was Nelson Goodman. Managers of the series were Barrie Bortnick (1968–69) and Frank Lloyd Dent (1969–71).

3. Two other descriptions of this series have appeared: Frank Lloyd Dent, "The Lecture-Performance: An Instrument for Audience Education," Technical Report no. 7, Harvard Project Zero; idem, "Zeroing in on Art," *Harvard Bulletin* 73, no. 11 (May 3, 1971): 41–44.

4. An illustrated description of the work of the Ina Hahn Dance Company with the "Art in the Making" series appeared in *Harvard Graduate School of Education Assocation Bulletin* 13, no. 4 (Summer 1969): 20–23.

5. Stephen Smoliar, "Snaking Along Sanders Basement," *Boston After Dark*, 11 March 1970, p. 26.

6. Kathleen Cannell, "Project Zero and the Arts," *Christian Science Monitor*, 24 April 1970, section 2, p. 14.

7. An illustrated description of this work was published in *Goal: The National Hockey League Magazine* (1974), pp. 14A–15A. The production of "Hockey Seen!" was partially funded by the Kempner Foundation.

8. For further information on the difficulties and potentials of audience education, see Chapter 10, "Building Greater Appreciation," in the Rockefeller Panel Report, *The Performing Arts—Problems and Prospects* (New York: McGraw Hill, 1965), John D. Rockefeller 3rd, Chairman of the Panel.

 Notes on
Contributors

Jeanne Bamberger is associate professor of education and music at MIT. She is co-author, with Howard Brofsky, of an introductory text in music, *The Art of Listening: Developing Musical Perception* (New York: Harper and Row, 3d. ed., 1975). Her recent articles include "The Luxury of Necessity" in *Papers from the Invitational Forum on the Education of Music Consumers*, National Association of Schools of Music, February, 1974; and "The Development of Musical Intelligence I: Strategies for Representing Simple Rhythms" in *Papers from the American Psychological Association Invitational Symposium on Music and Psychology, 1975*, edited by Thomas Bever (forthcoming).

Frank Dent has served as manager of the Project Zero lecture-performance series and more recently as director of the Rice Alumni Association. In that capacity he produced several further lecture-demonstrations in dance and drama. He has returned to Harvard to complete his doctoral degree.

Nathan Fox is a doctoral candidate at the Harvard Graduate School of Education.

Howard Gardner is co-director of Project Zero. He has published three recent books: *The Quest for Mind: Jean Piaget, Claude Lévi-Strauss, and the Structuralist Movement* (New York: Knopf, 1973), *The Arts and Human Development* (New York: Wiley, 1973), and *The Shattered Mind* (New York: Knopf, 1975). He is co-author, with Vernon Howard and David Perkins, of "Symbol Systems: A Philosophical, Psychological, and Educational Investigation," the lead article in *Media and Symbols: The Forms of Expression, Communication and Education*, 73rd Yearbook of the National Society for the Study of Education, ed. D. Olson (Chicago: University of Chicago Press, 1974).

Nelson Goodman founded and formerly directed Project Zero. He is professor of philosophy at Harvard, and was formerly at the University of Pennsylvania and Brandeis. He has been John Locke lecturer at Oxford, and Immanuel Kant lecturer at Stanford. His books are *The Structure of Appearance* (1951), *Fact, Fiction, and Forecast* (1954), *Languages of Art* (1968), *Problems and Projects* (1972). He also founded—and has written, designed, and produced works for—The Dance Center at the Harvard Summer School.

Vernon A. Howard received his Ph.D. in philosophy from Indiana University. He has held positions in philosophy and education at the University of Western Ontario, Harvard, and the University of London, where he now teaches aesthetics and the philosophy of science. His special interests are in the symbol systems of art and the philosophy of skills, on which latter topic he is currently writing a book entitled, "Skills: An Essay in Practical Epistemology."

John Kennedy is an assistant professor of psychology at Scarborough College, University of Toronto. He is the author of a recent book, *The Psychology of Picture Perception* (San Francisco: Jossey Bass, 1974). Some articles not mentioned in the bibliography to his paper include one on impossible objects, "Building the Devil's Tuning Fork," *Perception,* 1975, 4 (with Brooks Masteron), one on op-art brightness effects, "Attention, Brightness, and the Constructive Eye," in M. Henle (Ed.), *Vision and Artifact* (New York: Spranger, in press) and two on perceptual abilities of non-Western peoples, "Picture Perception in Africa," *Journal of Aesthetics and Art Criticism* (in press), "Picture Perception by the Songe of Papua," *Perception* (in press).

Søren Kjørup is a professor at the University Center of Roskilde, Denmark. He has authored in English the recent article "Doing Things with Pictures," *The Monist,* April 1974, *58* (2), and has published in Danish a book considering problems of aesthetics, *Aestetiske problemer: En indføring i kunstem filosofi* (Copenhagen: Scandanavian University Books/Munks-gaard, 1971); and a book on the semiotics of the cinema, *Filmsemiologi* (Copenhagen: Berlingske Forlag, 1975).

Paul A. Kolers is a professor of psychology at the University of Toronto. Author of numerous technical articles in perception and cognition, he has also written a monograph on the perception of motion (*Aspects of Motion Perception,* New York: Pergamon Press, 1972), and earlier contributed to and edited with Murray Eden a collection of papers on aspects of human and machine perception (*Recognizing Patterns,* Cambridge, Massachusetts; M.I.T. Press, 1968). His recent work has been concerned largely with understanding the similarities and differences that characterize perception of text and of pictures.

Diana Korzenik is chairperson of the Art Education Division, Massachusetts College of Art. Her recent publications include "Role-taking and Children's Drawing," *Studies in Art Education,* Spring 1974; "Changes in Representation in Children's Drawings," in *Proceedings from the Congress on the Psychopathology of Expression* (Basel: Kargen, 1975); "Creativity: Solutions to a Problem" *Studies in Art Education,* Spring 1976. She is a contributor to and editor of AFIRE (Art for Intergroup Relations Education) curriculum (5 titles), published by the Lincoln-Filene Center, Tufts University.

Barbara Leondar is associate dean, College of Liberal Arts, Boston University. Articles she has published include "Metaphor and Infant Cognition," *Poetics: International Review for the Theory of Literature,* 1975, *4* (2); "The Arts in Alternative Schools: Some Observations," *Journal of Aesthetic Education,* 1971, *5* (1); "Metaphor in the Classroom," in Ralph A. Smith (ed.), *Aesthetic Conceptions and Education* (Champaign: University of Illinois Press, 1970).

David Perkins is co-director of Project Zero. His special interests include creative process, critical abilities, errors in thinking, visual perception, and rhythmic capacities. His articles have appeared in the *Journal of Aesthetic Education, Cognitive Psychology, Perception and Psychophysics, Studies in the Anthropology of Visual Communication,* and other journals. He has developed an intensive course at Harvard Summer School entitled *The How of Art: Teaching Creative Process.* A sometime poet, he is just beginning to publish.

Graham Roupas is an assistant professor of philosophy at the University of Connecticut and has just completed his doctoral dissertation at Harvard University.

Beside their academic accomplishments, most authors gain a practical perspective from their amateur or semiprofessional involvement in the arts, including lieder singing, theatrical production, piano performance, poetry writing, painting, drama, and dance.

Index

Library of Congress Cataloging in Publication Data

Main entry under title:

The Arts and cognition.

Includes index.
1. Arts—Psychology—Addresses, essays, lectures. 2. Cognition—Psychology—Addresses, essays, lectures. I. Perkins, David. II. Leondar, Barbara.
NX 165.A79   700′.1   76-17237
ISBN 0-8018-1843-5